THE FARNESE GALLERY

PRINCETON MONOGRAPH
IN ART AND ARCHAEOLOGY
XXXVI
PUBLISHED FOR THE
DEPARTMENT OF ART AND ARCHAEOLOGY
PRINCETON UNIVERSITY

THE FARNESE GALLERY

BY JOHN RUPERT MARTIN

PRINCETON, NEW JERSEY

PRINCETON UNIVERSITY PRESS

1965

1880

PREFACE

MY AIM in writing this book has been to make a comprehensive study of the first great monument of Roman Seicento decoration—the Gallery of the Carracci in the Palazzo Farnese—and of its immediate predecessor, the Camerino Farnese.

The book has three parts. Part I is intended to form an introduction to the main subject. It opens with a brief account of the Farnese family and the Roman palace, and of the events leading up to the decoration of the Gallery. There follows a chapter on the Carracci themselves, in which the emphasis is, of course, laid on their period of service under the Farnese; the chief biographical sources for the artists are also considered here. Chapter 3 deals at some length with Annibale's first decorative project for the palace, the Camerino.

Part II is concerned entirely with the Farnese Gallery. A few words of explanation concerning the organization of this part of the book may not be amiss. The more I grappled with the complexities of this great cycle, the more I realized that no single approach to it would be adequate; hence the various methods of research and presentation which will be encountered in these chapters. The first problem to be dealt with, it seemed to me, was the dual one of the chronology of execution and the participation of Annibale's assistants. This, accordingly, forms the subject of Chapter 4. The next chapter contains an analysis of the decorative system of the Gallery, together with a discussion of the chief sources drawn upon by Annibale in fashioning his intricate solution. Chapters 6 and 7, which treat of the subject-matter of the cycle, are largely iconological in nature. Because the iconography of the Farnese Gallery has been generally ignored, it appeared to me the more necessary to pay special attention to this exceedingly difficult problem, involving as it does the artistic as well as the literary sources of Annibale's frescoes. About the rationale of the cycle as a whole I do not have serious doubts, but at the same time I am far from contending that my reading of it is accurate in every particular. Finally I have endeavored in Chapter 8 to elucidate the significance of the Gallery in the evolution of the Baroque by examining its influence on certain artists who were active in Rome during the first half of the seventeenth century.

Part III is devoted to the preparatory drawings for both the Camerino and the Gallery. Considerable space has been given to this subject, not only because of the intrinsic beauty of the drawings themselves, but also because they enable us to penetrate more deeply into the creative method of a great master. The book concludes with a catalogue of the drawings for the two cycles.

I began work on this subject about ten years ago. Much of the primary research was done in Rome during 1953-1954, at which time I also began to realize the formidable dimensions of the project that I had undertaken. The Mostra dei Carracci held at Bologna in 1956 was a twofold boon, first because I learned much from the exhibition itself, and secondly because it provoked a flurry of scholarly activity that I found both informative and stimulating. Study of the preparatory drawings was mostly carried out in print rooms in England and on the Continent during the spring and summer of 1958 and the summer of 1962. The pleasure of working with these originals compensated in some degree for the disappointing result of my search for documents. To be sure, I had some success in the Vatican Library, where I came across the letters concerning the Camerino addressed to Fulvio Orsini; but I learned virtually nothing from a lengthy perusal of the Farnese papers in the State Archives of Naples and Parma; and it was especially frustrating to be told that many of the documents discovered in Naples by Tietze had been destroyed in the second world war.

Without adequate illustrations a book such as this would fail of its purpose. The plates therefore cover the entire area of the frescoes in both the Camerino and the Gallery, and include all the preparatory drawings as well. Comparative illustrations, on the other hand, are relatively few in number. I have not thought it necessary to reproduce well-known monuments: the frescoed frieze of Palazzo Magnani is represented here, but not the Sistine ceiling.

Chapter 3 and parts of Chapter 11 first appeared in articles in the *Art Bulletin* (June 1956) and the *Bollettino d'Arte* (January-March 1959). These sections have been extensively revised in order to suit the present volume.

Since the literature on the Carracci has already reached sizable proportions it is obviously impossible for me to name the many authors from whose writings I have drawn profit. But I must mention three works to which I am particularly indebted. In the early stages of my investigation I had constantly beside me the fundamental study of the Farnese Gallery by Hans Tietze, which appeared in the Vienna *Jahrbuch* for 1906-1907, and which must still rank as one of the most notable achievements of art-historical scholarship. One may disagree with Tietze on many points—as indeed I have done—but it remains true that it was he who brought together the multifarious materials on which all subsequent studies of this subject must be based. When I first ventured into the tricky field of drawings I frequently turned for guidance to Rudolf Wittkower's catalogue of the Carracci drawings at Windsor, and to this was later added Denis Mahon's catalogue of the drawings loaned to the exhibition at Bologna.

To the many persons who gave me advice and criticism or who helped me to obtain photographs I owe the warmest thanks: Mr. Jacob Bean, Dr. Otto Benesch, Mme J. Bignami-Odier, Mr. P. S. Bird, Mme Jacqueline Bouchot-Saupique, Mme W. Bouleau-Rabaud, Mr. D. W. Buchanan, Mr. J. Byam Shaw, Dr. Maurizio Calvesi, Mlle M. L. Cornillot, Dr. Ivan Fenyö, Dr. Oreste Ferrari, Mlle Monique Geiger, Professor Cesare Gnudi, Professor Julius S. Held, Mr. Ralph Holland, Dr. Thomas P. Hoving, the late Sir Bruce Ingram, Professor Otto Kurz, the late Archibald G. B. Russell, Miss A. H. Scott-Elliot, Dr. Giulia Sinibaldi, Mr. Richard Spear, Mr. Philip Troutman, Professor J. G. van Gelder, Mlle Françoise Veron, M. A. Vidal-Naquet, Mr. Richard Wallace, Professor Rudolf Wittkower, and Mr. Thomas S. Wragg.

I am under a particular obligation to Roseline Bacou for invaluable assistance given to me in my study of the Carracci drawings in the Cabinet des Dessins of the Louvre; to William S. Heckscher, who read the typescript and, in addition to correcting errors and commenting on individual passages, proposed certain rearrangements in the text; to Denis Mahon, for his characteristic generosity in sharing with me his matchless knowledge of the Seicento; and to Erwin Panofsky, whom I can never sufficiently thank for the interest he has taken in this work and for the countless wise suggestions he has made for its improvement.

Her Majesty Queen Elizabeth II has graciously given permission to reproduce drawings from the Royal Collection at Windsor. The Duke of Sutherland (formerly the Earl of Ellesmere) has kindly permitted me to publish three drawings from his collection. Permission to reproduce drawings from the Devonshire Collection at Chatsworth has been granted by the Trustees of the Chatsworth Settlement. The cartoons by Agostino Carracci are reproduced by courtesy of the Trustees of the National Gallery, London, and the fragment of a cartoon by Annibale for the Camerino is reproduced with the permission of the Trustees of the British Museum. Messrs. Walter Gernsheim, Philip Hofer, and Carl Winter have kindly allowed me to reproduce works in their collections.

Many of the photographs of the Camerino and Gallery were taken by Renato Sansaini. The view of the Gallery reproduced as Fig. 38 was specially obtained for me by Ernest Nash. The drawings for the text illustrations were made by David Van Zanten. Harriet Anderson of the Princeton University Press has been unfailingly helpful in preparing the book for publication.

I am indebted to the Trustees of Princeton University for the academic leisure which has made possible the writing of this book. The initial research was undertaken during my tenure of a Bicentennial Preceptorship; additional grants for travel and photography were provided by the Research Fund and the Spears Fund of Princeton University.

J. R. M.

January 1964
Princeton, N.J.

PHOTOGRAPHIC SOURCES

Albertina, Vienna, Figs. 159, 161, 162, 163

Alinari, Florence, Figs. 1, 2, 30, 31, 273, 275

Alinari-Anderson, Rome, Figs. 18, 23, 89

Ashmolean Museum, Oxford, Figs. 100, 101

Biblioteca Reale, Turin, Figs. 113, 114, 222, 223

British Museum, Fig. 131

Cabinet des Dessins, Louvre, Figs. 104, 105, 106, 111, 115, 116, 118, 119, 120, 122, 123, 124, 127, 129, 130, 135, 136, 138, 144, 145, 148, 150, 151, 158, 160, 170, 172, 174, 176, 181, 182, 183, 185, 186, 188, 189, 195, 196, 197, 198, 199, 207, 209, 210, 211, 212, 218, 219, 228, 235, 236, 237, 239, 242, 247, 257, 261, 263, 264, 265, 266, 269, 271, 272

Colnaghi, London, Fig. 193

Courtauld Institute of Art, London, Fig. 203

Ernest Nash, Rome, Fig. 38

Gabinetto Fotografico Nazionale, Rome, Figs. 5, 6, 7, 8, 10, 11, 16, 17, 24, 36, 37, 39, 40, 41, 42, 43, 44, 45, 46, 47, 48, 49, 50, 51, 52, 53, 54, 55, 56, 57, 58, 59, 60, 61, 62, 63, 64, 65, 66, 67, 68, 69, 70, 71, 72, 77, 78, 79, 80, 81, 82, 83, 84, 92, 93, 94, 95, 96, 97, 98, 99, 178, 268

King's College, Newcastle, Fig. 240

Kunsthalle, Bremen, Fig. 215

Kupferstichkabinett, Berlin-Dahlem, Fig. 29

Leicester Museums and Art Gallery, Figs. 204, 217, 241

Metropolitan Museum of Art, New York, Figs. 103, 133, 276

Musée de Besançon, Fig. 184

Musée de Dijon, Fig. 112

Musée des Beaux-Arts, Budapest, Figs. 171, 175

Museum Boymans-van Beuningen, Rotterdam, Fig. 238

National Gallery, London, Figs. 190, 194

Royal Library, Windsor, Figs. 137, 152, 169, 180, 202, 224, 227, 232, 243, 245, 248, 249, 250, 251, 253, 254, 255, 258, 259, 260, 262, 270, 286, 289

Sansaini, Rome, Figs. 3, 4, 12, 13, 14, 15, 19, 20, 21, 22, 25, 26, 27, 28, 73, 74, 75, 76, 85, 86, 87, 88, 90, 91

Service de Documentation Photographique de la Réunion des Musées Nationaux, Figs. 121, 128, 141, 142, 146, 147, 149, 153, 157, 166, 192, 206, 213, 214, 221, 267, 281

Soprintendenza alle Gallerie, Florence, Figs. 167, 177, 225

Trustees of the Chatsworth Settlement, Figs. 156, 179

Victoria and Albert Museum, London, Fig. 288

Villani & Figli, Bologna, Figs. 9, 102, 107, 108, 109, 110, 117, 125, 126, 132, 134, 139, 140, 143, 154, 155, 164, 165, 173, 187, 191, 200, 201, 205, 208, 216, 220, 226, 229, 230, 231, 233, 234, 244, 246, 252, 256, 274

CONTENTS

ILLUSTRATIONS

THE PALAZZO FARNESE

THE CAMERINO FARNESE

THE FARNESE GALLERY

Unless otherwise stated, the drawings for the Camerino and the Gallery are attributed to Annibale Carracci.

DRAWINGS FOR THE CAMERINO

xvii

ABBREVIATIONS

BAGLIONE, *Vite*: Giovanni Baglione, *Le vite de' pittori, scultori et architetti dal Pontificato di Gregorio XIII del 1572 in fino a' tempi di Papa Urbano Ottavo nel 1642*, Rome, 1642.

BELLORI, *Vite*: Giovanni Pietro Bellori, *Le vite de' pittori, scultori et architetti moderni*, Rome, 1672.

MAHON, *Disegni: Mostra dei Carracci, Disegni*, catalogo critico a cura di Denis Mahon, 2nd ed., Bologna, 1963.

MAHON, *Studies*: Denis Mahon, *Studies in Seicento Art and Theory*, London, 1947.

MALVASIA, *Felsina*: Carlo Cesare Malvasia, *Felsina Pittrice, Vite de pittori bolognesi*, Bologna, 1678, 2 vols.

MANCINI, *Considerazioni*: Giulio Mancini, *Considerazioni sulla pittura* (ed. A. Marucchi and L. Salerno), Rome, 1956-1957, 2 vols.

TIETZE: Hans Tietze, "Annibale Carraccis Galerie im Palazzo Farnese und seine römische Werkstätte," *Jahrbuch der kunsthistorischen Sammlungen des allerhöchsten Kaiserhauses*, XXVI, 1906-1907.

WITTKOWER, *Carracci Drawings*: Rudolf Wittkower, *The Drawings of the Carracci in the Collection of Her Majesty the Queen at Windsor Castle*, London, 1952.

PART I
INTRODUCTION

CHAPTER 1 · THE PALAZZO FARNESE

WHEN the Farnese Gallery was opened, wrote the Abate Lanzi in 1795, "Rome beheld in it a certain grandeur, which might claim third place after the Sistine Chapel and the Stanze of the Vatican."[1] It was especially fitting, he might have added, that a fresco cycle judged worthy to rank with those of Michelangelo and Raphael should have been painted in the most impressive of all Renaissance palaces, the Palazzo Farnese (Fig. 1).

The Farnese Palace was begun in 1517 by Cardinal Alessandro Farnese (1468-1549), later to become Pope Paul III. When in 1534 he was elevated to the papacy he instructed his architect Antonio da Sangallo the Younger to enlarge the structure to a size that should be more in keeping with pontifical dignity. The great edifice was not to be finished until half a century later. By the time of Sangallo's death in 1546 the façade had been carried up to the base of the top story. In 1547 Michelangelo was appointed architect of the palace. He completed the façade, for which he designed the powerful cornice, and continued the building of the court and side wings. The last part of the palace to be erected was the rear wing (Fig. 2). It was probably begun in the 1560's by Michelangelo's successor Vignola; after the latter's death in 1573 the work was taken in hand by Giacomo della Porta. An inscription on the uppermost loggia of the garden façade records that the palace was completed in 1589.[2]

The lengthy period during which the palace was under construction coincides exactly with the zenith of the Farnese dynasty, which within the same span of years produced a great pope, a great cardinal, and a great captain. The unveiling of the Farnese vault in 1600 may be said to have signalized the completion of the palace: by that date the heroic epoch of the Farnese family was already past.

The rise of the Farnese to a station of power and influence was the work of Paul III, who conferred upon his illegitimate son Pier Luigi (1503-1547) the duchy of Parma and Piacenza. When Pier Luigi was murdered in 1547, the ducal crown passed to his son Ottavio (1521-1586), who however secured his title to it only after a bitter struggle. Two other sons, Alessandro and Ranuccio, were made cardinals at an early age.

Ranuccio Farnese (1530-1565), called Cardinal Sant'Angelo, was the first member of the family to make the Roman palace his permanent residence. Though the structure was far from complete, Ranuccio initiated a program of interior decoration, installing carved fireplaces and elaborate wooden ceilings in the larger rooms of the *piano nobile*. The most important of Ranuccio's projects was the decoration of the room over the main portal, the *salotto dipinto* (see text fig. 1, 2, page 7).

---

[1] Luigi Lanzi, *Storia pittorica della Italia*, 3rd ed., Bassano, 1809, II, p. 145.

[2] On the construction of the Palazzo Farnese see the admirable summary, with full bibliography, by J. S. Ackerman, *The Architecture of Michelangelo*, London, 1961, Catalogue, pp. 67-82.

Francesco Salviati was commissioned to paint here a cycle of frescoes, later completed by Taddeo Zuccari, glorifying the Farnese dynasty. One wall is devoted to the deeds of Pope Paul III, and the other to an earlier Ranuccio Farnese, general of the papal forces under Pope Eugenius IV.[3]

The name of Ranuccio was overshadowed by that of his elder brother Alessandro (1520-1589), known simply as "Cardinal Farnese" or "the great cardinal." Though he owed his position as cardinal and vice-chancellor of the Church to sheer nepotism, Alessandro was notwithstanding a man of rare ability and intelligence. He had a keen sense of the responsibility that attaches to high office, and in his day was acknowledged to be without peer as a Maecenas. His collection of antiquities was one of the largest in Rome. He purchased from the Chigi the villa which lies opposite the Farnese palace on the other bank of the Tiber and which henceforth was known as the Farnesina. He commissioned Vignola to build the Farnese Villa at Caprarola and the Church of Il Gesù in Rome. Some of the most important fresco cycles of the Mannerist era were created for him: for his Roman residence, the Palazzo della Cancelleria, Giorgio Vasari painted the apotheosis of Paul III in the Sala dei Cento Giorni;[4] and in the Villa at Caprarola Taddeo and Federico Zuccari carried out an even more extensive program in the Sala dei Fatti Farnesiani.[5] Alessandro was instrumental in bringing Titian to Rome in 1545-1546, at which time the Venetian master painted, among other Farnese portraits, the famous canvas of Pope Paul III with his *nipoti* Ottavio and Cardinal Alessandro Farnese (now in Naples). The great cardinal loved to surround himself with artists, scholars, and men of letters. Vasari tells of spending evenings at his court in the company of such *letterati* as Paolo Giovio, Annibal Caro, Francesco Maria Molza, Claudio Tolomei, and others. It was on one of these evenings, he relates, that Cardinal Farnese, acting upon a suggestion made by Giovio, proposed to the painter that he write the *Lives of the Artists*.[6]

Of all the humanists of the Farnese circle, the one most intimately acquainted with Sangallo's great palace was Fulvio Orsini (1529-1600). Illegitimate offspring of the princely family whose name he bore, Fulvio Orsini was a Canon of the Lateran. His long association with the Farnese began with his appointment as librarian to Cardinal Ranuccio; after the latter's death in 1565 he continued to occupy the same post under Cardinal Alessandro and, still later, under Cardinal Odoardo, who received the purple in 1591. Living in the Palazzo Farnese, Orsini not only supervised and augmented the family collection of antiquities, but amassed an impressive

[3] A. Venturi, *Storia dell'arte italiana*, IX, part 6, Milan, 1933, pp. 185 ff., figs. 107-113; see also the stimulating essay by E. K. Waterhouse, "Tasso and the Visual Arts," *Italian Studies*, III, 1946-1948, pp. 146 ff.

[4] E. Steinmann, "Freskenzyklen der Spätrenaissance in Rom, 1, Die Sala Farnese in der Cancelleria," *Monatshefte für Kunstwis-senschaft*, III, 1910, pp. 45 ff., pls. 11-13.

[5] Venturi, *op.cit.*, IX, part 5, figs. 509-511. On the meaning of the Caprarola cycle as a whole see F. Baumgart, "La Caprarola di Ameto Orti," *Studi Romanzi*, XXV, 1935, Introduction, pp. 77-95.

[6] Vasari, *Le vite* (ed. Milanesi), VII, pp. 681-682.

collection of his own. He died in 1600 at the age of seventy, leaving his most precious books to the Vatican Library and his other possessions to Cardinal Odoardo.[7]

The last great figure of the Farnese dynasty was the prince Alessandro (1545-1592), who in 1586 succeeded his father Ottavio as third Duke of Parma and Piacenza. Alexander of Parma, whose life was spent in the service of Philip II of Spain, and whom his contemporaries inevitably likened to Alexander the Great,[8] was without question the leading military genius of the age. He had fought at Lepanto under Don John of Austria, and was later sent to assist that commander in quelling the insurrection in the Netherlands. When Don John died in 1578, Alessandro was appointed to take his place as governor general of the Netherlands. The climax of his career came in 1585 with the capture of Antwerp, by which Parma secured the southern Netherlands for Spain and the Roman church. His plans for reconquering the Northern Provinces were thwarted by Philip's dream of invading England with the Invincible Armada. By the end of 1592, at the age of only forty-seven, Alessandro Farnese was dead, to be succeeded as Duke of Parma by his son Ranuccio (1569-1622).[9]

Farnese's second son, Odoardo (1573-1626), was early destined for the church, it being hoped that he would follow the example of his great-uncle Alessandro by becoming the leading cardinal of the papal court. Few careers can have had so auspicious a beginning. In 1591, newly created cardinal at the age of seventeen,[10] Odoardo took up residence in the Palazzo Farnese. He had at his disposal not only the magnificent palace and the other Farnese properties in Rome, but the Villa at Caprarola that had been Cardinal Alessandro's summer estate. Fulvio Orsini, who had long served the Farnese cardinals, took a special interest in the young man and assumed personal responsibility for his education.[11] Nor were his efforts misspent, for Odoardo soon won

---

[7] See the biographical sketch in Pierre de Nolhac, *La bibliothèque de Fulvio Orsini*, Paris, 1887, pp. 1-36.

[8] Famiano Strada, *De Bello Belgico*, Rome, 1648, Decas II, pp. 336 ff. See also the book of laudatory verses issued under the title *Raccolta di diverse compositioni sopra le Vittorie acquistate in Fiandra dal Serenissimo Alessandro Farnese Dvca di Parma, et di Piacenza, etc.*, Parma, 1586, *passim*, where Alessandro's service under Philip II of Spain is compared to that of Alexander the Great under his father Philip of Macedon.

[9] On Alessandro's military and political career see P. Fea, *Alessandro Farnese, Duca di Parma*, Rome, 1886, and L. Van der Essen, *Alexandre Farnèse*, Brussels, 1933-1937, 5 vols.

[10] Odoardo's birth date, often cited as 1574, was December 8, 1573, according to the baptismal notice in the Archivio di Stato at Parma (Casa e Corte Farnesiana, Odoardo Farnese, ser. II, busta 25, fasc. 3). He was therefore only seventeen when he became cardinal in March

1591. Yet it is sometimes said that he received this honor at the age of twenty-six (e.g., L. von Pastor, *History of the Popes* [ed. R. F. Kerr], XXII, London, 1932, p. 396; and Pierre de Nolhac, *La bibliothèque de Fulvio Orsini*, Paris, 1887, p. 23). The error can, I believe, be traced back to Alonzo Chacon (Ciaconius), who states that Odoardo was born in 1565, but also says (correctly) that he died on February 21, 1626, at the age of fifty-two—which of course agrees with 1573 but not with 1565 (*Vitae et Res Gestae Pontificum Romanorum et S.R.E. Cardinalium*, IV, Rome, 1677, cols. 229-230). The marriage of Odoardo's parents took place in 1565.

[11] Nolhac, *op.cit.*, pp. 22 f. See also Orsini's letter of February 8, 1593, to Duke Ranuccio Farnese (A. Ronchini and V. Poggi, "Fulvio Orsini e sue lettere ai Farnesi," *Atti e memorie delle RR. Deputazioni di Storia Patria per le provincie dell' Emilia*, nuova serie, IV, parte II, 1880, pp. 70 f.).

universal respect. The Venetian ambassador Giovanni Dolfin wrote of him in 1598: "Farnese is an angel of paradise; both through his goodness and his birth (the name of Cardinal Farnese being so esteemed in Rome and the Pope showing that he has such high regard for this family) he enjoys a great reputation at the Court, although he is still young."[12] Odoardo's appearance at this time is recorded in Annibale Carracci's painting *Christ in Glory with Saints* (Florence, Pitti), in which he is represented as a donor kneeling in prayer. Carracci's portrait agrees very well with the description of the cardinal by Alonzo Chacon, who says that he was tall, serious of mien, and had the prominent lower lip of the Habsburgs.[13] Modest and retiring by nature, Odoardo was reckoned a "cardinal of noble presence, worthy of having had for his great-great-grandfather Pope Paul III, worthy nephew of the great Cardinal Alessandro his uncle, and worthy son of the great and famous warrior Alessandro his father."[14]

Unfortunately, the picture of the cardinal which emerges from these eulogistic descriptions is an incomplete one. For the truth seems to be that Odoardo, though a man of unquestioned virtue and piety, lacked one of the essential qualifications of the ideal prince—generosity. There was a certain niggardliness in his nature—particularly evident in his unworthy treatment of Annibale Carracci—which was to mar his reputation as a liberal and discerning patron of the arts.

Though the external aspect of the palace has changed little, it is no longer possible to visualize the interior as it appeared in Odoardo's day. For here was housed the vast collection of antiquities and other works of art assembled by the Farnese during the sixteenth century, most of which are now to be seen in the museums of Naples.[15] At the time of Odoardo's arrival the collection was under the care of Fulvio Orsini, who in addition had here his own library and museum. We may perhaps form some idea of the magnificence of the Farnese possessions from the inventory of the palace drawn up in 1653, twenty-seven years after Odoardo's death.[16] Beneath the arcades of the court there stood, among other sculptures, the Farnese Hercules by Glycon and the much-admired Flora. Because of its great size the marble group known as the Farnese Bull was kept in a shed in the garden. The statue of Atlas supporting the globe occupied a room on the ground floor at the rear of the palace. The spacious

[12] "Relazione di Giovanni Dolfin tornato da Roma nel 1598," in E. Albèri (ed.), *Le relazioni degli Ambasciatori veneti al Senato,* ser. II, IV, Florence, 1857, p. 491.

[13] Chacon, *op.cit.*, col. 231: "Erat Odoardus Cardinalis Farnesius staturae procerae, aspectu gravi, & gravitatem prominente inferiore labio, ut Austriacum se ostenderet, mirabiliter affectabat."

[14] G. Bentivoglio, *Memorie e lettere* (ed. C. Panigada), Bari, 1934, p. 60.

[15] See the inventory of the Farnese antiquities made in 1568 for Cardinal Alessandro (*Documenti inediti per servire alla storia dei Musei d'Italia,* Florence-Rome, 1878-1880, I, pp. 72 ff.).

[16] P. Bourdon and R. Laurent-Vibert, "Le palais Farnèse d'après l'inventaire de 1653," *Mélanges d'archéologie et d'histoire, Ecole Française de Rome,* XXIX, 1909, pp. 145 ff. See also the description of the palace and its contents in Filippo Titi, *Descrizione delle pitture, sculture e architetture esposte al pubblico in Roma,* Rome, 1763 (1st ed., 1686), pp. 109 ff.

rooms of the state apartment on the first floor formed a veritable museum (see text fig. 1). The *sala grande* (1, 1) at the southeast corner of the palace contained, in addition to various ancient sculptures, the marble statue of the Duke Alessandro Farnese (Fig. 273), to which we shall return presently. One of the most impressive rooms of the *piano nobile* was the *sala degli imperatori* (1, 5), so called from the twelve

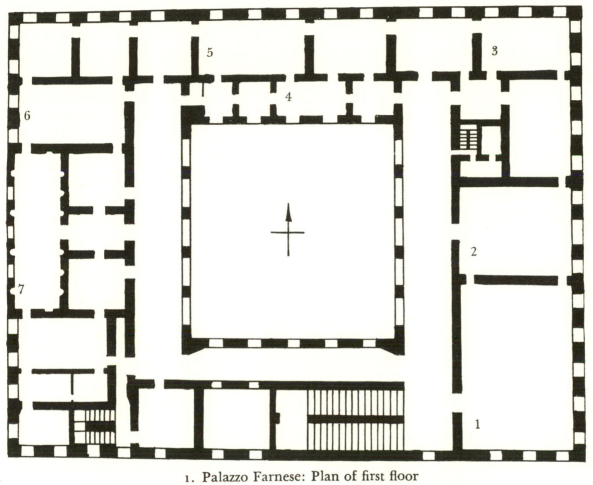

1. Palazzo Farnese: Plan of first floor

1. Sala grande	5. Sala degli imperatori
2. Salotto dipinto	6. Sala de' filosofi
3. Bedroom of Cardinal Ranuccio	7. Galleria Farnese
4. Camerino Farnese	

busts of Roman emperors which lined its walls; among these was the famous bust of Caracalla. The *sala de' filosofi* (1, 6), as its name indicates, was decorated with busts of ancient philosophers; but the spirit of high seriousness evoked by these sages must have been somewhat weakened by the presence in their midst of the Callipygian Venus. Here also was the great table of inlaid marble which is now in the Metropolitan Museum of New York.[17] On the second story were kept tapestries, services

[17] O. Raggio, in *The Metropolitan Museum of Art Bulletin*, XVIII, 1960, pp. 213 ff.

of crystal and silver, and paintings (including Titian's famous portraits of the Farnese). And finally there were on this floor the libraries, both of the Farnese and of Fulvio Orsini, with their incomparable wealth of books and master drawings.

The construction of the palace was now at an end, and Odoardo was able to give his attention to the interior. Two projects were uppermost in his mind. One was the decoration of the Gallery in the newly finished rear wing (1, 7); the other was the consecration of the *sala grande* at the front of the palace to the memory of his father, the Duke Alessandro of Parma.

The Gallery was intended to exhibit antique sculptures, the niches in the walls being filled with ten full-length statues and six busts (Figs. 32-34).[18] The architectural system of this room, in which the placing of pilasters and niches is determined by the external features of the garden façade (Fig. 2), was already in existence: what was still lacking was the applied decoration in stucco. Walter Vitzthum has recently discovered a drawing in the Berlin print room, evidently by Cherubino Alberti, for the walls of the Gallery (Fig. 29).[19] It unmistakably represents a section of the inner wall of the room, from the doorway in the middle to the last narrow bay at the left (cf. Volpato's engraving, Fig. 32). Comparison with the present state of the Gallery reveals that, although the architectural elements in the drawing are the same, the applied stucco ornament is of an altogether different order. Whereas the stuccoes projected in Cherubino's design are full of Mannerist conceits (particularly obvious in the lively and provocative attitudes of the figures), the decoration as actually carried out is more sedately classical in character (cf. Fig. 37): not only is the ornamental vocabulary more dependent on antique sources, but the figures assume simpler, more two-dimensional poses that serve to reinforce the flatness of the wall surface.

Vitzthum very reasonably conjectures that the Berlin drawing must date about 1594 or 1595. This was the period when Cardinal Odoardo was making plans for the decoration of the palace. Since Giovanni and Cherubino Alberti were then active in Rome, where they would shortly begin work on the frescoes of the Sala Clementina of the Vatican, it may be concluded that Odoardo asked them to submit a drawing for the Gallery. In the event, however, the design was not approved. Odoardo, it seems, decided to defer for the moment the stucco ornamentation of the Gallery. For there was another, more ambitious project that he wished to see carried out. This was the plan to commemorate his father's achievements by means of an elaborate decorative program in the *sala grande*, a program which should at the same time complement Salviati's fresco cycle in the adjoining room, the *salotto dipinto*. It is interesting that Odoardo did not employ Roman artists for this task; instead he turned to certain masters whose names were known to the Farnese court at Parma where he had been reared.

---

[18] For the identification of the statues in the Gallery see note 2 of Chapter 5.

[19] W. Vitzthum, "A Drawing for the Walls of the Farnese Gallery and a Comment on Annibale Carracci's 'Sala Grande,'" *Burlington Magazine*, cv, 1963, pp. 445-446.

The first step was to erect a sculptural monument to the victor of Antwerp. For this purpose Odoardo brought from Parma in 1594 the sculptor Simone Moschino, who was commissioned to carve a marble statue of the Duke Alessandro Farnese triumphing over Flanders and the River Scheldt and being crowned by Victory (Fig. 273). When the group was at last completed in 1598, it was placed in the *sala grande*. In the eighteenth century it was removed by the Bourbons to the palace at Caserta.[20]

Meanwhile Odoardo made preparations to cover the walls of this same room with an appropriate cycle of frescoes. The first documentary mention of this project appears in a letter written from Rome by Odoardo on February 21, 1595 to his brother the Duke Ranuccio in Parma: "I have resolved to have the *sala grande* of this palace painted with the deeds of the Duke our father of glorious memory by the Bolognese painters, the Carraccioli [*sic*], whom I have accordingly taken into my service, and whom I had come to Rome some months ago." In order that the artists may begin work promptly Odoardo asks if Ranuccio will send him a book of drawings illustrating their father's deeds, which, he believes, was dispatched to Parma from Flanders by the late Duke's secretary, Cosimo Masi.[21] "The Carraccioli" were of course Annibale Carracci and his brother Agostino. These were the artists who were to make the Farnese Gallery one of the principal monuments of Rome.

[20] Baglione, *Vite*, p. 377. On the history of Moschino's statue see H. Keutner, "Über die Entstehung und die Formen des Standbildes im Cinquecento," *Münchner Jahrbuch der Bildenden Kunst*, VII, 1956, pp. 164-167; and Vitzthum, *op.cit.*

[21] Naples, Archivio di Stato, Carte Farnesiane, fasc. 1324 (destroyed): "Serenissimo signor mio et fratello osservandissimo. Ho risoluto di far dipingere la sala grande di questo palazzo dell'imprese del signor duca nostro padre di gloriosa memoria dalli pittori Carraccioli Bolognesi, quali ho perciò condotti a miei servitii, et fatti venire a Roma alcuni mesi sono. Quest'opera ha bisogna di essere aiutata dal libro dei disegni delle imprese che il conte Cosimo Masi ha fatto venire di Fiandra per consignarlo a vostra altezza secondo mi scrisse alli mesi passati, che glielo dimandai. Anzi senza questo aiuto non veda si possa far cosa buona, supplico per tanto vostra altezza che si è giunto il detto libro con le robbe del conte Masi, ch'erano restate a dietro, mi faccia gratia di accordarmene per il tempo che sarà bisogna, perche con esso farò che li pittori cominciaranno a metter mano all'opera, la quale dovendo essere così per servitio di vostra altezza come mio, so che havera caro, che si effettui, et commanderà, che mi s'invii il libro subito, come di nuovo ne la supplico con ogni affetto, molto certo, che non mi negarà questa gratia della quale le resterò obligatissimo et senz'altro a vostra altezza bascio le mani. —Di Roma, li 21 di Febraro 1595.

"Di vostra altezza serenissima affettuosissimo servitore et fratello il Cardinale Farnese.

"Al serenissimo signor mio et fratello osservandissimo il signor duca di Parma et di Piacenza."

The letter is quoted by Tietze, p. 54.

CHAPTER 2 · THE CARRACCI IN THE SERVICE OF THE FARNESE

THE chief sources for the Carracci are found in the works of five seventeenth-century writers. The earliest is the *Treatise on Painting* composed between 1607 and 1615 by Monsignor Giovanni Battista Agucchi (1570-1632). Agucchi was a close friend of both Annibale Carracci and Domenichino, whose art provided the basis for his classical-idealist theory. Only a fragment of the treatise survives, but it contains an interesting and important account of the Carracci.[1]

Not much later than Agucchi's discourse is another treatise on painting (*Considerazioni sulla pittura*) by Giulio Mancini, which was written about 1620, but has only recently been published in full. Giulio Mancini (1558-1630) was a doctor (he became physician to Pope Urban VIII) and his views on art are those of a cultivated and well-informed layman. His treatise includes notices of Ludovico, Agostino and Annibale Carracci, all of whom he knew personally.[2]

The third biographer is Giovanni Baglione (1571-1644), who in 1642 published his *Lives of the Painters, Sculptors and Architects*, a volume intended to form a sequel to Vasari's *Lives*. The work comprises some two hundred biographies, many of them quite perfunctory. In his account of Agostino and Annibale Carracci, Baglione gives a summary description of the Farnese Gallery and names the principal subjects represented there.[3] The author was himself a painter and had undoubtedly known the Carracci brothers professionally.

In spite of their having been acquainted with the artists, Agucchi, Mancini and Baglione are less informative than two remarkable biographers of the later seventeenth century—the Bolognese Malvasia and the Roman Bellori.

Conte Carlo Cesare Malvasia (1616-1693) was the historian and ardent champion of the Bolognese painters, whose lives he recounted in his book *Felsina Pittrice* (1678). As might be expected, the work contains a very lengthy account of the Carracci, which is full of lively anecdotes and creates a convincing picture of the artists. Nevertheless *Felsina Pittrice* must be used with caution. For Malvasia's purpose in writing it is to enhance the reputation of Bologna, and to further this end he does not scruple on occasion to distort facts, suppress evidence, and even invent documents. Inevitably, this *campanilismo* leads the author into difficulties. Thus, for example, Ludovico is described as the greatest of the three Carracci because, one suspects, he alone was not lured away to Rome but remained faithful to Bologna. Malvasia's view of Annibale is particularly equivocal: though he clearly recognizes the genius of this master, he

[1] The fragment of Agucchi's treatise was published as part of the preface to the set of etchings by Simon Guillain after Annibale Carracci's drawings of the *Arti di Bologna* (1646). It has been reprinted in Mahon, *Studies*, pp. 231 ff.

[2] Mancini, *Considerazioni*, I, pp. 216-221.

[3] Baglione, *Vite*, pp. 105-109.

is obliged to argue that Annibale reached the pinnacle of his art in Bologna and that the Roman phase was a mere adjunct, contributing nothing to his development. "He went to Rome because he was called," Malvasia writes, "and for that reason only, not out of 'his desire and curiosity to see those statues' [he is here refuting Agucchi], which he had been quite able to do without in the *Almsgiving of St. Roch*, the *Resurrection*, the Sala Magnani and the like, the excellence of which he would never be able to equal again with all those new studies of his."[4]

Against this fervently pro-Bolognese and anti-Roman interpretation stands the more objective and considered estimate of the Carracci by Giovanni Pietro Bellori (1615-1696), a writer who in historical understanding and aesthetic perception far out-distances Malvasia. In his *Lives of the Modern Painters, Sculptors and Architects* (1672), Bellori selected twelve artists (beginning, as he put it, with "the restoration of painting by the hand of Annibale Carracci"), whose contributions he judged to be especially significant and whose works he analyzed with extraordinary care. In these admirable biographies there is a wealth of authentic detail: some of his subjects, such as Domenichino and Poussin, had been acquaintances of Bellori; in the case of those who, like the Carracci, had died before his time, he invariably consulted persons who had known them.[5] Annibale Carracci is the real hero of the book, and the Life of that artist provides a valuable corrective to Malvasia's highly colored account. There was, in Bellori's mind, no doubt that the Roman period was in every sense the culmination of Annibale's career. His descriptions of the great works of the Roman years, above all the Camerino and the Galleria Farnese, still form the indispensable starting-point for the study of these monuments.

Annibale and Agostino Carracci were already established masters when Cardinal Odoardo Farnese invited them to enter his service. The brothers had worked for many years in close collaboration with their cousin Ludovico in Bologna, where the three artists had founded a successful academy of painting. Ludovico Carracci (1555-1619) was the eldest and, in the beginning, the leading spirit of the group. His works of the decade 1585-1595, as for example the brilliant Bargellini altarpiece of 1588, have an undisputed place among the incunabula of the Baroque. In later years, perhaps feeling himself overshadowed by the superior genius of Annibale, his art suffered a marked decline in quality. Ludovico's greatest achievement was that he lifted the Bolognese school from the provincial level it had occupied during the period of Mannerism and transformed it into one of the most vital centers of Italian painting. Among his pupils were such artists as Guido Reni, Francesco Albani, and Domenico Zampieri called Domenichino.

Painting was only one of the accomplishments of Agostino Carracci (1557-1602). Though he was highly praised for such successful altarpieces as the *Communion of St. Jerome* (Bologna), Agostino was primarily trained as an engraver. All the early

[4] Malvasia, *Felsina*, I, p. 403.　　　　　[5] Bellori, *Vite*, Introduction.

accounts testify to his skill as a teacher; indeed to a man of his theoretical turn of mind the atmosphere of the Carracci Academy must have proved to be very congenial. He had several outstanding pupils: Giovanni Lanfranco and Sisto Badalocchio received their first instruction from Agostino when, near the close of his life, he was working for the Duke Ranuccio Farnese at Parma. But Agostino also had ambitions that lay outside the artistic profession. He took particular pride in his ability as a musician and as a man of letters, and obviously thought of these occupations as carrying greater social prestige than that of artist.

Annibale Carracci (1560-1609) was the youngest and most gifted member of the triad. Viewed as a whole, the course of Annibale's artistic development is clear and logical. From the very beginning he sought to fashion an idiom capable of replacing the sophisticated artificialities and outworn conventions of Mannerism. During the years 1585 to 1593 it was primarily to Correggio and the great Venetians that he looked for guidance. In the *Madonna enthroned with three Saints* of 1588 (Dresden) he showed himself to be the inheritor of the North Italian painterly tradition and already, though not yet in his thirtieth year, the dominant personality of the Emilian school. A significant change is perceptible in the *Christ and the Samaritan Woman* (Brera), painted in 1593: without having been to Rome, Annibale nevertheless here exhibits a marked orientation toward the art of the Roman High Renaissance and his style has become more classical. This monumental tendency is likewise evident in *St. Roch distributing Alms* (Dresden), the great canvas on which he was still working in 1595 when Cardinal Farnese summoned him to Rome. There he turned with enthusiasm to the study of Michelangelo, Raphael, and the antique. To the degree that his Roman grand manner was compounded of two main ingredients— North Italian colorism and Central Italian formal discipline—Annibale might be said to have effected in his art that union of *Colore* and *Disegno* which the theoreticians pictured as the highest goal of painting.

Although their work was chiefly made up of easel paintings, the Carracci occasionally collaborated in the decoration of patrician houses in Bologna. Their earliest joint project was the frescoed frieze with scenes of Jason and the Golden Fleece in the Palazzo Fava, completed in 1584. A second frieze in the same palace was devoted to the story of Aeneas. A few years later the three artists executed the beautiful frieze in the Palazzo Magnani (1588-1591), of which more will be said below. The Carracci also tried their hand at the decoration of palace ceilings. In 1592 they were commissioned by Cesare d'Este to furnish a set of four canvases for the Palazzo dei Diamanti in Ferrara: the paintings, which are now in Modena, were designed to be set in a coffered wooden ceiling and are redolent of the decorative manner of Veronese. The last collaborative cycle was carried out in 1593-1594 in the Palazzo Sampieri-Talon in Bologna, where the three Carracci painted six small frescoes on ceilings and fireplaces.

It is not to be wondered at that Cardinal Odoardo Farnese should have chosen

Annibale as the artist best qualified to realize his plans for the decoration of the Palazzo Farnese. Of the three Carracci Annibale was now the acknowledged leader, and Bellori is probably right in saying that he had already worked for the Farnese family in Parma.[6] The statement by Malvasia,[7] that the Duke Ranuccio wished to put Ludovico in charge of the work in the Roman palace, with Annibale in the role of assistant, may be dismissed as one of those fictions which the Bolognese writer (always eager to assert the superiority of Ludovico over Annibale) was only too prone to invent. Nor is there any reason to doubt that Annibale accepted Odoardo's offer chiefly because it would take him to Rome, where (in Bellori's words) "the fame of Raphael and the works of antiquity were a strong attraction to him."[8] He was now confident of his powers and firmly persuaded that only in the competitive atmosphere of Rome could he develop them to the full. Above all, he was to be given the opportunity to paint fresco cycles on a grand scale.

It is difficult, if not impossible, to reconstruct precisely the sequence of events that brought Annibale and Agostino Carracci into the service of Cardinal Farnese.[9] From Odoardo's letter of February 1595, in which he tells of his plans for the *sala grande*, we may infer that the brothers had arrived in Rome late in the year 1594 ("alcuni mesi sono") and were still there when Odoardo wrote. During this preliminary visit the two artists must have surveyed the work that was to be carried out and made all the necessary arrangements with the cardinal. Agostino took advantage of his stay in Rome to make an engraved copy of Barocci's *Aeneas and Anchises*.[10] Both artists then returned to Bologna, no doubt in order to complete works begun previously. Annibale's chief task, we know, was to finish his monumental canvas, *St. Roch distributing Alms*, for which he had received the commission some years earlier from the Company of St. Roch in Reggio. In July 1595 he wrote from Bologna to a member of the company to explain the difficulties he was experiencing in bringing the work to completion, and to tell of the agreement that he had made to enter Cardinal Farnese's service in Rome at the end of the summer.[11] By November 8, 1595, Annibale was already settled in Rome: the Duke Ranuccio, writing on that date to his brother Odoardo, speaks of Annibale as residing in the Farnese Palace and refers

[6] Bellori, *Vite*, p. 30. In this connection one might hazard the conjecture that Annibale's *Vision of St. Eustace* (Naples, Pinacoteca) was painted for the ducal court at Parma about 1585; at a much later date we find it listed among the works of art in the Farnese Palace in Rome (Inventory of 1653, cited by G. C. Cavalli in the Catalogue of the *Mostra dei Carracci*, 3rd ed., Bologna, 1958, p. 179, no. 61), but since it belongs to the early period of the artist the most likely explanation is that Odoardo himself brought the canvas to Rome from Parma. Possibly the fact that he had just been created Cardinal-deacon of Sant'Eusta-chio gave added interest to the subject of the picture.

[7] *Felsina*, I, p. 403.

[8] Bellori, *Vite*, p. 30.

[9] The problem is dealt with by Tietze, pp. 54 and 57.

[10] Agostino's print, the preparatory drawing for which is in Windsor Castle, is dated 1595. See Wittkower, *Carracci Drawings*, p. 113, no. 99.

[11] Reggio Emilia, Archivio Opere Pie, Congregazione San Rocco. The letter was published by F. Malaguzzi Valeri in *Archivio storico dell'arte*, v, 1892, pp. 135-137.

to him as "your painter."[12] As for Agostino, he seems to have moved to Rome only in the latter part of 1597.[13] Documentary evidence shows that he received payment in October of that year for a portrait of the Duke Ranuccio "which he has presented to Cardinal Farnese."[14] The supposition is that Agostino himself brought the picture to Rome when he set out to join his brother there.

When Annibale entered Farnese's service in 1595 he was thirty-five years of age. His appearance may be judged from the self-portrait in the Uffizi, painted only a few years before, which tells of an unassuming but sensitive and reflective nature; though inclined to be somewhat melancholic, he possessed a keen sense of humor and was famous for his witticisms. As the official artist of Cardinal Farnese Annibale was given quarters in the palace. "Arriving in Rome," writes Bellori, "he presented to the Cardinal in the name of the Duke [Ranuccio] the painting of St. Catherine done in Parma. He was graciously received by this noble lord and was treated with the rank of gentleman, with ten scudi per month and portions for himself and two young men: this is what they call in Rome the bread and wine which it is customary to distribute daily to members of the court."[15] But Annibale's style of life may not in fact have been quite so gentlemanly as Bellori would have it. A certain Giovanni Battista Bonconti, writing from Rome in August 1599, gives this account of the artist's existence: "M. Annibale Carracci receives from his [cardinal] no more than ten scudi per month, and portions for himself and a servant, and a little room under the roof. And for this he toils and pulls a cart the whole day like a horse, and does loggias, rooms and salons, pictures and altarpieces, and works that are worth a thousand scudi. He is worn out with hard work and has little taste for such servitude."[16] There is no reason to question the veracity of this description. The cardinal's parsimoniousness is fully confirmed by the sculptor Moschino, who in 1594 wrote to the Duke Ranuccio to complain that he was not being properly paid.[17] But though Annibale doubtless felt some dissatisfaction with his mode of life, it must not be imagined that he tried

[12] Naples, Archivio di Stato, Carte Farnesiane, f. 724, cited by Tietze, pp. 107 f., note 2.

[13] Agostino's engraved portrait of the Bolognese naturalist Ulisse Aldrovandi (B. 137), which was surely executed in Bologna, can be dated to 1596 because it specifies the age of the subject (born in 1522) as seventy-four.

[14] Parma, Archivio di Stato, Mastri Farnesiani, c. 286, cited by Tietze, p. 126. This may be the portrait listed in an inventory of paintings in the Palazzo del Giardino at Parma c. 1680: "Un ritratto del Sermͦ sig.ʳ Duca Ranuccio I.º armato con frappa al collo, la destra sopra un tavolino con tappeto turchino, la sinistra sopra un elmo di ferro, di

Agostino *Carazza*" (G. Campori, *Raccolta di cataloghi ed inventarii inediti*, Modena, 1870, p. 230).

[15] Bellori, *Vite*, pp. 30 ff.

[16] Malvasia, *Felsina*, I, p. 574. Some forty-five years later the French painter Pierre Mignard, who had come to Rome in the service of Cardinal Alphonse de Richelieu, was quartered in the very room formerly occupied by Annibale (Mazière de Monville, *La vie de Pierre Mignard, premier peintre du Roy*, Amsterdam, 1731, p. 18).

[17] A. Ronchini, "Francesco e Simone Moschini," *Atti e memorie delle RR. Deputazioni di Storia Patria per le Prov. Mod. e Parm.*, VIII, 1876, p. 107.

in any way to rise above his station. He was an artist, and took a professional pride in his work; having no ambition to become a gentleman, he was content to be looked on simply as a painter. He preferred to avoid the society of courtiers and to lead a withdrawn existence in the palace with his pupils, devoting all his energies to painting.[18]

In all of this Annibale presents a notable contrast to his brother Agostino, who, because he was less devoted to his art, felt a need to be regarded as a gentleman. Being ashamed of the fact that their father had been a humble tailor, Agostino characteristically sought to ennoble the family name by inventing for it an emblematic device.[19] The difference between the two brothers is nicely illustrated by an anecdote told by Bellori. "Going up one day from the Gallery to his apartment, Annibale chanced to meet his brother and was annoyed to see him strolling in the company of several *cavalieri*. Calling him aside, as if he had some important matter to discuss with him, he whispered in his ear, 'Remember, Agostino, that you are a tailor's son.' Later when he reached his rooms he took a piece of paper and drew on it a picture of their father with his spectacles threading a needle, with the name Antonio written above, and beside him their old mother with the scissors in her hand. When the drawing was finished he sent it to his brother. Agostino was so upset and offended by it that not long afterward (several other incidents having meanwhile taken place) he broke with Annibale and left Rome altogether."[20]

That the collaboration of the two brothers came to an end as the result of disagreements between them is attested by all the biographers. But their explanations vary. According to Monsignor Giovanni Battista Agucchi, who was personally acquainted with Annibale and whose account of the affair must be the earliest that we have, the quarrel was fomented by someone (unnamed) who wanted to see the two artists divided. Agostino, he says, freely acknowledged that the task of completing the Gallery was better left to Annibale as the more experienced painter.[21] The physician Giulio Mancini, on the other hand, makes it appear that the fault lay chiefly with Annibale, who is pictured as having provoked the altercation out of jealousy of Agostino's skill; but Mancini also notes that Agostino was able to do relatively little work in fresco because it caused him difficulty in breathing.[22] A somewhat similar view is adopted by Malvasia, who enlivens his account of the affair by reproducing part of a letter said to have been written by Annibale to Ludovico shortly after Agostino's departure from Rome; the break came about (Annibale is quoted as saying) through "the unbearable conceit of Agostino, who got me upset and confused by never being satisfied with anything I did and by always looking for faults. What is more, by continually bringing poets, story-writers, and courtiers up on the scaffold he was

[18] Bellori, *Vite*, p. 71.
[19] *Ibid.*, p. 114.
[20] *Ibid.*, p. 71.
[21] G. B. Agucchi, *Trattato*, reprinted in D.

Mahon, *Studies*, p. 255.
[22] G. Mancini, *Considerazioni sulla pittura*, I, p. 217.

both a hindrance and a disturbance to me, with the result that he neither did anything himself, nor allowed others to do anything." This explanation, adds Malvasia, was patently invented by Annibale to conceal the real source of the trouble, which was his own jealousy.[23] Both Bellori and Malvasia, it may be noted, imply that the person who promoted the disagreement was Annibale's pupil, Innocenzo Tacconi.[24]

In leaving Rome, Agostino did not quit the service of the Farnese. It was doubtless through the good offices of Cardinal Odoardo that arrangements were made for him to enter the employ of the Duke Ranuccio in Parma.[25] Agostino had already painted two portraits of the duke, who seems to have admired his work and been well-disposed toward him.[26] The rolls of the ducal court at Parma show that he took up his duties there on July 1, 1600.[27] The artist was not to occupy his new position for long. His chief project, the fresco decoration of a ceiling in the Palazzo del Giardino, was interrupted by his death, which occurred on February 23, 1602.[28] Almost a year later, in January 1603, the members of the Accademia degli Incamminati (as the Academy of the Carracci came to be called) held an impressive memorial service in the Chiesa dell'Ospedale della Morte in Bologna. A volume published at Bologna in the same year contains a full account of the solemn ceremony.[29] In the middle of the church was erected a huge column decorated with emblems and allegorical paintings in praise of Agostino (see Fig. 280). The funeral oration was pronounced by Lucio Faberio, a friend of the Carracci, who had served as secretary of the Academy.

Despite the cardinal's careful plans the fresco cycle glorifying the Duke Alessandro Farnese was never executed. It has always been assumed that Odoardo intended this cycle to be painted in the Gallery at the rear of the palace and that for some reason

[23] Malvasia, *Felsina*, I, p. 404.

[24] Bellori, *Vite*, p. 82; Malvasia, *Felsina*, I, pp. 571 f.

[25] Bellori, *Vite*, p. 111. Agucchi says that Agostino went first to Bologna and from there to Parma (*Trattato*, in Mahon, *Studies*, p. 255). This is also reported by Baglione, *Vite*, p. 105.

[26] Agostino's two portraits of Ranuccio are mentioned by both Bellori (*Vite*, p. 111) and Lucio Faberio in his funeral oration (Malvasia, *Felsina*, I, p. 429). The first picture was paid for in 1597 (see note 14 above); Agostino himself seems to have taken this to Rome as a gift from the duke to Cardinal Farnese. The second portrait must have been done in Rome: Faberio says (*loc.cit.*) that it was painted *in absenza*. This is undoubtedly the picture for which payment was made in July 1599; it commemorated the duke's recovery from a serious illness the year before (documents

cited by Tietze, p. 126, note 3).

[27] Parma, Archivio di Stato, Ruoli Farnesiani, 1599-1603, Reg. 9, cited by Tietze, p. 127, note 4.

[28] Parma, Archivio di Stato, Ruolo de Provigionati del 1599-1603, cited by Tietze, p. 130, note 5.

[29] *Il Funerale d'Agostin Carraccio fatto in Bologna sua patria da gl' Incaminati Academici del Disegno scritto all' Ill.mo et R.mo Sig.r Cardinal Farnese*, Bologna, 1603. The engravings are by Guido Reni and Francesco Brizio. The text is reprinted in Malvasia, *Felsina*, I, pp. 407-433. The statement in the catalogue of the *Mostra dei Carracci* (3rd ed., p. 90) that the memorial service was held in January 1602 (i.e. before Agostino's death) is plainly due to an oversight. Unfortunately the same error is repeated in the catalogue of the exhibition *L'ideale classico del Seicento in Italia*, Bologna, 1962, p. 50.

he later decided to change the subject-matter from family history to fable.[30] This assumption is certainly incorrect.

In the first place when Odoardo speaks of *la sala grande* he is plainly referring, not to the Gallery, but to the great hall which rises through two stories at the southeast corner of the palace (text fig. 1, 1, page 7).[31] Here, significantly, stood the marble group by Simone Moschino representing Alessandro Farnese crowned by Victory and triumphing over Flanders and the Scheldt (Fig. 273). The ample walls of this room afforded an ideal surface for a narrative cycle. In the Gallery, on the other hand, the only uninterrupted surface was the vaulted ceiling, and this would have been ill suited to such a program. It can never have been Odoardo's intention to decorate the Gallery with scenes from the life of the Duke of Parma.

Secondly, it is clear that the plan to paint such an historical cycle was not abandoned but merely postponed, probably because the indispensable book of drawings sent by Masi from Flanders had not been received in Rome. By the summer of 1595 Odoardo was already making plans for another project, the decoration of the Camerino (text fig. 1, 4, page 7), and when Annibale Carracci arrived in Rome later in the year he at once began work on that room. From the Camerino he turned directly to the the ceiling of the Galleria, a task which occupied him for several years. What then happened is best told in Bellori's words: "The cardinal desired that he should paint in the *sala* the heroic deeds of the great Alexander Farnese, who had died not many years before in Flanders, and he also intended to employ him in repainting the cupola of the Church of the Gesù in Rome. . . .[32] But these noble intentions were not to be realized, nor was this Roman Alexander to have his Apelles." For, as the biographer goes on to explain, the cardinal decided to recompense Annibale for the works that he had executed since coming to Rome. Before this could be done, however, a sycophantic Spanish courtier, one Don Juan de Castro, took it upon himself to calculate the total value of the wages and the bread and wine received by the artist over the period in question, and to deduct this amount from the proposed remuneration. Odoardo was accordingly persuaded by this gentleman to pay Annibale the insultingly small sum of 500 *scudi d'oro*, which were brought to his room in a saucer.[33] It was an unfortunate decision, which was not only to deprive the cardinal of the proposed

[30] E.g., Tietze, pp. 53 f.

[31] W. Vitzthum has come to the same conclusion (*Burlington Magazine*, Oct. 1963, p. 446).

[32] The dome of the Gesù, later to be repainted by Gaulli, was originally frescoed by Giovanni de Vecchi (Baglione, *Vite*, p. 128; see also P. Pecchiai, *Il Gesù di Roma*, Rome, 1952, pp. 76 f., 104 ff.). One wonders what solution Annibale would have adopted for the cupola.

[33] Bellori, *Vite*, pp. 66 f. Cf. also Baglione,

Vite, p. 108. Mancini (*Considerazioni*, I, p. 218) says only that Annibale considered himself inadequately recompensed. Odoardo's unjust treatment of the artist is alluded to by Poussin in a letter of 1642 addressed to Sublet de Noyers (C. Jouanny, *Correspondance de N. Poussin*, Paris, 1911, pp. 140 f.). The most scathing denunciation of Cardinal Farnese's behavior is that of Bernini (M. de Chantelou, *Journal du voyage du Cavalier Bernin en France* [ed. L. Lalanne], Paris, 1885, p. 59).

fresco cycle upon which he counted so much, but was even to place in jeopardy the plans for completing the Gallery. For Annibale, physically exhausted after his work on the vault and profoundly upset by Agostino's defection, reacted sharply to his patron's callous and ungrateful behavior and fell into a state of depression which prevented him from resuming work on the Gallery for a lengthy period.[34] As for the other fresco projects which the cardinal had in mind—the Alessandro Farnese cycle and the repainting of the dome of the Gesù—these came to nothing. "Such," concludes Bellori, "is the unhappiness that befalls courts, princes, and fine arts alike when certain persons oppress others in order to gain advantage for themselves, and claim first place in favor by driving out virtue with ignorance and presumption."[35]

But worse trouble was to follow. Early in the year 1605, not long after recommencing work on the Galleria, Annibale's health broke down completely and he was stricken with a kind of paralysis which caused a temporary loss of memory and even of the power of speech.[36] A good deal is known about the artist's circumstances in the period immediately following his collapse, because it was at this time that Cesare d'Este, Duke of Modena, commissioned a painting from him, and there exists in the State Archives at Modena a lengthy correspondence detailing the efforts which were made to induce Annibale to execute the work. On March 12, 1605, Cardinal Farnese himself wrote to the duke: "When Annibale Carracci has recovered from a serious illness which he has had these past days and which still keeps him from painting, Your Highness's request will be attended to. . . . This may be within a month, as the doctors hope that by that time Carracci will be completely restored to health."[37] The doctors' prognosis was too sanguine. In fact Annibale never fully recovered, and (though at the time no one could have foreseen this) his career as a painter was virtually at an end. By the summer of 1605 he had forced himself to begin work on the painting for the Duke of Modena; but during the succeeding months he proved to be incapable, physically and mentally, of bringing it to completion, and at length the ill-fated project had to be abandoned.[38]

As soon as his health allowed him to move, Annibale quitted the Farnese palace. In August 1605 the agent of the Duke of Modena found him living in seclusion "dietro le vigne de' Riarij alla Lungara."[39] During the last years he changed his place of residence in Rome several times. Bellori speaks of a house on the Quirinal where now stands the Church of San Carlo alle Quattro Fontane;[40] in 1607 he is registered

[34] This and other problems of chronology are dealt with in Chapter 4.

[35] Bellori, *loc.cit.*

[36] Mancini, *Considerazioni*, I, p. 218.

[37] Modena, Archivio di Stato, Carteggio dei Principi, busta 96. Cited by Tietze, p. 147, note 1: "Quando Annibale Caracci sia rihavuto d'una infirmità mortale che ha havuto li giorni passati, et che lo tiene tuttavia interdetto dalla pittura, Vostra Altezza resterà servita . . . et questo potrà esser fra un mese, sperando i medici, ch'in questo tempo esso Caracci sia per rivalidarsi affatto."

[38] Documents cited by Tietze (pp. 147-149) and by Cavalli (Catalogue of the *Mostra dei Carracci*, pp. 96-99).

[39] Modena, Archivio di Stato, Corrisp. Esteri, busta 124. Cited by Tietze, p. 148, note 1.

[40] Bellori, *Vite*, p. 67; Malvasia, *Felsina*, I, p. 442.

as living in the parish of S. Lorenzo in Lucina.[41] Though Annibale would perhaps
have preferred to be left alone, there were certain professional obligations which he
could not avoid. He was still a member of the Academy of St. Luke, and seems to
have made an effort to attend its meetings.[42] In addition he was master of a busy workshop, the members of which looked to him for guidance. There is evidence, too, of
the genuine affection which Annibale's pupils felt for him. In August 1607 Sisto
Badalocchio and Giovanni Lanfranco dedicated to him a set of engravings which
they had made after the Raphael frescoes in the Vatican Loggie.[43] Almost a year later,
in July 1608, there was a pathetic attempt by a group of students to rouse the master
from his state of melancholy and interest him in painting once more.[44] Ironically, it
must have been just about this time that Carracci, realizing that he could never hope
to regain his powers of body and will, decided to entrust to his assistants the task of
completing the Galleria Farnese.

Annibale's condition, aggravated by what Bellori calls *disordini amorosi*, deterio-
rated markedly during the spring of 1609 and he was advised to seek a change of air in
Naples. Finding no improvement there he returned after a short time to Rome, where
he died on July 15, 1609.[45] He was buried, as he had wished, in the Pantheon.

Seeing his plans for a cycle of frescoes honoring the Duke Alessandro thus thwarted,
Cardinal Farnese presumably gave up the idea altogether. The dauntless Malvasia
suggests, however, that Odoardo may now have tried to induce Ludovico to take over
the task. He even claims to have seen four large drawings by Ludovico for the cycle
in question; but these, he adds, had been made some years earlier in response to a
plea for help from Annibale.[46] There is probably no truth in the story, which sounds
rather like a postscript to Malvasia's report that the Galleria was first offered to Ludovico.

Did Annibale himself make any sketches for the proposed cycle in the *sala grande*?
The great repositories of Carracci drawings in Windsor Castle and the Louvre contain no groups of studies that might be connected with such a project. The black
chalk drawing by Annibale in the Louvre (Inv. 7314) representing Alessandro Farnese on horseback was not designed for an historical subject but is a study for Carracci's large equestrian portrait of the duke which was later transported, with the

---

[41] Stati d'anime, 1607, fol. 23. Cited by J.
Bousquet, "Documents sur le séjour de Simon
Vouet à Rome," *Mélanges d'archéologie et
d'histoire, Ecole Française de Rome*, LXIV,
1952, p. 289, note 3.

[42] In October 1607, for example, he made
a contribution for the feast of St. Luke (Rome,
Archivio dell'Accademia di San Luca, vol.
42, Entrata e Uscita del Camerlengo, fol. 34
v.). Bernini, who came to Rome as a boy about
1605, later told of meeting Annibale and accompanying him to the Academy, where the

latter was asked to pose the model (Chantelou, *Journal*, p. 34).

[43] Bellori, *Vite*, pp. 96 ff.; Malvasia, *Felsina*,
I, p. 519 f.

[44] Mahon, *Disegni*, pp. 167 f., no. 248.

[45] Mancini, *Considerazioni*, I, p. 219; Baglione, *Vite*, p. 108; Bellori, *Vite*, pp. 76 f.
Monsignor G. B. Agucchi, who closed Annibale's eyes, described his last hours in a letter
to a friend (Malvasia, *Felsina*, I, p. 445).

[46] Malvasia, *Felsina*, I, p. 447.

other Farnese possessions from the Roman palace, to Parma.[47] From the lack of graphic material it may be concluded that Annibale made no extensive preparations for the Alessandro Farnese cycle.

[47] Campori, *Raccolta di cataloghi*, p. 209: "Ritratto del Serm̃o Sig. Duca Alessandro armato a cavallo con bastone di comando alla destra e duoi soldati in lontananza, del *Carazza*." I do not know what has become of this painting.

CHAPTER 3 · THE CAMERINO FARNESE

THE decision to paint the ceiling of the Camerino instead of proceeding with the original plans for the Alessandro Farnese cycle was taken before the summer of 1595. The frescoes glorifying their father's deeds would have to wait until the arrival of the book of drawings which Odoardo had asked Ranuccio to send him; in the meantime Annibale Carracci was to be given as his first task the decoration of the cardinal's own study.

It was not unusual, some years ago, to speak disparagingly of the Camerino Farnese, and to describe its frescoes as unworthy of their author. The subjects, it was said, were too heavily burdened with recondite symbolism to be congenial to Annibale's forthright and practical nature. The result, inevitably, was a failure, which was only redeemed by the more felicitous decoration of the Gallery in the same palace. That the Camerino was highly thought of in the Seicento counted for nothing: Bellori's enthusiastic praise, for example, was to be attributed to the fact that, as a man of letters, he took such delight in the erudition of the program that he was blind to its artistic defects.

If today it has become possible to discuss the Camerino without enumerating its shortcomings, this is chiefly due to two things. The first, of course, is the fact that the interest in the art of the Carracci has progressed to the point where it is no longer regarded as inherently decadent and inferior, but can be openly and unreservedly enjoyed. Secondly, studies in the field of iconology have served to correct the notion that literary content is somehow detrimental to the work of art. We now find it less often assumed that artists of the sixteenth and seventeenth centuries felt constrained and hampered in their expression by having to follow subjects invented for them by others. Looked at as sheer decoration, the Camerino is a charming and highly successful interior. It is impossible to believe that Annibale executed this work in a merely perfunctory and routine fashion, or that he was indifferent to (not to say embarrassed by) the subject matter.

What is more, the Camerino is of special interest in that it tells us a good deal about Annibale's early response to the stimulus of Rome. The general effect of the decoration is still Correggiesque, recalling in certain respects the Camera di San Paolo in Parma. But the new impressions of the Roman environment have already left their mark. Particularly evident is Annibale's careful study of antique sculpture, both statuary and relief. This is not hard to explain. Living in the Farnese Palace the master was in daily contact with one of the richest collections of antiquities that the city could offer. No less obvious is the influence of Raphael, whose narrative compositions must have exerted at this stage a decisive effect on the formation of Annibale's classical style. But Michelangelesque elements are also present here. For the artist has already come under the spell of the Sistine ceiling, and has accordingly introduced more than one reminiscence of Michelangelo's *ignudi*. The Camerino is the first monument of Annibale's Roman grand manner, and the indispensable prelude to the Galleria Farnese.

Malvasia's assumption that Annibale and Agostino worked side by side in the Camerino is not confirmed by the evidence. Agostino does not appear to have joined his brother in the Palazzo Farnese until the autumn of 1597, by which time the decoration of the Camerino was already complete, nor is there anything to suggest his hand among the preparatory drawings.[1]

The Camerino is on the first, or principal, floor of the palace (text fig. 1, page 7); it measures slightly more than fifteen by thirty feet.[2] Light is admitted through two windows overlooking the central court. These are matched by two doors on the opposite wall; there is also a door at each end of the room. The rather complex structure of the coved ceiling can best be understood from a diagram (text fig. 2). The coving is penetrated by six triangular spandrels—two on each side and one at each end—where

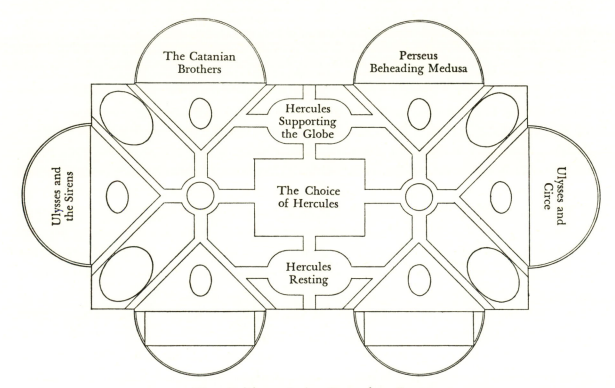

2. The Ceiling of the Camerino Farnese

semicircular lunettes rise above the doors and windows. In the center of the field a rectangular area contains a painting on canvas. On either side of this, along the shorter axis of the ceiling, are two spaces of oval shape (properly oblong, with semi-

[1] Malvasia, *Felsina*, I, p. 404. The hypothesis of an intervention by Agostino in the Camerino has been tentatively revived by Roberto Longhi (in *Paragone*, no. 89, 1957,

p. 42).

[2] According to F. de Navenne, 4.8 x 9.4 meters (*Rome et le palais Farnèse pendant les trois derniers siècles*, Paris, 1923, I, p. 72).

circular ends). These variously shaped areas are defined by moldings of gilt stucco, which are connected to form a structural network over the ceiling as a whole. The decoration below the cornice is modern. The coving, the lunettes, and the spandrels are plainly visible in Figs. 3 and 4, which also show the four Cardinal Virtues in the corners. Toward either end of the ceiling there is a medallion containing the *impresa*, or personal device, of Cardinal Odoardo Farnese—three purple lilies and a scroll with the motto ΘΕΟΘΕΝ ΑΤΞΑΝΟΜΑΙ (Fig. 16).

Especially beautiful is the grisaille ornament which fills the various irregular sections of the vault. It is painted with feigned lighting so as to simulate stucco, the illusion of plasticity being such that the design seems actually to be raised in high relief. This chiaroscuro decoration consists principally of elegant rinceaux, strikingly classical in appearance, among which are interspersed masks, fauns, satyrs, putti, and the like; here and there can be seen a conventionalized lily, heraldic emblem of the Farnese family. The work is of infinite variety, each compartment being full of delightful surprises. For example, in each of the areas which enclose the central rectangle (Figs. 5-8) we find a Michelangelesque faun holding a cornucopia, a putto supporting a garland, and a goat-legged satyr who seems to converse with a little bird perched on a branch of the foliage. The seated attitude of the satyr appears to have been inspired by the figure of Pan in the antique marble group of *Pan and Olympus* in the Farnese collection, a work which frequently suggested motives to Annibale In the adjoining compartment is a female satyr, or Panisca, in the same attitude. Almost unnoticed within the curving arabesques are four little medallions representing deeds of Hercules. In each of the triangular spandrels (Figs. 19-22) there appears an oval containing an allegorical figure; the ovals are painted in imitation of gilt bronze relief and are placed within a laurel wreath supported by decorative figures.

There is an interesting study at Windsor for the decorative parts of the vault (No 2, Fig. 102), in which it is possible to recognize most of the features of the ceiling as it was actually carried out. The drawing contains no hint, however, of the medallions with the labors of Hercules, nor of the Cardinal Virtues; these elements must therefore have been late additions to the program.

We turn now to the principal subjects.[3] The theme of the ceiling is Virtue, set forth allegorically in various scenes from mythology—"immagini della Virtù," Bellori calls them.[4] All were designed, as we shall see, to honor the young Cardinal Farnese,

---

[3] The individual subjects are described by Bellori (*Vite*, pp. 33-44). See also Tietze, pp. 65-71; A. Foratti, *I Carracci nella teoria e nella pratica*, Città di Castello, 1913, pp. 263-269; H. Bodmer, "Die Fresken des Annibale Carracci im Camerino des Palazzo Farnese in Rom," *Pantheon*, XIX, 1937, pp. 146-149; and J. R. Martin, "Immagini della Virtù: the Paintings of the Camerino Farnese," *Art Bul-*letin, XXXVIII, 1956, pp. 91-112. Detailed engravings of the ceiling were made in the seventeenth century by Pietro Aquila (*Imagines Farnesiani cubiculi cum ipsarum monocromatibus et ornamentis Romae in ædibus Sereniss. Ducis Parmensis ab Annibale Carraccio aeternitati pictae, à Petro Aquila delineatae incisae*, Rome, n.d.).

[4] *Vite*, p. 33.

whose personal device is an integral part of the decorative scheme. The scenes which occupy the middle area of the vault (cf. text fig. 2) are devoted to Hercules as the type and champion of Virtue.

THE CHOICE OF HERCULES (FIG. 9)

The central painting is the canvas representing the *Choice of Hercules*. The original, now in the Pinacoteca Nazionale at Naples, has been replaced in the vault of the Camerino by an indifferent copy (cf. Figs. 5-8).[5] The picture illustrates the apologue invented by Prodicus of Ceos, as described by Xenophon (*Memorabilia* II. 1, 21 ff.) and other ancient writers.[6] The adolescent Hercules, seated in a place of solitude, saw two women appear before him. Vice sought to lure him along the easy path of indolence and pleasure; Virtue counseled him to take the arduous road of duty and honor. Confronted with this dilemma Hercules at length chose virtue.

Carracci's presentment of the episode is clear, logical, and instantly understandable; it is easy to see why this became the "canonical formulation" of the subject, from which henceforth it was hardly possible to deviate.[7] The nude, beardless Hercules, frowning in his indecision and clasping a mighty club, sits on a rock in the middle of the scene. At his left the elegant figure of Voluptas, seductively clad in swirling and diaphanous garments of yellow hue, indicates the sweet but false delights that await him along the "primrose path of dalliance": a book of music, masks, musical instruments, and playing cards—and, deep within the grove, clusters of grapes. On the other side stands the sterner figure of *Virtus*, holding a sword[8] and pointing upward along the stony way that leads to the mountaintop, where the winged horse Pegasus can be seen amidst the trees. She wears a pale red mantle over a light blue tunic. Seated at her feet is a poet wreathed with laurel; holding an open book before him, he seems to promise eternal fame for Hercules if he will choose the way of goodness. The outcome, to be sure, is obvious. Already the hero's eyes are turned toward Virtue, and the palm tree behind him is, as Bellori observes, a "presagio ben certo delle sue vittorie."[9]

It has been convincingly shown that the composition depends primarily on the

[5] The canvas was detached from the ceiling and sent to the Farnese collection in Parma in 1662 (see A. Filangieri di Candida, "La Galleria Nazionale di Napoli," *Le Gallerie Nazionali Italiane*, V, 1902, p. 267, note 5, no. 3). In the eighteenth century, when the Bourbons of Naples inherited the Farnese collections, the painting was removed to the palace of Capodimonte.

[6] The classic study of this subject is that by E. Panofsky, *Hercules am Scheidewege und andere antike Bildstoffe in den neueren Kunst*, Leipzig-Berlin, 1930.

[7] *Ibid.*, pp. 124 ff.

[8] The sword is the *parazonium*, which appears as an attribute of *Virtus* on Roman coins (e.g. those of Galba and Vitellius) showing *Honos* and *Virtus* (H. Mattingly, *Coins of the Roman Empire in the British Museum*, I, London, 1923, p. 357 and pl. 58, 10; p. 375).

[9] *Vite*, p. 35. On the palm tree as a symbol of rebirth and victory over death, see G. B. Ladner, "Vegetation Symbolism and the Concept of Renaissance," *De artibus opuscula XL: Essays in Honor of Erwin Panofsky*, New York, 1961, pp. 303-322.

antique marble relief of *Hercules and the Hesperides*,[10] well known in Rome during the sixteenth century and now in the Villa Albani: from this source Carracci derived the simple rhythmic grouping of a seated male figure (in both instances Hercules) between two standing women, the triangular pattern formed by the heads, the rock on which the hero sits, and the tree rising behind him. In the attitudes of the figures the two sources of Annibale's classicism—antiquity and the Roman High Renaissance—are fully apparent. Panofsky has shown, with admirable succinctness, that the seated Hercules "combines the motives of the Ludovisi Mars and the Hermes fastening his Sandal with the pose of the *ignudi* above Isaiah." Similarly, the poet laureate is "a synthesis of an antique river god and the Cumaean Sibyl transformed into a male figure."[11] *Voluptas*, finally, depends directly on the figure seen from the back in Marcantonio's engraving after Raphael, the *Judgment of Paris*.

The subject was not wholly new to Annibale. In the Palazzo Sampieri (now Talon) in Bologna he had painted only a few years earlier a ceiling fresco showing Hercules guided by Virtue.[12] But this is a far more elaborate conception. The masks beside Vice are familiar symbols of deceit.[13] The particular association of the two masks, one young and fresh, the other old and bearded, with sensual love and its deceptive pleasures, is unquestionably derived from an allegory by Michelangelo: the *Venus and Cupid*, a composition executed after his cartoon by Pontormo and copied by other Mannerist artists during the sixteenth century.[14] There the two masks were shown hanging beside an altar. In Carracci's canvas this feature is echoed in the draped altar upon which the masks lie; the younger face, moreover, is partly concealed behind the bearded one, exactly as in the Michelangelesque composition. Two kinds of music are contrasted here: on the side of Virtue are heard the lofty strains of epic poetry, and on the other the base and trivial music of the tavern and the gaming-house.[15]

There is no doubt that the painting was intended as an allusion to Odoardo Farnese himself, although the figure of Hercules is of course in no sense to be regarded as a portrait. It was not uncommon for princes of the period to be likened to the virtuous hero of ancient fable. Giovanni Savorgnano employs just such a metaphor in a poem addressed to the young Odoardo, opening with the lines:

> *Giovanetto real, novello Alcide,*
> *Che i serpi uccisi del fecondo Egitto.*[16]

[10] Panofsky, *op.cit.*, pp. 127 f., fig. 66.

[11] *Ibid.*, p. 126, note 1.

[12] Tietze, p. 62, fig. 5; F. Malaguzzi Valeri, in *Cronache d'arte*, I, 1924, fig. 6.

[13] See Cesare Ripa, *Iconologia*, Siena, 1613, s.v. "Bugia," "Fraude," "Inganno," and "Imitatione."

[14] H. Thode, *Michelangelo, Kritische Untersuchungen über seine Werke*, Berlin, 1908-1913, II, pp. 324 ff. C. de Tolnay, *Michelangelo*, III, *The Medici Chapel*, Princeton, 1948, pp. 108 f., 194 ff.

[15] For the combination of playing cards and musical instruments to signify reprehensible amusements see Ripa, *op.cit.*, s.v. "Scandolo": "Un vecchio . . . terrà con la destra mano . . . un mazzo di carte da giuocare, con la sinistra un leuto, & alli piedi vi sarà un flauto, & un libro di musica aperto."

[16] *Raccolta di diverse compositioni sopra le vittorie acqvistate in Fiandra dal Serenissimo Alessandro Farnese Dvca di Parma, et di Piacenza, . . . ,* Parma, 1586 (dedicatory poem).

As the Duke Alessandro Farnese, by his martial exploits, recalls Jupiter's victory over the Titans, so also his son, like a new Hercules (Alcides), is destined to rid the world of monsters and giants. "Heaven hath also ordained palms for thee," the poet assures Odoardo.[17] A similar imagery is evoked by the palm tree in Carracci's painting.

Prodicus' story of the choice of Hercules enjoyed special favor among courtly writers because a felicitous compliment to some noble youth could easily be devised by casting him in the principal part. Thus, for example, the Dutch historian Stephanus Vinandus Pighius chose the title *Hercules Prodicius* for his account of the life and travels of the young Prince Carl Friedrich of Cleves.[18] For Odoardo, moreover, the role of "Prodician Hercules" was especially apt. As a boy, the example that had been held before him as most worthy of emulation was that of his great-uncle, Cardinal Alessandro Farnese (1520-1589), a man of cultivation and learning, equally distinguished as a prince of the church and as a patron of artists and men of letters. The author of the poem *La Caprarola* (around 1585) expresses the hope "that with this honor my illustrious lord Odoardo may imitate the kingly deeds of his uncle Alessandro."[19] It is quite evident that in Odoardo's case to choose the path of virtue and honor meant to follow in Cardinal Alessandro's footsteps. And, it may be added, there were later those who believed (or pretended to believe) that he had actually succeeded in rivaling his great-uncle as a Maecenas. Traiano Boccalini speaks, with characteristic irony, of "the great splendor of *Edward* Cardinal *Fernese*, who by a Princely generosity, and profuse liberality used towards all men, had made the Court, and the whole Nobility of *Rome* so in love with him, as he was now more honoured and observed in anothers Popedom, then the great *Alexander* Cardinal *Fernese* was formerly in the Popedom of his Uncle, *Paul* the third."[20]

The example of Cardinal Alessandro is, in point of fact, expressly alluded to in the painting. For the winged horse serves not only as a symbol of "fame as the consequence of virtue,"[21] but also as a reference to Alessandro himself, who bore an *impresa* showing Pegasus on Mount Parnassus, to signify his patronage of *letterati*.[22] The same two meanings—fame engendered by virtue, and the fostering of arts and letters—are combined in the figure of the poet who fixes his gaze on the young Hercules, and promises to sing his praises forever.

[17] *Ibid.*: ". . . palme prescritto / Ben'ancho hà il cielo à te."

[18] *Hercules Prodicius, seu principis iuventutis vita et peregrinatio*, Antwerp, 1587.

[19] F. Baumgart, "La Caprarola di Ameto Orti," *Studj Romanzi*, xxv, 1935, p. 122, stanza 84. The "honor" refers to the cardinalate with which Odoardo was to be invested.

[20] *Ragguagli di Parnaso* (ed. G. Rua), II, Bari, 1912, p. 253. I quote from the English translation by Henry, Earl of Monmouth (*Advertisements from Parnassus*, London, 1656, p. 351).

[21] On this see Panofsky, *op.cit.*, p. 117.

[22] The *impresa*, which was invented by Molza, is described by Annibal Caro (*Delle lettere familiari del Commendatore Annibal Caro . . .*, Padua, 1742, II, p. 366). Cf. also *ibid.*, I, p. 217: "Avvertite, che quel Pegaso vuol dire il Cardinal Farnese, per esser sua Impresa." Caro himself, it may be added, designed a Pegasus device for the future Duke Alessandro, to show that he desired to emulate his uncle the cardinal (*ibid.*, II, pp. 141 f.).

The *Choice of Hercules*, manifestly designed both as a compliment and as an exhortation to the young Odoardo, sets the keynote for the entire cycle. Closely linked in subject matter to this first scene are the two oval frescoes flanking it, both of which have to do with the same virtuous champion.

HERCULES BEARING THE GLOBE (FIG. 10)

Once again the hero occupies the middle of the composition. But now he appears as a mature, bearded man, wrapped about with the lion skin and kneeling beneath the weight of a huge sphere, the surface of which bears the signs of the zodiac and the constellations. On the left and right are seated two astronomers, their lower limbs enveloped in loose draperies; one holds an armillary sphere in his outstretched right hand, and the other works with a pair of compasses on a tablet while he observes the globe of heaven.

The fable of Hercules taking Atlas' burden upon his own shoulders is variously explained in mythographical literature, the most frequent interpretation being that Atlas was an astronomer from whom Hercules learned the science of the heavens.[23] This, as Bellori tells us[24] and as the two astronomers at the sides confirm, provides the meaning of Annibale's fresco. Hercules is to be understood as the philosopher, the seeker after wisdom, symbolized by the celestial sphere. The theme is a recurrent one in the Cinquecento. A fresco by Agostino Carracci in the Palazzo Sampieri-Talon represents both Hercules and Atlas supporting the globe.[25] In the emblem book of Achille Bocchi (1555) a similar imagery had already been associated with the Farnese. One of the illustrations, labeled "pro maximo Farnesio" (presumably Cardinal Alessandro), shows Hercules and Atlas standing over a celestial sphere: the first takes measurements with a pair of compasses, while the other reads from a book.[26] In the accompanying verse Hercules is described as typifying the active life and Atlas as representing the contemplative ("hic videt, alter agit"). In the Camerino fresco, however, Atlas is absent, and Hercules assumes the contemplative role.

The two astronomers are not easily identified: even Bellori is silent on this point. Bodmer calls them Pythagoras and Euclid.[27] The sphere, however, probably designates the figure at the left not as Pythagoras, but as Ptolemy. It is true that he is without the crown which (as in Raphael's *School of Athens*) sometimes distinguishes that personage; but the crown is by no means an invariable attribute. Indeed it is probable that by this time Ptolemy's royal lineage was recognized as mythical. In sixteenth-century editions of his work Ptolemy is usually portrayed wearing a simple cap.[28] As

[23] Servius on Virgil's *Aeneid* I, 745. On this subject see also E. Panofsky, *Studies in Iconology*, New York, 1939, pp. 20 f., note 10.

[24] *Vite*, p. 35.

[25] *Ibid.*, p. 106. F. Malaguzzi Valeri, in *Cronache d'arte*, I, 1924, fig. 8.

[26] Achille Bocchi, *Symbolicarum quaestion-*

um libri quinque, Bologna, 1555, Symb. CX. This was pointed out by Tietze, p. 67, note 2.

[27] Bodmer, in *Pantheon*, XIX, 1937, p. 147.

[28] E.g. in the frontispieces of the *Geographia universalis vetus et nova, complectens Claudii Ptolemaei Alexandrini enarrationis libros viii*, Basel, 1545, and *La geografia di Claudio*

regards the second figure, the compasses form a suitable attribute for the mathematician Euclid, who also wrote a treatise on astronomy (the Φαινόμενα). Raphael represents him with both compasses and tablet in the *School of Athens*.

The two sages are placed so that their attitudes effectively complement each other, one being seen from the back and the other from the front. Their postures are an echo (in reverse) of the pair of *ignudi* above the Persian Sibyl of the Sistine; the figure of Euclid, at the right, also contains an unmistakable reminiscence of the seated St. Andrew in the left foreground of Raphael's *Transfiguration*. Hercules with the globe, on the other hand, was obviously inspired by the famous Farnese Atlas, now in Naples, which had been acquired many years earlier by Cardinal Alessandro.[29] The astronomical signs visible on the sphere are identical with those of the sculptured globe. Carracci's kneeling figure, one of the most impressive of the cycle, was perfected only after lengthy study and experiment.[30] In Bellori's eyes it was a consummate achievement: and the proof of this, he writes, was that when Albani and Domenichino had to represent such a subject they could do no more than copy Annibale's Hercules.[31]

HERCULES RESTING (FIG. 11)

In the second oval Hercules is seen resting from his labors. He is half reclining on a rocky ledge, behind which is a grove of trees; his chin is supported by his clenched left hand, and in his right he grasps a long dagger, the point of which is pressed against the rock. The position of the hero's legs is reminiscent of the Adam in the creation scene of the Sistine. His club and bow and arrows lie on the ground at his feet. Around him are the evidences of his labors. The tawny hide of the Nemean lion is draped over his loins and cushions his elbow; the three golden apples of the Hesperides rest beneath his leg; in the middle of the scene is the antlered head of the Arcadian stag; then appear the three snarling, barking heads of the dog Cerberus, who is chained to a large block of stone; and finally, in the lower left, there emerges the great snout of the Erymanthian boar. Seated upon the block and sharply silhouetted against the sky is a winged sphinx, who looks fixedly at Hercules. An inscription on

Ptolemeo Alessandrino, Venice, 1548; and in the title page of the *Tabulae geographicae Cl: Ptolemaei ad mentem autoris restitutae & emendatae per Gerardum Mercatorem . . .*, Cologne, 1578.

[29] R. Lanciani, *Storia degli scavi di Roma e notizie intorno le collezioni romane di antichità*, Rome, 1903, II, p. 163. Bellori, who notes the derivation, speaks of the Farnese statue as Hercules (*Vite*, p. 81). A very different source was proposed by Mariette, who mistakenly believed that Annibale's Hercules was based on an engraving in Bocchi's emblem book showing Atlas supporting the heavens

(Symb. CXXXVIII). The attitudes of the two figures are in fact not much alike. See P. J. Mariette, *Abecedario* (ed. by P. de Chennevières and A. de Montaiglon), Paris, 1851-1853, pp. 320 f.

[30] For the preparatory drawings see Nos. 1, 12, 13, 14 and 15 (Figs. 100, 101, 114-117).

[31] *Vite*, p. 81. Albani's subject must be the *Hercules bearing the globe, assisted by Apollo and Mercury*, which was engraved by Villamena, and for which there is a preparatory drawing at Chatsworth. Cf. Malvasia, *Felsina*, I, p. 123. I have been unable to trace the work in question by Domenichino.

the stone below her reads: ΠΟΝΟΣ ΤΟΥ ΚΑΛΩΣ ΗΣΥΧΑΖΕΙΝ ΑΙΤΙΟΣ, which may be translated: "Toil is the bringer of sweet rest."

Ancient sources tell of no encounter between Hercules and the Sphinx. It is probable, then, that she is meant to exemplify the perils undergone by the hero in his fight against evil; according to Hyginus,[32] the Sphinx was of the same parentage as several of the monsters overcome by Hercules. Moreover, it was Juno, author of Hercules' tribulations, who sent the Sphinx to plague Thebes. But we shall see later that there was still another reason for her presence here.

Bellori informs us that this scene, with its signs of toil and struggle, denotes the active life, whereas the other fresco, showing Hercules bearing the globe, stands for the contemplative life.[33] This results in a pleasant paradox, for the hero rests when he is meant to typify action, and labors when he signifies contemplation. Bellori's interpretation is no doubt correct; but it can perhaps be carried a step further. Is it possible that the central group of three paintings, all dealing with Hercules, was designed as a tripartite allegory of the virtuous life?

The notion that there are not merely two but three modes of human life appears in the late antique writer Fulgentius;[34] he defines them as contemplative, active, and sensual, and finds them exemplified in the Judgment of Paris by the three contending goddesses, Minerva, Juno, and Venus respectively. The idea is further developed and enriched by the Florentine Neoplatonists of the Quattrocento, especially by their leading thinker, Marsilio Ficino. In the dedicatory letter preceding his commentary on Plato's *Philebus*, addressed to Lorenzo de' Medici, Ficino draws a parallel between the Judgment of Paris and that of Hercules, remarking that whereas the former was confronted with three goddesses, and hence with three ways of life, Hercules was required to choose only between Venus and Juno, that is, between the "sensual" and "active" life.[35] "Scorning Venus," says Ficino, "Hercules followed courageous virtue under Juno." For it was due to Juno, as we recall, that the Herculean labors had to be performed.

Needless to say, Carracci's three paintings do not depend simply on Ficino's words: Venus and Juno, for instance, are nowhere represented. This is a new and original

---

[32] *Fabula* 151.

[33] *Vite*, p. 37.

[34] Mythologiae II, 1 (De judicio Paridis): "Philosophi tripartitam humanitatis voluerunt esse vitam, ex quibus primam theoreticam, secundam practicam, tertiam philargicam voluere: quas nos Latine contemplativam, activam, voluptariam nuncupamus. . . ." Similar definitions are found in Mythographus Secundus, 206 (G. H. Bode, *Scriptores rerum mythicarum Latini tres*, Celle, 1834, I, p. 144) and Mythographus Tertius, II, 22 (*ibid.*, p. 241). Cf. also Panofsky, *Hercules am Scheidewege*, pp. 59 f.

[35] "Tres esse vitas, nemo ratione vivens dubitat, contemplativam, activam, voluptuosam. . . . Duae [deae] tantum occurrisse traduntur Herculi, Venus scilicet, atque Iuno. Hercules neglecta Venere, animosam sub Iunone virtutem est secutus" (*Marsilii Ficini Florentini . . . opera*, Basel, 1576, I, pp. 919 f.). The theme recurs, in another form, in Francesco Colonna's *Hypnerotomachia Poliphili* (Venice, 1499): Poliphilus is confronted by three gates inscribed *gloria dei, mater amoris,* and *gloria mundi,* which plainly correspond to the contemplative, sensual, and active lives respectively.

complex, in which Hercules plays the chief role throughout. Nevertheless the influence of such Neoplatonic speculation on the three kinds of life is clearly perceptible. The central painting (Fig. 9) illustrates the fundamental moral choice—the rejection of the *vita voluptuosa* and the decision to follow the life of virtue. But virtue in turn has two aspects: the *vita contemplativa* (Fig. 10), which is the life of wisdom, the liberal arts and religion; and the *vita activa* (Fig. 11), which is the life of power and authority, and of human affairs in general. Both, it is implied, are proper to a prince of the church.

THE OTHER SCENES OF HERCULES

The Hercules cycle of the Camerino is not limited to these three principal scenes. Four little roundels, neatly contained within the volutes of the foliate ornament, form a group enclosing the central painting (Figs. 5-8). These medallions, which illustrate four of the Herculean labors, are executed in the same grisaille as the surrounding field and give the same illusion of stucco relief. The two lower ones (i.e. near the lower corners of the *Choice of Hercules*) represent, on the right, the strangling of the Nemean lion (Fig. 8) and, on the left, the fight with the Lernaean hydra (Fig. 6), in which the hero sears the monster's severed necks with a flaming torch. The two upper medallions, which are inverted, depict on one side the slaying of Antaeus (Fig. 5), and on the other Cerberus being dragged out of the smoke and flame of the underworld (Fig. 7). It has already been pointed out that Carracci's design for the ceiling (Fig. 102) makes no provision for these medallions, which must have been added subsequently to the program. The only one of the series that seems to have a classical prototype is that of the Nemean lion (Fig. 8), which may be derived from a relief of the type of that in the Villa Medici.[36]

In these little pictures Hercules appears as *monstrorum domitor*; here he actually performs those valiant deeds which are only alluded to in the larger scenes. In particular, they illustrate the consequences of the hero's decision to take the toilsome path of virtue. For the labors can be interpreted both in the physical and spiritual sense: Servius insists that Hercules' strength is more properly that of the mind than of the body.[37]

What determined the selection of these particular episodes from the list of Hercules' deeds? The answer may be that they were intended to symbolize the Four Elements, or, to put it more precisely, the triumph of Virtue over the Elements.[38] That the Hydra, for instance, could denote Water hardly requires to be demonstrated: the explanation of the fable offered by Servius[39] and others after him is that Hercules

---

[36] A. von Salis, "Löwenkampfbilder des Lysipp," *112. Winckelmannsprogramm der Archäologischen Gesellschaft zu Berlin*, 1956, pp. 9 ff., Abb. 5.

[37] Servius on Virgil's *Aeneid* VI, 395.

[38] This was suggested to me by Professor Panofsky. E. Wind has drawn attention to a somewhat similar iconography in Raphael's Stanza della Segnatura (*Journal of the Warburg Institute*, II, 1938-1939, pp. 75 ff.).

[39] Servius on *Aeneid* VI, 287: ". . . nam Hydra, ab aqua dicta est, id est, ἀπὸ τοῦ ὕδατος."

stopped a lake from flooding. Cerberus, who was brought up from the lower world, might stand for the element Earth; once again Servius specifically makes the identification: "Nam Cerberus terra est."[40] The Nemean lion, to pursue the same reasoning, may be taken to represent Fire. In the series of the four temperaments engraved by Virgil Solis, the choleric humor appropriately includes among its attributes both a lion and flames.[41] Astronomy provides a similar association. For the lion is the mansion of the sun, and when the sun enters the sign of the lion (usually identified as the Nemean lion) the fiery heat of summer results.[42] There remains Antaeus, who met his death by being held suspended in the air, and who may therefore refer to that element.

Two further scenes of Hercules have still to be considered. In each of the two window-embrasures the soffit of the lintel is decorated in imitation of stucco. Over the right-hand window there is represented the infant Hercules strangling the serpents in his cradle (Fig. 15); on either side of this center panel are two Farnese emblems, the unicorn and the lily. On the soffit of the other window is pictured the death of Hercules on the funeral pyre on Mount Oeta (Fig. 13). These two subjects mark the beginning and the end of the Hercules cycle in the Camerino. The precocious child who, even in his cradle, destroys the evils which beset him presages the dauntless hero of mature years. The final scene illustrates the apotheosis of Hercules, as he looks up to heaven to receive the reward of immortality for his life of toil and feats of virtue. Here we may be reminded of Savorgnano's verses, cited above, in which the boy Odoardo is likened to the infant Hercules who slays the serpents, and for whom heaven has already prepared a reward.[43]

Each of the spandrels over the windows contains an allegorical figure within a gilt oval. In the one at the right (Fig. 15) is seen a winged female figure blowing a trumpet and running. This is of course the familiar type of Fame.[44] The male figure in the other oval (Fig. 13) is probably to be explained as the personification of Honor, here conceived as the complement of Fame. He is a winged youth, holding a wreath in his right hand and a scepter or staff in his left; the identification of the figure as Honor is confirmed by its resemblance to Annibale's painting of this subject in Dresden.[45]

The lunettes on the side next the court are less than a semicircle in area because the windows encroach upon them from below. The right-hand lunette (Fig. 14) shows a winged Victory in flight, looking at the spectator and holding a laurel wreath

[40] *Ibid.*, VI, 395.

[41] Reproduced in E. Panofsky and F. Saxl, *Dürers 'Melencolia I,'* Leipzig-Berlin, 1923, Abb. 50.

[42] Mythogr. Tertius, 15, 5 (Bode, *op.cit.*, I, p. 254). Cf. also Ripa, *Iconologia*, s.v. "Luglio."

[43] Cf. note 16 *supra*. The same two subjects are represented on the cover of the Farnese casket made for Card. Alessandro (A. de Ri-

naldis, in *Bollettino d'arte*, 2nd ser., III, 1923, fig. on p. 153).

[44] Cf. Ripa, *Iconologia*, s.v. "Fama."

[45] Cf. Malvasia, *Felsina*, I, p. 502: "L'Onore in aria, giovane ignudo con un'asta in mano, e varie corone." The painting is reproduced in the catalogue of the Mostra dei Carracci (no. 80) with the inaccurate title *Il Genio della Fama*.

in her outstretched hands. She is painted *al naturale* against a background of blue sky, in contrast to the *Infant Hercules* on the soffit directly below, who is in chiaroscuro. The second lunette (Fig. 12) contains a similar Victory, with a laurel wreath in her left hand and a palm branch in her right to denote Hercules' ultimate triumph and apotheosis. Such figures are a familiar type in Cinquecento art, serving indifferently both as angels in scenes of martyrdom and as personifications of Victory in profane subjects.

ULYSSES AND CIRCE (FIG. 17)

The lunettes at either end of the room are devoted to a second mythological hero—Ulysses. The first lunette represents the adventure with Circe. The scene takes place in a spacious loggia, the architectural features of which are copied almost exactly from the arcaded court of the Farnese palace itself.[46] The sorceress, clad in a loose garment which leaves one breast uncovered, sits languidly on a bed or throne raised on a high marble base, the side of which is sculptured with Venuses and Cupids in amorous embrace. The magic wand rests point downward in her relaxed right hand, while with her left she proffers the charmed drink to Ulysses. Half hidden in the shadows behind her are two large vessels containing the poison. Ulysses, holding a long spear in his hand, stands with one foot on the step of the throne as he takes the cup from Circe. He has a short, curly beard, and wears a chlamys over his armor, the cuirass of which is decorated with a pair of opposed griffins (a common motive on Roman armor). Behind Ulysses, and concealed by him from the eyes of Circe, is the god Mercury, recognizable by the caduceus, and winged cap and sandals. With his right hand he slyly places the moly in the cup so as to render the potion harmless. And in the corner lies one of Ulysses' luckless companions who has been transformed by the enchantress—a nude human figure with a swine's head.

In composing this scene Annibale undoubtedly remembered Pellegrino Tibaldi's fresco of *Ulysses and Circe* in the Palazzo Poggi at Bologna.[47] The personages occupy the same positions: the enchantress at the left, the hero in the middle, and the bewitched companion in the right foreground. In the attitude of this last figure, moreover, may be seen further proof of the connection between the two frescoes (although Annibale characteristically suppresses the pronounced Mannerist contortion of the legs). In other respects, however, the two conceptions differ sharply. In contrast to Tibaldi's fantastically complex interior, peopled by gesticulating figures in curiously postured attitudes, Carracci has imagined the hall of Circe to be a plausible palace in which the actors—even the god Mercury—are disposed in natural attitudes that can be rationally explained.[48] This is the lesson of Raphael. Indeed a composition

[46] Annibale also represented the Farnese arcade in his *Vision of St. Francis*, in the collection of John Pope-Hennessy (reproduced in the catalogue of the Mostra, no. 91).

[47] G. Briganti, *Il manierismo e Pellegrino Tibaldi*, Rome, 1945, fig. 114.

[48] A Carraccesque drawing of this subject at Windsor (Wittkower, *Carracci Drawings*, p. 104, Cat. 35, pl. 5) combines features taken both from Tibaldi and from Annibale. The figure of Ulysses drawing his sword is plainly derived from Tibaldi's fresco. But the atti-

such as the *Dream of Pharaoh* in the Vatican Loggie offers many points of similarity to Annibale's fresco.

ULYSSES AND THE SIRENS (FIG. 18)

At the other end of the room is Ulysses' adventure with the Sirens. The ship, propelled by burly oarsmen, draws near to the fatal island, on which can be seen the three Sirens and, along the beach, the bones of their victims. The vessel is painted gold, and bears on its side a relief of Neptune riding in his chariot and attended by sea deities. Ulysses, his eyes fastened on the Sirens, is tied hand and foot to the mast, from which he struggles to break loose. But Minerva stands close behind him, fully armed, and places her hand on his shoulder—an act of supernatural guidance which complements that of Mercury in the Circe episode (Fig. 17). In the stern of the ship one of Ulysses' companions puts his hand to his ear, as if striving to catch the Sirens' song, while the steersman turns to look up at him inquiringly.

The general meaning of the two Ulysses subjects is clear enough: they illustrate how, with divine guidance (Mercury and Minerva), evil temptation may be resisted and its disastrous consequences averted. But for a more precise definition of their significance we must examine the allegorical figures which are centered in the spandrels over each lunette. Each one represents a female figure in a half-reclining attitude. They serve the same function as the putti who appear in the ovals of Correggio's Camera di San Paolo:[49] that is to say, they form a kind of commentary on the scenes directly below.

In the gold oval above *Ulysses and Circe* (Fig. 19) a young woman is seated, her right hand resting on her knee and her left holding a bird. The bird is undoubtedly a turtledove, the emblem of marital fidelity, because when it has lost its mate it never seeks another;[50] the young woman is thus a personification of Chastity.[51] The meaning of the scene in the lunette below is that Ulysses, aided by Mercury, remains faithful to his wife Penelope by resisting the wiles of Circe (whose throne is suitably decorated with erotic images). This is supported by Servius' identification of Circe as a harlot, who "by her blandishments led men from a human into a bestial existence."[52]

The young woman in the oval (Fig. 20) above *Ulysses and the Sirens* balances an armillary sphere in her upraised right hand, and grasps a serpent with her left. We

tude of Circe can only come from the Camerino fresco, which is also the source of the architectural setting and of such details as the vessels containing the poisoned drink. The drawing has been attributed to a pupil of Ludovico about 1600 (Mahon, *Disegni*, p. 39, no. 33), and to Albani (F. Arcangeli, in *Arte Antica e Moderna*, no. 4, 1958, p. 356, pl. 129c).

[49] E. Panofsky, *The Iconography of Correggio's Camera di San Paolo*, London, 1961, pp. 47 f., 53 f., 68 f., etc.

[50] Cf. Giovanni Pierio Valeriano, *Hieroglyphica, seu de sacris Aegyptiorum aliarumque gentium literis commentarii*, Lyons, 1610, XXII, 16.

[51] Cf. Ripa, *Iconologia*, s.v. "Castità."

[52] Servius on Virgil's *Aeneid* VII, 19. Cf. also Mythogr. Secundus, II, 212. (Bode, *op.cit.*, I, p. 146): "Hanc [sc. Circen] Ulyxes innocuus transit, quia sapientia libidinem contemnit. Unde et uxorem habere dicitur Penelopen castam, quod omnis castitas sapientiae conjungatur."

have not far to look to find the meaning of this figure, because she appears in Cesare Ripa's *Iconologia* as the personification of Intelligence: the sphere and the snake signify that "in order to understand lofty and sublime things it is first necessary to go along the ground, as the serpent does."[53] The sphere as a symbol of higher wisdom we have already observed in *Hercules bearing the globe* (Fig. 10). Here again the allegorical figure elucidates the picture below. The adventure with the Sirens demonstrates how the native intelligence of Ulysses, aided by the celestial wisdom of Minerva, is successful in outwitting the seducers. For the Sirens, like Circe, are prostitutes seeking to lure the unwary.[54] Together, the two lunettes can be said to constitute another allusion to Cardinal Odoardo Farnese as the virtuous prince, whose innate chastity and intelligence, fortified by heavenly assistance, enable him to pass unharmed through all temptations.

PERSEUS AND MEDUSA (FIG. 23)

The fables continue in the two lunettes on the side opposite the windows. One of these represents the Beheading of Medusa. Perseus, entirely nude except for the helmet of invisibility and Mercury's winged sandals, has seized the Gorgon by her snaky locks, and already presses the hooked scimitar to her throat; in order to avoid her petrifying glance he turns his head and looks at her image as it is reflected in the polished shield held by Minerva. The goddess, helmeted and with an ample cloak over her armor, leans on a spear and watches Perseus at his grisly work. A little to the rear stands Mercury with caduceus and winged cap, also looking at the shield. Medusa is seated on a rock where she has been sleeping; her arms are thrust out in sudden surprise, and her face wears an expression of agony.[55] Her two sisters recline in attitudes of sleep upon the boulders at the right side. The fresco has suffered heavily, and in its present state is only a travesty of the original.[56]

The triangular spandrel over this lunette, like those already described, contains a gold oval within which is an allegorical figure (Fig. 21). Here a woman stands with feet crossed, leaning with her left arm on a column, and holding a long spear in her right hand. The type is derived ultimately from Roman coins of Macrinus,[57] on which it represents Securitas, the column in particular denoting firmness. These coins were well known in the sixteenth century: Ripa has a description of one,[58] and Sebastiano Erizzo, in his book on ancient numismatics, publishes an engraving

[53] Ripa, *op.cit.*, s.v. "Intelligenza": "Donna vestita d'oro, che nella destra mano tenga una sfera, e con la sinistra una serpe . . . mostra che per intendere le cose alte, e sublimi, bisogna prima andar per terra come fa la serpe."

[54] Servius on Virgil's *Aeneid* v, 864.

[55] Wittkower has pointed out that the head and gestures of Medusa reflect Annibale's interest in the Niobid sculptures which he saw in Rome and of which he made several drawings (*Carracci Drawings*, p. 149, pl. 55).

[56] I reproduce here (Fig. 23) the Anderson photograph of 1934, taken before the recent restoration. In the process of repainting Medusa has suffered the loss of her right knee and right thumb; similar blunders have disfigured the entire surface of the fresco.

[57] Mattingly, *Coins of the Roman Empire in the Brit. Mus.*, v, London, 1950, pp. 501 ff., nos. 40, 54, 77, 105, 122, 126; pls. 79, 10 and 17; 80, 12, etc.

[58] *Iconologia*, s.v. "Sicurtà, o Sicurezza."

of a coin of Macrinus with the same figure inscribed as *Securitas Temporum*.[59] Security forms an appropriate accompaniment to *Perseus and Medusa*. Fulgentius describes the slaying of the Gorgon as the victory of virtue, aided by wisdom, over terror.[60] And when terror is vanquished, security prevails.

Although the personification of Securitas is antique, the immediate model for the figure is modern. Specifically, Annibale seems to have studied Marcantonio's engraving of Fortitude (B. 389) in order to impart to his figure the desired degree of classical grace and poise. The resemblance to the print is particularly marked in the stance and in the handling of the drapery across the thighs.

THE CATANIAN BROTHERS (FIG. 24)

The second lunette along the side wall presents a quite different subject. Here we see illustrated the story of the brothers Amphinomus and Anapius of Catania, who, when an eruption of Aetna destroyed the city, carried their parents through the flames with such fearless devotion that the fire and lava gave way before them, and all reached safety. In the middle of the scene one of the brothers advances toward the spectator, bearing his father upon his back. Behind him the second brother carries their mother, whose face and gestures betray her fear.[61] In the distance can be seen the exploding volcano and the city of Catania in flames. An unexpected intruder in this scene is the giant Polyphemus (inexpertly repainted), reclining at the left side, and surrounded by his flock of sheep; he grasps the shepherd's crook in his hand, and the reed-pipe lies beside him. It would seem that Polyphemus is intended primarily to localize the scene at Aetna, for it was here that the Cyclopes were said to assist Vulcan in forging Jupiter's thunderbolts. At the same time he also establishes a link between this subject and those dealing with Ulysses, whose encounter with the Cyclops is thus indirectly alluded to.

The gilt oval that appears in the spandrel over this lunette (Fig. 22) shows a standing woman holding a cornucopia in her left hand, while with her right she grasps the handle of a ship's rudder, the blade of which passes behind her. To her right is a stork with one leg raised. These attributes identify the figure as *Pietas*. The type is derived, like that of *Securitas*, from Roman coins.[62] The important element is the stork, which is used as a symbol of piety because it never deserts its parents when they have become old and feeble.[63]

The appropriateness of the personification needs no emphasis, because the theme of the *Catanian Brothers* is manifestly that of filial piety. The subject, though it is

[59] *Discorso di M. Sebastiano Erizzo sopra le medaglie de gli antichi*, Venice, 1568, p. 643.

[60] *Mythologiae* I, 26. Cf. also Mythogr. Primus, I, 130 (Bode, *op.cit.*, I, p. 42); Mythogr. Secundus, II, 113 (*ibid.*, p. 113); and Mythogr. Tertius, 14, 3 (*ibid.*, pp. 251 f.).

[61] Here, as in the figure of Medusa, Wittkower has drawn attention to the influence of the Niobid group (*Carracci Drawings*, p. 149).

[62] E.g., those of Mark Antony (H. A. Grueber, *Coins of the Roman Republic in the British Museum*, London, 1910, II, p. 402; III, pl. CIV, 6-8).

[63] See Valeriano, *Hieroglyphica*, XVII, 1; and Ripa, *op.cit.*, s.v. "Gratitudine" and "Pietà."

known on ancient coins,[64] is not a common one. It may seem puzzling that the same meaning was not expressed through a more familiar episode, such as Aeneas carrying his father Anchises from the burning city of Troy. The explanation must be that the story of the Catanian Brothers was chosen as a compliment to both Odoardo and his brother Ranuccio, not to Odoardo alone. It is significant that the same subject occurs—and carries a similar meaning—in the fresco cycle by Rosso Fiorentino in the Gallery of Francis I at Fontainebleau.[65]

Bodmer has drawn attention[66] to a large chalk drawing by Annibale which is undoubtedly a preparatory study for one of the lunettes in the Camerino. The subject, later rejected from the cycle, is the Slaying of the Chimera (No. 40, Fig. 138). Bellerophon, clad in armor and mounted on the winged horse Pegasus, charges through the air toward the monster and drives a lance into its jaws. The fire-breathing Chimera, pictured as a lioness with a dragon's tail, and with a horned goat's head protruding from its back, rears up to meet his attack. The scene is closed by a grove of trees at the left; and several buildings, one of them a temple, can be distinguished in the distance. The drawing shows a few alterations and adjustments, the most important of which have to do with Bellerophon's right arm and lance.

It is not difficult to see how this subject was to have been fitted into the program of the Camerino, the theme being the familiar one of virtue triumphant over vice.[67] It would seem, moreover, to have been conceived as a pendant to *Perseus and Medusa*. For Bellerophon is mounted on Pegasus; and Pegasus, the symbol of fame, was born from the Gorgon's blood when she was slain by Perseus—a fitting sequel, since virtuous actions beget fame. "Virtus enim, dum terrorem amputaverit, famam generat," says Fulgentius.[68] And we may recall, finally, that Pegasus was also a Farnese emblem.[69] It may thus be concluded that *Bellerophon and the Chimera* (since it depends iconographically on *Perseus and Medusa*) was originally intended to occupy the place in the cycle now filled by the *Catanian Brothers*. The substitution was made, as I have suggested above, in order to provide a subject that might allude to both Odoardo and Ranuccio.

THE CARDINAL VIRTUES

In the corners of the vault, finally, are seen the four Cardinal Virtues (cf. Figs. 25-28), in which the observer was no doubt expected to perceive a punning reference

[64] G. F. Hill, *Coins of Ancient Sicily*, Westminster, 1903, pp. 205 f.

[65] D. and E. Panofsky, "The Iconography of the Galerie François I at Fontainebleau," *Gazette des Beaux-Arts*, ser. 6, LII, 1958, pp. 135 ff., fig. 32. It is here shown that the Catanian story commemorates the filial devotion of Francis I's two sons.

[66] Bodmer, "Camerino," p. 147.

[67] Ripa, *op.cit.*, s.v. "Virtù."

[68] *Mythologiae* I, 26.

[69] See note 22 above. Odoardo's father, Duke Alessandro, was represented as Bellerophon killing the Chimera on a metal token issued in 1587 in commemoration of his victories in the Netherlands. See G. van Loon, *Histoire métallique des XVII provinces des Pays-Bas . . .*, The Hague, 1732, I, p. 366; and Ireneo Affò, *La Zecca e moneta parmigiana illustrata . . .*, Parma, 1788, p. 193, pl. 5, XLIII.

to Cardinal Odoardo Farnese, "vero amatore delle virtù," as Ripa calls him.[70] They do not appear in the Windsor study for the ceiling (Fig. 102), and must therefore, like the Hercules medallions, have been a late addition to the cycle. Each figure is set within an oval surrounded by a garland of fruit, the whole being in grisaille so as to feign stucco. Iconographically, they conform exactly to the recipes of Cesare Ripa. At the left of *Ulysses and Circe* stands the sprightly form of *Justice*, clad in fluttering draperies (Fig. 25); she has a balance in her left hand and a sword uplifted in her right.[71] On the right side is the equally lively figure of *Temperance*, looking back over her shoulder, with a palm branch and a bridle as her attributes (Fig. 26).[72] At the other end of the room, *Fortitude* appears on the left of *Ulysses and the Sirens* (Fig. 27); she carries a spear and a shield on which can be discerned a lion attacking a boar.[73] And on the right side of the same scene is *Prudence* (Fig. 28), a young woman with two faces, who looks in a mirror and has a serpent wound about her arm.[74]

In devising these allegorical figures Annibale found it convenient to turn for inspiration to the set of Virtues engraved by Marcantonio (B. 386-392). The series, which includes the three theological as well as the four cardinal virtues, was engraved, as Vasari relates,[75] from the designs of Raphael.

The clearest instance of this relationship is afforded by the fresco of *Prudence* (Fig. 28), in which the position of the head and arms, and the arrangement of the drapery, carried diagonally across the body and gathered in a large knot at the hip, establish beyond question the dependence on Marcantonio's engraving of the same virtue (B. 392); the mirror (specified by Ripa) appears as an attribute of Prudence in Raphael's fresco in the Stanza della Segnatura.

Justice (Fig. 25), with her sword and balance, her striding attitude and agitated draperies, is similar to Marcantonio's engraving of *Justice* (B. 388); the figure has been turned at a different angle, so as to be seen somewhat more from the front than from the back. There is perhaps also an echo here of the engraving of *Temperance* (B. 390).

Carracci's *Temperance*, however (Fig. 26), owes little to this print (if we discount the flying fold of drapery seen in both). The pose seems to have been suggested rather by Marcantonio's *Faith* (B. 387). On the left thigh of *Temperance* the drapery has been bunched into a thick fold and looped over a narrow band of cloth; this curious detail finds a parallel in Marcantonio's print of *Justice*.

For his *Fortitude* (Fig. 27) Annibale did not rely on Marcantonio's engraving (B. 389), since this follows a different iconographical tradition. Instead he availed himself

---

[70] *Iconologia*, s.v. "Virtù heroica."
[71] *Ibid.*, s.v. "Quarta Beatitudine" and "Giustitia retta."
[72] *Ibid.*, s.v. "Temperanza."
[73] *Ibid.*, s.v. "Fortezza": "Donna armata . . . nella destra mano terrà un'asta . . . & nel

braccio sinistro uno scudo, in mezo del quale vi sia dipinto un leone che s'azzuffi con un cignale."
[74] *Ibid.*, s.v. "Prudenza."
[75] G. Vasari, *Le vite*, ed. Milanesi, Florence, 1878-1885, v, p. 413.

of the engraving of *Temperance*, altering the attributes, but making little change in the stance and the costume. As to Marcantonio's *Fortitude*, this, we recall, had already served as the model for the figure of *Securitas* in another section of the ceiling (Fig. 21).

Who was the author of this program? We may be certain, first of all, that it was not Annibale Carracci himself. The task of the artist was not to devise the subject matter, but to execute in fresco a plan drawn up for him by a man of letters. The decoration of the Farnese palace at Caprarola offers an instructive example of the collaboration of author and painter in the sixteenth century.[76] There the leading spirit of the enterprise was Cardinal Alessandro Farnese's secretary, Annibal Caro (1507-1566), two of whose letters setting forth parts of the program have survived.[77] They illustrate very well the elaborate and precise instructions which were customarily drawn up by humanists for the benefit of artists. Nothing of the literary content of the program was left to the painter; his function in this respect was one of passive and unhesitating acceptance. We have no reason to think that it was otherwise with Annibale Carracci in the Camerino.

The evidence of early writers is of little use to us here. The *Trattato* of Giulio Mancini does not even mention the Camerino in the account of the Carracci.[78] Giovanni Baglione has a brief description of the room in his life of Annibale (1642), but says nothing of its authorship.[79] The first writer to supply any information of this sort is Giovanni Pietro Bellori. The great historian and theorist of Seicento art, writing many years after the events he describes, makes a somewhat ambiguous statement concerning Carracci's literary adviser. "Meanwhile," he says, "[Annibale] prepared himself for the Gallery. But since in the meantime he painted the Camerino in the same palace, we shall take note of this room first, treating it in such a way that while describing the paintings individually we shall be able at the same time to set forth the moral of the argument, which is most praiseworthy, and in which, beyond the erudition of Agostino, it is thought that he was aided by his friend Monsignor Gio: Battista Agucchi, a man celebrated in every branch of letters. . . . In this room, then, amid various decorations of feigned stucco, he set forth his moral paintings, following the wisdom of the ancient poets, and symbolized the actions of virtue with most beautiful inventions."[80] This passage has often been interpreted as meaning that Agucchi was responsible for the program of the Galleria Farnese.[81]

[76] On this subject see Baumgart, "La Caprarola di Ameto Orti," Introduction, pp. 77-95; and J. Seznec, *The Survival of the Pagan Gods*, New York, 1953, pp. 291 ff.

[77] The first, addressed to Taddeo Zuccari, describes the scheme to be followed for the cardinal's bedroom (Caro, *Lettere familiari*, II, pp. 336 ff.). The other is addressed to Onofrio Panvinio and contains the program for the cardinal's study (*ibid.*, pp. 455 ff.).

[78] Mancini, *Considerazioni*, I, pp. 218 ff.

[79] Baglione, *Vite*, p. 106.

[80] Bellori, *Vite*, p. 32.

[81] E.g., Tietze, p. 90. Tietze also points out that, after Bellori, most writers agree in naming Agucchi as Carracci's literary adviser in the Gallery.

But this is not what Bellori says: in point of fact his words apply only to the Camerino, and not to the Gallery.[82]

What is still more important is that in naming Agucchi Bellori is plainly not sure of himself but is merely recording what is thought to be true (*si tiene*). Agucchi, after all, was an accomplished man of letters, with a deep interest in artistic matters; his admiration for Annibale was well known; and both were of Bolognese origin. What could be more natural than that Agucchi should have had a hand in formulating the program of the Camerino? Nevertheless there are reasons for believing that Bellori is in error on this point.

Agucchi himself, in his *Trattato*, does not specifically mention the Camerino, but is content to include it anonymously among "several little rooms and a very large gallery" painted in fresco by the Carracci brothers.[83] Of his own contribution he says nothing. Such reticence (if he had really provided the *libretto*) might be ascribed to a seemly ecclesiastical modesty, but taken in conjunction with Bellori's uncertainty it seems only to confirm that Agucchi had no part in the project. There is still another reason for regarding Agucchi's participation as unlikely. At the time when the program of the Camerino was being formulated (i.e. in 1595) he was only twenty-five years old, younger than Annibale Carracci by a decade, and surely not yet worthy to be called *celebre in ogni studio di lettere*. Was it necessary for Cardinal Odoardo to call upon so young a man for so erudite a task? Was no one else available? The old humanist circle brought together by Cardinal Alessandro Farnese had by this time, it is true, virtually disappeared: Francesco Molza was long dead, the veteran Annibal Caro had died in 1566, and Onofrio Panvinio two years later. But one member of that group still survived and remained active in the service of the Farnese family: Fulvio Orsini (1529-1600). And Orsini, as I mean to show, furnished the program for the Camerino.[84]

Orsini's reputation as a humanist was international. The friend and correspondent of Justus Lipsius, Cardinal Granvelle, Carlo Sigonio, John Sambucus, and other distinguished personages, he was equally accomplished as historian, philologist, and archaeologist. Of his many books, two in particular may be mentioned here. In 1570 he published his volume of ancient portraits, the *Imagines et elogia virorum illustrium*.[85] This was followed, in 1577, by his great work on numismatics, the *Familiae*

[82] Despite his mention of Agostino, Bellori does not seem to have believed, as did Malvasia (*Felsina*, I, p. 404), that both brothers worked in the Camerino. Malvasia's error was corrected by Vincenzo Vittoria (*Osservazioni sopra il libro della Felsina Pittrice*, Rome, 1703, pp. 51 ff.). See note 1 above.

[83] Agucchi, *Trattato*, in Mahon, *Studies*, p. 254.

[84] Some years ago Navenne proposed Orsini's name in connection with the Camerino, but for no more cogent reason than that he was

still in the service of the Farnese when it was painted (*Rome et le palais Farnèse pendant les trois derniers siècles*, I, p. 72).

[85] *Imagines et elogia virorum illustrium et erudit. ex antiquis lapidibus et nomismatibus expressa cum annotationib. ex bibliotheca Fulvi Ursini*, Rome, 1570. For a critical evaluation of Orsini's iconographic studies see J. H. Jongkees, *Fulvio Orsini's Imagines and the Portrait of Aristotle* (Archaeologica Traiectina IV), Groningen, 1960, pp. 3-16.

Romanae,[86] written in collaboration with his friend, the learned Spanish bishop Antonio Agustín. But Orsini was first and foremost a collector—of books, manuscripts, coins, gems, inscriptions, marbles, paintings, and drawings. His library, reconstructed by the patient researches of Nolhac, included 300 Latin and 162 Greek manuscripts as well as important manuscripts in the vernacular; of his printed books he thought it worth while to bequeath to the Vatican Library only those containing marginal notes by learned men.[87] His collection of antiquities, now hopelessly dispersed, counted over 400 engraved gems, more than 150 inscriptions, several thousand Greek and Roman coins, and fifty-eight marble busts and reliefs.[88] In addition, he owned a large number of paintings and drawings, including works by Michelangelo, Raphael, Titian, and El Greco.[89]

As a humanist in the service of the Farnese cardinals, Orsini had long had experience in the invention of programs for fresco cycles. At Caprarola, under Caro's general supervision, he had early assumed responsibility for part of the work: in October 1564 Caro writes that he has mislaid Orsini's notes containing the plan for one of the rooms, and consequently cannot explain to Taddeo Zuccari what is required.[90] After Caro's death it was no doubt Orsini who took charge of the project as a whole. In 1573 we find him writing to Cardinal Alessandro concerning the proposed astronomical theme of the Sala del Mappamondo.[91] For the ceiling of this room, it may be observed, Orsini did not himself write the *libretto*, but sent for Alessandro's approval a scheme prepared by his friend, M. Orazio Trigini de' Marij. Careful scholar that he is, Fulvio assures the Cardinal "che la dottrina e la pratica di questo mio amico è buona e fondata su boni autori"; moreover, Trigini possesses an illustrated manuscript of Hyginus showing the constellations.[92]

The letters which Fulvio wrote in his later years make it clear that he took a paternal interest in Odoardo, and that he hoped to see him become, like his great-

---

[86] *Familiae Romanae quae reperiuntur in antiquis numismatibus ab urbe condita ad tempora divi Augusti, ex Bibliotheca Fulvi Ursini. Adiunctis Familiis XXX ex libro Antoni Augustini Ep. Ilerdensis*, Rome, 1577.

[87] P. de Nolhac, *La bibliothèque de Fulvio Orsini*, Paris, 1887.

[88] P. de Nolhac, "Les collections d'antiquités de Fulvio Orsini," *Mélanges d'archéologie et d'histoire, Ecole Française de Rome*, IV, 1884, pp. 139-231.

[89] *Idem*, "Une galerie de peinture au XVIe siècle: les collections de Fulvio Orsini," *Gazette des Beaux-Arts*, XXIX, 1884, pp. 427-436; E. du Gué Trapier, "El Greco in the Farnese Palace, Rome," *Gazette des Beaux-Arts*, LI, 1958, pp. 73-90.

[90] "Un folletto mi ha levata dinanzi quella nota che V.S. mi lasciò delle istorie de la Sala,

e per diligenza che abbia fatta, non la ritruovo. Vi prego a mandarmene subito un'altra, se n'avete copia, o così a mente scrivetene parte, acciò possa pensare a gli riscontri de le figure di sopra: chè con messer Taddeo non posso risolver cosa alcuna senz'essa. . . ." (*Prose inedite del Commendator Annibal Caro pubblicate ed annotate da Giuseppe Cugnoni*, Imola, 1872, pp. 165 f.). Cf. also Caro's letters to Orsini dated June 9 and 30, 1565 (*ibid.*, pp. 166 ff.).

[91] A. Ronchini and V. Poggi, "Fulvio Orsini e sue lettere ai Farnesi," *Atti e memorie delle RR. Deputazioni di Storia Patria per le provincie dell'Emilia*, nuova serie, IV, parte II, 1880, p. 53 (Lettera VI) and pp. 54 ff. (Lettera VIII).

[92] *Ibid.*, p. 53 (Lettera VI).

uncle Alessandro, the first cardinal of Rome. In 1593 he writes to Ranuccio, Duke of Parma, that Odoardo frequently visits him at his apartment, where the two pass the evening discussing ancient history and literature. It is considered, Orsini goes on to say, "that if he continues to follow the path that he has started upon he will surely become the splendor of this court, owing to the strong inclination that he shows for matters serious and heroic."[93] The metaphor of the path that leads to glory is one that recurs in the *Choice of Hercules*.

Orsini's services as *letterato* to Odoardo must have begun in earnest with the latter's elevation to the cardinalate in 1591, and his taking up residence in the family palace in Rome. One of Fulvio's first duties seems to have been the invention of an *impresa* or personal device for the young cardinal.[94] This *impresa*, as we have already seen, is prominently displayed in the Camerino, where it appears twice within a medallion on the vault (Fig. 16): a purple lily (or iris) with the motto ΘΕΟΘΕΝ ΑΤΞΑΝΟΜΑΙ. That the device is actually the work of Orsini is proved by a letter, dated August 4, 1592, written by Odoardo (at the moment in Parma) to Fulvio in Rome. The minute of the letter reads in part: "I was very much pleased by the *impresa* of the plant of purple lilies, with the motto in either Greek or Latin; since both have the same meaning I prefer the Latin, as being more witty according to what you say. I thank you for this *impresa*, and because from the subtlety of your wit one could expect nothing but what is perfect and good, there is no need for me to say more about it to you."[95]

In choosing the lily Fulvio was of course making use of the heraldic charge—the *giglio*—of the Farnese family. But the device also has particular reference to Odoardo

[93] *Ibid.*, pp. 70 f. (Lettera XXIV): ". . . non è oscuro il giuditio, che si fa di questo Sig.re, cioè: che, se continuarà di camminare nella via cominciata, debba esser lo splendore di questa Corte, per la molta inclinatione che mostra alle cose serie et eroiche. . . ." Although Odoardo had been cardinal for almost two years when this was written, he had only recently passed his nineteenth birthday.

[94] On the Farnese *imprese* in general see Caro's letter of January 15, 1563, to the Duchess of Urbino (*Lettere familiari*, II, pp. 364 ff.).

[95] Vat. cod. 9064, fol. 335. Minute of letter from Cardinal Odoardo Farnese to Fulvio Orsini. It is written in a secretary's hand, with several alterations and corrections. The opening sentence refers to Odoardo's brother, Prince Ranuccio, recently returned from military service under their father Alessandro, Duke of Parma.

"Al Sr. Fuluio Orsino.

"Il contento che V.S. ha sentito della mia ricuperata salute, et giuntam.te del ritorno del

Sr Principe mio fr[at]ello in Italia, mi è talmente noto che non ha bisogno di alcuna dimostratione, solo mi resta di sentirlene obligo, sicome faccio, et ringratiarla dell'uno, et dell'altro. Mi è piaciuta grandem.te la impresa della pianta de Gigli paonazzi, con il motto ò greco, ò latino, et come che l'uno, et l'altro facciano il medesimo senso, à me piace più il latino, come più spiritoso secondo lei dice. Io la ringratio di detta impresa, et perche dalla finezza del suo ingegno non si poteua aspettar se non cosa perfetta, et buona, io non mi estenderò in dirgliene altro. Io farò cadere· in proposito di ragionar di V.S. col Sr Principe, et con quell' occasione farò fede à S.A. del piacere, che lei ha sentito della sua felice tornata, et le basciarò per parte sua le mani, sicome à lei di buon cuore mi racc.do."

On the reverse (fol. 335 v.), in another hand: "[15]92 / Parma 4 Agosto / Al Sr Fuluio Orsino."

Cited by Martin, "Immagini della Virtù," Appendix I, pp. 111 ff.

himself. The color of the lilies (*gigli paonazzi*) is surely to be connected with his recent elevation to the purple. And likewise the motto, θεόθεν αὐξάνομαι, "I grow by God's aid," is probably an allusion to his youthfulness: Odoardo had been created cardinal, as we know, at the age of seventeen. The imagery is derived from Matthew 6:28: καταμάθετε τὰ κρίνα τοῦ ἀγροῦ, πῶς αὐξάνουσιν, "Consider the lilies of the field, how they grow." It will be observed that the *Greek* version of the motto was finally agreed upon despite Odoardo's expressed preference for the Latin.⁹⁶ Another shade of meaning is supplied by Picinelli, who explains in his emblem book that the purple lily or iris denotes "advancement in virtue," because it grows more fragrant each day.⁹⁷

The fact that Orsini invented the Cardinal's *impresa* does not, of course, prove that he also wrote the program for the Camerino cycle. But in this matter there is some further documentary evidence to be considered.

In August 1595 Odoardo wrote two letters from Parma, where he evidently spent the summer months, to Orsini in Rome; both have to do with the decoration of a *camera* in his Roman palace. The minute of the first letter is dated August 8. Odoardo begins by saying that his brother, the Duke Ranuccio, regrets that he has been unable to find a position for the nephew of the Bishop of Pozzuoli. He then continues: "I am glad that the paintings and stuccoes of my room are being attended to, as you inform me. Since I hope to be in Rome before it is finished, I shall wait till then to decide whether there will have to be inscriptions to explain the scenes [*historie*] which will be in it, or whether the scenes will have to be left without inscriptions. Meanwhile I am not displeased to hear your plan; on the contrary I thank you for it. . . ."⁹⁸

⁹⁶ It would probably have read "Dei auxilio cresco" or something similar. Cf. the Vulgate passage: "Considerate lilia agri quomodo crescunt." For a very similar metaphor see the words addressed to Odoardo (not yet elected cardinal) in the poem "La Caprarola" by Ameto Orti: "At tu cresce puer: tua te iam provocat ostro / Roma . . ." (Baumgart, "La Caprarola di Ameto Orti," p. 122, stanza 84).

⁹⁷ F. Picinelli, *Mondo simbolico, o sia università d'imprese scelte, spiegate, ed illustrate con sentenze, ed eruditioni sacre, e profane*, Milan, 1653, p. 337.

⁹⁸ Vat. cod. 9064, fol. 336. Minute of letter from Cardinal Odoardo Farnese to Fulvio Orsini. The hand is that of a secretary, seemingly the same as in the minute of August 4, 1592 (cf. note 95 above).

"Al sʳ Fuluio Orsino.

"Illʳᵉ et R. sʳᵉ. Hauendo rinouato col sʳ Duca mio fr[at]ello l'uffᵒ che io feci i mesi passati con S.A. per l[ette]re à fin che l'Apollonio nipote di Monsʳ Vescouo di Puzzolo fosse prouisto di qualche uffᵒ nello stato di

Abruzzo, l'A. Sua si è scusata meco di hauerne promessi à tanti, ch'è certa di non poterli sodisfar tutti in questa prossᵃ distributione, et che però tratta dell'impossibile che possa dar cosa alcuna al nipote di esso Monsʳᵉ. V.S. sarà dunq. contenta di riferirlo à Monsʳ sudᵒ facendolo certo, che mi rincresce di non hauerle potuto procurare le satisfattiⁿⁱ ch' egli desideraua, et che sarò tanto più pronto à darli segni in altre occⁿⁱ della mia buona uolontà.

"Mi piace che si attende agli stucchi et pitture della mia Camᵃ come V.S. m'auisa. Et per che io spero d'essere à Roma nanti che sia finita, riseruo all'hora di risoluermi se ci si haueranno da fare le l[ette]re per intelligenza dell'Historie che saranno in essa secondo che V.S. mi propose, ò pure se si hauerà da lasciar l'historie senza l[ette]re. Intanto non mi è spiaciuto d'intendere il pensiero di V.S. anzi ne la ringratio, si come faccio anco dell' auiso che mi ha dato che l'Ambʳᵉ Cesʳᵉ si fosse inuitato à uenir à star con lei due hore il pᵒ d'Agosto. La quale uenuta si sarà

Fulvio replied promptly, asking for the Cardinal's wishes regarding the stucco ornament of the room, as becomes clear from the minute of Odoardo's second letter, which is dated August 22, 1595: "In reply to what you wrote me in your letter of the eleventh concerning the stuccoes of my room, my answer is the same as what I told you orally, namely, that I very much liked certain rooms that I had seen belonging to the Duke of Urbino, and that I like them a great deal more now that I have been there and have considered them more carefully than the other times. Although Cavaliere Thomaso[99] will perhaps be able to remember them clearly, nevertheless I want to tell you that the compartments [*lo scompartimento*] of these rooms are entirely plain, except in the corners, where an oak is entwined, which encroaches a little on the space of the compartment so as to make a most beautiful effect. I should like the compartments, then, to be fashioned in this way and to remain otherwise plain. I leave to you, however, the decision whether to replace the oak with a vine, palm, or olive, and likewise whether to use more or less gold, provided that in the space of the compartments there shall be nothing but the foliage which will be entwined in the corner."[100]

We have now to determine whether these letters actually refer to the Camerino. I believe that they do, and furthermore that they identify Fulvio Orsini as the author of the program. We shall have to remember, in considering them, that we possess only the less important part of the correspondence: the problem would be much

stata per altro che per pigliarsi gusto [*above this is written*: godersi] con lei. V.S. mi farà piacere ad auisarmelo. Et con questo fine mi le rac^do di cuore."

Then, in another hand: "1595 / Parma 8 d'Agosto / Al s^r Fuluio Orsino."

Cited by Martin, *op.cit.*, Appendix, II, p. 112.

[99] I have been unable to identify this personage, who must have been a member of Odoardo's household.

[100] Vat. cod. 9064, fol. 337. Minute of letter from Cardinal Odoardo Farnese to Fulvio Orsini, written in the same hand as the minute of August 8, 1595 (cf. note 98). The "Venus" of which Odoardo speaks at the end of his letter presumably formed part of his collection of sculptures.

"Al s^r Fuluio Orsino.

"Ill^re et Reu^do S^re. Per risposta di quello che V.S. mi ha scritto con la l[ette]ra sua de gli XI. intorno à gli stuchi della mia Camera, replico à V.S. quel. med^mo che le dissi à bocca, cio è che à me piaceuano infinitam^te certe Camere che haueuo uiste del Sr Duca d'Vrbino, et molto più mi sono piaciute adesso che son passato di là, che le ho considerato

più diligentem^te dell'altre uolte. Et se bene il Cau^re Thomaso ne potrà hauer forse fresca mem^a non lasciarò con tutto ciò di dire à V.S. che lo scompartimento di dette camere è tutto schietto, eccetto che negli angoli intorno à quali s'aggira una quercia, che uiene à pigliar' un poco del uano dello scompartimento, et à far' un' effetto belliss°. Di questa maniera adunq. uorrei che fosse lauorato lo scompartimento et nel resto restasse schietto. Rimetto però à V.S. il mettere in luogo della quercia ò uite ò palma, ò oliua come anco il mettere più oro ò manco oro, pur che nel uano dello scompartim^to non sia altro che il fogliame che starà auolto all'angolo.

"Intorno al resto che V.S. mi ha scritto con la sud^a l[ette]ra non ho che risponderle se non che il tutto ho inteso uolentieri, et mi è stato car^mo l'auuertimento ch'ella mi ha dato per conto della mia Venere. Et per fine prego Dio che le conceda ogni contento."

On the outer sheet (fol. 338 v.) in another hand: "1595 / Parma 22 d'Agosto / Al s^r Fuluio Orsino."

Cited by Martin, *op.cit.*, Appendix III, p. 112.

simpler if we had Fulvio's letter setting forth his *pensiero*. But then if Odoardo had remained in Rome there would be no correspondence whatever.

The date alone—August 1595—is significant. Annibale Carracci cannot have begun work on the Camerino frescoes until late in 1595. In July of that year he was in Bologna, where he wrote of his obligation to enter Cardinal Farnese's service in Rome at the end of the summer.[101] It was just at this time that the plans for the decoration of the Camerino must have been taking shape. The fact, moreover, that Odoardo speaks of *historie* proves that it was not merely a question of some minor ornamental work, but of a cycle of scenes which, as he notes, might have to be provided with explanatory inscriptions. One can well imagine his wondering if a subject such as Amphinomus and Anapius might not need to be identified.

It appears, from Odoardo's mention of *stucchi et pitture*, that Fulvio had intended from the start to use some form of stucco ornament, whether real or fictitious. In this matter the cardinal seems to have had ideas of his own, to judge from his letter of August 22.[102] He would like, he says, to have an oak decoration entwined in the corners of the compartments, a scheme suggested by certain rooms belonging to the Duke of Urbino.[103] In the event, Odoardo's plan was modified, and the vault was ornamented not with plaster relief but with a rich system of rinceaux in *stucco finto*. The fact should not be overlooked, however, that in the corners of the central compartments there is a garland of oak leaves (cf. Figs. 5-8).

It remains now to consider some other evidence, which, together with that of the documents, will suffice, I believe, to confirm the attribution to Fulvio Orsini of the *libretto* of the Camerino. Of the subjects represented there, several can be shown to have been of particular interest to him.

Perhaps the most striking example is the *Hercules resting* (Fig. 11). This, as can be seen at a glance, depends directly on an engraved gem in the collection of Orsini himself (Fig. 278).[104] The relationship between the two was long ago recognized: in

[101] F. Malaguzzi Valeri, in *Archivio storico dell'arte*, v, 1892, pp. 135-137.

[102] This letter is cited (without the correct Vatican signature) and in part translated into French by Navenne, who fails however to perceive that it is dated (*Rome et le palais Farnèse*, I, pp. 9 ff.). Navenne is misled by the mention of *stucchi* and *camera* into supposing that the reference is to Cardinal Ranuccio's bedroom in the Palazzo Farnese. Beneath the fresco by Daniele da Volterra runs a narrow stucco frieze which (Navenne believes) must be an addition devised by Fulvio Orsini for Cardinal Odoardo. Needless to say, this is impossible: the stucco ornament is contemporary with Daniele's fresco. Cf. M. L. Mez, "Una decorazione di Daniele da Volterra nel Palazzo Farnese a Roma," *Rivista d'arte*, XVI, 1934, pp. 276-291.

[103] Where were these rooms? There is nothing in the Ducal Palace at Urbino that corresponds to Odoardo's description (cf. Pasquale Rotondi, *Il Palazzo Ducale di Urbino*, Urbino, 1950-1951). In a letter to the writer, Dr. Rotondi points out that the oak mentioned by Odoardo was the heraldic emblem of the Della Rovere family, and suggests therefore that the rooms in question might have been on the top floor of the palace, which was completed under the Della Rovere. If so, their decoration has evidently not survived.

[104] In the inventory drawn up by Orsini himself the gem is described as follows: "Corniola ouata grande di color non bello, con Hercole a sedere, et alcuni animali da lui

the mid-eighteenth century Mariette explicitly stated that Annibale had copied Orsini's gem.[105] In order to meet the demands of the long oval field, Carracci has actually created a wholly new composition. The Sphinx assumes much greater importance; magnified in size and seated upon a higher base, she fixes her gaze on the resting hero. Hercules, for his part, leans back in a half-sprawling attitude and returns her glance. The tension thus established between the two is not even hinted at in the intaglio, where the Sphinx is not only smaller, but faces in the opposite direction. The other modifications are of a minor sort. The horses of Diomedes (behind Hercules in the gem) have disappeared, and Cerberus and the stag have been inserted in the expanded space between Hercules and the Sphinx. But the boar's head, the club, the apples, the bow and arrows, the lion skin, and the dagger held by the hero, all have their counterpart in the gem, from which even the Greek inscription[106] has been copied (but with the solecism ΚΑΛΟΣ corrected to ΚΑΛΩC). One can picture Fulvio proudly exhibiting to Annibale the precious cornelian which was to serve as model for the painting. The gem itself is lost, but to judge from the engraving it seems to have been of Renaissance workmanship and not an ancient original. Professor Erik Sjöqvist has suggested to me that it might have been modeled after the Belvedere torso, which was believed to represent Hercules.

Another subject in which it is possible to discern the personal interest of Orsini is that of the *Catanian Brothers* (Fig. 24). We know that this story, rare though it may be in Renaissance art, had long been familiar to Fulvio from his textual and numismatical studies, and even enters into his private correspondence. As early as 1560 his friend Antonio Agustín wrote to him from Palermo to describe some Sicilian coins. "I have another coin in bronze," the letter reads in part, "of which I think I have found a beautiful interpretation, although the coin itself is not beautiful, but ugly and badly preserved. On one side is the head of a woman more modest than beautiful; on the other side two youths carry two persons on their shoulders. I think it is a coin of Catania, and the head that of Piety,[107] the two youths being those two brothers who carried their father and mother out of the land in a fire, of whom mention is made by Pausanias, Book IX,[108] and Vergil, or some other author, at the end of the poem *Aetna: Namq. optima proles Amphion fraterq. pari sub munere*

domati, con lettere greche che dicono la fatiga esser cagione d'honesto riposo, ΠΟΝΟC ΤΟΥ ΚΑΛΩC ΗCΥΧΑΖΕΙΝ ΑΙΤΙΟC, da M. Jacomo Passaro" (Nolhac, "Les collections d'antiquités de Fulvio Orsini," *Mélanges*, IV, 1884, p. 153).

[105] P. J. Mariette, *Traité des pierres gravées*, Paris, 1750, I, p. 35. The stone belonged to Pierre Crozat (idem, *Description sommaire des pierres gravées du cabinet de feu M. Crozat*, Paris, 1741, p. 35), and was later acquired by the Duc d'Orléans (G. de La Chau and G. Le Blond, *Description des principales pierres*

gravées du cabinet de S. A. S. Monseigneur le Duc d'Orléans, Paris, 1780, I, pp. 273-278, and pl. 86). Other gems show variants of the same composition; cf. Mariette, *op.cit.*, II, pp. 84-85, and T. Worlidge, *A Select Collection of Drawings from Curious Antique Gems . . .*, London, 1768, pl. 150.

[106] *Corpus Inscr. Graec.* No. 7296.

[107] In reality it was the young Dionysos, but, as Agustín says, his coin was badly preserved (cf. Hill, *Coins of Ancient Sicily*, pl. XIV, 16).

[108] Actually Book X.

fortes etc.[109] I believe there was some variety in the names among the historians. You might do me the favor of ascertaining, both from coins and from books, whether I am right or not."[110] Presumably Orsini informed him that his interpretation was substantially correct. Fulvio's own collection, as we learn from the inventory, included an example of this very coin.[111] In his *Familiae Romanae* of 1577 (written with the aid of Agustín), he drew attention to another antique representation of the Catanian brothers, in this instance on a Roman coin of Sextus Pompey, which he illustrated in an engraving, explaining that to the ancients the two brothers were a symbol of piety.[112]

The *Choice of Hercules* (Fig. 9) was another theme with which Orsini had earlier been concerned. In the *Imagines illustrium* of 1570 he published an engraving of a herm representing a young man with Hercules' club and lion skin; an inscription on the base likened him to the youthful Hercules of Prodicus' story.[113] In the accompanying text Orsini took occasion to write a brief account of Prodicus, and to quote Cicero's version of the allegory.[114] The herm is the same as that described by Stephanus Pighius in his *Hercules Prodicius*, where it is also reproduced in an engraved frontispiece.[115]

The happy idea of adapting the compositional scheme of *Hercules and the Hesperides* for the *Choice of Hercules* may very well have come from Orsini, with his specialized knowledge of ancient monuments. It has already been suggested, concerning the *Choice of Hercules*, that the two masks seen at the right among the attributes of *Voluptas* were derived from Michelangelo's *Venus and Cupid*, in which two quite similar masks denote the deceptiveness of the joys of love. This is not mere speculation, however; for we know that the cartoon of Michelangelo's allegory was

[109] *Aetna* 624 ff.

[110] Vat. cod. 4104 (fol. 327): ". . . Ho in bronzo un' altra medaglia della quale penso hauer trouato una bella interpretatione, benche essa non è bella, ma brutta, et mal conseruata. Di un canto è la testa di una donna più honesta che bella, dell altro canto doi giouani portano due persone sopra li humeri. Io credo che sia moneta di Catania, et la testa della Pietà, li duoi giuouani quelli duoi fratelli che portarono suoi padre et madre fuora della terra in un incendio de quali fa mentione Pausania lib. IX. et Vergilio ouero altro auttore nel Aetna alla fine Namq. optima proles Amphion fraterq. pari sub munere fortes et c. Credo nelli nomi fusse uarietà fra li historici. V.S. mi fara gratia di chiarirsi et con medaglie et con libri, se sono fuor di strada, ouero in essa. . . ." The entire letter is printed (though with numerous alterations in spelling and wording) in *Anecdota litteraria ex mss. codicibus eruta*, II, Rome, 1773, pp. 353-357.

[111] "Ma. de Catanesi con testa di giouine et nel rouerscio li dui fratelli che portano il padre et la madre in collo" (Nolhac, "Les collections d'antiquités," p. 216).

[112] Orsini, *Familiae Romanae*, p. 206: ". . . Amphinomum & Anapia Catanenses fratres, quibus pietatem antiqui significabant." For the coin see Grueber, *Coins of the Roman Republic in the Brit. Mus.*, III, pl. CXX, 5-8.

[113] Orsini, *Imagines et elogia virorum illustrium*, pp. 60-61.

[114] *De Off.* I, 32, 118.

[115] *Hercules Prodicius*, pp. 16 f. Pighius' engraving, like Orsini's, shows the herm with the head restored. The original herm is lost. See E. Mandowsky and C. Mitchell, *Pirro Ligorio's Roman Antiquities*, London, 1963, pp. 83 f., no. 61, pl. 33.

actually owned by Orsini himself.[116] We may imagine it being offered, like the engraved gem, as a model to be used by Carracci.

The theme of the active and contemplative life, illustrated in the Camerino by *Hercules resting* and *Hercules bearing the globe*, was no novelty in Farnese iconography. At Caprarola, as Baumgart has shown,[117] this antithetical symbolism was developed on a monumental scale, one half of the great palace being devoted to various manifestations of the active life, and the other to the glorification of the contemplative life. Orsini had been charged at Caprarola, as we know, with the Sala del Mappamondo. Here were represented the celestial realm (the constellations, the signs of the zodiac, the four seasons, etc.) and the terrestrial realm (the four quarters of the globe, the explorers, etc.), the whole symbolizing the contemplation of the cosmos. It is not surprising that a similar theme recurs in the Camerino, in the fresco of *Hercules bearing the globe*.

On more than one occasion, as we have seen, it was Fulvio's own collection that furnished a model to the painter. Similarly, the subject of the *Catanian Brothers* was no doubt suggested by ancient coins. Whether some of the other scenes were likewise motivated by objects in Orsini's possession it is perhaps impossible to say with certainty; but there are several parallels in subject matter which may not be due to coincidence. Even a cursory survey of Fulvio's inventory is sufficient to show that he possessed an unusually large number of objects having to do with Hercules. There was, for example, a marble tablet with the hero's deeds carved in relief and inscriptions in Greek.[118] The infant Hercules strangling the serpents was represented on six Greek coins[119] and two incised gems[120] owned by him. Other objects depicted Hercules with the Nemean lion,[121] with Cerberus,[122] and the hydra.[123] These were probably made available to Carracci.

Allegorical figures derived from coins, such as *Victoria*, *Securitas*, and *Pietas*, all of which figure in the Camerino, would certainly have been known to Orsini from his experience as a numismatist. Annibal Caro, writing to Fulvio in 1562, described a Roman coin showing *Pietas* with cornucopia, rudder and stork,[124] i.e. with precisely the same attributes as she has in the fresco (Fig. 22). On a Greek silver coin in Orsini's

---

[116] Nolhac, "Les collections d'antiquités," p. 176, no. 60: "Quadro grande corniciato di noce, con Venere et Cupido, di mano del med° [Michelangelo]." The cartoon is now in Naples; it was published by E. Steinmann, "Cartoni di Michelangelo," *Bollettino d'arte*, v, 1925, pp. 8 ff., fig. 2. Tolnay thinks it a copy, probably by Bronzino, of Michelangelo's original cartoon (*Michelangelo*, III, p. 195).

[117] "La Caprarola di Ameto Orti," pp. 84 f.

[118] Nolhac, "Les collections d'antiquités," p. 184, no. 35: "Tauoletta di basso rilieuo di marmo con historie di Hercole piena di lettere greche."

[119] *Ibid.*, p. 189, nos. 43-45; p. 202, nos. 476-477; p. 203, no. 492.

[120] *Ibid.*, p. 158, no. 105; p. 165, no. 252.

[121] *Ibid.*, p. 216, no. 130; p. 225, no. 406 (coins).

[122] *Ibid.*, p. 213, no. 55 (coin); p. 157, no. 82 (gem).

[123] *Ibid.*, p. 203, no. 500 (coin).

[124] Caro, *Lettere familiari*, II, p. 332: "Ve ne sono bene infinite con questo: PIETAS. . . . In M. Antonio Triumviro; con la sinistra tiene un corno di dovizia; con la destra, come un timone; e appresso è una picciola cicogna."

cabinet was illustrated the beheading of Medusa by Perseus;[125] two other coins[126] represented Bellerophon and the Chimera, a subject which was at first to have been included in the Camerino cycle. But enough has been said to show the importance of this collection for the iconography of the cycle.

It may seem strange that Orsini's role as literary adviser to Annibale Carracci should have been totally forgotten. The fact is largely due, as we have pointed out above, to Bellori, who first introduced the name of Agucchi into this context, and whose word was accepted as authoritative by later writers. Orsini himself probably looked on such work as being of only secondary importance compared to the antiquarian studies to which his life was mainly devoted; the writing of a program was merely one of the duties expected of a humanist in the service of a cardinal. For Carracci, however, the association may have been an invaluable one. He must surely have thought it fortunate that, at the very time when, as a newcomer in Rome, he was striving to acquire a deeper understanding of classical style than was possible in Bologna, he could draw upon the immense erudition of one of the greatest archaeologists of his day.

[125] Nolhac, *op.cit.*, p. 205, no. 566.   [126] *Ibid.*, p. 191, no. 107; p. 214, no. 80.

PART II
THE FARNESE GALLERY

CHAPTER 4 · THE CHRONOLOGY OF THE FARNESE GALLERY AND THE ROLE OF ANNIBALE'S WORKSHOP

WHEN Annibale Carracci moved into the Farnese palace in 1595, his patron had evidently not yet come to a firm decision regarding the decoration of the Gallery in the rear wing. Cherubino Alberti had, it is true, submitted a design for the *stuccatura* (Fig. 29), but his solution was not put into effect. We have seen, moreover, that it was not the Gallery, but the *sala grande*, that Cardinal Farnese had in mind when he invited Annibale into his service. No doubt the cardinal expected that when the Camerino was finished the artist would be able to begin work directly on the project that was of the greatest concern to Odoardo—the Alessandro Farnese cycle in the *sala grande*. But when that project had once again to be postponed, he concluded that the painter's talents would be best employed in the Gallery which still stood unfinished at the rear of the palace, and Annibale was therefore commissioned to fresco the ceiling and walls of this room.

Thus began, in this unceremonious way, the most monumental undertaking of Annibale's career, the masterpiece on which his fame chiefly rests. It is strange to reflect that so little is known of the circumstances in which this great project was realized: the Farnese archives yield no documents that mark the commencement or even the termination of the work; there are no records of payments which might enable us to follow its progress; we hear of no unveiling. This lack of what might be called primary documentation makes it extremely difficult to trace the successive stages of the decoration. For it means that we must attempt to construct a reasonable chronology from other, less satisfactory kinds of evidence.

The general sequence of events is nevertheless clear enough. The decoration of the Farnese Gallery was carried out in three stages. The first stage was the painting of the vault; this immense work went forward rapidly in an extraordinary surge of creative energy. The second stage, which followed after a considerable lapse of time, saw the execution of the large Perseus frescoes on the end walls. Another lengthy hiatus intervened before work was resumed on the third and final phase, the painting of the various frescoes of the lateral walls and the caryatids beneath the Perseus subjects. It is also clear that the generally accepted view, according to which the Gallery was terminated in 1604, must now be revised. The weight of evidence obliges us to conclude that the final elements of the decoration were only completed in 1608.[1]

---

[1] It is encouraging to find that Denis Mahon's conclusions regarding the chronology of the Gallery are in many respects similar to mine; see his "Note sur l'achèvement de la Galerie Farnèse et les dernières années d'Annibal Carrache," in the catalogue of the exhibition *Dessins des Carrache, Musée du Louvre*, Paris, 1961, pp. 57-61. Cf. also Gian

I. THE CEILING

A fresco cycle of the scale and complexity of the Farnese ceiling can only have been brought into being through the close collaboration of artist and literary adviser. Although an iconographical plan must have been drawn up, at least in outline form, before Annibale began to work on the project, many important questions still remained unsettled. We know, for example, that the disposition of the main subjects was not fixed at the outset: Annibale's earliest studies for the broad framework of the ceiling do not place the *Bacchanal* in the center (Figs. 151-152). We may imagine decisions of this sort as being made in informal discussions, no doubt extending over a considerable period.

The name of the *letterato* who composed the program of the vault is not recorded in the sources. Bellori's erroneous mention of Agucchi in connection with the Camerino[2] has frequently been interpreted as meaning that it was he who advised Annibale on the subject matter of the Farnese ceiling; but this conclusion must be regarded as unwarranted (though Agucchi may have been called upon at a later stage in the decoration of the Gallery). Yet the problem is perhaps not insoluble. For it is virtually certain that the distinguished humanist who conceived the cycle of the Camerino was also responsible for that of the Farnese vault. Indeed it would have been strange if the task had been entrusted to anyone but Cardinal Farnese's librarian, Fulvio Orsini. Orsini died on May 18, 1600. By that time, as will shortly appear, the greater part if not all of the ceiling was already finished.

It is true that in the Gallery we do not sense the personal intervention of Fulvio Orsini to the same degree as in the Camerino, where a number of subjects can be shown to be directly inspired by objects (notably coins and gems) in Fulvio's own possession. In part this can be explained by the difference in scale between the two cycles: in the intimate, cabinet-like atmosphere of the Camerino it is fitting that many of the paintings should reveal their derivation from miniature works of art, whereas in the Gallery, at least as regards the larger frescoes, it was necessary to turn to models of a more monumental character than could be found in Orsini's collection. Even so, if we examine the cycle more carefully we shall discover unmistakable signs of Orsini's influence. It is to the smaller frescoes that we must look to see reflections of his interest in the minor arts. The medallions, for example, markedly resemble bronze coins, and it cannot be mere coincidence that subjects like *Europa and the Bull* and *Hero and Leander* are well known on Greek coins. Among the carved gems owned by Orsini were representations of Marsyas,[3] Leander,[4] Ganymede,[5]

Carlo Cavalli in the catalogue of the exhibition *L'ideale classico del Seicento in Italia*, Bologna, 1962, pp. 50 f.

[2] *Vite*, p. 32.

[3] Nolhac, "Les collections d'antiquités de Fulvio Orsini," *Mélanges*, IV, 1884, p. 162, no. 189.

[4] *Illustrium imagines ex antiquis marmoribus, nomismatibus, et gemmis expresse: quae extant Romae, maior pars apud Fulvium Ursinum, editio altera . . . ,* Antwerp, 1606, Appendix, pl. L.

[5] Nolhac, *op.cit.,* p. 162, no. 181. Orsini also owned a copy by Daniele da Volterra after

and Hyacinthus,[6] all of which figure on the ceiling. As librarian and custodian of the Farnese collections he had access to such works as Perino del Vaga's drawing of the *Triumph of Bacchus* (Fig. 281), from which Annibale was to take many of the ideas—both formal and iconographic—which are developed in his fresco. It was undoubtedly Orsini who impressed upon him the symbolic significance of the Bacchus-Alexander theme in Farnese imagery.

The meager evidence at our disposal suggests that Annibale set to work on the Farnese ceiling in 1597. The Camerino had been completed, and if we are right in assuming that Agostino arrived in Rome in October of that year, this would indicate that everything was then in readiness for the great task. Unluckily we have no reports of the Gallery at this time: the *Avvisi* are silent, nor do guidebooks and accounts by travelers contain anything that might shed light on the beginnings of the work. We look in vain for information in the famous *Itinerarium Italiae* by François Schott, the first edition of which was published at Antwerp in 1600. Because his itinerary of Rome depends heavily on Boissard's *Roman Topography* of 1597, Schott gives a brief account of the Farnese palace and its antique sculptures, but says nothing of the Gallery.[7] The German architect Heinrich Schickhardt visited the Farnese palace in 1599 but probably did not see the Gallery, since he makes no mention of it in the book which he published a few years later; his silence probably indicates that the room was closed to visitors while the vault was being painted.[8]

Though it may be impossible to uncover any precise information about the commencement of the ceiling frescoes, we are not left entirely in the dark concerning their termination. For on this matter a certain amount of evidence can be assembled. We shall first examine the literary sources.

On October 26, 1601, a young Moravian nobleman named Zdenek Waldstein paid a visit to the Palazzo Farnese and recorded in his diary what he saw there.[9] On entering the palace he was first struck by the two huge statues of Hercules which stood in the court. He was then taken upstairs to the principal rooms where he was shown, among other things, a model of the bridge of boats that Alessandro Farnese had em-

---

Michelangelo's famous drawing of Ganymede (*ibid.*, p. 178, no. 97).

[6] *Ibid.*, p. 162, no. 193.

[7] F. Schott, *Itinerarii Italiae rerumq. Romanorum libri tres*, Antwerp, 1600. On the history of this book see E. S. de Beer, "François Schott's 'Itinerario D'Italia,'" *The Library*, new series, XXIII, 1942-1943, pp. 57-83. The first edition of the book to include a notice of the Farnese Gallery is the Italian version published by Bolzetta in 1610.

[8] H. Schickhardt, *Beschreibung einer Raiss, welche der . . . Herr Friderich Hertzog zu Württemberg . . . i. J. 1599 . . . auss dem Land zu Württemberg in Italiam gethan*, Tübingen,

1603. Cited by Tietze, p. 125, note 4.

[9] On Waldstein and his diary see J. A. F. Orbaan, *Bescheiden in Italië omtrent Nederlandsche Kunstenaars en Geleerden*, The Hague, 1911, I, pp. 170 ff., no. 185; *idem*, *Rome onder Clemens VIII*, The Hague, 1920, pp. 126 ff.; and J. Odier, "Voyage en France d'un jeune gentilhomme morave en 1599 et 1600," *Mélanges d'archéologie et d'histoire*, Ecole Française de Rome, XLIII, 1926, pp. 140 ff. (the last-named particularly useful). The journal, at one time the property of Queen Christina of Sweden, passed after her death to the Vatican Library (MS Reg. lat. 666).

ployed for the siege of Antwerp, and Moschino's statue of the Duke crowned by Victory. After describing more of the family treasures Waldstein continues: "In a certain room [there was] a ceiling or roof so skillfully decorated with paintings that on first entering it you would have said they were sculptures."[10] Only two rooms in the palace had painted ceilings—the Camerino and the Galleria. But Waldstein's words can hardly be taken to apply to the Camerino, which because of its small size he would surely have called *cubiculum*. Moreover, the fact that he speaks of the sculptural effect of the decoration makes it virtually certain that what the young Czech traveler saw was the Farnese Gallery; it made much the same impression on John Evelyn, who wrote of the frescoed figures of the ceiling that he was unable "to determine whether they were flat, or emboss'd."[11] Although as a description of the Gallery Waldstein's brief account admittedly leaves much to be desired, it appears nevertheless to be the earliest mention that we have of the frescoes of the vault.

It was some seven months later, at the end of May 1602, that Ludovico Carracci arrived in Rome from Bologna for a short visit. We have no reliable account of the state in which he found his cousin's project at that time. Our only informant is Malvasia, who, in order that the older artist may share some of Annibale's glory, unblushingly declares that during a fortnight's stay in Rome Ludovico "adjusted and corrected" the whole of the Farnese Gallery and personally painted the nude youth beside the medallion of *Pan and Syrinx* (Fig. 51).[12] Needless to say, the story of Ludovico's intervention is purely fictitious. In any event it may be deduced from Waldstein's diary that the scaffolding had been taken down before this date.

We next hear of the frescoes in the funeral oration read by Lucio Faberio at the memorial service for Agostino Carracci in January 1603: "Go and admire the Diana [*sic*] and the Galatea, two frescoes which he painted in the Gallery of the illustrious Cardinal Farnese, where his brother Annibale, who has painted all the rest, deserves eternal praise for having increased the number of the beauties of Rome, for citizens and foreigners alike."[13]

[10] Bibl. Vat., MS Reg. lat. 666, fol. 291 r.: "In conclavi quodam tectum sive pavimentum picturis adeo artificiose ornatum, ut in introïtu primo sculpturas esse diceres." Since *pavimentum* normally denotes a pavement consisting of stones set in mortar, its use to describe a ceiling is unorthodox, to say the least. Possibly Waldstein means to allude to the plaster covering of the vault. In any event, the phrase *tectum sive pavimentum* leaves no doubt that he is referring to a ceiling. Professor Panofsky has pointed out to me that the use of the word *pavimentum* to designate a roof-covering of stone occurs in the anonymous *Bellum Alexandrinum* 1, 3: "aedificia et structuris ac fornicibus continentur tectaque sunt rudere aut pavimentis."

[11] *The Diary of John Evelyn* (ed. E. S. de Beer), Oxford, 1955, II, p. 215. See also the description of the Gallery by the English painter Richard Symonds, who was in Italy in 1650-1651: "All ye Colours of ye naked bodyes has no black in ym, they come off so round, they seeme reall flesh mighty gay and glorious" (Brit. Mus. Egerton MS 1635, fol. 18; cited by L. Salerno, "Seventeenth-Century English Literature on Painting," *Journal of the Warburg and Courtauld Institutes*, XIV, 1951, p. 245).

[12] *Felsina*, I, p. 406. Malvasia's statement was repudiated by Vittoria, *Osservazioni*, p. 53.

[13] *Il funerale d'Agostin Carraccio*, p. 40 (reprinted in Malvasia, *Felsina*, I, p. 431): "Ite, e mirate . . . la Diana, e la Galatea, due quadri

Almost contemporary with Faberio's oration is the important notice of the Gallery which Carel van Mander included in his *Schilderboeck*: "Among other [artists] there is one called Carracci, living in the palace of the illustrious Cardinal Farnese, where he has done various fine things, especially a beautiful gallery, which is so excellently painted in fresco that it is said that this manner surpasses those of all other masters, and that its beauty cannot be described."[14] The *Schilderboeck* was published only in 1604, but the privilege is dated 1603, and the information concerning Carracci, which Van Mander received from a correspondent in Rome, may be even earlier.

A remark by G. B. Passeri in his Life of Domenichino shows that by August 1604 the Farnese Gallery had begun to be generally known in Rome.[15] The passage in question has usually been cited (in my view wrongly) as proving that the entire decoration of the Gallery—the walls as well as the vault—was terminated by this date,[16] but at least it cannot be disputed that by 1604 the ceiling was visible in its completed form and had become a familiar monument.

If these were our only sources of information we should probably conclude that the ceiling was finished and the scaffolding taken down in 1601, or (if it were doubted that the room described by Waldstein was really the Gallery) by 1602 or 1603 at the latest. But there is additional evidence which not only tends to confirm Waldstein's report but also establishes that the huge task required an even shorter period of time. The frescoes of the vault were actually completed as early as 1600.

There is, firstly, the fact that the date MDC is inscribed beneath the scene of *Polyphemus and Galatea* at one end of the ceiling.[17] This was unquestionably meant, as Bellori says,[18] to mark the completion of the vault. A terminal date of 1600 is

a fresco ch'egli dipinse nella galleria dell'Illustriss. Cardinal Farnese, dove il suo fratello Annibale, che tutto il resto v'ha dipinto; hà con eterna sua lode accresciuto a fuorastieri, e terrazani il numero delle bellezze di Roma."

[14] Carel van Mander, *Het Schilderboeck*, Haarlem, 1604, fol. 190 v.-191 r.: "Onder ander isser eenen geheeten *Caratz*, woonende tot den doorluchtigen Cardinael *Farnees*, alwaer hy verscheyden fraey dingen heeft ghedaen/die seer uytmuntende zijn/insonderheyt een schoon gallerije/die so uytnemende geschildert is op t' nat/datter geseyt wort/dat dese maniere die van alle ander Meesters te boven gaet/en dat de schoonheyt niet uyt te spreken is." The text is reprinted, with commentary, in H. Noë, *Carel van Mander en Italië*, The Hague, 1954, pp. 292 ff.

[15] *Die Künstlerbiographien von G. B. Passeri*, ed. J. Hess, Leipzig-Vienna, 1934, p. 24 and note 4.

[16] Cf., for example, L. Salerno, in Mancini,

Considerazioni sulla pittura, ed. Marucchi and Salerno, II, p. 102.

[17] The inscription is not visible from the floor of the Gallery. I am grateful to D. W. Buchanan, Esq., and A. Vidal-Naquet, Attaché at the French Embassy in Rome, for their kindness in verifying its existence. It is doubtless due to a mere slip of the pen that Gian Carlo Cavalli describes the inscription as being beneath the so-called *Galatea* painted by Agostino (Catalogue of the exhibition *L'ideale classico del Seicento in Italia*, Bologna, 1962, p. 50).

[18] Bellori, *Vite*, p. 59. See also Vincenzo Vittoria, *Osservazioni*, p. 53. I cannot agree with Navenne (*Revue des Deux Mondes*, March 1900, p. 196) and Tietze (pp. 125 ff.) that the date has anything to do with the marriage of the Duke Ranuccio to Margherita Aldobrandini, which took place in Rome on May 7, 1600. What is more, Tietze's reasons for believing that the vault could not have

absolutely consistent with the literary sources cited above. What is more, it accords perfectly with what is known of Agostino's participation in the project. His two frescoes (which owing to their position in the lower zone of the vault were among the latest to be painted) were incontestably completed before July 1600, since by that time he was already in Parma in the service of Duke Ranuccio.

Another guide to the dating of the Farnese vault is furnished by Agostino's engraving *Omnia vincit Amor* (B. 116),[19] which represents Cupid overcoming Pan and is dated 1599 (Fig. 276). The composition is made up of elements taken from works by Annibale. The two nymphs at the right side, who cling to each other as if in fear while they watch the contest, are copied from Annibale's painting, *Diana and Callisto*, now in the Ellesmere Collection.[20] (We may note in passing that these same figures reappear, in slightly altered form, as the two Nereids at the extreme left of Agostino's fresco of *Glaucus and Scylla*, Fig. 60). The group of Pan and Cupid, on the other hand, clearly imitates Annibale's roundel of the same subject on the vault of the Gallery (Fig. 48); Agostino's preparatory drawing for the engraving resembles the fresco still more closely in that Pan's upraised hand is pressed against Cupid's face.[21] Since the engraving bears the date 1599 it follows that the corresponding section of the Farnese frieze must be of about the same period: the design, if not the actual execution, of the frescoed medallion can be safely assigned to 1599.

The first frescoes to be painted were of necessity those at the top of the vault, namely, the *Bacchanal* and the two flanking octagonal scenes of *Pan and Diana* and *Paris and Mercury*. In all probability they were done during the period 1597-1598. When in due course the time came for Annibale's assistants to paint the ornamental frames around the latter pictures, it was discovered that the octagons were not perfectly regular, and wedge-shaped sections were therefore added at two corners of each fresco (Figs. 65-66).

Although it is impossible to reconstruct the exact sequence in which the remaining parts of the ceiling were executed, an examination of the decorative figures leads to the conclusion that, at least as far as they are concerned, Annibale worked from the southern end toward the north (from top to bottom in the view of the ceiling reproduced as Fig. 36). One striking proof of this is to be seen in the pairs of satyrs who are seated on the frames of the large pictures at either end. Those at the south, over the scene of *Polyphemus and Galatea* (Fig. 67), are in simple profile poses, as if the artist had wished to avoid unnecessary complications. By contrast, the satyrs at the opposite end of the Gallery (Fig. 68) are more advanced in conception and must belong to a later phase: the figures assume lively twisting attitudes and look up toward

been finished by 1600 seem to me to be inconclusive.

[19] Reproduced in A. Petrucci, "L'incisione carraccesca," *Bollettino d'Arte*, serie IV, XXXV, 1950, fig. 6 (p. 135).

[20] Reproduced in *Burlington Magazine*, CII,

1960, p. 129, fig. 39.

[21] Frankfurt, Städelsches Kunstinstitut, inv. no. 4059 (H. Bodmer, "Die Entwicklung der Stechkunst des Agostino Carracci," *Die graphischen Künste*, N.F.,V, 1940, p. 68, fig. 32).

the vault. Annibale has now become surer of the spatial properties of the ceiling, both real and illusionistic, and is accordingly able to exploit these properties more freely through such things as pose and direction of gaze. There are other signs of the artist's initial inexperience, before he fully mastered the various technical problems posed by the ceiling. Thus, for example, in the pair of embracing atlantes to the left of *Polyphemus and Galatea* (Fig. 40) Carracci has encountered difficulty in co-ordinating the arms of the two figures. They were probably the first of the series to be carried out in fresco, for the other three pairs exhibit no such lack of adjustment. No differences of this sort are apparent among the seated *ignudi*, but it is noteworthy that the most accomplished (and hence presumably the latest) figures are to be found near the northern end of the Gallery (cf. Figs. 47 and 48).

One of the most extraordinary facts about the Farnese ceiling is that most of it was painted by Annibale himself. Agostino is known to have done the two large *quadri riportati* over the middle of the longitudinal walls; the remainder, as Lucio Faberio remarked in 1603,[22] is almost entirely the work of Annibale.

Agostino's authorship of the *Aurora* (Fig. 59) and the so-called *Galatea* (Fig. 60) is supported by incontrovertible evidence, both literary and stylistic. They are unhesitatingly attributed to him in all the biographical sources, from Faberio on.[23] Nor do the frescoes themselves leave any room for doubt. For despite their manifest dependence on the monumental style of Annibale, the distinguishing characteristics of Agostino's dry and pedantic manner are plainly visible: the "pneumatic" plumpness of the putti and the female figures; the ropelike treatment of the musculature of the male figures; the interest in silhouettes; and the cool coloration. The preparatory drawings and cartoons (Figs. 188-192, 194) are likewise indisputably by Agostino's hand.

About the other members of Annibale's workshop at this period we know very little. As early as November 1595 the Duke of Parma had asked Cardinal Farnese to take into his service, in company with Annibale, a young painter named Ottavio Pincolini.[24] But nothing more is heard of this artist. The chief of Annibale's assistants, after Agostino, was Innocenzo Tacconi of Bologna. Tacconi was a nephew of Ludovico, and seems to have presumed upon this relationship to exercise an undue influence over the master; it was he, according to both Bellori and Malvasia, who fostered the discord between Annibale and Agostino that led to the latter's departure.[25] Soon after the rupture, in 1600 or 1601, Tacconi was entrusted with the frescoes on the vault of the Cerasi Chapel in Santa Maria del Popolo in Rome, for which Annibale

[22] *Il funerale d'Agostin Carraccio*, p. 40 (reprinted in Malvasia, *Felsina*, I, p. 431). See note 13 above.

[23] *Ibid.* Mancini, *Considerazioni*, I, p. 217. Baglione, *Vite*, pp. 105, 107. Bellori, *Vite*, pp. 55, 57, 110 f.

[24] Naples, Archivio di Stato, Carte Farnesiane, f. 724. Cited by Tietze, p. 107.

[25] Bellori, *Vite*, p. 82. Malvasia, *Felsina*, I, pp. 571 f. Innocenzo appears as a boy in the portrait of the Tacconi family painted by Ludovico about 1590 (catalogue of the *Mostra dei Carracci*, 3rd ed., Bologna, 1958, pp. 115 f., no. 10).

had prepared the designs.[26] Doubtless he had already assisted Annibale in a similar capacity in the Gallery. The medallions, for example, may well have been painted by Tacconi after drawings by Annibale; many of the figures in these roundels (cf. Figs. 47, 49, 50) are of the same slight and delicate build, and have the same diminutive hands and feet, as those of the Cerasi frescoes.[27] To other lesser assistants, finally, was left the task of painting the architectural features, the ornament, the picture frames, and the minor decorative figures.

Even when allowance has been made for the parts done by collaborators, Annibale's personal share in the enterprise remains an extraordinary one. There is no doubt that all the principal scenes and the more important accessory figures (notably the atlantes and the *ignudi*) were executed by the master himself. Bellori tells the revealing story that when Annibale was dissatisfied with the final result in fresco he would tear down whole sections of the *favole* and *partimenti* and patiently do all the work over again, even making fresh sets of drawings and cartoons.[28] He alone, moreover, devised the complex decorative system and prepared the numerous preliminary designs that were needed for a cycle of this magnitude. Only in the case of Agostino's two frescoes were the preparatory drawings not made by Annibale, and even here he exercised close supervision, making at least one change in his brother's plans.[29] As was pointed out above, the tale told by Malvasia of Ludovico's participation is totally without foundation. All things considered, the planning and execution of the Farnese vault must have been for Annibale a period of intense and sustained effort. We can readily imagine that the difficulties he encountered during this operation brought him to a state of nervous irritability and fatigue. This is actually confirmed, as it happens, by Bonconti's letter of August 1599, which provides an eye-witness's account of Annibale's arduous life at this very period.[30] Even the quarrel with Agostino, when seen in this light, can be understood as a symptom of the emotional strain experienced by the artist under the formidable pressures of the task confronting him.

The ceiling completed, there now ensued a necessary break in the project of frescoing the Gallery. The removal of the scaffolding made it possible, as Mahon has noted,[31] for the *stuccatori* to carry out the ornamentation of the walls, a task which no doubt required considerable time. From this moment Annibale appears to have relaxed somewhat his personal control of the decorative ensemble. It is quite obvious that he cannot have been responsible for the design of the stucco-work, which is

[26] Baglione, *Vite*, p. 312. Bellori, *Vite*, pp. 82 f.

[27] See L. Steinberg, "Observations in the Cerasi Chapel," *Art Bulletin*, XLI, 1959, pp. 183 ff., figs. 3-5.

[28] *Vite*, p. 81.

[29] See the drawings for *Glaucus and Scylla* (Nos. 82 and 83).

[30] Malvasia, *Felsina*, I, p. 574: "M. Annibale Carrazzi . . . lauora, & tira la caretta tutto il dì come vn cauallo, & fà loggie, camare & sale, quadri, & ancone, & lauori da mille scuti, & stenta, & creppa, & hà poco gusto anchora di tal seruitù."

[31] Mahon, "Note sur l'achèvement de la Galerie Farnèse," p. 59. The story of Annibale's working and eating with the *muratori* (Bellori, *Vite*, p. 76) must belong to this period.

thin and almost two-dimensional in appearance and reflects nothing whatever of his inventiveness and plastic energy. Bellori was likewise conscious of the mediocre quality of the stuccoes when he wrote that they were not executed from the *buon disegno* of the master.[32] We must therefore consider the possibility that Annibale was for some reason unable personally to superintend the work of the *stuccatori*.

It is significant that several misfortunes fell upon the artist just at this period. The first was Agostino's angry departure from Rome. Exactly when this took place is unknown, except that it was before the end of June 1600. Almost contemporaneous with Agostino's defection was the death of Fulvio Orsini, which occurred in May of the same year. The seriousness of this dual calamity should not be underestimated. It meant that Annibale, already suffering from the effects of prolonged overwork and emotional tension, was suddenly deprived both of his principal assistant and of the literary adviser upon whom he depended for the subject matter of the fresco cycle. For even though the vault was finished, there was still work to be done on the walls.

Furthermore, it may have been at this inopportune moment that Cardinal Farnese, seeing the great project temporarily brought to a halt, chose to recompense his artist for the work thus far accomplished by offering him the miserly sum of 500 *scudi d'oro*.[33] The bitter disappointment felt by Carracci, who was "by nature melancholic and highly nervous," whose "spirit was exhausted," and who now looked to his patron for some tangible proof of his appreciation, has been described by Bellori.[34] What actually happened, we may surmise, was that Annibale fell ill and was for some time incapacitated. It was the first breakdown, the forerunner of that total physical collapse which was to overtake the master a few years later. The stuccoes were completed without Annibale's supervision, and resumption of work on the fresco cycle had to be further postponed. To make matters worse, there came word early in 1602 of Agostino's death. Later, as the artist regained his strength, other projects began to claim his attention, above all the Aldobrandini lunettes and the Herrera chapel. It cannot have been before 1604 that he addressed himself once more to the decoration of the the Farnese Gallery.

During this period, when work was suspended on the Gallery, Annibale's workshop underwent some reorganization. Tacconi, who may have become senior assistant after Agostino's withdrawal, was soon overshadowed by a group of abler artists, all of whom were recruited from Emilia during the years 1601-1602. Three painters came

[32] *Vite*, p. 61. But Bellori mistakenly concluded that the stuccoes antedated the frescoes ("essendo stati lauorati prima").

[33] Mahon has also suggested (*loc.cit.*) that the "fatal incident" may have occurred during the interval that followed the termination of the vault. It is to be emphasized that the biographers offer no reliable indication of the date of the episode but are simply making a guess. Baglione's account has it that the sum

of 500 scudi was meant to cover ten years of continuous labor (*Vite*, p. 108). Bellori says that Annibale had been in Rome for eight years, thus seeming to imply a date of 1603 (*Vite*, p. 67). But these remarks should not be interpreted literally, because both writers assumed that Odoardo's reckoning was made after the completion of the entire Gallery, which was almost certainly not the case.

[34] *Vite*, p. 67.

to Rome from the Carracci studio in Bologna. Of these Francesco Albani and Domenichino became close adherents of Annibale;[35] Guido Reni, the third member of the Bolognese party, was too independent a spirit to play a subordinate role, and never entered Annibale's Roman *bottega*. There were also the two Parmesan artists, Giovanni Lanfranco and Sisto Badalocchio, who moved to Rome after the death of Agostino at Parma in February 1602 and were lodged in the Farnese palace.[36] The youngest newcomer was Agostino's natural son, Antonio Carracci, who had been born in 1589 and who now after his father's death was adopted by Annibale.[37] It cannot have been Annibale's intention at this stage to entrust to his pupils any of the important frescoes in the Gallery: there were other tasks for them to perform. Tacconi, working from Annibale's designs, had recently completed the vault of the Cerasi chapel in Santa Maria del Popolo; Domenichino would soon carry out three frescoes in a garden loggia of the Farnese palace; Albani and others would be called upon to assist the master in the Aldobrandini lunettes and the Herrera chapel; and Lanfranco would paint the frescoes of the Camerino degli Eremiti.

II. THE PERSEUS FRESCOES

Although Orsini did not live to see the Perseus frescoes take shape on the end walls of the Gallery, it is likely that he had earlier selected the subjects and discussed with the artist their relationship to the paintings of the vault. When Annibale, deeply embittered by his employer's conduct, and no doubt feeling much less enthusiasm for the enterprise, at length felt capable of resuming work he set about making the requisite preparatory drawings for the Perseus scenes. That he had not yet fully recovered is apparent from the fact that the earliest of these drawings reveal a perceptible falling off in quality.[38]

The first to be painted was the fresco of the *Combat of Perseus and Phineus* (Fig. 78). If there were any doubt that some years had elapsed between the completion of the ceiling and the beginning of work on the lower part of the Gallery this scene would be enough to dispel it. As compared to the *Bacchanal*, for example (Fig. 69), with its rhythmic grace and subtly varied postures, the *Perseus* seems harsh and lacking in resiliency: the heroic figures are uncompromisingly posed in stable attitudes, movement is suppressed, and even the colors are strangely muted. At the same time these stylistic peculiarities do not mean, as Tietze argued, that the fresco was executed by Domenichino.[39] The differences between this work and the paintings of the vault

[35] Mancini, *Considerazioni*, I, pp. 241 ff. Bel(l)ori, *Vite*, p. 292.

[36] Mancini, *op.cit.*, I, p. 247. Bellori, *Vite*, pp. 95, 366 f.

[37] Mancini, *op.cit.*, I, pp. 218, 220 f. Baglione, *Vite*, p. 150. For Antonio's birthdate see L. Salerno, "L'opera di Antonio Carracci," *Bollettino d'Arte*, XLI, 1956, p. 30 and note 1.

[38] Tietze (pp. 151 ff.) considered them to be by Domenichino. Wittkower, while rightly insisting on Annibale's authorship, has remarked on the curious lack of brilliance in drawings such as No. 136 (Fig. 249) and No. 137 (Fig. 250) (*Carracci Drawings*, p. 137).

[39] Tietze, pp. 149 ff. In his opinion, both Perseus frescoes are the work of Domenichino.

are to be accounted for by the changes taking place in Annibale's manner as he moved toward the more severe and monumental classicism of the late period. It is worth noting, too, that Albani, who was certainly well-informed about the Farnese frescoes, was satisfied that Annibale was the author of the *Perseus and Phineus*, from which he made a copy in pen and ink of "the figure who drawing back his arm to hurl the spear is turned into stone, by Annibale in the Galleria Farnese."[40] Domenichino also admired the fresco. The kneeling figure of Phineus finds a close parallel in his *Vision of St. Jerome*, painted at Sant' Onofrio in 1604-1605[41] (which would indicate that Carracci's fresco was painted no later than 1604); and the striding attitude of Phineus' captor is no less plainly reflected in the soldier pushing back the crowd in Domenichino's *Flagellation of St. Andrew* of 1608 (San Gregorio Magno).

Toward the end of 1604 work was begun on the *Perseus and Andromeda* (Fig. 77), which because of its uneven quality is more problematical than its pendant, the *Perseus and Phineus*. The expressive figure of Andromeda chained to the rock can only have been executed by Annibale himself. Tietze, who attributed the entire work to Domenichino, found her to be both "übergross" and "überlang."[42] But these qualities are characteristic of Annibale's later paintings, such as the *Assumption* in the Cerasi Chapel and the *Domine, quo vadis?* in the National Gallery in London. The least satisfactory part of the painting is the group of spectators gathered on the shore at the right, the ill-proportioned figure of King Cepheus being particularly disturbing. In the end it is difficult to resist the conclusion that another hand than Annibale's must have participated in the making of the fresco. As Mahon has pointed out, moreover, since the master would certainly not have permitted his assistants to paint the figures in a major composition unless compelled to do so by circumstances beyond his control, there is reason to believe that it was while he was at work on this very fresco that Annibale was stricken by the paralysis which we know overcame him early in 1605.[43] In this emergency it would have been necessary for an assistant, making use of the master's preliminary drawings, to complete the painting to the best of his ability.

Who was the pupil who (if this reconstruction of events is correct) was summoned to finish off the work? It seems almost certain that it must have been Domenichino, whose intervention at a later date in the final phase of the decoration of the Gallery is absolutely authenticated. Now in his twenty-fourth year, he had already acquired some experience in fresco, and may well have been working on the non-figurative parts of the *Andromeda* even before the master's illness. This might explain its curiously pale coloring, which finds a close analogy in the three frescoes painted by

[40] Malvasia, *Felsina*, ii, pp. 243 f. The drawing was one of a number of figures in action, selected from Titian, Raphael, and others, which were to be used as illustrations for a projected treatise on painting.

[41] The borrowing was observed by Passeri, who remarked that "in quelle Istorie [il Domenichino] si servisse di alcuna figura de Caracci della Galeria di Farnese" (Passeri, *Vite* [ed. Hess], p. 25 and note 1).

[42] Tietze, p. 150.

[43] Mahon, "Note sur l'achèvement de la Galerie Farnèse," pp. 58 f.

Domenichino in a garden loggia of the palace; one of these, the *Venus and Adonis*, had earned him Annibale's praise.[44] In short, that Domenichino had a hand in the *Andromeda* scene could be accepted without reservation if it were not for the fact that Bellori, who was thoroughly familiar with the artist's share in the Gallery, fails to mention it. It is of course possible that Bellori considered it unnecessary to cite a work which Domenichino had merely brought to completion.

In any event it is clear that Annibale's collapse early in 1605 precipitated a second and even more serious crisis in the great undertaking. If the *Perseus* was already finished, and if the *Andromeda* had been carried to such an advanced stage that what remained to be done could be entrusted to a pupil, it was unfortunately true that work had not even begun on the smaller paintings planned for the walls. For these there were only a number of drawings by Annibale, ranging in finish from the cartoon for the *Virgin with the Unicorn* to the preliminary sketches for the eight little mythological subjects and the *Virtues*. In these circumstances the decision seems to have been taken, probably by Cardinal Farnese, to suspend work on the Gallery until Annibale should once again be able to take charge. For Odoardo at first believed, as we learn from his letter of March 12, 1605, that the artist would recover quickly.[45] A year later, however, we find him writing that Annibale has still done no painting for him since his illness.[46]

III. THE FINAL PHASE: THE MINOR FRESCOES

It was not until the last stage of the decoration of the Gallery that Annibale's pupils were given a significant role in the execution of the frescoes. Even a cursory glance is sufficient to convince the observer that the paintings on the lateral walls (Figs. 92-99), as well as the six caryatids (Figs. 79-84) beneath the Perseus frescoes, are the work of assistants. Nor is it difficult to understand how this came about. As time wore on, and Annibale still gave no sign of being able to resume painting, it became obvious that it would be left to the members of his school, armed with his drawings and perhaps turning to him for advice, to bring the Gallery to completion. Two main problems confront us here: one is the problem of attribution, and the other is that of the date.

It would be interesting to know, for instance, which frescoes (if any) were assigned to Francesco Albani. He enjoyed Annibale's favor, and collaborated with him on the Aldobrandini landscape lunettes. As regards his participation in the Gallery we have only Passeri's casual remark that Carracci employed him "in alcune cose della sua Galeria de' Farnesi";[47] but this ought probably to be discounted since Passeri is speaking of the period before Annibale's illness when his pupils were given no in-

[44] Bellori, *Vite*, p. 292. The attitude of Domenichino's Venus, moreover, is very like that of Cassiopea in the *Andromeda* fresco.

[45] Modena, Archivio di Stato, Carteggio dei Principi, busta 96, cited by Tietze, p. 147, note 1.

[46] *Ibid.*, busta 97, cited by Tietze, p. 149.

[47] Passeri, *Vite* (ed. Hess), p. 264.

dependent tasks in that project. When the master became incapacitated early in 1605, Albani was charged with the bulk of the execution of the Herrera Chapel,[48] and this responsibility may have prevented him from taking any part in the Gallery. It seems likely, on the other hand, that Giovanni Lanfranco, one of the most gifted and original artists of the Carracci circle, must have acquired some experience in the Gallery; but the biographers in their account of his early Roman period speak only of his paintings in the Camerino degli Eremiti, datable about 1605.[49] The most shadowy figure of all is Lanfranco's colleague, the talented but negligent Sisto Badalocchio, concerning whose early work in Rome we have almost no information, except that he appears to have had a hand in the Herrera Chapel.[50] The sole member of Annibale's school about whose activity in the Gallery we possess definite information is Domenichino, and it is accordingly with that artist, whom the ailing Annibale seems to have looked upon as in some sense his heir, that we must begin.

In his description of the Farnese cycle Bellori specifies that Domenichino painted the *Virgin with the Unicorn* (Fig. 89) from Annibale's cartoon.[51] This is wholly credible. The cartoon, it is evident, had been made by Annibale before his collapse in 1605; thereafter, finding himself incapable of mural painting, he appointed Domenichino to translate it into fresco. It is also clear that Domenichino would not have regarded this task as beneath his dignity, for at this period he was seeking to immerse himself in the art of Annibale and, more particularly, in the style of the Farnese vault. Nevertheless, in spite of its strongly Annibalesque character, Domenichino's authorship of the fresco reveals itself in such things as the cooler tonality and in the gentler, more lyrical mood.

Of Domenichino's further share in the Gallery Bellori says only that he "worked on" the six green-bronze caryatids beneath the Perseus scenes.[52] The biographer seems to have chosen his words carefully; for the figures are plainly not all by the same hand. The three *ignudi* at the north, i.e. beneath *Perseus and Phineus* (Figs. 79-81), are superior in quality to the other three, and may therefore reasonably be ascribed to Domenichino. The figures are disposed symmetrically, the outer ones being in profile and the center one *en face*; each captive is seated within a shallow semicylindrical niche upon a thickly folded mass of drapery, one end of which also serves to cushion his head and shoulders against the weight from above. The ornamental band beneath each niche is painted in imitation of the stucco panel on the side walls. The three caryatids at the opposite end, under the *Andromeda*, are by another and markedly less competent hand (Figs. 82-84). Ungainly and ill-proportioned, they have evidently been made in imitation of the first set. Whoever their author, it was not Domenichino,

---

[48] See D. Posner, "Annibale Carracci and his School: the Paintings of the Herrera Chapel," *Arte antica e moderna*, no. 12, 1960, pp. 397-412.

[49] Bellori, *Vite*, p. 367. Passeri, *Vite* (ed. Hess), p. 140. See L. Salerno, "The Early Work of Giovanni Lanfranco," *Burlington Magazine*, XCIV, 1952, pp. 188 ff., figs. 2-6.

[50] Bellori, *Vite*, pp. 68 f. See Posner, *op.cit.*, p. 403.

[51] Bellori, *Vite*, p. 61.

[52] *Vite*, p. 64.

who would not have been guilty of the crudities that are so conspicuous in the two outer figures.

Tietze's attribution[53] to Domenichino of the four Virtues at the extremities of the long walls is, I believe, fully confirmed by an analysis of the preparatory drawings (see Chapter 11). Before he was stricken Annibale had done no more than to make a few initial sketches, and from these Domenichino later prepared detailed studies to be translated into fresco. Further corroboration of his responsibility for these figures is to be found in Domenichino's decoration of the Camera di Diana at Bassano di Sutri, where the central subject of the ceiling, representing *Latona with her Children Diana and Apollo*, is simply an adaptation of the Farnese oval with Charity suckling two infants (Fig. 76).[54] The fact that the artist gave such prominence to this group lends support to the hypothesis that the Virtue on which it depends is his own invention.

We turn now to the eight little mythological scenes distributed four to a side along the lateral walls.[55] For these Annibale had likewise dashed off a number of rapid pen sketches, which were subsequently utilized by his pupils in executing the frescoes. Unfortunately there is nothing in the sources to tell us who these pupils were or how the subjects were divided amongst them. Since they are not all by the same hand Tietze is clearly mistaken in attributing the whole series to Domenichino.[56] Yet there are indications that he played a part—perhaps a leading part—in bringing these little pictures to completion.

We may take as a starting-point the scene of *Diana and Callisto* (Fig. 93), situated on the left of the principal door on the inner wall. As was observed by Brugnoli,[57] Domenichino had recourse to this composition when in 1609 he was at work on a similar subject in the Giustiniani palace at Bassano di Sutri: in the fresco of *Diana and Actaeon* the graceful, half-reclining posture of the goddess and the motive of the nymph partly submerged in the pool depend so unequivocally on the Farnese panel as to make it appear that he was responsible for both pictures. This supposition is strengthened by the pronounced similarity in color which links the *Diana and Callisto* to the neighboring *Virgin with the Unicorn* (Fig. 89), a fresco known to have been executed by Domenichino. The same preference for a cool, rather grayish tonal-

[53] Tietze, p. 153.

[54] M. V. Brugnoli, "Gli affreschi dell'Albani e del Domenichino nel palazzo di Bassano di Sutri," *Bollettino d'Arte*, XLII, 1957, pp. 274 f., fig. 10. The chalk drawing in the Louvre (Inv. 7373 verso), which Tietze (p. 153) understandably took to be a sketch by Annibale for the oval of *Charity*, is in fact a study by Domenichino for the fresco at Bassano. See J. R. Martin, "Disegni del Domenichino," *Bollettino d'Arte*, XLIV, 1959, p. 43, fig. 9.

[55] In the following pages I am particularly

indebted to Denis Mahon, with whom I had the opportunity to discuss this problem a few years ago, and who has subsequently set forth his views in the article already cited, "Note sur l'achèvement de la Galerie Farnèse," in the catalogue of the exhibition, *Dessins des Carrache, Musée du Louvre*, pp. 57-61.

[56] Tietze, pp. 152 ff.

[57] Brugnoli "Gli affreschi dell'Albani e del Domenichino nel palazzo di Bassano di Sutri," p. 274.

ity is seen again in the *Daedalus and Icarus* (Fig. 92) at the left end of the inner wall. Of the four scenes on the side opposite the windows, then, there is reason to ascribe to Domenichino the two at the left of the *Virgin with the Unicorn.*

It might seem only reasonable to conclude that if Zampieri painted *Diana and Callisto* he must also have been responsible for its sequel, the *Transformation of Callisto* (Fig. 94), on the right of the doorway, but this possibility is ruled out by the quite different coloration of the two scenes. In the latter the flesh tints are noticeably warmer, and there are touches of red in the shadows; in addition the rocky background is somewhat lighter than in the *Diana and Callisto*. Inasmuch as these ruddier flesh tints likewise appear in the adjoining scene of *Mercury and Apollo* (Fig. 95), Mahon is probably correct in attributing this subject (the fourth and final fresco on the inner wall) to the same hand.[58] Who was the author of these two scenes? A certain heaviness of touch shows that it cannot have been Albani, who had already arrived at a style full of grace and refinement. I should like to suggest that the executant might have been Annibale's nephew Antonio Carracci. At the time when these pictures were painted Antonio would have been about nineteen; and this might serve to explain their relative ineptness of draughtsmanship.[59]

Whereas the four little paintings on the side facing the windows bear the impress of Annibale's classical manner in their emphasis on the sculptural properties of the human figure, those on the outer wall are characterized by their looser, more "painterly" treatment. It is in fact already possible to see in these two parallel series an early instance of the duality of *Disegno* and *Colore* in the art of the Seicento. None of the paintings over the windows, significantly, can be attributed to Domenichino: the light here being decidedly poor he no doubt felt disinclined, as Annibale's deputy, to put his hand to works which would not easily be seen. To substantiate this it is only necessary to look at the scene farthest left on the window wall—*Arion and the Dolphin* (Fig. 96)—in which the brushwork is obviously much too spirited for Domenichino; nor does the vivid blue setting against which Arion's yellow drapery stands out so sharply have anything in common with the subdued palette used for *Daedalus and Icarus*. The bold modeling of the face in patches of light and dark is especially revealing. The only member of the Carracci circle who was capable of such pictorial freedom was Domenichino's rival Lanfranco.

To Lanfranco must also be given the panel at the extreme right of the outer wall representing *Hercules freeing Prometheus* (Fig. 99). The nudes are vigorously drawn, the foreshortened body of Prometheus being particularly fine. The stony gray shade of the mountain changes to a light green in the lower corners, and the leaden sky is effectively relieved by a strip of bright blue along the top.

The scene of *Minerva and Prometheus* (Fig. 97) is unquestionably the weakest of

[58] Mahon, "Note sur l'achèvement de la Galerie Farnèse," p. 60.

[59] For an analysis of Antonio's early style see L. Salerno, "L'opera di Antonio Carracci," *Bollettino d'Arte*, XLI, 1956, pp. 30 ff.

the quartet on this side. A certain negligence in draughtsmanship, especially in the two male figures, may cause us to think of Sisto Badalocchio, whose hasty workmanship and lack of experience in fresco are specifically mentioned by Bellori.[60] But there are other and more cogent reasons for considering Sisto as the executant. The figure of Minerva, with its small head and diminutive features, is a familiar type in early paintings by this artist;[61] and the architecture at the left is remarkably similar to that seen in Badalocchio's fresco of *St. Diego preaching*, formerly in the Herrera Chapel.[62]

There remains the picture of *Hercules and the Dragon* (Fig. 98). In spite of a superficial resemblance to *Hercules freeing Prometheus*, the draughtsmanship and modeling are somewhat hard and insensitive. It is probable that here again we have to do with the workmanship of Sisto.

The emblematic devices that accompany the mythological subjects were likewise executed by members of Annibale's workshop. Our illustrations (Figs. 85-88) reproduce the four *imprese* on the inner wall; a duplicate set appears on the opposite wall. Mention must be made, finally, of the little frescoed panels which decorate the soffits of the lintels over the three windows. The octagonal compartment over the middle window simply bears the patron's name in gold letters on a blue ground: ODOARDVS CAR. FARNESIVS (Fig. 37). The other two panels are lozenge-shaped. One shows a *Battle of Sea Gods* (Fig. 90) and the other a *Nymph and Triton* (Fig. 91), the latter recalling in some respects Agostino's fresco of *Glaucus and Scylla*.

We have endeavored to show that work on the lower part of the Farnese Gallery was brought to a standstill by Annibale's serious illness in 1605, and that thenceforth the master played no direct role in the project, leaving the remaining frescoes to be carried out entirely by his disciples. The question that now confronts us is: when were these last paintings executed?

John Pope-Hennessy has remarked[63] that, if we are to believe Bellori, Domenichino did not paint the *Virgin with the Unicorn* (and presumably his other frescoes in the Gallery as well) until he had completed the scenes of Apollo for the Villa Aldobrandini at Frascati. Annibale was so impressed by his work there, Bellori writes, that "he employed him in the Farnese Gallery, allowing him to paint over a door the Virgin with the Unicorn, which Domenichino copied from the master's cartoon with so much skill that Annibale himself could not have shown more."[64] Bellori is

[60] *Vite*, pp. 68 f. See also Agucchi's comments on Sisto (Malvasia, *Felsina*, I, p. 518).

[61] L. Salerno, "Per Sisto Badalocchi e la cronologia del Lanfranco," *Commentari*, IX, 1958, pp. 44 ff.

[62] Posner, "Annibale Carracci and his School," p. 403, pl. 136a.

[63] *The Drawings of Domenichino in the Collection of His Majesty the King at Wind-sor Castle*, New York, 1948, p. 15.

[64] Bellori, *Vite*, p. 295: "Per le quali opere [the frescoes of the Villa Aldobrandini] Annibale scorgendo Domenico tuttauia più intento, & vigoroso nell'arte, si riuolse ad amarlo efficacemente, e l'adoperò nella Galeria Farnese, dandogli à colorire sopra vna porta la Vergine dell'Alicorno, la quale egli imitò dal cartone del maestro con tanta felicità, quanta

of course not infallible, and it is conceivable that in this instance, as in certain others, he is simply wrong. The received view has been that the Aldobrandini cycle must fall within the period 1605-1606. The commission was given to Domenichino, as Bellori relates, by Cardinal Pietro Aldobrandini at the suggestion of Giovanni Battista Agucchi, who was then his *Maggiordomo*.[65] Passeri adds that the frescoes were painted in the beginning of the pontificate of Paul V, who was elected Pope in 1605;[66] and this accords very well with the fact that for the scene of the *Contest of Apollo and Marsyas* Domenichino made use of a drawing by Annibale (still preserved) which cannot be much later than that date.[67] Recently, however, the traditional dating of the Aldobrandini frescoes has been challenged.[68] It would thus be unwise, while critical opinion on the subject is still divided, to use the Frascati cycle as evidence for the date of Domenichino's activity in the Galleria Farnese. Fortunately other evidence is at hand.

Several signs point to the period 1607-1608 as the time when Annibale, still unable after several years to address himself to the task of monumental painting and probably sensing that his career was drawing to a close,[69] resolved to name Domenichino as his successor. It was for this reason that he recommended to Cardinal Farnese that Domenichino should receive the commission to decorate the Chapel at Grottaferrata,[70] begun in 1608, and even gave him some assistance in the planning of the cycle.[71] It is significant too that when in the same year Annibale saw the two frescoes painted

Annibale stesso non hauerebbe vsata maggiore."

[65] Bellori, *Vite*, p. 295. Agucchi became *Maggiordomo* in 1604 (cf. Mahon, *Studies*, p. 112).

[66] Passeri, *Vite* (ed. Hess), p. 26.

[67] Ellesmere Collection, no. 51. See Mahon, *Disegni*, pp. 96 f., no. 127.

[68] In a recent documentary study, Klaus Schwager has proposed re-dating Domenichino's frescoes at Frascati to the period 1613-1614, chiefly for the reason that they are not mentioned in an account of the Villa by Cardinal Pietro Aldobrandini, believed to have been written in 1611 ("Kardinal Pietro Aldobrandinis Villa di Belvedere in Frascati," *Römisches Jahrbuch für Kunstgeschichte*, IX-X, 1961-1962, pp. 289 ff.). Evelina Borea, who was earlier informed of Dr. Schwager's findings, reached a similar conclusion (in *Paragone*, No. 123, March 1960, pp. 12 f.), without however attempting to reconcile the new hypothesis with the evidence supporting the earlier dating. Against their interpretation may be set the arguments put forward by Denis Mahon ("Note sur l'achèvement de la Galerie Farnèse," pp. 57-61), G. C. Cavalli

(in the catalogue *L'ideale classico*, pp. 75 f.), and Luigi Salerno (in *Burlington Magazine*, May 1963, pp. 194 ff.), all of whom have re-affirmed, on stylistic and other grounds, a dating of 1605-1606. The problem clearly merits further study.

[69] The seriousness of Annibale's mental and physical condition in July 1608 may be judged from the effort made by several of his pupils (among them Sisto Badalocchio) to compel him to begin painting again. See Mahon, *Disegni*, pp. 167 f., no. 248.

[70] Baglione, *Vite*, p. 382. Bellori, *Vite*, p. 296. Passeri, *Vite* (ed. Hess), p. 29. L. Serra has established that the work was carried out between 1608 and 1610 (*Domenico Zampieri detto il Domenichino*, Rome, 1909, pp. 30 ff.).

[71] A drawing at Windsor proves conclusively that Annibale took some responsibility for the design of the Grottaferrata frescoes (Wittkower, *Carracci Drawings*, p. 148, no. 359, pl. 84). The sculptor Algardi told Malvasia that Annibale had painted the head of the epileptic boy in Domenichino's fresco of *St. Nilus curing an Epileptic Boy* (Malvasia, *Felsina*, I, p. 501).

at San Gregorio Magno by Domenichino and Guido Reni he made no effort to conceal the fact that he regarded Domenichino's as the better work.[72] These signal marks of favor make it all the more probable that this was also the time when he appointed Domenichino to superintend the final stages of the Farnese Gallery.

Finally we must recall once more the decoration of the Camera di Diana in the Giustiniani palace at Bassano di Sutri, which was carried out by Domenichino while the impressions of the Farnese Gallery were still very fresh in his mind. Since the frescoes at Bassano were painted in the summer of 1609,[73] it follows that his work in the Gallery cannot have been much earlier than 1608.

Annibale thus lived to see the Galleria at last completed. It can hardly be imagined that the sight gave him much pleasure. His patron had shown small gratitude; he had quarreled irreconcilably with his brother; his health was ruined; and he had had to endure the humiliation of entrusting to his assistants work that he was no longer capable of performing.

[72] Bellori, *Vite*, pp. 303 f.

[73] When the summer heat became oppressive Domenichino interrupted his work at Grottaferrata in order to repair to Bassano, from which he wrote to Cardinal Farnese on the last day of July 1609 (Serra, *Il Domenichino*, p. 31). On September 30 he received a payment of 125 scudi for the ceiling of the Camera di Diana at Bassano (Brugnoli, "Gli affreschi dell'Albani e del Domenichino," p. 277, Appendice di documenti, IV). By this date he had already returned to Grottaferrata, as was reported in a letter by Agucchi (Malvasia, *Felsina*, II, p. 331).

CHAPTER 5 · THE DECORATIVE SYSTEM

THE Gallery (Figs. 30-31), situated at the rear of the palace in the wing overlooking the Tiber (cf. Fig. 2 and text fig. 1, page 7), is a long, narrow room, about sixty-six feet in length and twenty-one feet in width. The ceiling, which at its apex is a little over thirty-two feet high, is a barrel vault, the ends being coved in the same manner as the sides.[1] The principal entrance is a doorway in the middle of the inner wall; each end wall has two doors, of which the inner one is false. A generous light is admitted by three tall windows; this is now supplemented by concealed electric lighting along the cornice. In order to simplify the problem of orientation we shall speak of the Gallery as running north and south, with the windows on the west.

The side walls, subdivided into wider and narrower bays by a series of Corinthian pilasters and niches, are covered with stucco decoration heightened with gold. The stucco work is especially profuse along the upper part of the walls, where circular niches containing antique busts alternate with small frescoed panels. By contrast, the lower zone today looks rather bare and empty. The original appearance, however, with ten full-length statues occupying the niches, was certainly very different (Fig. 34). The statues, heartlessly removed by the Bourbons,[2] have been replaced by sixteenth-century busts of Roman emperors. It is not a happy effect, because the busts, even though mounted on tall pedestals, do not adequately fill the niches. They also create an impression of monotony in that they offer no contrast to the busts in the circular recesses above.

---

[1] Letarouilly gives the dimensions as 20.14 m. x 6.59 m. (*Edifices de Rome moderne*, II, pl. 117). Bellori (*Vite*, p. 44) describes the room as being 90 palmi in length and 28 palmi in width; the Roman palmo being 8.796 inches, this gives a length of 65.8 feet and a width of 21.35 feet. The height may be judged from Letarouilly's drawings and from a note by Navenne (*Rome et le palais Farnèse pendant les trois derniers siècles*, Paris, 1923, I, p. 77) that it measures 9.8 m.

[2] Since to the best of my knowledge the statues which originally stood in the Gallery have not all been previously identified, I have thought it useful to name them here, and to indicate their present whereabouts.

On the wall opposite the windows (Fig. 32), from left to right:

1. *Satyr and Infant Dionysus*. London, British Museum, no. 1656. A. H. Smith, *A Catalogue of Sculpture in the Department of Greek and Roman Antiquities*, London, 1892-1904, III, pp. 57 f.

2. *Antinous*. Naples, Museo Nazionale, Inv. 6030. A Ruesch, *Guida illustrata del Museo Nazionale di Napoli*, no. 983.

3. *Apollo*. Naples, Mus. Naz., Inv. 6262. Ruesch no. 675.

4. *Hermes*. London, Brit. Mus., no. 1599. Smith, *op.cit.*, pp. 37 ff.

5. *Dionysus*. Naples, Mus. Naz., Inv. 6318. Ruesch no. 263.

6. *Satyr and Infant Dionysus*. Naples, Mus. Naz., Inv. 6022. Ruesch no. 253.

On the window wall (Fig. 33), from left to right:

1. *Ganymede and the Eagle*. Naples, Mus. Naz., Inv. 6355. Ruesch no. 278.

2. *The so-called Antonia*. Naples, Mus. Naz., Inv. 6057. Ruesch no. 988.

3. *Draped female figure*. Naples, Mus. Naz., Inv. 6269. Ruesch no. 225.

4. *Eros*. Naples, Mus. Naz., Inv. 6353. Ruesch no. 275.

I have not attempted to identify the six busts which were placed in the circular niches.

The entire scheme of decoration depends, ultimately, on the fenestration. For the three windows have determined the spacing of the pilasters and niches on the long walls, and these in turn have governed the ordering of the frescoes on the ceiling. Alternating with the windows on the outer wall (Fig. 33) are four narrow bays, each one framed by pilasters and each containing a shell-headed niche. Above each window is a hemispherical recess containing a sculptured bust; over each niche is a cartouche and a rectangular panel in fresco. These units establish a fundamental alternation of round and rectangular, and of sculpture and painting, that will be echoed in the decoration of the vault. The system is slightly varied on the inner wall (Fig. 32), where the wider spaces corresponding to the windows are occupied by two niches (the second and fifth) and the doorway. But the rhythmic sequence of wider and narrower bays remains unchanged, and the upper zone of the wall presents the same alternation of painting and sculpture, and of rectangular and circular elements, that is seen on the opposite side. At either end of the lateral walls is a narrow bay containing a coat of arms carved in stucco and, lower down, an oval fresco of a Virtue (Figs. 73-76). It is a structural peculiarity of the Gallery that the two bays at the northern end, and the ovals within them, are noticeably narrower than those at the south.

The end walls are decorated in a very different manner (cf. Fig. 35). Instead of the architectural system of pilasters and niches, a single large fresco spans almost the whole width of the wall, its massive stucco frame resting directly on the lintels of the doors. The weight also appears to be sustained by three atlantes, painted to resemble bronze, who are seated within simulated niches.

Here and there may be seen the signs and symbols of the Farnese. At the ends of the long walls are the coats of arms of Cardinal Farnese and his brother Ranuccio, Duke of Parma (Fig. 38); and on the soffit of the lintel over the middle window appears the name of the patron himself: ODOARDVS CAR. FARNESIVS (Fig. 37). Almost unnoticed amid the profusion of decorative features on the walls are the emblems of the Farnese family (Figs. 85-88), who have thus as it were set their seal upon the Gallery. Another family emblem is the large fresco over the entrance door representing the *Virgin with the Unicorn* (Fig. 89).

The frescoed vault (Fig. 36) may be thought of as comprising two zones. The first is the coved part of the ceiling directly above the cornice, which we may call, with Bellori,[3] the frieze. The second is the almost horizontal field at the top of the vault, which is occupied by a series of *quadri riportati* (literally "transferred pictures"), so called because they resemble framed easel paintings which have been removed from their normal position on a wall and set in place upon the ceiling; it can be seen that these *quadri riportati* are not confined to the upper zone of the vault but extend downward at four points so that they overlap the frieze (cf. text fig. 3).

The frieze consists of a kind of parapet which rests on the cornice and is itself

[3] Bellori, *Vite*, p. 45.

crowned by a heavy Doric entablature (the latter visible only at the corners). The entablature is supported by stone-colored atlas herms, sixteen in number, which, it will be observed, are simply extensions of the wall pilasters (cf. Fig. 32); they thus serve to establish an organic connection between the feigned architecture of the vault and the real architecture of the room. In the enframed spaces between the herms

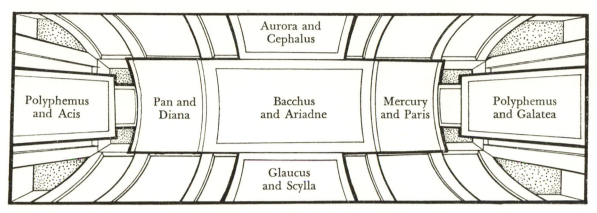

3. The Ceiling of the Farnese Gallery

there appear, alternately, bronze medallions with figure subjects in simulated relief and rectangular paintings in polychrome. Each medallion is flanked by a pair of nude youths, painted in natural colors, who sit in animated postures upon marble blocks protruding from the bases of the herms (cf. Fig. 47). Their function, ostensibly, is to carry the weighty festoon of fruits and flowers that undulates along the base of the frieze. It is typical of the endless variety of the ceiling that the grotesque masks fastened to the festoon are of two kinds: those beneath the monochrome medallions are naturally colored whereas those beneath the paintings are of terracotta. The heavy festoon held by the youths finds an echo in the chaste bay-leaf garland which is suspended from goats' heads and shell-masks placed above the panels of the frieze. The figure decoration of this zone is completed by pairs of putti, painted *al naturale*, who rest on the upper rim of each medallion. Between them is placed an ox-skull as a central motif. The frieze disappears from sight at four points (i.e. over the middle of each wall) where large framed paintings have been set in front of it. There is also an interruption in the corners of the vault; here the frieze parts slightly to disclose a view of a balustrade on which cupids are standing against the open sky. The balustrade is presumably to be thought of as continuing in both directions *behind* the frieze and not simply as bridging the gap at the angle. The two herms at each corner, one youthful and the other bearded, interlock their arms, thereby giving an impression of extra strength and support.[4]

[4] It is tempting to think that this conceit might have been suggested by an engraving in Achille Bocchi's emblem book, which shows the corner of a palace, to which are attached herms of Athena and Mercury with arms linked (*Symbolicarum Quaestionum Libri Quinque*, Symb. CII).

Despite the penetration of the frieze at the corners, the Doric architrave which rests upon it continues unbroken. This architrave in turn supports a vaulted ceiling, of which we are given only a glimpse behind the satyrs sitting on the frames of the Polyphemus pictures (Figs. 67-68). The effect is that of a vault within a vault, the fictitious one being a smaller repetition of the real ceiling of the Gallery. We see little of the smaller vault, however: it is spanned by four marble ribs into which are fitted three large framed pictures, and these screen most of the higher zone from view.

These pictures are the *quadri riportati*, portable paintings which have been fixed to the architectural framework as if to suggest that a gallery of pictures had been moved to the ceiling. It did not escape Bellori's notice that in the upright paintings of this series Annibale had employed a low point of view so as to prevent them from seeming top-heavy;[5] this is particularly evident in the frescoes of *Pan and Diana* and *Paris and Mercury* (Figs. 65-66), where the considerable expanse of sky undeniably tends to reduce the illusion of weight. There are in all nine *quadri riportati*; they are of various sizes, and are arranged in the form of a cross, the arms of which rest on the cornice at the ends and sides of the Gallery (Fig. 36 and text fig. 3, above). In order to provide a greater illusion of support for these pictures, Annibale has made certain adjustments within the frieze. At the corners of the *Bacchanal*, which is not only the largest, but in addition is mounted in a simulated marble frame of massive proportions, he has stationed four atlas herms of exceptionally powerful physique. This sturdy quartet is reinforced, moreover, by four full-length atlantes, likewise stone-colored, whose task it is to aid in bearing the weight of the adjoining pictures. The two small pictures of *Ganymede* and *Hyacinthus* (Figs. 67-68) have plainly been inserted in order to close the gap that would otherwise exist between the *quadri riportati* on the crown of the ceiling and the vertical paintings at the ends. They are flanked by two satyrs of mischievous aspect, who are seated holding bunches of fruit on the frame of the large upright picture.

The complex organism of the ceiling combines three independent systems of decoration. It is well to insist on this at the outset: no analysis of the Farnese vault can be wholly satisfactory that does not take account of the quite diverse traditions that have here been fused into a new and unified whole. The first is the architectonic system, which is mainly derived from the Sistine ceiling of Michelangelo and which provides the fundamental structural framework. The second is the system of the frieze, in origin a form of mural decoration, which has been closely integrated with the first, or architectonic system. The third is the system of *quadri riportati*, which has similarly been interlocked with the architectonic framework. Needless to say, I

[5] *Vite*, p. 64. Bellori carefully distinguishes between this low angle of sight and the perspective foreshortening of the structural features, although he observes that the two harmonize very well with each other.

do not mean to imply that the Farnese ceiling was created by any such deliberate or calculated process of combination, but only that the final conception incorporates and holds in equilibrium the essential features of several different systems of decoration.

For Annibale Carracci, as for countless other artists, the Sistine ceiling was an abundant source of ideas. In the great architectonic framework of the chapel, with its range of scenes spread along the level crown of the vault, Annibale perceived a scheme that could be adapted to the Gallery. The feigned entablature of the Farnese ceiling clearly owes its inspiration to the mighty painted cornice of the Sistine; and the four beams that bridge the central field were likewise suggested by the broad divisions between the Genesis scenes of the chapel. There is also evidence to show with what care Annibale studied the figure inventions of the Sistine. In two drawings at Windsor we find him making copies after figure groups in the lunettes.[6] In the Farnese Gallery itself (as every commentator has duly remarked from the time of Bellori on)[7] the most conspicuous proof of Annibale's indebtedness to the Sistine ceiling is to be seen in the *ignudi*—the seated youths arranged in pairs facing each other on either side of a bronze medallion. Instead of occupying the central field, however, these figures have been shifted to the already crowded lower zone, that of the coving or frieze.

The decoration of the coving, as has already been said, follows the tradition of the mural frieze designed for rooms with flat ceilings. Annibale's adaptation of this system to the Gallery was made feasible by the fact that the lower zone of the vault, unlike that of the Sistine Chapel, is not broken up by intervening triangular spandrels, but presents an even and nearly vertical surface. His conception of this part of the decoration may best be understood by comparing it to the frieze of the Palazzo Magnani, painted by the Carracci in collaboration about 1588-1591.[8] This great fresco, which has aptly been termed "the Adam and Eve of Baroque decoration,"[9] contains in germ several of the ideas that were to be developed by Annibale in the Farnese ceiling. The Magnani frieze consists of a series of narrative scenes punctuated by groups of decorative figures; the severity of the rectangular pictures is further relieved by ornamental features such as masks and festoons, which are suspended both above and below the frieze proper. As can be seen at once, the Farnese frieze

[6] Both drawings are reproduced in E. Steinmann, *Die Sixtinische Kapelle*, Munich, 1901-1905, II, figs. 204-205.

[7] Bellori, *Vite*, pp. 79 f. Annibale is here commended for preferring the *ignudi* of the ceiling to the "manneristic anatomies" of the Last Judgment, and thereby demonstrating how best to make use of Michelangelo's art.

[8] E. Bodmer, "Gli affreschi dei Carracci nel Palazzo Magnani ora Salem a Bologna," *Il Comune di Bologna*, XX, no. 12, Dec. 1933,

pp. 3-20.

[9] D. Mahon, "Eclecticism and the Carracci: Further Reflections on the Validity of a Label," *Journal of the Warburg and Courtauld Institutes*, XVI, 1953, p. 341. The importance of the Magnani frieze for the Farnese ceiling has been emphasized by A. Foratti, "L'organismo decorativo del soffitto nella Galleria Farnese," *Il Comune di Bologna*, XIX, 1932, pp. 33 ff.

adheres essentially to the same scheme, the introduction of the bronze medallions serving only to create a still more varied effect. But the most remarkable feature of the Magnani frieze is the prominence given to the *partimenti*, the points of support dividing the pictures (cf. Fig. 274). In contrast to the Jason frieze painted a few years earlier in the Palazzo Fava, where the scenes are separated by a single standing figure,[10] here the division is marked by a whole cluster of decorative figures in different media.[11] Each group is dominated by a seated atlas of white marble; on either side stand two living children holding the festoons that hang below the frieze, and behind the atlas are two bronze-colored youths who reach out toward the masks suspended above the pictures. In this lively grouping of sitting and standing figures who perform different tasks, as well as in the interplay of various illusions, the *partimenti* of the Magnani frieze directly foreshadow those of the Farnese ceiling.[12] But the relationship can be shown to be even more explicit: the attitude of the bronze boys standing with arms extended and one leg crossed over the other is virtually repeated in the full-length atlantes of the Gallery who share with the termini the burden of supporting the architrave (cf. Fig. 43).

Inevitably, the frieze is overshadowed by the huge *quadri riportati* which extend over the length and breadth of the vault. Large framed pictures of this kind were no novelty in Roman fresco-painting. Annibale doubtless knew Francesco Salviati's frescoes in the Palazzo Sacchetti, where the story of David is narrated in a series of paintings with heavy gold frames suspended before a feigned columnar architecture. It was perhaps from this cycle that Annibale took the device, employed so effectively in the Gallery, of framed paintings overlapping a continuous architectural background. Even more important were certain vaults of Raphael's Loggie in the Vatican, in which Carracci must have admired the perspective effect of *quadri riportati* seen against the sky.[13] But it seems to have been a Bolognese work, rather than a Roman one, that was uppermost in his mind when he applied himself to the task of ordering the principal scenes of the Gallery. Pellegrino Tibaldi's decoration of the Sala d'Ulisse in the Palazzo Poggi (Fig. 275) has long been recognized as one of the primary sources of the Farnese ceiling. In his life of Tibaldi, the Bolognese writer Malvasia makes a great point of this tribute to the artist's genius: "The Carracci," he writes, "would always send their pupils to draw in this room . . . and it is certain that before beginning work on the Farnese Gallery Annibale had a sketch sent to him of this rich and well-ordered ceiling."[14] Tibaldi's fresco decoration[15] comprises

[10] See S. Ostrow, in *Arte antica e moderna*, No. 9, 1960, pp. 68 ff., pls. 21-25.

[11] Foratti, *op.cit.*, figs. 1-3.

[12] This relationship was perceived by Bellori, who writes of the Farnese frieze: "Seguitò egli l'ordine delle sale di Bologna, mà con più ordinate, e peregrine inventioni etc." (*Vite*, p. 47).

[13] K. Lanckoronska, "Zu Raffaels Loggien," *Jahrbuch der kunsthistorischen Sammlungen in Wien*, N.F. IX, 1935, pp. 111-120, figs. 75-76.

[14] *Felsina*, I, p. 193: "[I Carracci] mandarono sempre i loro scolari a disegnare le figure del detto Salotto . . . , ed è certo, che prima di porsi al lavoro della Galleria Farnese, fece Annibale trasmettersi uno schizzo di sì guidicioso, e ricco scomparto." A similar statement appears in Malvasia's life of Annibale (*ibid.*, p. 466).

[15] F. Würtenberger, "Die manieristische

five *quadri riportati* arranged in a cruciform pattern, the four corners of the ceiling being treated illusionistically as if open to the air. The scheme is manifestly derived from those perspective vaults in Raphael's Loggie which have been mentioned above. But because the Poggi ceiling is oblong rather than square, the central rectangle assumes greater importance and the chief painting of the cycle is accordingly situated there. In addition, the open corners have been enlivened by the insertion of Michelangelesque *ignudi* seen in drastic foreshortening upon the balustrades.

The narrow openings in the angles of the Farnese Gallery, where cupids appear on a low balustrade as if *en plein air*, are frequently cited as demonstrating Annibale's obligation to Tibaldi. Equally conclusive evidence is to be found in the arrangement of the *quadri riportati*. Although the Gallery is very much longer in proportion to its width than the Sala d'Ulisse, Carracci has nevertheless retained the fundamental cruciform disposition by increasing the number of pictures along the longitudinal axis from three to seven (text fig. 3, p. 71). The central picture, moreover, is still the dominant one. It is not difficult to conceive of this Tibaldesque system as an entity complete in itself—the nine framed pictures assembled crosswise, the rest of the ceiling being open to the sky, with only a narrow balustrade visible along the perimeter. We may then imagine the entire system as being superimposed upon, or as interlocking with, the architectonic structure of the ceiling: the pictures in the center are inserted into the structural framework prepared for them, and the others are made to stand in front of the frieze. The balustrade, however, runs *behind* the frieze and thus emerges into view only at the corners.

Although the "open" corners with their balustrades seen in perspective were plainly suggested by Tibaldi's ceiling, it was precisely at these points that Annibale was obliged to deviate most sharply from the Bolognese model. The chief difficulty lay in the fact that the vault of the Gallery, unlike those of the Sala d'Ulisse or the Loggie, is not relatively low, but rises from the cornice in a steep arc. This surface, as Annibale discovered, lent itself more readily to a frieze-like treatment *à la* Palazzo Magnani than to an illusionistic penetration of the enclosing ceiling. Since the angles of the vault had, therefore, to be thought of as predominantly vertical rather than horizontal surfaces, he reduced the openings to their present narrow dimensions, thereby avoiding an insoluble problem of illusionism.

When we begin to consider the sources drawn upon by Annibale for the decorative figures of the Farnese ceiling we are likely to think first of the use of antique models. The bulging muscular physique of some of the termini (cf. Figs. 43 and 46) was probably inspired by the powerful frame of the Farnese Hercules; indeed we know that Annibale was making sketches of the famous statue at the very time that he was designing the atlantes (cf. Figs. 228 and 230). And though the seated youths are as a rule Michelangelesque rather than antique in origin it can be seen that one of them (Fig. 48) recalls the pose of the Ludovisi Mars. But above all it is the termini

Deckenmalerei in Mittelitalien," *Römisches*   73 f., fig. 30.
Jahrbuch für Kunstgeschichte, IV, 1940, pp.

of feigned marble that proclaim their affinity to ancient originals, and there is of course no doubt that Annibale knew and imitated sculptured herms of this sort. That he intended to create an impression of antique statuary is proved by the inclusion of several damaged or broken figures, the most remarkable of which is the herm at the right of *Diana and Endymion* (Fig. 44), whose right arm is missing near the shoulder. Here, it would seem, Carracci has sought to reproduce the actual rather than the ideal condition of ancient sculpture.[16] But we are surely mistaken if we think that this reflects a purely antiquarian attitude on the part of Annibale: his main purpose, unquestionably, was to make still more tenuous the boundary between the real and the illusory.

We ought not perhaps to conclude that the atlantes were derived solely from the antique. Annibale's imagination might also have been stimulated, as Calvesi has shown, by the curious series of herms engraved by Agostino Veneziano (B. 301, 303, and 304). Among them appear three figures with arms broken off close to the shoulder; two herms wear a Herculean lionskin, and one of them also carries a club; another is pictured with arms folded, and still another is wrapped in a heavy cloak. An evident relationship has also been noted between one of the standing *ignudi* (Fig. 44) and Marcantonio's engraving of a man supporting a column base (B. 476).[17] It is likewise possible, to turn from prints to the field of monumental art, that the lively attitudes of the termini at the angles were prompted by the atlas herms adorning the dado of Raphael's Stanza dell'Incendio: it may suffice to compare the atlas at the left of *Polyphemus and Galatea* (Fig. 61) to the herm at the extreme right beneath the fresco of the *Fire in the Borgo*. At least one of the termini, finally, may owe something to Michelangelo; the impressive figure beside the tondo with *Orpheus and Eurydice* (Fig. 50), whose arms are enveloped in a cloak, may well have been inspired by the heavily robed herms on the Tomb of Julius II.

Nowhere can the potent influence of Michelangelo on Annibale be more clearly assessed than in the seated youths of the Farnese frieze. That these figures trace their descent from the *ignudi* of the Sistine has long been established; in some instances, moreover, the family resemblance is very marked. The pose of the adolescent sitting at the right of *Polyphemus and Galatea* (Fig. 41) is closely related to that of the *ignudo* on the right above the Persian Sibyl; his companion, on the left of *Polyphemus and Galatea* (Fig. 40), derives from the youth on the left above the Erythraean Sibyl. In the same manner the attitude of the figure seated at the right of *Polyphemus and Acis* (Fig. 39) can be seen to be studied from the *ignudo* on the left over the prophet Ezekiel. Two other figures, those at the right of *Orpheus and Eurydice* (Fig. 50) and at the right of *Europa and the Bull* (Fig. 53), appear to have been adapted from the

---

[16] Cf. the amusing comment by Domenichino on these "breakages" as reported in a letter by Agucchi (Malvasia, *Felsina*, II, p. 330). The passage is discussed by Mahon, *Studies*, p. 123.

[17] M. Calvesi, in *Commentari*, VII, 1956, pp. 275 ff., figs. 29-36.

youth on the left above the Persica. These are a few of the more striking parallels: confrontation of the two series reveals further points of resemblance between them. Within the Sistine cycle Annibale did not confine his attention exclusively to the *ignudi*; in the attitude of the adolescent beside the medallion of *Salmacis and Hermaphroditus* (Fig. 52) there is plainly a reminiscence of the prophet Jonah.

In designing the pairs of children who recline against the medallions, Annibale perhaps had in mind the bronze-colored nudes occupying the triangular fields over the spandrels of the Sistine ceiling.[18] The postures are in many cases similar, and the use of the ox-skull as a central feature corresponds to the ram-skull which appears between Michelangelo's figures. But whereas the latter are somber and lost in gloom, playing only a minor role in the decoration, Annibale has characteristically made his putti extremely lively and playful, and has given them a place of prominence in the frieze.

Revealing though it may be to analyze the sources drawn upon by Annibale for the Farnese Gallery, we must not make the error of supposing the result to be simply an ingenious compilation of solutions invented by others. (We touch here upon the vexed question of the "eclecticism" of the Carracci.) The extraordinary unity of this complex cycle is in no sense merely the product of its constituent parts, but was imposed upon it by the skill and artistry of the designer. The various "derivative" components have undergone a thorough metamorphosis, so that, while retaining—as was intended—something of the flavor of their original context, they have at the same time become integral parts of a new setting.

We may illustrate this point by referring to the transformation of elements taken from Michelangelo. In the Sistine ceiling Michelangelo shrank from illusionism, preferring not to draw the ultimate consequences of his own architectonic conception. Annibale, on the other hand, familiar with the methods of *quadratura* painting developed during the later sixteenth century,[19] has not hesitated to apply them throughout his design. All the plastic forms of the decoration—architecture, human figures, sculpture, bronze reliefs, even the picture frames—are foreshortened so as to conform to the view from below. And this consistent perspective treatment, in conjunction with the uniform system of lighting from below, makes the vault (what the Sistine does not pretend to be) an organic continuation of the real architecture of the walls.[20] It is instructive, in this connection, to compare Annibale's solution with a Mannerist fresco cycle such as that by Jacopo Zucchi in the Palazzo Ruspoli in Rome, which

[18] C. de Tolnay, *Michelangelo*, II, *The Sistine Ceiling*, Princeton, 1945, pls. 196-218.

[19] See H. Posse, "Das Deckenfresco des Pietro da Cortona im Palazzo Barberini und die Deckenmalerei in Rom," *Jahrbuch der preussischen Kunstsammlungen*, XL, 1919, esp. pp. 126 ff.; and Würtenberger, *op.cit.*, pp. 61 ff.

[20] Strictly speaking, it is not correct to say

that the principal mythological subjects have been exempted from this illusionistic treatment. For these framed pictures do not exist in isolation but are to be seen from the same point of view and under the same conditions of placement and lighting as the "three-dimensional" parts of the decoration.

likewise contains numerous borrowings from the Sistine.[21] The difference is obvious at once. In Zucchi's fresco the rational, architectonic quality of the design has been largely sacrificed, and the organic relationship of walls and ceiling thereby obscured, in a picturesque proliferation of parts. The Farnese ceiling, for all its unclassical crowding and complexity, displays no such lack of articulation: the function of each element in the design is explicitly defined, and the organic connectedness of the whole is in no way impaired.

It has already been noted that the structural system of the wall is continued into the vault. An extraordinary transmutation takes place here, as the purely architectural forms of the pilasters re-emerge, beyond the cornice, in the half-human shapes of the herms. These, being of simulated stone, at once establish a relationship with the antique statues in the niches below (Figs. 32-33). But the statues, although free-standing and wholly human in form, are somehow less alive than the herms, which are after all only painted fictions. A further complication is introduced by the *ignudi*, who are represented as figures of flesh and blood. And lastly there are the bronze atlantes of the end walls—feigned figures in feigned niches (Fig. 79-84). In the same way, the alternating units of the frieze—a circular relief and a square painting—are plainly intended to be seen in juxtaposition to the row of circular niches and rectangular panels on the wall just below the cornice. The relationship, characteristically, is a staggered one: the bronze medallion with its simulated relief appears above the little frescoed panel, and the large framed painting stands over the circular niche with its sculptured bust.

Beyond doubt the most brilliant and original of all of Annibale's inventions is that of superimposed systems of decoration. Through a subtle placing of overlapping forms, there is built up an impression of shifting masses, moving from the ends toward the center, where the eye is at last brought to rest on the largest and most stable pictures. The phenomenon can be observed both in the frieze and along the top of the vault. It is hardly necessary to add that this dynamic method of unification was not derived from any other scheme of decoration, but is a unique solution conceived by Annibale himself. Least of all does it depend on the Sistine ceiling, where the principle of organization is simple and uncomplicated, and the rhythmic progression from one scene to the next is regular and continuous.[22] Yet, despite the wealth of figures, pictures, and architecture that is crowded into the vault, the observer experiences no sensation of oppressive weight or enclosure. The whole spectacular edifice, with its gay colors, its open corners and its shifting layers of illusion, seems to be lightly poised—like a house of cards, as Tietze has aptly remarked.[23] And over

---

[21] F. Saxl, *Antike Götter in der Spätrenaissance. Ein Freskenzyklus und ein Discorso von Jacopo Zucchi*, Leipzig-Berlin, 1927. See also Würtenberger, *op.cit.*, pp. 81 ff., fig. 37.

[22] The contrast between the Sistine ceiling

and the ceiling of the Farnese Gallery was summed up, in a justly famous passage, by Heinrich Wölfflin in his *Renaissance und Barock* (4th ed., Munich, 1926, p. 67).

[23] Tietze, p. 73.

all of this intricate and complex structure there rises another, higher vault, of which we are given only a glimpse at either end of the ceiling.

To pass from the Camerino into the Galleria, Cesare Gnudi has written, "is like passing from early spring to full summer."[24] The difference between the two is not simply one of scale. Through its restraint and simplicity, and through the delicacy of its ornamental passages, the decoration of the Camerino inspires a mood of intimacy and reflection. The Gallery, by contrast, is at once more complex and more exuberant. From the moment that he enters this "gallery of magnificence and pleasure,"[25] the observer is conscious of a festive atmosphere. This may be attributed to such things as the wit and variety of the *ornamenti*, the seductive grace of the fables and, not least, the entrancing brightness of the colors. The frescoes of the ceiling, in particular, give an extraordinary impression of luminosity. The seventeenth-century English virtuoso Richard Symonds was struck by this quality when he wrote: "All ye Colours of ye naked bodyes has no black in y^m, they come off so round, they sceme reall flesh mighty gay and glorious. Terra verde & lacca seeme ye colours of ye deepe shadowes."[26] It is not so much that the individual colors are brilliant, as that the total effect suggests the conditions of a sunny day. What might be called the "natural" colors—blue, green, yellow, and white—are noticeably prominent, whereas the purely decorative hues, especially the reds, roses and violets of the draperies, are generally more pastel-like in quality, as if their intensity had been lessened by the blond light of day that is suffused throughout the vault.

There is another factor that contributes immeasurably to the spirit of the Gallery, and that is the unexpectedly assertive character of the accessory figures, who are not content to play a merely passive role as decorative adjuncts, but make their presence felt in an unmistakable way. This insubordination is especially conspicuous in the satyrs who sit on the frames of the Polyphemus pictures and in the pairs of frolicking putti on the medallions. The seated *ignudi* are in much closer proximity to the observer than are the corresponding figures of the Sistine. They are also utterly different in mood, possessing none of that spiritual tension that imparts to Michelangelo's youths their almost superhuman quality; comparison shows the Farnese figures to be more earthly and their energy to be of a more physical sort. Because they are painted illusionistically and appear to receive their light from the windows of the Gallery, they are accepted as existing, not in an ideal or universal realm, but in our own space and time.

Paradoxically, however, it is not the "living" but the "inanimate" figures that do most to create the psychological atmosphere of the Gallery. The marble termini, rising incongruously from their pillar-like bases, and condemned to perpetual im-

---

[24] Introduction to the catalogue of the *Mostra dei Carracci*, 3rd ed., Bologna, 1958, p. 41.

[25] Jonathan Richardson, Sr. and Jr., *An Account of the Statues, Bas-reliefs, Drawings and Pictures in Italy, France, &c. with Remarks*, 2nd ed., London, 1754, p. 143.

[26] Brit. Mus. Egerton MS 1635, fol. 18; quoted by L. Salerno in *Journal of the Warburg and Courtauld Institutes*, XIV, 1951, p. 245.

prisonment within the architectural complex, are nevertheless provocatively alert and animated. Some, with arms upraised and head turned to the side, appear to sway from the hips. Others, as if conscious of the spectator's gaze, look down at him with smiles, winks or frowns according to their fancy. And the paired herms at the angles display their agility by interlacing their arms. Unlike the herms, who carry out their task with a certain insouciance, the full-length caryatids apparently find their burden oppressive. With heads bent sharply beneath a cushion of drapery, they twist and turn restlessly, shifting their weight from one foot to the other and entwining their arms about the ornamental garland. Are they also perhaps a little embarrassed by the intimate love-scenes that are represented in the paintings beside them? The result of this "animation of the inanimate" is that the decorative figures of the frieze assume greater prominence than the mythological subjects to which they are nominally subservient. It is not only the bronze-green roundels that are thus overshadowed; even the four brilliantly colored paintings (Figs. 43-46) cannot, because of their strongly classical composition, prevail over the Baroque exuberance of the accessory figures. It will be observed, however, that this inversion of the normal relationship between picture and decoration is confined to the frieze. The sovereignty of the principal scenes is not threatened by the unsubmissive demeanor of the auxiliary figures: the *Triumph of Bacchus and Ariadne* and the Polyphemus fables dominate the Gallery by reason of their size, their commanding positions and compositional vigor.

Although the frescoes of the Farnese Gallery are in generally sound condition, it is obvious to the spectator that they have undergone numerous repairs and restorations. Bellori describes two serious faults which developed in the seventeenth century and the drastic measures which were taken to correct them.[27] The first consisted of a longitudinal fissure extending along the middle of the vault and downward through the end walls. This was attributed to the weight exerted on the Gallery from above, which tended to push the rear wall outward; in order to arrest this movement the wall was anchored to the inner structure of the palace by means of iron chains passing above and below the Gallery. In many parts of the fresco the final coat of plaster (the *intonaco*) had become detached from its base (the *arricciato*). The damage was especially severe at the southern end where, according to Bellori, the fresco of *Perseus and Andromeda* (Fig. 77) was beginning to fall to pieces; in fact this scene shows more signs of repair than any other in the Gallery. The task of securing the *intonaco* to its base was undertaken by Giovanni Francesco Rossi, whose method was to drive T-shaped nails into the fresco; each nail was later covered with gesso and the patch colored to match its surroundings. Rossi inserted no fewer than 1300 nails of this kind in the Gallery, and such was his skill, Bellori reports, that the painter Carlo

[27] G. P. Bellori, *Descrizzione delle imagini dipinte da Rafaelle d'Urbino nelle Camere del* *Palazzo Apostolico Vaticano*, Rome, 1695, pp. 81 ff.

Maratti himself was unable to discover, even from the scaffolding, where they had been placed. Today, unhappily, Rossi's handiwork is much more in evidence (cf. Fig. 66). It must be remembered, however, that without his efforts a considerable part of the surface of these frescoes would undoubtedly have perished.

The second fault was caused by moisture which had worked its way through a gap in the wall over the exterior cornice and soaked part of the frieze above the windows. The area most seriously affected was that of the medallion of *Salmacis and Hermaphroditus* and the adjacent *ignudo* (Fig. 52), which has been much repainted. To prevent further leakage a protective roof of sloping marble slabs was placed over the exterior cornice, which is still plainly visible on the rear façade of the palace (Fig. 2). In spite of such measures there has been further deterioration due to humidity in the roundel of *Cupid and Pan* and in the atlas herm at the right, part of whose torso is modern (Fig. 48).

It is not only the restorers who have left their mark on the Gallery. There are also some inscriptions on the ceiling, so placed as to be almost invisible from the floor, which tell of the presence of artists sent to study and make copies there. The block on which is seated the nude youth at the right of *Polyphemus and Galatea* (Fig. 61) bears the words: L'ANNO 1667 È STATA COPIATA. This inscription, hitherto unnoticed, commemorates the laborious task undertaken by four *pensionnaires* of the newly founded French Academy in Rome, who reproduced the frescoes of the vault in a set of canvases which were installed on a ceiling in the palace of the Tuileries.[28]

Still another French artist has left a record of his activity in the Farnese Gallery. On the central post of the balustrade which serves as a pedestal for the *Cupids struggling under the Wreath* (and almost hidden within the veining of the marble) appears the inscription in red letters: TARAVAL 1760 (Fig. 40). The painter Hugues Taraval (1729-1785), having won the Prix de Rome, arrived at the French Academy in Rome in November 1759.[29] It was just at this time that the director, Natoire, had succeeded in obtaining authorization for his *pensionnaires* to draw and study in the Gallery,[30] and Taraval was obviously one of those who availed themselves of this privilege. Why he chose to paint his name on the ceiling is a mystery; but since he cannot have been entrusted with any work of restoration we may conclude that it was done merely as a prank. This becomes even more likely when we discover that his name occurs twice among the graffiti on the lower part of the walls.[31]

---

[28] Bellori, *Vite*, p. 65: "In questo tempo è stata imitata da gli Academici Regij, che studiano in Roma trasportate le fauole in tele ad olio, per ornarne vn altra Galeria nel palazzo del Louro, che si fabbrica di nuouo alla magnificenza di S. M." The copies were made by Pierre Mosnier, Jean-Baptiste (not Michel) Corneille, François Bonnemer, and Louis-René Vouet (the son of Simon Vouet). See *Mémoires inédits sur la vie et les ouvrages*

des membres de l'Académie Royale de Peinture et de Sculpture, Paris, 1854, II, p. 13; and H. Lapauze, *Histoire de l'Académie de France à Rome*, Paris, 1924, I, p. 23.

[29] *Correspondance des Directeurs de l'Académie de France à Rome*, XI, Paris, 1901, p. 319.

[30] *Ibid.*, pp. 326, 362, and 365.

[31] On the band of stucco ornament beneath the oval of *Temperance* we read: "Hugues Taraval 1760"; and on the corresponding

What use was made of the Gallery? No information has come down to us from the time of Odoardo. But in the inventory of 1653 we find listed among the contents of the room three keyboard instruments: a *gravi organo di cipresso*, a *cimbalo vecchio*, and a portative organ.[32] Their presence suggests that the Gallery was used as a music room.

Even without knowledge of the instruments one might have concluded that the Farnese Gallery was dedicated to music. The situation could not be more appropriate: the pleasant, well-lit room, its windows overlooking the garden, makes an ideal setting for musical performances. It is significant, moreover, that the theme of music is a recurrent one throughout Carracci's cycle of frescoes. The sounds of organ and harpsichord thus found an agreeable echo in the syrinx and lyre of the fables on the vault.

In the National Gallery in London there is a painted panel by Annibale representing *Bacchus and Silenus*,[33] which would appear because of its odd shape to have been made for a musical instrument, possible a *clavicembalo*. The style is that of the Farnese frescoes, and the subject—the young Bacchus playing the syrinx to amuse Silenus—is perfectly in harmony with the iconography of the cycle. It is tempting to believe that this panel might have belonged to one of the keyboard instruments in the Farnese Gallery.

panel beneath *Justice*: "Taraval 1761."

[32] Bourdon and Laurent-Vibert, "L'inventaire de 1653," *Mélanges*, 1909, pp. 180 f.

[33] See the notice by G. C. Cavalli in the catalogue of the *Mostra dei Carracci*, 3rd ed., Bologna, 1958, pp. 221 ff., no. 97.

CHAPTER 6 · THE ICONOGRAPHY
OF THE CEILING

IT may seem astonishing that a Roman cardinal of the later sixteenth century should have permitted a great room in his palace to be adorned with love scenes from classical mythology. How can the Farnese Gallery, with its pagan subject matter and its nude figures represented in various amorous encounters, be reconciled with the spirit and teaching of the Counter-Reformation?[1] The invectives of theologians like Cardinal Paleotti and Antonio Possevino against "indecent and lascivious" paintings would appear to have been uttered in vain. No doubt there were some who found the Gallery scandalous. This indeed was the view expressed by La Bruyère in his *Caractères* (1688): "That the filthy stories of the gods, Venus, Ganymede, and the other nudities of Carracci, were made for princes of the Church, and those who call themselves successors of the Apostles, the Farnese palace offers proof."[2] But this unfavorable judgment is an exception. Far from raising a storm of protest, the Farnese Gallery seems to have been from the moment of its unveiling the object of praise by churchmen and laymen alike.

The earliest accounts, such as those by Lucio Faberio, Carel van Mander, and Giulio Mancini, take little notice of the subject matter of the cycle. Agucchi's catalogue of the merits of the Gallery includes such things as the "nobiltà de' soggetti" and the "viva espressione degli affetti," but there is not a word about the individual scenes or the meaning of the whole.[3] And Baglione (1642), though he names the principal *favole*, likewise makes no attempt to interpret them.[4]

No comprehensive description of the frescoes appeared until Giovanni Pietro Bellori addressed himself to the task with his customary energy and thoroughness. Bellori wrote two commentaries: the first was prepared to accompany the engraved plates of the Gallery by Carlo Cesio (1657);[5] the second and somewhat fuller account forms part of the biography of Annibale Carracci in the *Vite* (1672).[6] The latter was soon acknowledged to be the authoritative source of information concerning the Farnese Gallery and as such was widely consulted.[7]

[1] E. Mâle, *L'Art religieux après le Concile de Trente*, Paris, 1932, pp. 3 f.

[2] Jean de la Bruyère, *Les Caractères*, Paris, 1692, p. 574: "Que les saletez des Dieux, la Venus, le Ganimede, & les autres nuditez du Carache ayent esté faites pour des Princes de l'Eglise, & qui se disent successeurs des Apostres, le Palais Farnese en est la preuve." A similar sentiment was expressed by Salvator Rosa in his satire *La Pittura* (vv. 703-705): "Gl'impudichi Caracci, e i Tizziani / Con figure di chiassi han profanati / I Palazzi de'Prencipi Christiani" (G. A. Cesareo, *Poesie e lettere

edite e inedite di Salvator Rosa*, Naples, 1892, I, p. 249).

[3] *Trattato*, reprinted in Mahon, *Studies*, p. 257.

[4] Baglione, *Vite*, p. 107.

[5] *Argomento della Galeria Farnese dipinta da Annibale Carracci disegnata & intagliata da Carlo Cesio*, Rome, 1657 (hereinafter cited as *Argomento*). The text is reprinted in Malvasia, *Felsina*, I, pp. 437-442.

[6] Bellori, *Vite*, pp. 44-66.

[7] E.g., F. Titi, *Descrizione delle pitture, sculture e architetture esposte al pubblico in

The argument, as Bellori defines it, is "human love governed by celestial love."[8] This, I believe, is substantially correct. But in his interpretation of individual scenes Bellori is frequently unreliable. One difficulty lay in the fact that he was unable to discover a unifying theme within each set of pictures (the medallions, the rectangular panels of the frieze, and so forth) and therefore was driven to make unlikely combinations of scenes from different categories. He argues, for example, that in the fables of Hercules and Iole, Diana and Endymion, and Polyphemus and Galatea we are to see Love's power to subjugate the strong, the chaste, and the brutish; it sounds plausible enough, until we realize that this supposedly coherent set is in reality composed of two panels from the frieze and one of the large *quadri riportati* at the ends. Or again, he writes, the embraces of Jupiter and Juno, Aurora, and Galatea signify Love's universal power; but this grouping is even more disparate, combining as it does Agostino's two paintings with a single subject from the frieze. Bellori himself is plainly uneasy about these irregular combinations, and twice remarks that the order of subjects in the Gallery is not clear and logical as in the Camerino, but that the arrangement is evidently determined by decorative rather than iconographical considerations.[9] A second flaw in Bellori's analysis results from his tendency to interpret the *favole* in a pejorative sense: the *Bacchanal*, with its emphasis on intoxication, represents profane love; the medallions, almost without exception, denote lustful desires. Jonathan Richardson's comment on the Gallery, after reading Bellori's account, may seem apposite here: "Throughout Concupiscence generally prevails, and over all Ranks and Degrees; but Virtue Rarely."[10] It is a strange fact that Bellori, who described the Farnese Gallery as a *"nobilissimo poema,"*[11] should at the same time have believed that the principal scenes of the cycle depicted the triumph of profane love.

Early in this century Bellori's interpretation of the cycle, which had long gone unchallenged, was subjected to critical scrutiny by Hans Tietze and declared to be overdrawn. Tietze found it difficult to believe that a detailed program had been prepared for the Gallery, and argued that it was absurd to look for allegorical significance in each and every scene. In his view the three middle pictures—the *Aurora*, the *Bacchanal*, and the so-called *Galatea*—formed a unit glorifying the power of love "in cielo, in terra, in mare." To go beyond that was to become lost in vain speculation. "For Annibale," he concluded, "the interest in these scenes did not lie in the philosophical systems *that interpreters might ascribe to them*, but in the opportunity that they afforded to represent nude figures in a variety of lively attitudes."[12]

These conclusions, founded as they are on the impressive scholarship of the great

Roma, Rome, 1763, pp. 112 ff.; Jonathan Richardson, Sr. and Jr., *An Account of the Statues, Bas-reliefs, Drawings and Pictures in Italy, France &c., with remarks*, 2nd ed., London, 1754, pp. 135 ff.

[8] *Vite*, p. 65: "l'amore humano regolato dal celeste."

[9] *Vite*, pp. 48 and 65.

[10] Richardson, *op.cit.*, p. 141. No irony seems to have been intended.

[11] *Vite*, p. 64.

[12] Tietze, pp. 76 f., 89-94 (my italics).

Austrian art historian, have generally been received with favor. Yet it must be said that they are not wholly convincing. In the first place (as Tietze himself admits) it had long been customary for the humanists of the Farnese court to prepare detailed programs whenever a new fresco cycle was to be painted. It would be strange indeed if Odoardo Farnese, having relied upon Fulvio Orsini to furnish an iconographical plan for the Camerino, should then have decided that nothing of the sort was needed for the Gallery, despite the fact that this was to be a much larger and more ambitious project. In the second place we are surely not entitled to conclude, merely because the cycle is difficult to fathom, that it follows no coherent program. Tietze's thinking on this point, one suspects, has been colored by the doctrine of *l'art pour l'art*. And lastly, we might ask, why is it so often assumed that the painter was solely interested in the representation of nude figures? Annibale was certainly not blind to the beauty of the human form, but as an artist trained in the tradition of history painting he was also very much concerned with expression; in fact the rendering of the *affetti* is one of the things that the seventeenth century found most worthy of praise in the Gallery.

Tietze was undoubtedly right in insisting that a detailed iconographical program was not fully worked out in advance: there was no complete libretto which could be simply delivered to the artist with instructions to translate it into visible form. The preparatory drawings make it clear that several important features of the cycle were not specified at the outset but must have been subsequently decided upon. But this is not to say that an iconographical plan did not exist, or that the choice and disposition of subjects were left entirely to the whim of the artist. We must rather understand the program of the Farnese vault as the product of close and continuing collaboration of artist and literary adviser. Only through such a partnership could the complex iconography and the equally complex design of the ceiling have been so harmoniously wedded.

Bellori remains our most reliable cicerone to the iconography of the cycle. Despite the many obvious faults that mar his exegesis of the Farnese Gallery it must be granted, I think, that his ideas are fundamentally sound. He realized above all that the key to the entire program lay in the theme of Heavenly and Earthly Love. Was there perhaps current in Rome an oral tradition to this effect? This would seem to be indicated by the fact that even though Bellori understood the thematic basis of the cycle he was unable to give a detailed exposition of it. It is regrettably true that in his reading of the fables he frequently missed the point and attributed to Profane Love those victories that belong properly to Sacred Love. In most instances, however, such blunders, though amusing, are not of a fundamental kind. What is important is that Bellori's conception of the Gallery as a whole is a just and balanced one. He is no pedant, whose only thought is for the intellectual and moral content of the frescoes; on the contrary he dwells at length on their beauty and inexhaustible variety. If he insists that allegory is an essential ingredient of the program it is because he understands that the Gallery was intended to give both pleasure and instruction:

the purpose of the allegory, he says, is to make the fables not only enjoyable but edifying, "mescolando il diletto col giovamento."[13] The more we reflect upon the personality of Odoardo Farnese, his sense of dedication and high purpose, his feelings of responsibility as a scion of an honored family, the more evident does it become that Bellori's interpretation of the Galleria Farnese is fundamentally correct. These pagan fables, which parade before our eyes a spectacle full of sensuous charm and cheerful eroticism, are at the same time a mere painted curtain masking a deeper meaning—the Triumph of Divine Love.

We are too ready, perhaps, to take this as evidence of hypocrisy, and to regard the allegorical content of the program as a token gesture of compliance with the strict moral standards of the Counter-Reformation. These allegories mean nothing to us; therefore (it is reasoned) they meant nothing to those for whom they were invented, but were simply a pious fiction which made it possible to represent pagan subjects without fear of ecclesiastical censure. No doubt such charges are occasionally justified; but they are decidedly not applicable to the Farnese Gallery, and in addition may serve only to obscure the fullest meaning of the cycle. It has never been sufficiently emphasized that in these frescoes Annibale has given form to an authentic Baroque idea—the revelation of the spiritual through the medium of the sensual. The central theme is the power of divine love to exalt and transfigure the human soul. This mystical idea finds its supreme expression in the *Triumph of Bacchus and Ariadne* (Fig. 69), where the mortal Ariadne, caught up in a *furor divinus*, is deified by the love of the god.[14]

I. THE CONTEST OF HEAVENLY AND EARTHLY LOVE

"Before describing the mythological scenes," Bellori begins, "we may conveniently consider the Cupids painted so as to resemble living figures in the four corners of the Gallery above the cornice; for on them depend the entire meaning and allegory of the work. Here the artist sought to represent in various emblematic ways the conflict and reconciliation between the two Loves defined by Plato—Heavenly and Common Love."[15] Bellori alludes here to the Platonic doctrine of the Twin Venuses, one celestial (Ἀφροδίτη Οὐρανία) and one common (Ἀφροδίτη Πάνδημος), which originated, as he says, with Plato himself, and was elaborated by the Florentine philosopher Marsilio Ficino in his *Commentary on Plato's Symposium*.[16] For each Venus there exists a corresponding Cupid, one representing heavenly and the other earthly love.

---

[13] Bellori, *Vite*, p. 65.

[14] A recent attempt to establish a connection between the Farnese Gallery and the *Hypnerotomachia Polifili* can only be described as ingenious but unconvincing. See E. Quaranta, "Influenze probabili del 'Polifilo' sugli affreschi dei Carracci in Palazzo Farnese," *Amor di Libro, Rassegna di bibliografia e di erudizione*, v, 1957, pp. 18-30.

[15] *Vite*, pp. 47 f.

[16] Marsilio Ficino, *Commentarium in Convivium Platonis*, ii, 7. I have used here the edition by R. Marcel, *Marsile Ficin, Commentaire sur le Banquet de Platon*, Paris, 1956, pp. 153 ff. For an illuminating discussion of this doctrine see E. Panofsky, *Studies in Iconology*, New York, 1939, pp. 141 ff.

The difference between them is epitomized by Vincenzo Cartari in his manual of mythology: "Of the heavenly Venus was born the heavenly Cupid, and that divine Love which raises the human mind to the contemplation of God . . . . The other Love was born of the second Venus, whom Plato calls common, worldly, and earthly; and he is in like manner common and earthly, and full of human lust, as the fables tell."[17]

The four images in the corners are to be understood, then, as illustrating the contest of Sacred and Profane (or Heavenly and Earthly) Love. The sequence begins with the two Amori fighting to gain possession of a palm branch; in the second episode they are pulling each other's hair; in the third Divine Love seeks to take the torch away from Earthly Love; the outcome is pictured in the last scene, where the two are reconciled and kiss each other.

The *Fight for the Palm* (Fig. 39) depends, as Panofsky has shown,[18] on an illustration in Cartari's *Imagini* (Fig. 279).[19] This at once introduces an anomalous note, because Cartari's engraving was not meant to represent Heavenly and Earthly Love, but the very different pair called Eros and Anteros.[20] In antiquity the primary meaning of Eros and Anteros was Love and Love Returned. The *locus classicus* is found in Pausanias (*Description of Greece*, VI 23, 3, 5), who says that in the gymnasium at Elis Anteros was represented trying to wrest a palm branch from Eros, the implication being, it would seem, that Love-in-return ought to show no less zeal than Love himself. This meaning of Anteros as Love Returned was fully understood in the sixteenth century; Cartari, for example, explains that the Elean group described by Pausanias signified *Amore reciproco*.[21] But at the same time there was also current another interpretation, according to which Anteros was the god of divine love, as opposed to earthly love. That this mistaken notion found wide acceptance was largely due to the influence of Andrea Alciati. In his famous emblem book, first published in 1531, Alciati defined Anteros as *amor virtutis*, saying that he has nothing to do with the common Venus, but raises men's minds to the heavens; instead of Cupid's weapons, he carries four wreaths symbolizing the virtues.[22] In a second emblem Anteros is pictured overcoming "the other Cupid" whom he has bound to a tree, while the victim's bow and arrows are thrown into a fire.[23]

---

[17] Vincenzo Cartari, *Imagini delli dei de gli antichi*, Venice, 1674 (1st ed., 1556), pp. 239 f.: "Due [Amori] furono posti da Platone, si come ei pose due Veneri parimente; L'una celeste della quale nacque il celeste Cupido, e quel divino Amore, che soleva l'animo humano alla contemplatione di Dio. . . . Nacque questo Amore . . . dell' altra Venere, la quale chiama Platone volgare, mondana, e terrena; volgare parimente, e terreno, e pieno di lascivia humana, secondo che finsero le favole."

[18] E. Panofsky, "Der gefesselte Eros," *Oud Holland*, L, 1933, pp. 193 ff.

[19] V. Cartari, *Le imagini de i dei de gli antichi*, Lyons, 1581, p. 420. The same episode is represented in Agostino Carracci's painting, *Amore reciproco*; cf. O. Kurz, in *Journal of the Warburg and Courtauld Institutes*, XIV, 1951, p. 226, pl. 42a.

[20] Panofsky, *op.cit.*; see also R. V. Merrill, "Eros and Anteros," *Speculum*, XIX, 1944, pp. 265-284.

[21] *Imagini delli dei* (ed. of 1674), p. 242.

[22] Andrea Alciati, *Emblematum Liber*, Emblema CIX (CX).

[23] *Ibid.*, Emblema CX (CXI).

It is in this moralizing sense, and not in the orthodox antique sense of reciprocal love, that we must interpret Carracci's Cupids fighting for the palm. Even though they appear in the classical guise of Eros and Anteros, they are in reality, as the context makes clear, the twin Loves of Platonic doctrine—*Amor terrenus* and *Amor divinus*.[24]

In the *Struggle under the wreath*, as we may call it (Fig. 40), the two Cupids are locked in combat and pulling each other's hair; one of the wrestlers is trying to trip his opponent. Suspended overhead is a shining laurel wreath which sheds its rays upon the struggling pair. The wreath as an attribute of Divine Love seems to have been suggested by Alciati's emblem book.[25] For an explanation of the radiance surrounding it we may turn to a passage in Cartari: "Divine love is like the sun, which sheds its rays throughout the universe. . . . As the sun creates warmth wherever it touches, so does Love kindle those souls which it approaches, so that they turn with ardent desire to heavenly things."[26] Bellori's commentary on the fresco is strikingly similar in tone. The radiant laurel wreath, he writes, "means that victory over brutish appetites exalts men to heaven, and it also shows that this splendor is characteristic of Celestial Love, which gently warms the soul without tormenting it with impure fire, as is symbolized in the next image by the burning torch."[27]

With these words Bellori introduces the third episode, the *Fight for the Torch* (Fig. 41). The burning torch is a venerable symbol of Love's power to inflict pain, and thus forms an appropriate attribute of *Amore volgare*. The scene may have been inspired by Cartari's illustration (Fig. 279), in which there appears, besides Eros and Anteros, a third Cupid extinguishing a torch in a river. This is *Amor Lethaeus*, who is described by Ovid (*Remedia Amoris*, 549-554) as the god who heals the wounds of love by quenching its flame in the cold waters of forgetfulness. Cartari, whose account of the subject is wholly accurate,[28] does not make the blunder of supposing that this deity is only Divine Love in another guise. But having already seen Anteros and Eros transmuted into Sacred and Profane Love, we can easily understand how *Amor Lethaeus*, the god who extinguishes the flame of carnal passion,

[24] Panofsky has remarked (*op.cit.*, p. 196) on the hesitant attitude taken by Bellori toward the Eros-Anteros group of Annibale, in which the seventeenth-century commentator of course perceived the affinity to the Elean group described by Pausanias. In his *Argomento della Galeria* (1657) Bellori interpreted the pair in the proper antique sense as an allegory of *amor mutuo* (in Malvasia, *Felsina*, I, p. 438). But in the *Vite* of 1672 (p. 48) he was much less emphatic, saying only that "Anteros was believed to punish unjust Love," a deliberately ambiguous statement that can be construed as referring either to the authentic Eros-Anteros tradition or to the Neoplatonic idea of Sacred and Profane Love. For the source of the term *Amore ingiusto* see Panofsky, *loc.cit.*

[25] Alciati, *op.cit.*, Emblema CIX.

[26] Cartari, *Imagini* (ed. of 1674), p. 240: "Amore divino . . . è come il Sole, il quale sparge i suoi raggi per l'universo. . . . Et come il Sole riscalda ovunque tocca, così Amore accende quelle anime, alle quali si accosta, onde con infiammato desiderio si rivolgono alle cose del Cielo."

[27] Bellori, *Argomento* (in Malvasia, *Felsina*, I, pp. 437 f.).

[28] Cartari, *op.cit.*, p. 243. See Agostino's painting, *Amore Letheo*, in Vienna (Kurz, *op.cit.*, p. 228, pl. 44a).

might by the same alchemy be converted into *Amor Coelestis*. As Bellori interprets the fresco, Common Love is hiding the torch behind his back so that Heavenly Love shall not take it from him and put out its flame. But since the two Cupids are identical in outward appearance it might equally well be argued that Heavenly Love has already seized the torch and is fending off his adversary's efforts to recapture it.

The concluding scene (Fig. 42) illustrates the Union of Sacred and Profane Love. After a lengthy struggle *Amor divinus* has succeeded in disarming his opponent, and the two Cupids, now reconciled, smilingly embrace each other. The palm branch which they were earlier fighting over rests against the balustrade. The meaning is plain: only when Earthly Love is governed and held in check by Heavenly Love can the two live in harmony. Wittkower has observed[29] that the postures of the pair are closely modeled after Cartari's *Eros and Anteros* (Fig. 279). Paradoxical as it may seem, Annibale found the tame poses of Cartari's fighting Cupids more adaptable to a gentle embrace than to a scene of struggle, for which he accordingly invented a much livelier pair of figures (Fig. 39).

Bellori is surely right in maintaining that these four images provide the key to the entire work. For the unifying theme of the Gallery is not, as some have believed, simply "the power of love" but precisely "Sacred and Profane Love." This is not meant to imply that the program can be easily explained; but it may at least serve as a reminder that the cycle is something more than a haphazard selection of erotic stories from mythology.[30]

II. THE FRIEZE

Omnia vincit Amor: et nos cedamus Amori.

Virgil, *Eclogue* x, 69

The frieze consists, as we have seen, of an alternate sequence of paintings and bronze medallions. We may begin with the polychrome panels ("quadri coloriti al naturale": Bellori), which depict four amorous encounters exemplifying the power of love.

THE FOUR PAINTED PANELS

JUPITER AND JUNO (FIG. 43)

Jupiter, wearing a pale violet mantle that covers the lower part of his body, is seated on a softly cushioned bed; with one leg drawn up and the other resting on the floor he turns to embrace his bride, who has already placed one knee on the marital couch. Looking up amorously into Juno's eyes the god puts his right hand on her shoulder

[29] Wittkower, *Carracci Drawings*, p. 139, under no. 307.

[30] Tietze, while admitting (pp. 89-90, 104) that the Cupids in the corners conform to the types of Heavenly and Earthly Love, categorically rejects Bellori's explanation that they are fundamental to the meaning of the entire cycle. That they have a merely decorative function is proved, he says, by the fact that they do not appear in the preliminary drawings for the ceiling. This point is discussed in Chapter 11.

and with his left grasps her thigh. The eagle at his feet, clutching the thunderbolt in its claws, discreetly turns its glance away from the divine pair. As she approaches her ardent lord Juno has partially disrobed, but with breast uncovered she still modestly holds a blue garment around her. In the shadows behind her can be seen the peacock with plumage spread.

Tietze mistakenly believed that Juno holds an apple in her left hand;[31] in reality it is only a fold of the mantle which she carries draped over her hand. One feature does require explanation, however, and that is the band of patterned cloth that Juno wears beneath her breasts. This is surely the girdle of Venus—"the broidered, fair-wrought girdle"—which Juno borrowed from her in order to arouse Jupiter's passion.[32] "Give me now love and desire," were Juno's words to Venus, "wherewith thou dost overcome all the immortals, and mortal men."

The fresco has always been admired. Félibien found it a commendable example of *l'expression de l'amour*.[33] The existence of a copy in the Borghese Gallery also testifies to its popularity.[34] Annibale's indebtedness to the Raphaelesque tradition, and particularly to the frescoes of the Loggia di Psiche in the Farnesina, is plainly evident in these two splendid figures. We may note, in addition, a close dependence on Agostino Veneziano's engraving of *St. John the Evangelist* (B. XIV, 93), which is to be seen in the position of Jupiter's legs, in the arrangement of the drapery, and even in the placing of the eagle between his feet. But as Foratti has observed[35] there is also present, both in the head and in the attitude of Jove, a reminiscence of the *Laocoön*. It is interesting that Annibale should twice have made use of this tormented pose to convey the force of amorous passions (cf. Fig. 63).

DIANA AND ENDYMION (FIG. 44)

Under Diana's magic spell, the shepherd Endymion has fallen asleep against a grassy slope, his plump legs drawn up and his head supported on his left arm. The yellow mantle which is wrapped about his body also serves to cushion his elbow. His right hand has relaxed its grip, and the fingers rest nervelessly against the staff. The moon-goddess, the crescent gleaming in her hair, glides downward upon a cloud to embrace the enchanted youth. So noiselessly does she caress her beloved that even the sleeping dog curled up beside his master is not awakened. Half hidden in the foliage at the left, two amoretti observe the scene approvingly. One, holding the fatal arrow in his hand, smiles with delight to see the most chaste goddess subject to his power; the other parts the branches and makes a sign of silence by putting his finger to his mouth.

---

[31] Tietze, p. 78.

[32] Homer, *Iliad* XIV, 197-223. The connection was noted by A. Pigler, *Barockthemen*, Budapest and Berlin, 1956, II, p. 136.

[33] A. Félibien, *Entretiens sur les vies et sur les ouvrages des plus excellens peintres anciens et modernes*, 2nd ed., Paris 1685-1688, II, p. 18.

[34] P. della Pergola, *Galleria Borghese. I dipinti*, I, Rome, 1955, p. 21, no. 17, fig. 15. L. Salerno suggests an attribution to Antonio Carracci (*Bollettino d'Arte*, XLI, 1956, pp. 35 f.).

[35] A. Foratti, *I Carracci nella teoria e nella pratica*, Città di Castello, 1913, p. 283.

Although the myth of Selene and Endymion must have been well known to him from antique sarcophagi, Annibale has made no attempt to reproduce a classical prototype. Instead, as may be seen from the pose of Endymion, there is a clear reminiscence here of the Raphaelesque fresco of *Venus and Adonis* in the bathroom of Cardinal Bibbiena, a composition engraved by both Marcantonio and Agostino Veneziano (B. 484 and 485).

HERCULES AND IOLE (OR OMPHALE) (FIG. 45)

The scene illustrates the humiliation of Hercules, brought about by his infatuation for Iole. "He whom not a thousand wild beasts . . . , whom Juno could not overcome, is overcome by Love."[36] The mighty hero, incongruously clad in feminine silks of violet hue and with a golden band about his arm, sits playing a tambourine ("il rotondo timpano lascivo": Bellori) as he gazes ardently into the eyes of his beloved. The imperious Iole, seated beside him with one leg placed across Hercules's thigh, has donned his lion-skin and supports herself with his great club. Her left hand is placed on the hero's shoulder. From a loggia behind her, Cupid, armed with his bow, gestures laughingly toward Hercules whom he has thus humbled; this incident was taken, as Bellori observes,[37] from Tasso's *Gerusalemme Liberata* (Canto XVI, 3).

Since Hercules is described in the textual sources as spinning yarn, most works of art accordingly show him holding a spindle.[38] Here, however, he is pictured striking a tambourine. In making this substitution Annibale plainly means to allude to the sensual nature of the hero's passion: in the *Choice of Hercules* (Fig. 9), painted a few years earlier in the Camerino, the tambourine is included among the attributes of *Voluptas*.

Annibale's propensity to turn for inspiration to antiquities in the Farnese collection is nicely illustrated here. The way in which Iole puts her hand on Hercules' shoulder and looks at him intently shows that the artist has studied the little marble group of *Hercules and Omphale*, now in Naples. For the figure of the hero, however, he found a more imposing model in the *Farnese Hercules*, from which he took not only the powerful physique and the curly hair and beard, but even the inclination of the head.

VENUS AND ANCHISES (FIG. 46)

The goddess of love is seated on an ornate golden bed, over which hang violet curtains. She is nude, except for a veil wound about her head, one end of which she presses to her breast; her garments and jewelry may be seen lying upon the chair at the left. The unexpectedly modest demeanor of Venus contrasts sharply with the eagerness of Anchises, who, seated on the bed beside her, boldly lifts the goddess's leg

[36] Ovid, *Heroides* IX, 25 f.: "Quem non mille ferae . . . , Non potuit Iuno vincere, vincit Amor."

[37] *Vite*, p. 58. See on this subject E. K. Waterhouse, "Tasso and the Visual Arts," *Italian Studies*, III, 1946-1948, p. 156.

[38] As in the ceiling panel by Pintoricchio now in the Metropolitan Museum in New York (B. Burroughs, in *Bulletin of the Metropolitan Museum*, XVI, January 1921, Part II, p. 10, fig. on p. 7).

over his thigh in order to remove her sandal (having already, it would seem, disposed of the other). Standing close to Venus and leaning with folded arms against her leg is her son Cupid, whose mischievous grin shows plainly that he is the cause of her fall. That from this union sprang the founder of the Roman race is indicated by the words of Virgil inscribed on the footstool, GENVS VNDE LATINVM (*Aeneid*, I, 6). The lofty peak visible in the distance may be taken to represent Mt. Ida.

The scene agrees closely with the text of the Homeric *Hymn to Aphrodite*, the theme of which is that not even Venus can escape Love's dominion. In order that Aphrodite might not boast that she had caused the gods to be smitten with passion for mortals, while she herself remained untouched, "Zeus sent into her heart sweet desire of Anchises." The poem describes how "with downcast eyes she crept towards the bed," which was covered with the skins of animals, and how Anchises "took from her body her shining jewels, brooches, and twisted armlets, earrings and chains . . . and unclad her of her glistering raiment, that he laid on a silver-studded chair."[39]

Bellori thought that Annibale had drawn his inspiration for the scene from an antique marble.[40] But he was probably mistaken in this, for, as Calvesi has recently observed, the composition depends in part on an invention by Raphael, the *Marriage of Alexander and Roxana*, which is known both through drawings and an engraving by Caraglio.[41] Annibale's Venus resembles the figure of Roxana in pose and in such details as the braided hair and the arrangement of the veil. Even the motive of the *déchaussement* of Venus was plainly suggested by the action of the cupid who, in the Raphaelesque composition, removes the slipper from Roxana's foot. According to Bellori the motto *Genus unde Latinum* refers not only to the birth of Aeneas but also to the antiquity of the Farnese. This idea would not seem to be very plausible—until we recall that Salviati had painted a fresco in the same palace representing Ranuccio Farnese in the guise of Aeneas receiving arms from his mother Venus.[42] It is thus conceivable that Annibale intended to allude, if only indirectly, to the same theme.

These four frescoes are clearly meant to demonstrate the invincible power of Love, who holds dominion over mortals and immortals alike: *omnia vincit Amor*. The mighty Hercules is rendered weak and effeminate; even this paragon of virtue becomes the slave of a sensual passion. The chaste Diana is inflamed with love for the shepherd Endymion. Venus herself, the very goddess of love, is not immune to Cupid's darts, and yields herself to Anchises. Jupiter and Juno, usually quarrelsome, are here united by amorous desire.

It is in keeping with the richness and variety of the cycle that these four panels can

[39] *Hymn to Aphrodite*, 45 ff. The passages quoted are from the translation by A. Lang, *The Homeric Hymns*, New York, 1899, pp. 168 ff.

[40] *Vite*, p. 57.

[41] M. Calvesi, "Note ai Carracci," *Commentari*, VII, 1956, p. 275, pl. LXXIII, figs. 16-17.

On the several versions of this subject cf. A. E. Popham and J. Wilde, *The Italian Drawings of the XV and XVI Centuries at Windsor Castle*, London, 1949, p. 316, no. 809.

[42] Reproduced in A. Venturi, *Storia dell'arte italiana*, IX, part 6, Milan, 1933, p. 189, fig. 107.

be viewed in different relationships. They may be grouped, first of all, into two complementary pairs. In the two scenes toward the north the male is aggressive and the female submissive. Jupiter draws Juno to his couch in a marital embrace; on the opposite side Venus sits modestly on the bed while Anchises removes her clothing. In the two scenes at the south the roles are reversed: the male is passive and the female takes the lead. The sleeping Endymion is caressed by Diana; and Hercules is made to play the woman while Iole dons the lion-skin and wields his club. Other combinations are presently perceived. Two of the scenes depict love between equals, whereas the other two tell of love between unequals. The two amorous deities, Jupiter and Juno, are in this respect comparable to the two mortals, Hercules and Iole, who appear diagonally opposite; the relationship is underlined by the fact that Hercules' muscular build echoes, and amplifies, the powerful frame of Jupiter. In the same way the union of the goddess Venus and the mortal Anchises has its counterpart in the love of Diana for Endymion. Still another grouping can be made on the basis of figure-composition. On the east, or inner wall the compositional scheme is fundamentally pyramidal, each pair of figures being so placed that the heads meet at the apex of a triangle. On the west, or window wall a different compositional mode is employed: in each panel the two persons sit in more or less upright positions, the woman resting her leg on the man's thigh; in addition both Iole and Anchises wear the hero's lion-skin.

THE BRONZE MEDALLIONS

Alternating in contrapuntal fashion with the polychrome panels are the medallions painted in imitation of bronze relief. There are twelve of these tondi—four on each side, and two at each end (the latter visible only as segments of circles). A glance at the arrangement of subjects (taken in most instances from the *Metamorphoses* of Ovid) shows that the medallions are to be grouped in pairs, each one being complemented by that which faces it on the other side of the Gallery. The system is slightly varied at the ends, where each pair of segmental medallions (if I may use this term) forms a unit complete in itself. But this involves no fundamental change, for each of these roundels can be thought of as belonging to the adjacent longitudinal series, and hence as finding its complement in the series opposite.

Whereas the unifying theme of the four polychrome paintings might be defined as the power of Profane Love, the bronze medallions, by contrast, are intended to show forth the power of Sacred Love. They are to be read, that is to say, in an allegorical or moralizing manner. It has already been noted that most of the subjects are drawn from the *Metamorphoses*. Three scenes, however, do not come from that source,[43] which alone should be enough to convince us that the cycle of medallions was not intended simply as a literal illustration of the Ovidian fables. Indeed it must be concluded that the underlying textual source was not Ovid's poem at all, but one of

---

[43] *Cupid and Pan, Hero and Leander,* and the *Judgment of Paris.*

those Christianized versions of it which may be grouped under the name of the *Moralized Ovid*.[44] For it is only in a text of this kind that we can discover all the subjects represented in the medallions. This reliance on what would appear to be a "mediaeval" interpretation of the *Metamorphoses* might seem to be most improbable in the closing years of the Cinquecento, the more so because such moralizations of Ovid (though not the original works of Ovid themselves) had been expressly banned by the Council of Trent.[45] But not even the authority of the *Index Librorum Prohibitorum* could have been effective in extirpating so ingrained a mode of thought; and it is a fact that allegorized versions of Ovid continued to be produced and read throughout the later sixteenth century.[46] Having previously seen how Alciati's moralizing interpretation of Eros and Anteros was able to intrude itself into the iconography of the Gallery, we are prepared to understand that the Ovidian myths might undergo the same treatment. Half a century and more later, when Bellori wrote his commentaries on the Gallery, moralistic versions of this sort were no longer in vogue. This is why Bellori's explanations of the medallions are almost invariably wide of the mark.

In the following description, we may conveniently begin at the north end of the Gallery with the tondo that occupies the space to the left of *Jupiter and Juno*.

APOLLO AND MARSYAS (FIG. 47)

The subject is *Apollo flaying Marsyas* (*Metamorphoses* vi, 382-400). The satyr who rashly challenged Apollo to a musical contest is fastened by his wrists to a tree; a goatskin mantle hangs from his shoulders, and the pan-pipe, the cause of his undoing, is suspended from a branch. Apollo, armed with a knife, personally administers the punishment, and is already stripping the skin from his victim's thigh. The lyre rests on the ground at his feet. The form of the satyr, whose arms are pinioned above his head and whose legs are human, not caprine, is adapted from the antique Marsyas type, as exemplified by the statue in Florence. The reclining figure holding a cornucopia, tentatively identified by Tietze as Marsyas' disciple Olympus,[47] is in reality a personification of the river Marsyas which was formed by the tears of the satyr's followers. The resemblance to antique river gods such as those of the Capitol is especially marked.[48] The frescoed medallion is in good condition, but the youth at the left shows a large damaged patch on the left arm.

---

[44] The group includes the French *Ovide Moralisé*, and the *Moralized Ovid* in Latin by Pierre Bersuire (Berchorius). For the first see C. de Boer (ed.), "Ovide moralisé. Poème du commencement du quatorzième siècle," *Verhandelingen der K. Akademie van Wetenschappen, Afd. Letterkunde*, n.s., xv, 1915; xxi, 1920; xxx, 1931; xxxvii, 1936; xliii, 1938. The Latin version by Bersuire is best known in the editions attributed to the Dominican Thomas Waleys (or Walleys), e.g., *Metamorphosis Ovidiana moraliter a Magistro Thoma Waleys anglico de professione predicatorum sub sanctissimo patre Dominico explanata*, Paris, 1515. For other moralizing commentaries on Ovid see J. Seznec, *The Survival of the Pagan Gods*, New York, 1953, pp. 91 ff.

[45] F. H. Reusch, *Die Indices Librorum Prohibitorum des sechzehnten Jahrhunderts*, Tübingen, 1886, p. 275.

[46] Seznec, *op.cit.*, p. 96.

[47] Tietze, p. 81.

[48] H. Siebenhüner, *Das Kapitol in Rom*, Munich, 1954, pp. 48 ff., 91, Abb. 23. For a

To Bellori *Apollo flaying Marsyas* signified "the light of wisdom, which takes away from the soul its bestial outer hide."[49] There can certainly be no doubt that the scene represents in general the victory of good over evil; but, as the *Moralized Ovid* explains, it also denotes specifically the punishment that is meted out to foolish and presumptuous persons who contend against their betters.[50] A more elaborate allegory is offered in Anguillara's translation of the *Metamorphoses* (1584): he who does not fear God, but strives against him, is quickly reduced to helplessness and becomes as unsteady as the water of a river.[51] Herein lies the probable explanation of the river god seen in the medallion. But the allegory is further enriched by another element that we shall find to be recurrent throughout the cycle—an element of musical symbolism. Even in antiquity the victory of the celestial lyre over the sensual pipe signified the triumph of reason over carnal passions and orgiastic cults. The prominence given to the musical instruments in Carracci's roundel is unquestionably intended to demonstrate the subjugation of the satyr's shrill and impure music by the quiet strains of Apollo's lyre, which transports the soul to heaven.[52]

The symbolic implications of the Marsyas fable were not unknown to the Farnese. After the recovery of Piacenza from Spain in 1556, the Duke Ottavio Farnese issued a commemorative medal on the reverse of which appeared the Flaying of Marsyas, with the motto CUM DIIS NON CONTENDENDUM.[53]

CUPID AND PAN (FIG. 48)

The medallion directly opposite, on the other side of the vault, represents *Cupid overcoming Pan*, and is clearly meant as the counterpart to *Apollo and Marsyas*. The winged god of love, grasping Pan by one of his horns, has forced him to the ground, and stands with his foot on his victim's thigh. The pair are framed by two trees: Pan's reed-pipe hangs in that at the left, and Cupid's bow and arrow are seen in the other. The surface of the medallion and the surrounding area has been damaged, probably by moisture; the torso of the atlas at the right is almost wholly repainted.

The struggle of Pan and Cupid does not come from the *Metamorphoses*, but is, sig-

similarly foreshortened view, cf. Heemskerck's drawing of the river gods of the Capitol (C. Hülsen and H. Egger, *Die römischen Skizzenbücher von Marten van Heemskerck*, Berlin, 1913-1916, I, fol. 45 r.). Claude Lorrain includes a river god in his *Landscape with the Flaying of Marsyas* (collection Earl of Leicester).

[49] *Vite*, p. 66. *Idem, Argomento* (in Malvasia, *Felsina*, I, p. 441).

[50] Waleys, *Metamorphosis Ovidiana*, fol. 56.

[51] *Le metamorfosi di Ovidio ridotte da Gio: Andrea dell' Anguillara in ottava rima . . .*, Venice, 1584, p. 213: "La favola di Marsia ci dà ad intendere, che, quando vogliamo contendere con Iddio, non lo temendo come deve esser temuto, la sua omnipotenza ci fa presto

conoscere, che siamo più flussibili che non è un fiume, togliendoci tutte le forze co'l privarci della gratia sua; di modo, che, cadendo in terra il nostro vigore, si converte nell'acqua del fiume, laquale non si ferma giamai."

[52] A. Michaelis, "Apolline e Marsia," *Annali dell'Instituto di Corrispondenza Archeologica*, XXX, 1858, pp. 298 ff. See also F. W. Sternfeld, "The Dramatic and Allegorical Function of Music in Shakespeare's Tragedies," *Annales Musicologiques*, III, 1955, pp. 265-282.

[53] I. Affò, *La Zecca e moneta parmigiana . . .*, Parma, 1788, p. 177, note 112; pl. 3, no. XVII. A. Armand, *Les médailleurs italiens des quinzième et seizième siècles*, 2nd ed., Paris, 1883-1887, I, p. 223, no. 11.

nificantly, included in the *Moralized Ovid*.[54] The proper title of the subject is "Love conquers all"—*omnia vincit Amor* (Virgil *Ecl.* x, 69) the figure of Pan standing both for the deity of that name and for "all" (the Greek Πᾶν).[55] Although in mythographical and emblematic literature Cupid conquering Pan generally signified the power of love over universal nature,[56] the episode also acquired a moralizing meaning in that it served to symbolize the victory of divine love over carnal passions.[57] For example, when Annibale represented the subject as a relief on a vase in the Bridgewater *Danaë* (now destroyed), it was intended as a chastity motive.[58] That the Farnese medallion must be understood in the same sense, the analogy to the tondo of *Apollo and Marsyas* makes fully evident. Both scenes celebrate the victory of spiritual love over the bestial lower nature; Marsyas and Pan are vanquished and their lascivious music silenced.[59]

The subject of Cupid struggling with Pan was frequently represented by the Carracci. It first appears in a fresco by Agostino, originally in the Palazzo Magnani, the preparatory drawing for which is in Windsor.[60] From this source Annibale may have taken the attitude of Pan, who kneels with one hand on the ground while trying with the other to fend off his opponent. The posture of Cupid, however, owes nothing to Agostino's design, but has another parentage altogether. The motive, originating in antique Medea sarcophagi, acquired a new currency through being revived by Michelangelo, who employed it for the figure of the infant Christ in the marble tondo now in the Royal Academy in London.[61] Since the type was widely adopted during the Cinquecento there is perhaps no need to look for the immediate source of Annibale's figure. The fact nevertheless remains that the Farnese Cupid finds a remarkably close parallel in Michelangelo's Christ Child. It is not, after all, inappropriate that Annibale's "relief" medallion should resemble an actual sculptured tondo; if a relationship could be shown to exist between them, this would only serve to underline the essentially spiritual meaning of the fresco.

It will be recalled, finally, that Annibale's group of Cupid and Pan was copied by Agostino with only slight changes in his engraving *Omnia vincit Amor* (Fig. 276), which is dated 1599.

BOREAS AND ORITHYIA (FIG. 49)

The second medallion on the inner wall, partly "concealed" by the overlapping

---

[54] Cf. Waleys, *op.cit.*, fol. 13 v.: "Cum amore [Pan] pingebatur luctatus, sed ab eo victus erat."

[55] Servius on Virgil's *Eclogue* II, 31.

[56] E.g., Cartari, *Imagini* (ed. of 1674), p. 251.

[57] A. Bocchi, *Symbolicarum Quaestionum de universo genere . . . libri quinque*, Bologna, 1555, Symb. LXXV: "Pan victus a Cupidine in lucta cadit. (Omnia cui cedant, divino cedat Amori.)"

[58] Panofsky, "Der gefesselte Eros," pp. 193 ff.

[59] It is difficult to account for Bellori's explanation (*Argomento*, in Malvasia, *Felsina*, I, p. 441), which is that "when reason is subordinated to lust our mind becomes monstrous and bestial."

[60] Wittkower, *Carracci Drawings*, pp. 111 f., no. 94, pl. 26.

[61] Panofsky, *Studies in Iconology*, p. 172, note 3; C. de Tolnay, *Michelangelo*, I, Princeton, 1947, pp. 104 f., 162 f.

frame of the adjoining painting, represents *Boreas abducting Orithyia* (*Metam.* VI, 682-710). The nude, bearded north wind, his wings outspread, clasps his arms about his beloved as he transports her high above the earth.

Bellori, for whom the medallions signify in general "the vices and evil effects of profane love," explains the rape of Orithyia by Boreas as "the unbridled reign of the lustful."[62] Yet it must be said that there is little in this graceful picture to warrant so censorious an interpretation. The expression and gestures of the wind god do not so much suggest lust as mercy and tenderness, nor does Orithyia struggle against her captor. In short it is evident that we must look for a more favorable allegory than that proposed by Bellori. One such interpretation, typical of its kind, is to be found in the fourteenth-century *Ovide moralisé*, where Boreas is compared to Christ who descended to earth in order to deliver the human soul from the bondage of sin, "dont il resort a grant victoire, montans en celestial gloire."[63] We shall not be wrong if we regard this scene as an example of spiritual ravishment: Orithyia illustrates the rapture of the soul, transported to heaven by divine love.

For the figure of Orithyia Annibale has once again made use, consciously or unconsciously, of the posture of the infant Christ in Michelangelo's marble tondo.

SALMACIS AND HERMAPHRODITUS (FIG. 52)

The medallion that serves as the counterpart to *Boreas and Orithyia* represents the fable of *Salmacis and Hermaphroditus*. As Ovid relates (*Metam.* IV, 285-388), the nymph Salmacis, when she saw Hermaphroditus bathing in her fountain, fell in love with him and, embracing him, begged of the gods that she might be united to him forever. The wish was granted, and the two were merged into one form combining the characteristics of male and female. The youth then prayed that henceforth anyone bathing in the pool should be similarly enfeebled and made half man.

The fresco was extensively damaged by moisture in the seventeenth century and has obviously undergone considerable restoration. The *ignudo* at the right has been badly rehandled, the foreshortened left leg being only a travesty of Annibale's draughtsmanship (cf. the preparatory drawing, Fig. 217). In the medallion itself a particularly clumsy piece of restoration has transformed the foliage on the bank of the pool into what looks like curtains; the original appearance of this section can be better appreciated from Cesio's engraving (Fig. 277). It was perhaps this illogical feature that led Tietze to doubt whether the scene actually represents Salmacis and Hermaphroditus.[64] But there need be no uncertainty: the two embracing figures, whose feet are immersed in the pool, can only be the pair in question.

[62] Bellori, *Argomento* (in Malvasia, *Felsina*, I, p. 441).

[63] De Boer (ed.), "Ovide moralisé," *Verhandelingen*, XXI, 1920, p. 372.

[64] Tietze, p. 84. It may be noted in passing that the painting by Scarsellino in the Bor-

ghese Gallery, always described as "Diana and Endymion," in reality likewise represents Salmacis and Hermaphroditus (P. della Pergola, *Galleria Borghese, I dipinti*, I, p. 67, no. 117).

That the story of Salmacis and Hermaphroditus was regarded as a suitable pretext for a "fantasia oscena e lasciva" we know from Marino's letter to Ludovico Carracci, in which it is suggested that the artist compose a painting showing the two figures "ignudi e abbracciati in mezzo della fontana."[65] For Annibale's medallion, however, some meaning must be sought which will be more in harmony with that of its counterpart, *Boreas and Orithyia*. In the Latin text of the *Moralized Ovid* we read that the fable is an allegory of the Incarnation: Hermaphroditus is to be understood as the Son of God, to whom is joined human nature (Salmacis) within the Virgin's womb (the fountain); from this union of two natures, divine and human, a single person results.[66] Somewhat simpler, and certainly less startling, is the explanation offered by Lodovico Dolce, who says that the myth represents "the miraculous union which the soul makes with God, by forsaking these transitory and mortal things and ascending to the contemplation of things divine."[67] This is probably the sense of Annibale's fresco.

Of both the Boreas and Salmacis medallions we may say that their theme is the mystery of heavenly love, through which the human soul is caught up and absorbed into the divine.

ORPHEUS AND EURYDICE (FIG. 50)

The fifth tondo contains the familiar story of *Orpheus and Eurydice* (*Metam.* x, 11-63). The musician, holding the lyre beneath his arm, looks back in dismay as Eurydice vanishes from his sight amid the infernal smoke; his foot is still raised to mark the interrupted ascent from the underworld, while he flings out his arm in a vain attempt to grasp his wife.

Bellori's explanation runs as follows: "Eurydice, who is returned to Hades through looking back, denotes the inconstancy of our human nature, which, when it has just been restored to the light by the harmony of wisdom, sometimes reverts to sensual appetites and goes back to the shades of sin."[68] It may seem curious that Bellori should speak of Eurydice as looking back, since the whole point of the original fable centers on Orpheus' weakness in turning round before he has left the underworld; it is nevertheless a fact that in the moralized versions the disaster is generally attributed to the woman rather than to the man. The anonymous *Ovide moralisé*, for example, interprets Orpheus as Christ, who descends from heaven in order to deliver the human soul from the "dark prison of hell"; Eurydice, on the other hand, typifies those who by reverting to their evil ways have forfeited all hope of salvation.[69] This is one of

[65] G. Bottari and S. Ticozzi, *Raccolta di lettere sulla pittura, scultura ed architettura*, Milan, 1822-1825, VII, pp. 25 ff. See also Wittkower, *Carracci Drawings*, p. 109, Cat. 88.

[66] Waleys, *op.cit.*, fol. 43.

[67] L. Dolce, *Le trasformationi tratte da Ovidio . . .*, Venice, 1561 (1st ed., 1553), p. 102: "Si può prender per Hermafrodito la

mirabile unione, che fa l'anima con Dio, lasciando queste cose transitorie e mortali, e poggiando alla contemplatione delle Divine."

[68] *Argomento* (in Malvasia, *Felsina*, I, p. 441).

[69] De Boer (ed.), "Ovide moralisé," *Verhandelingen*, XXXVII, 1936, pp. 21 ff. A briefer allegory in Waleys, *op.cit.*, fol. 80. It is inter-

the few occasions when Bellori's interpretation exactly corresponds to that of the allegorized Ovid.

Not to be overlooked as a celestial symbol in this scene is Orpheus' lyre, the instrument of harmony and enlightenment which is also associated with Apollo.

PAN AND SYRINX (FIG. 51)

Facing *Orpheus and Eurydice* is the tondo with *Pan and Syrinx* (*Metam.* I, 689-712). Annibale has chosen the moment when the god Pan, thinking he has caught the nymph Syrinx in his arms, finds instead that he has succeeded only in grasping the marsh reeds into which she has been transformed so as to escape his embrace. Ovid goes on to tell how from these reeds the god fashioned the Pan-pipe, or syrinx, as it was called in memory of the nymph. Instead of the usual putto reclining upon the medallion there appears here an infant satyr, whose goat-legs echo those of Pan.

In keeping with the system of paired medallions, the allegorical sense of the fable may be expected to agree closely with that of the corresponding scene of *Orpheus and Eurydice*. The *Ovidius moralizatus* offers the following exposition: "The nymph [Syrinx] may signify the sinful and stubborn soul, which despises the love of the shepherd god, that is Christ, and turns to the rivers, that is, to worldly pleasures. But these finally change her into a reed, that is, into an empty and weak person."[70] Is it conceivable that in one medallion Pan can signify the lower nature of man subjugated by divine love and in another the love of Christ for a human soul? It *is* conceivable only if we bear in mind a fundamental principle of allegory, namely, that meanings are not fixed in an absolute way, but that it is context that determines which of several meanings shall apply in a given instance. Thus it is that Pan overpowered by Cupid takes on unfavorable significance because he offers a parallel to Marsyas punished by Apollo. Contrariwise it is by analogy to Orpheus that Pan frustrated in his pursuit of Syrinx denotes heavenly love thwarted by human frailty. Another factor linking the two subjects is the musical symbolism implicit in each. Eurydice, who will not heed the celestial strains of the lyre, is comparable to Syrinx, transformed by her worldliness into the vain and empty reed-pipe—the *fistula diaboli*, as it is called in the *Moralized Ovid*.[71]

EUROPA AND THE BULL (FIG. 53)

The last of the medallions over the inner wall represents the *Rape of Europa* (*Metam.* II, 846-875). Her garments fluttering gracefully behind her, Europa is borne through the sea by the bull and grasps his horns with both hands as she looks back to the shore.

esting that Rubens' interpretation of the fable should agree with that of the moralized Ovid: in his painting in the Prado it is not Orpheus but Eurydice who looks back.

[70] F. Ghisalberti, "L' 'Ovidius Moralizatus' di Pierre Bersuire," *Studi Romanzi*, XXIII, 1933, p. 106. Cf. also Waleys, *op.cit.*, fol. 25.
[71] Waleys, *op.cit.*, fol. 25.

The beautiful allegory in the *Moralized Ovid*[72] relates that Jupiter is Christ, who, out of his love for the human soul (Europa), has descended to earth, his incarnation being symbolized by the bull, the animal of sacrifice. Europa, clinging fast to him, is carried from the shores of this world through the sea of penitence to the everlasting bliss of Paradise. The analogy to the *Rape of Orithyia* (Fig. 49), both in the underlying allegory and in Carracci's pictorial imagery, is a striking one, and serves to reinforce the fundamental unity of the series of medallions.

It was suggested by Tietze that this subject might have been modeled after an antique statuary group such as the *Nike Sacrificing a Bull* in the Vatican Museum.[73] The resemblance between the bull in the fresco and that in the marble group is certainly very marked; perhaps Annibale intended in this way to allude to the sacrificial motive of his subject. The attitude of Europa, like that of Orithyia, may remind us once again of Michelangelo's marble tondo, where the infant Christ appears in a similar posture.

HERO AND LEANDER (FIG. 54)

Leander is seen swimming in the Hellespont, while ahead of him Cupid has already reached the shore of Sestus and is clambering up the bank. Hero, holding a lamp, looks down from her tower as her lover draws near. Bellori, who almost invariably misses the sense of these roundels, offers a typically disapproving interpretation: "Leander, who under the guidance of Love is submerged in the water, shows forth the sea of troubles and misfortunes of that god's followers."[74]

Although the story of Hero and Leander does not appear in the *Metamorphoses*, it is nevertheless included in certain versions of the *Moralized Ovid* (no doubt because the poet speaks of the two lovers in the *Heroides*, XVIII-XIX). A characteristic allegory is that of Pierre Bersuire (Berchorius), who identifies Leander as mankind traversing the sea of this mortal life. Hero signifies divine wisdom, and her torch the light of faith and doctrine which guides mankind to Paradise.[75] The tragic conclusion of the story is simply ignored. It is obvious that this subject was selected in order to serve as a complement to the *Rape of Europa*. In both roundels the human soul is enabled, through the agency of divine love, to cross the perilous sea and reach the celestial haven.

It was probably Fulvio Orsini's idea that the composition should be made to resemble coins of Sestus and Abydos on which this subject is represented.[76] In the

[72] Ghisalberti, *op.cit.*, p. 109; Waleys, *op.cit.*, fol. 33.

[73] Tietze, p. 83. For the group in question see W. Amelung, *Die Sculpturen des Vaticanischen Museums*, II, Berlin, 1908, pp. 339 f., no. 130, pl. 33.

[74] Bellori, *Argomento* (in Malvasia, *Felsina*, I, p. 441).

[75] Ghisalberti, *op.cit.*, p. 117. See also De

Boer (ed.), "Ovide moralisé," *Verhandelingen*, XXI, 1920, pp. 78 ff.

[76] See particularly a bronze coin of Septimius Severus from Abydos, which shows Leander swimming at the lower left and Hero with her torch at the top of a round tower (W. Wroth, *British Museum, Catalogue of Greek Coins of Troas, Aeolis, and Lesbos*, London, 1894, p. 7, pl. III, 2). The connection

attitude of Cupid climbing up the bank there is an amusing reminiscence of the *grimpeur* in Michelangelo's *Battle of Cascina*; the figure in question was copied in two prints by Marcantonio Raimondi (B. 487 and 488).

Nowhere in his descriptions of the Gallery does Bellori name the subjects of the four medallions at the ends of the vault. The omission is understandable, to be sure, for less than half of their surface is visible. Since it was part of Annibale's intention to create the illusion of an accidental overlapping we are permitted to glimpse only fragmentary compositions, and identification is thus made extremely difficult. Some aid is furnished by "Lucius Philarchaeus," who in the eighteenth century wrote a descriptive text to accompany Cesio's engravings and attempted to identify these enigmatic scenes.[77]

JASON AND THE GOLDEN FLEECE (FIG. 56)

One of the partly hidden roundels presents little difficulty. It is the one on the right of *Polyphemus and Galatea*, which plainly represents Jason taking the Golden Fleece from the tree, while the guardian dragon lies helpless at its foot (*Metam.* VII, 149-158). The scene should be compared to the Carracci fresco of the same subject in the Palazzo Fava,[78] from which Annibale has virtually copied the central episode. According to the (easily predictable) allegory offered by the *Moralized Ovid*, Jason denotes the Saviour who delivers mankind (the Golden Fleece) from the clutches of the devil (the dragon).[79] The fable is thus similar in all essential respects to that of *Orpheus and Eurydice*.

SCENE OF ABDUCTION (FIG. 55)

The counterpart to this subject—on the other side of *Polyphemus and Galatea*—shows a man wearing helmet and body armor who is carrying a girl in his arms. It is difficult to know precisely which mythological episode is intended here.[80] It is obviously a scene of abduction, and as such must admit of the same interpretation as the other subjects of this sort. We shall not be far from the mark if we regard this scene as yet another allegory of Christ delivering the human soul from bondage. There is no need to stress the fact that such a meaning is entirely in harmony with the adjacent medallions, the *Rape of Europa* and *Jason and the Golden Fleece*.

At the opposite end of the Gallery two roundels are similarly concealed in part by the frame of *Polyphemus and Acis*:

was noted by Tietze, pp. 84 f.

[77] *Ædium Farnesiarum Tabulae ab Annibale Caraccio depictae a Carolo Caesio aeri insculptae atque a Lucio Philarchaeo explicationibus illustratae*, Rome, 1753.

[78] S. Ostrow, "Note sugli affreschi con 'Storie di Giasone' in Palazzo Fava," *Arte antica e moderna*, no. 9, 1960, p. 71, pl. 24 c.

[79] Waleys, *op.cit.*, fol. 58 v.

[80] Lucius Philarchaeus proposes "Theseus abducting Hippolyta, or Helen" (*Ædium Farnesiarum Tabulae*, pp. XLVII f.), but these episodes are too obscure and would therefore be out of place in this cycle.

THE JUDGMENT OF PARIS (FIG. 57)

The medallion on the left side shows a seated youth, nude except for a mantle that covers his back; his right arm is extended, and a shepherd's crook rests against his shoulder. This is beyond doubt the shepherd Paris in the very act of awarding the golden apple to Venus;[81] the similarity to the figure of Paris in Marcantonio's famous engraving (B. 245) is too striking to be overlooked.

Although Ovid makes no mention of the Judgment of Paris in the *Metamorphoses*, the tale proved too susceptible to edifying exposition to be omitted from the *Moralized Ovid*. Of the several meanings that have attached themselves to the fable most emphasize the human weakness shown by Paris in slighting the two worthy goddesses and giving the prize to Venus. This fallibility is neatly expressed in the following couplet from the *Ovide moralisé*:

> *Par vain delit, qui l'amusa,*
> *Le mal prist, le bien refusa.*[82]

PAN AND APOLLO (FIG. 58)

The complementary roundel also represents a seated figure, whose goat-legs show him to be a satyr. His arm is raised, and he wears a cape or mantle. Behind him stands a youthful figure (is it a boy or a girl?) with a shepherd's crook. Here, I believe, we are to see Pan playing the reed-pipe in his contest with Apollo, as Ovid relates in the eleventh book of the *Metamorphoses* (153 ff.). The attitude of the figure is consistent with this interpretation; and the shepherd's crook serves to designate him as *ovium custos*. The youthful figure at his side would appear to be either Daphnis, to whom Pan taught music,[83] or perhaps one of the nymphs charmed by the sound of his pipe.[84] If further confirmation is needed, it may be found in Annibale's drawing of the *Judgment of Midas* (Ellesmere Collection),[85] where the seated figure of Pan, wearing a mantle and holding the syrinx, is remarkably similar. The hidden portion of the roundel may be understood to contain Apollo with his lyre, and perhaps also King Midas who, for preferring the music of Pan, was rewarded with ass's ears.

The *Moralized Ovid* explains that the fable is directed "against those rude and bestial persons who favor the singing of the rustic Pan over that of the heavenly Apollo: . . . the sayings and deeds of bestial men give them more pleasure than the acts of saints and religious men."[86] It now becomes clear that these two subjects form

---

[81] This is also suggested by Lucius Philarchaeus (*op.cit.*, p. XLVII).

[82] De Boer (ed.), "Ovide moralisé," *Verhandelingen*, XXXVII, 1936, p. 178. See also Waleys, *op.cit.*, fols. 88 v., 89 r.

[83] Servius on Virgil's *Eclogue* V, 20.

[84] Ovid, *Metam.* XI, 153 ff.

[85] P. A. Tomory, *The Ellesmere Collection of Old Master Drawings*, Leicester, 1954, p. 22, no. 51; Mahon, *Disegni*, pp. 96 f., no. 127.

The drawing was used by Domenichino for one of his frescoes in the Villa Aldobrandini at Frascati.

[86] Waleys, *op.cit.*, fol. 86: "Applica hec contra rudes et bestiales qui approbant plus canticum panos ruricole quam apollinis celicolle: . . . magis eis placent illa que dicunt et faciunt homines bestiales quam que agunt sancti et spirituales homines."

a pair having to do with mistaken judgments. The all-too-human error of Paris, in deciding for Venus and the love of Helen, is to be compared to the stupidity of Midas, who found Pan's pipes superior to Apollo's lyre. We must also take note of the way in which these "fragmentary" roundels are linked to the main series of medallions along the sides of the vault. That series begins, as we recall, with *Apollo flaying Marsyas*, the theme of which is plainly related to the adjoining *Contest of Pan and Apollo*. Similarly, the opposite medallion of *Cupid overcoming Pan* signifies the victory of divine love over sensual passions, and may therefore be said to "correct" the error made by Paris.

The frieze thus serves as an introduction to the cycle, setting forth the theme of the Twin Loves. Whereas the painted panels exemplify in a direct way the conquests of Profane Love, the medallions illustrate in allegorical fashion the workings of Divine Love. The ox-skull adorned with a chaplet that appears above each medallion reinforces its spiritual meaning. For this motive (as Guillaume du Choul explains in his *Religion des anciens Romains*, Lyons, 1581, pp. 316-318) is a symbol of piety.

III. AGOSTINO'S FRESCOES

Closely allied in meaning to the medallions of the frieze are the two large *quadri riportati* executed by Agostino Carracci. They give the illusion of having been set in front of the frieze, the middle sections of which are as a result forever concealed from view. One of Agostino's frescoes poses a perplexing iconographical problem; this is the so-called *Galatea*, which will be treated below. The other represents the *Rape of Cephalus by Aurora* (*Metam.* VII, 694-713).

AURORA AND CEPHALUS (FIG. 59)

Descending on a cloud from the heights, the goddess of the dawn has succeeded in thrusting the reluctant youth into her golden chariot. Cephalus, who can think only of Procris, averts his head and raises his arms in a futile gesture of resistance as he attempts to escape from Aurora's embrace. His dog, meanwhile, looks up at him in puzzlement. Aurora is appropriately clad in rose-red garments. In her enamored state she is neglectful of her duty as precursor of Apollo, whose brilliant light is already visible at the horizon: the two white steeds, eager to begin the journey across the sky, stamp and rear impatiently; and an Amoretto with a basket of roses (emblems of the dawn's rays) looks round at his tardy mistress as if urging her to depart.[87] In the foreground Aurora's ancient husband Tithonus lies asleep, wrapped in a mantle of violet hue. The side of the chariot is adorned with a relief showing a seated female figure being crowned by putti and a Victory; this is perhaps to be connected with Homer's description of Aurora as "golden-throned."

The fresco contains several unusual passages. One is the stippled shading on the

---

[87] The two horses are specifically mentioned by Homer (*Odyssey* XXIII, 244 ff.). Cartari speaks both of these and of the baskets of red and yellow roses (*Imagini*, ed. of 1674, p. 51).

belly and forequarters of the nearer of the two horses. Especially interesting is the treatment of the fold of drapery that flutters above Aurora's legs: here Agostino seems to have made a number of little round depressions in the surface of the *intonaco*. This technique was perhaps suggested by Raphael's *Disputa*, the uppermost section of which is similarly dotted. The deep blue repaint which until recently covered much of the fresco has now been removed, so that the sky once more gives an impression of luminosity.

Calvesi, discussing the possible influence of prints on Agostino's composition, observes that the attitude of Aurora, as she reaches out to embrace Cephalus, may have been suggested by the amorous wife of Potiphar seeking to seduce Joseph in Marcantonio's engraving (B. 9).[88] The horses, with their diminutive heads and arbitrary proportions, have a distinctly Mannerist flavor: they may remind us, for example, of the elegant rearing horse in the *Conversion of St. Paul* (Vienna), attributed to Niccolò dell'Abbate and more recently to Parmigianino.[89]

Interesting analogies have been shown to exist[90] between Agostino's fresco and Gabriello Chiabrera's melodrama, *Il rapimento di Cefalo*, written to celebrate the marriage of Marie de' Medici to Henry IV in 1600.[91] It is a striking fact that both works allude to the disruption of the universal order by Aurora's passion for Cephalus. This indeed is the leading theme of Chiabrera's drama: Love's power is such that even the eternal rhythm of night and day is halted; only when the god causes Cephalus to return Aurora's love can the regular order of the cosmos be resumed. The author leaves no doubt that for Cephalus the choice lies between earthly and celestial love. It behooves him therefore to forsake the mortal Procris and to ascend with the goddess to immortality.[92]

So closely is this situation paralleled by Agostino's *Rape of Cephalus* that one might be tempted to conclude that the painter drew inspiration from Chiabrera's drama. An objection to this hypothesis arises from the fact that the two works are almost exactly contemporaneous: the melodrama, first published in 1600, was performed in October of that year; and Agostino's fresco was completed before July 1600. To explain how Agostino might have had knowledge of Chiabrera's text thus becomes difficult, though perhaps not impossible.[93] Before leaving the question of the supposed relation-

[88] Calvesi, in *Commentari*, VII, 1956, p. 270, fig. 10. Marcantonio's print, it should be added, copies Raphael's fresco of this subject in the Loggie. Calvesi's further suggestion, that the sleeping Tithonus derives from a figure in a print by Fantuzzi after Primaticcio (*ibid.*, fig. 11), is much less convincing. Agostino might have taken the pose from ancient sculpture (e.g., the "Dead Persian" in Naples), or from Annibale, who employs it, for instance, in his *Resurrection* of 1593 (Louvre). Cf. Wittkower, *Carracci Drawings*, p. 141, no. 323,

pl. 77.

[89] Cf. S. J. Freedberg, *Parmigianino, his Works in Painting*, Cambridge, Mass., 1950, pp. 76 f., 178 ff., fig. 65.

[90] I. Lavin, "Cephalus and Procris," *Journal of the Warburg and Courtauld Institutes*, XVII, 1954, pp. 278 ff.

[91] Ed. by A. Solerti, *Gli albori del melodramma*, Milan-Palermo-Naples, 1905, III, pp. 29 ff.

[92] Solerti, *op.cit.*, p. 43.

[93] Cf. Lavin, *op.cit.*, p. 283.

ship between Agostino and Chiabrera we must take note of a significant difference in the treatment of the fable. Unlike the drama, the painting contains no hint of a happy outcome. Cephalus' expression and gestures make it entirely evident that he will never yield to Aurora's seductive caresses.[94] This need not surprise us. For Agostino is simply adhering to Ovid's text, which specifies that the goddess abducted the youth against his will (*invitumque rapit*).

If we now attempt to interpret this scene within the context of the cycle, it becomes clear that Cephalus is a favored mortal who might, like Orithyia, be mystically abducted to celestial bliss;[95] but who chooses, like Eurydice and Syrinx, to cling instead to earthly delights. By rejecting the *amore celeste* he provokes the ire of the goddess and—though this is not illustrated—brings disaster and unhappiness upon himself. Even the tragic death of Procris only shows how fleeting and deceitful are the pleasures of this world.

The myth of Aurora and Cephalus was to figure in the memorial service held for Agostino Carracci in Bologna in 1603. Among the emblematic paintings composed for that occasion by members of the Carracci Academy was one by Lionello Spada representing the *Rape of Cephalus* (Fig. 280, no. 5, lower right). Aurora's abduction of the youthful hunter was chosen to symbolize Agostino's sudden departure from this world to a deserved place among the stars, a meaning reinforced by the motto *Sic virtus ad sydera rapit*.[96] It can scarcely be doubted that in selecting this subject Spada had in mind Agostino's fresco in the Farnese Gallery.

GLAUCUS AND SCYLLA (FIG. 60)

Opposite the *Aurora and Cephalus* stands the second fresco by Agostino, the subject of which has long been in doubt. The composition takes the form of a procession of sea deities advancing toward the right. The group is headed by a Triton, his body twisted in a vigorous contrapposto as he blows a shell-trumpet; close by an Amoretto covers his ears to shut out the blare, and a dolphin with open mouth spouts forth a stream of water. In the center a slender and graceful girl reclines upon the back of a sea monster who clasps both arms about her and turns his head as if in annoyance at the trumpeter. The girl makes no effort to respond to his embrace, but with an expression of indifference raises her arms, delicately holding in one hand a fluttering veil which the wind fills out behind her. She is followed by three Nereids riding upon dolphins, one of whom looks out at the observer and points to the girl. The gesture serves to underline the action of Cupid who, as he flies over the group, takes

---

[94] I cannot agree with Lavin (*ibid.*, p. 280) that Cephalus is "somewhat coy perhaps, but not really reluctant."

[95] The *Ovide moralisé* goes so far as to identify Aurora as the Virgin Mary (De Boer, ed., "Ovide moralisé," *Verhandelingen*, xxx, 1931, p. 100).

[96] *Il funerale d'Agostin Carraccio*, pp. 15-16.

The emblematic subjects were engraved by Guido Reni. The text is reprinted in Bellori (*Vite*, p. 126) and in Malvasia (*Felsina*, I, pp. 414 f.). Rubens represented *Aurora and Cephalus* in one of the sketches for the Torre de la Parada (London, Nat. Gall., wrongly identified as "Diana and Endymion").

aim at the maiden with bow and arrow. The composition is completed by several other Amoretti; two are in flight, carrying a torch and a bundle of arrows, and two are swimming in the water, where they act as escort for the two principals.

There has never been certainty as to what mythological subject is here represented. In the past the name most frequently given to the painting was "Galatea," no doubt because of its patent resemblance to Raphael's fresco of that title in the Villa Farnesina. The earliest reference to the work appears in the funeral oration delivered by Lucio Faberio during the commemorative service for Agostino in January 1603. In his eulogy of the artist Faberio urges his listeners to go and admire "the Diana and the Galatea" in the Farnese Gallery.[97] Faberio's knowledge of the Gallery is a little hazy. By "Diana" he means of course the fresco of *Aurora and Cephalus*, which he has evidently confused with *Diana and Endymion*. He is probably also wrong about the name "Galatea."

Nevertheless Faberio's words carried some weight, and by the time that Baglione wrote his *Lives* (1642) "Galatea" had become the accepted title.[98] Not long afterward, however, Bellori seems to have felt some doubts about its correctness. In his first account of the Farnese cycle (1657), he is plainly unable to make up his mind. "Galatea," he writes, "or perhaps Venus borne over the ocean by the sea god Cymothoë, is accompanied by the Graces on dolphins and by flying Cupids with a torch and arrows."[99] Later, in the *Vite* of 1672, Bellori decides firmly for Galatea, although he is somewhat disturbed by the absence of her customary shell-chariot.[100] Pietro Aquila, whose engravings of the Farnese Gallery were published in 1674, identified the scene as Venus riding upon Triton, thus reviving Bellori's first notion.[101] The same interpretation was adopted by Lucius Philarchaeus in his commentary on the Cesio engravings.[102]

Richard Förster rightly objected to the identification of the principal figure as Venus, remarking among other things that Venus would certainly not tolerate the caresses of so unlikely a lover as Triton. He proposed to see in the girl merely a sea nymph or, if a name were needed, Salacia embraced by Portunus.[103] Tietze went even further, maintaining that it was fruitless to speculate about the meaning of the scene because no specific subject had been intended; for him the fresco was simply a procession of anonymous sea deities, concocted of elements taken from Raphael's *Galatea*, and having no other purpose than to illustrate the power of love in the element of

[97] *Il funerale*, p. 40 (reprinted in Malvasia, *Felsina*, I, p. 431).

[98] Baglione, *Vite*, pp. 105, 107.

[99] *Argomento*, in Malvasia, *Felsina*, I, pp. 439, 441. Bellori seems to refer here to Claudian, *Epithalamium de Nuptiis Honorii Augusti*, ll. 128 ff. But Venus rides upon Triton: and Cymothoë is a Nereid pursued by Triton, not a sea god.

[100] *Vite*, p. 55. This interpretation is adopted by Félibien, *Entretiens*, 2nd ed., II, p. 68.

[101] *Galeriae Farnesianae Icones Romae in Aedibus Sereniss. Ducis Parmensis . . . a Petro Aquila delineatae incisae*, Rome, 1674, pl. 6.

[102] *Ædium Farnesiarum Tabulae*, p. XVII, pl. IX.

[103] R. Förster, *Farnesina-Studien*, Rostock, 1880, p. 53.

water.[104] This idea must be emphatically rejected. Everything that is known of the relationship between artist and writer in the preparation and execution of a fresco cycle makes it evident that in no circumstances would a painting of this size and prominence be treated as a merely decorative or anonymous composition. The exact subject, to be sure, may elude us, but this means only that our iconographical analysis is insufficient.

A moment's reflection will show that the scene cannot represent either Galatea or Venus. Not only does Galatea have her place elsewhere in the cycle, but the embrace of the sea creature rules out the unlikely possibility that she might reappear here. As for Venus, Förster has shown conclusively that she cannot be the figure in question. Salacia and Portunus, Cymothoë and Triton and the like may be dismissed as being mythologically unimportant or without narrative interest. In searching for the answer to this enigma we may best be guided by analogy. The fresco of *Aurora and Cephalus*, of which this is the pendant, indicates that the subject must come from Ovid's *Metamorphoses*, and that it must deal with unrequited love, preferably between a mortal and a deity. The only fable that conforms both to these requirements and to the marine setting of the picture is that of Glaucus and Scylla (*Metam.* XIII, 898-968; XIV, 1-74). Glaucus the fisherman had recently been transformed into a sea divinity when he beheld the maiden Scylla bathing *sine vestibus* in the water, and at once fell in love with her; despite his protestation that he was no monster or wild beast but a god, she scorned his advances and fled. But Scylla, like Cephalus, could not with impunity rebuff the love of a deity. When Glaucus in desperation applied to Circe to aid him in his suit, the sorceress (who herself loved Glaucus) took revenge by causing Scylla to be changed into a hideous monster. The analogy to *Aurora and Cephalus* is complete, save that the sexes of the principals are reversed. The moral is the same: those who are so devoted to worldly pleasures that they will not accept heavenly love forfeit eternal bliss and come to a miserable end.[105] In both pictures, moreover, we see only the failure of the mortal to respond to the divine embrace; the fatal consequences are not illustrated.

The story of Glaucus and Scylla is not unknown in sixteenth and seventeenth century art. A typical conception is that by Salvator Rosa,[106] who shows the two figures only, at the moment when Scylla is escaping from the grasp of her lover. In expanding the episode into a complex, multi-figured procession Agostino (or Annibale, since he was in charge of the work) undeniably took liberties with the text. There are several reasons for this elaboration of the basic narrative. The first is the shape of the picture itself, which demands a long horizontal composition. Whereas in the *Aurora*

[104] Tietze, pp. 76 f.

[105] The *Ovide moralisé* is even more explicit: Glaucus is the Saviour, and Scylla the Synagogue who will not heed his attempts to win her (De Boer, ed., "Ovide moralisé," *Verhandelingen*, XXXVII, pp. 475 ff., XLIII, pp. 16

ff.).

[106] T. Bodkin, "A Note on Salvator Rosa," *Burlington Magazine*, LVIII, 1931, pp. 91 ff., pls. I and II. Rosa represented the fable in an etching as well as in painting.

and Cephalus this requirement could easily be met by the inclusion of the chariot and horses, in the *Glaucus and Scylla* it was necessary to resort to additional figures in order to fill out the space. The second reason is that these supernumeraries all find some justification in the text of Ovid. (This is also true of Tithonus in the Aurora fresco, who strictly speaking ought not to be present at all.) Cupid, for instance, shoots an arrow at Scylla in an unsuccessful attempt to smite her with love for Glaucus; the Amorino with the torch has already given up trying to inflame her and is flying away. The three Nereids at the left are surely those sea nymphs to whom Scylla boasted of her rejected suitors (*Metam.* XIII, 735-737).

Far outweighing in importance any such literary references, however, are the formal borrowings from Raphael's *Galatea*. As has already been noted, it is precisely the obvious relationship between the two works that has tended to obscure the meaning of Agostino's fresco. Cupid with his bow and arrow is a virtual replica (but with the position of the legs reversed) of the leftmost putto in the group of three in Raphael's painting. Scylla's upraised arm and veil are plainly taken from the Nereid embraced by the Triton in the left foreground of the *Galatea*; the latter figure, in turn, is the prototype of the trumpeting Triton in *Glaucus and Scylla* (designed however by Annibale, not Agostino).[107] Likewise from Raphael is the putto riding on a dolphin just below Scylla, who closely resembles the boy guiding Galatea's shell-chariot. The Amoretto with the sheaf of arrows in the upper left corner is derived from the putto standing beside Vulcan in the *Wedding of Cupid and Psyche*, also in the Farnesina.

Certain elements in Agostino's fresco can be paralleled in sixteenth-century engravings. It is possible, for example, that both the pose of the nude Scylla and the flying figure of the Cupid with the torch were suggested by Agostino Veneziano's print of *Venus reclining on a Dolphin* (B. 239). The putto who covers his ears to shut out the sound of the conch blown by the Triton may remind us of a similar motive in one of the ovals of Correggio's Camera di San Paolo at Parma.[108] In addition to such borrowings, however, it is more than probable that Agostino turned for inspiration to antique sarcophagi, especially those decorated with a "sea-thiasus"—a frieze of Nereids and sea monsters. The type may be illustrated by a sarcophagus in the Vatican,[109] which contains several motives similar to those in the Glaucus fresco.

It is significant, finally, that the art of Annibale has left its impress on this fresco. The two Nereids at the left side are derived from the pair of nymphs who are seen, huddled together, in Annibale's painting of *Diana and Callisto*;[110] the same figures

---

[107] See Annibale's drawing for this figure (No. 83, Fig. 193).

[108] Panofsky, *The Iconography of Correggio's Camera di San Paolo*, fig. 18.

[109] A. Rumpf, *Die Meerwesen auf den antiken Sarkophagreliefs* (Die antiken Sarkophagreliefs, v, pt. 1), Berlin, 1939, pp. 63 f.,

no. 146, pl. 47. See also the Lateran sarcophagus (*ibid.*, p. 36, no. 91, pl. 36), and the sarcophagus in Palazzo Giustiniani (*ibid.*, p. 53, no. 126, pl. 44).

[110] *Burlington Magazine*, CII, 1960, p. 129, fig. 39.

were copied even more literally by Agostino in his print of 1599, *Omnia vincit Amor* (Fig. 276).

Since the publication of Tietze's fundamental study of the Gallery, it has been customary to regard Agostino's two frescoes as being grouped with the central picture of *Bacchus and Ariadne* to form a set of three demonstrating the universal sovereignty of Eros. For it was Tietze's idea that the Bacchic procession represented the power of Love on earth, the *Aurora and Cephalus* his power in the air, and the so-called *Galatea* his power in the water. This explanation will no longer suffice. In the first place it does not take account of the complexity of the program, which is concerned with much more than the power of love. Furthermore the Bacchic scene is meant to offer a contrast, not a parallel, to the other two subjects. And lastly, it must be evident that if Annibale had thought of these three frescoes as making a coherent group he would not have assigned two of them to his brother, thereby sacrificing stylistic unity.

IV. THE LOVE OF POLYPHEMUS

One of the most striking features of the Gallery is the effect produced by the two monumental paintings at the ends of the vault, which seem, by their size and force, to dominate the entire length of the room (Figs. 61-62). They have as their subject the myth of Polyphemus and Galatea (*Metam.* XIII, 738-897). In Ovid's poem the tale is told by Galatea herself to the maiden Scylla, whose encounter with Glaucus occupies, as we have seen, a similar place in the middle of the longitudinal frieze.

POLYPHEMUS AND GALATEA (FIG. 63)

The first scene, at the south end, represents *Polyphemus wooing Galatea*. The nude Cyclops is seated on the rocky promontory described by the poet. Twisting his powerful frame he supports himself on his elbow and rests one leg against his staff. As he lifts his mouth from the reed-pipe he gazes amorously at Galatea with his single eye and begins to sing to her of his love. The soft foliage overhead makes an appropriate pastoral setting for the deceptive sweetness of Polyphemus' serenade. The fresco does not correspond to Ovid's text in all respects: there is, for example, no sign of Acis, although Ovid writes that Galatea lay in her lover's arms while she listened to the giant's song. It is evident that for the group at the right side Annibale has followed instead the description of Philostratus (*Imagines* II, 18),[111] where there is no mention of Acis: "The nymph sports on the peaceful sea, driving a team of four dolphins yoked together and working in harmony [only one is visible here]; and maiden-daughters of Triton, Galatea's servants, guide them, curbing them if they try to do anything mischievous or contrary to the rein. She holds over her head against the wind a light scarf of sea-purple to provide a shade for herself and a sail for her chariot . . . ; her hair is not tossed by the breeze, for it is

---

[111] This was pointed out by Förster, *Farnesina-Studien*, pp. 51 f.

so moist that it is proof against the wind."[112] Galatea, unmoved by Polyphemus' music, looks coolly at her monstrous suitor, but the Nereid beside her stares at him in open-mouthed admiration, "expressing," as Bellori puts it, "her pleasure at his song."[113]

In the attitude of Polyphemus Annibale acknowledges the formative effect upon his monumental style of both Michelangelo and antique sculpture. The upper part of the figure is adapted from the *ignudo* seated on the right above the Libyan Sibyl; the torso and legs, however, are modeled after the *Laocoön*. Such adaptations are never arbitrary or without significance. The spiritual unrest of the Sistine youth and the physical torment of *Laocoön* have appropriately been combined to create an image of passionate yearning and frustration. The figure of Galatea, who leans indolently against her companion and raises her left hand to her shoulder, may contain a reminiscence of Michelangelo's *Aurora* in the Medici Chapel. The similarity is particularly marked in the turn of the head and in the graceful action of the hand that is lifted to grasp the drapery; but even Galatea's cap-like coiffure recalls in some respects the headdress worn by Aurora.[114]

POLYPHEMUS AND ACIS (FIG. 64)

In the second painting, *Polyphemus slaying Acis*, Annibale follows the text of Ovid closely. The giant, who before had been all tenderness and amorous desire, is now transformed by jealous rage and despair. Seizing a mass of rock and balancing himself on one foot, he is on the point of hurling it at the fleeing Acis, whose fate is plainly inescapable; Galatea, further away, is saved by throwing herself into the sea. This is one of the most effective paintings of the entire cycle: the towering form of the Cyclops, seen at the crucial moment of equilibrium before his mighty energy is unleashed, is an unforgettable image of pent-up rage and murderous force. In the distance the fiery eruption of Aetna (also mentioned by Ovid) makes a fitting accompaniment to the giant's burning fury.

To Bellori the figure of Polyphemus seemed yet more admirable because it conformed to the scientific observations on movement set down by Leonardo da Vinci in his *Trattato della Pittura*. The first publication of the treatise was that of Du Fresne in 1651;[115] it was this edition that Bellori had before him when he wrote the following comment:[116]

But in addition to the grand manner Annibale has here left us an example of force-

---

[112] Philostratus, *Imagines* II, 18 (Cyclops), transl. by A. Fairbanks, Loeb Classical Library.

[113] *Vite*, p. 59.

[114] There is a copy of *Polyphemus and Galatea*, in tempera on tile, in the collection of the Earl of Leicester (reproduced in *Catalogue of an Exhibition of Italian Art of the Seventeenth Century, Burlington Fine Arts Club*, London, 1925, p. 21, no. 14, pl. II).

[115] *Trattato della Pittura di Lionardo da Vinci, novamente dato in luce con la vita dell'istesso autore, scritta da Rafaelle du Fresne . . . ,* Paris, 1651.

[116] *Vite*, p. 60.

ful motion as described by Leonardo da Vinci, and several times repeated, in his *Treatise on Painting*, when he speaks of the use of force to deliver a great blow: "When a man prepares to make a forceful motion, he bends and twists as much as he can in the direction contrary to that where he wishes the blow to fall, and thus he prepares a force as great as is possible for him."[117] And in the chapter on movement: "If someone is to throw spears or rocks, having turned his feet toward the target, he twists and bends and moves himself from there to the opposite side, where, when he gathers his strength, he returns with speed and ease to the point where he lets the weight leave his hands."[118] Thus Polyphemus, by twisting and bending backward with his arms, but with one foot forward, gathers strength and prepares to throw; the right leg is placed on the ground so as to sustain the heavy weight, and the left leg, extended in the opposite direction to that of the arms, is bent at the knee. And this he does in order to center his weight above the foot which rests on the ground; for, as Leonardo teaches, without bending in this way he would neither be able to use his strength nor to throw.[119]

Manuscript copies of Leonardo's treatise were being circulated during the sixteenth century, and Annibale might well have known passages from it such as those cited by Bellori. According to an anecdote told by Félibien, Carracci regretted that he had not read Leonardo's precepts on painting when he was young, declaring that they would have saved him twenty years' work.[120]

Bellori says of the Polyphemus episodes that they demonstrate the power of love to subdue even the most savage breasts.[121] This explanation is obviously inadequate, if only because Polyphemus, far from being subdued, is shortly aroused by jealousy to a state of uncontrollable fury. A more satisfactory interpretation can perhaps be arrived at by considering the relationship of these two subjects to the frescoes of *Aurora and Cephalus* and *Glaucus and Scylla*, of which the underlying theme is the rejection of divine love and the dangers inherent therein. It will be perceived at once that the story of Polyphemus and Galatea presents a certain similarity to these myths: through her refusal of the Cyclops' proffered love, Galatea incurs his wrath and sees her beloved Acis slain. But there is a significant point of difference. For Polyphemus, unlike Aurora and Glaucus, is not a god but a wicked monster, the personification of impiety and brutish appetites. He despises the gods: Galatea calls him *magni cum dis contemptor Olympi* (*Metam.* XIII, 761), and he himself boasts of his scorn for Jupiter (*ibid.*, 857). In the *Ovide moralisé* we find him identified, naturally enough, as the devil.[122] Even his music is reprehensible, for he plays upon

---

[117] Bellori here quotes from the *Trattato*, p. 66, cap. CCXXXIII. I have availed myself of the English translation by A. Philip McMahon, *Treatise on Painting by Leonardo da Vinci*, Princeton, 1956, I, p. 140, no. 368.

[118] Quoted from the *Trattato*, pp. 50 f., cap. CLXXXII.

[119] Cf. *Trattato*, p. 75, cap. CCLXII.

[120] Félibien, *Entretiens*, 2nd ed., I, p. 515.

[121] *Argomento*, in Malvasia, *Felsina*, I, p. 441; *Vite*, p. 65.

[122] De Boer (ed.), "Ovide moralisé," *Verhandelingen*, XXXVII, pp. 467 ff.

the pan-pipe, the instrument of sensual and lustful natures. (It is significant that Pan appears in one of the medallions beside the picture of *Polyphemus and Acis*) The love of the Cyclops, then, is neither divine nor human, but bestial.

This reading of the Polyphemus scenes finds corroboration in the two little pictures which are placed above them so as to form a transition to the paintings in the center of the vault. Each has a green frame adorned with golden shells and ram's heads.

GANYMEDE AND THE EAGLE (FIG. 68)

Over the fresco of *Polyphemus and Acis* is the *Rape of Ganymede* (*Metam.* x, 155-161). Because of his love for Ganymede, Jupiter has assumed the form of an eagle. Spreading its powerful wings and fastening its talons around the youth's legs (which are protected from injury by a fold of drapery) the great bird soars upward with its burden. Ganymede, whose body is extended diagonally across the picture, places his arm around the eagle's neck and looks intently into its eyes.

The Rape of Ganymede has a long history as a symbol of celestial ravishment.[123] There can be no doubt that in this setting Ganymede denotes the human soul abducted by divine love. Inevitably there comes to mind the beautiful drawing of Ganymede by Michelangelo, now known to us only through copies; Annibale was certainly familiar with the composition, for Fulvio Orsini owned a copy by Daniele da Volterra after Michelangelo's drawing.[124] But the differences between the two conceptions are more revealing than the similarities. Panofsky has said of Michelangelo's design that it shows Ganymede "in a state of trance without a will or thought of his own, reduced to passive immobility by the iron grip of the gigantic eagle, the posture of his arms suggesting the attitude of an unconscious person or a corpse."[125] Carracci's figure, on the other hand, does not play a merely passive role, but a willing and cooperative one, as is made clear by his embrace of the eagle and by the steadfast gaze with which his eyes are fixed upon its face. Both the gesture of the youth and his relationship to the eagle may have been suggested to Annibale by the sculptural group of *Ganymede and the Eagle*, now in Naples, which formerly occupied one of the niches in the Farnese Gallery itself (cf. Fig. 33).

This example of celestial love, in which the human soul enters willingly into spiritual union with its creator, stands in sharp contrast to the brutish concupiscence of Polyphemus, who impiously refuses to acknowledge a higher love, but desires only to satisfy his lust.

To the Farnese family Ganymede and the eagle carried still another connotation,

[123] For the various meanings that have been applied to the myth see Panofsky, *Studies in Iconology*, pp. 212 ff. Among the emblem books see especially Alciati, *Emblematum liber*, Embl. iv; and A. Bocchi, *Symbolicarum quaestionum libri quinque*, Bologna, 1574, Symb. LXXVIII and LXXIX.

[124] Nolhac, "Les collections d'antiquités,"

Mélanges, iv, 1884, p. 178, no. 97: "Disegno senza cornice, col ratto di Ganimede rapito, in f°, di mano di Danielle, copiato da Michel°." The best replica of the Ganymede drawing is in Windsor (Popham and Wilde, *The Italian Drawings of the XV and XVI Centuries at Windsor Castle*, p. 265, no. 457, fig. 103).

[125] Panofsky, *op.cit.*, p. 216.

which we may be sure was not overlooked here. A medal issued in the time of Pope Paul III shows Ganymede watering the Farnese lilies while resting his hand against Jove's eagle. The inscription above, which contains a pun on the name Farnese, reads: ΦΕΡΝΗ ΖΗΝΟΣ (the dowry of Zeus); below is written ΕΥΡΑΙΝΕΙ (he waters well). The reference is to the generosity of the Pope in granting to his son Pier Luigi the Duchies of Parma and Piacenza in 1545.[126]

APOLLO AND HYACINTHUS (FIG. 67)

The companion picture, placed above the scene of *Polyphemus and Galatea* at the other extremity of the Gallery, represents Apollo and Hyacinthus flying heavenward after the fatal incident described by Ovid (*Metam.* x, 162-219). Apollo, carrying the lyre in his right hand, grasps Hyacinthus by the wrist to bear him aloft; the youth is seen from the back, with his head turned to look at Apollo, and he holds in his hand the flower which marks his transformation.

The myth of Hyacinthus forms the logical counterpart to that of Ganymede, which it immediately follows in the *Metamorphoses*. It is true that in the poem Apollo does not abduct Hyacinthus; Ovid says only that the god would have set him in the sky if fate had not prevented it:

Te quoque, Amyclide, posuisset in aethere Phoebus,
tristia si spatium ponendi fata dedissent. (*Metam.* x, 162 f.)

But this does not affect the allegorical meaning of the subject. For Hyacinthus, according to the *Moralized Ovid*, was changed by Apollo into a celestial flower.[127] In the present context, therefore, the scene carries the same significance as the *Rape of Ganymede*; Hyacinthus is likewise the beloved human soul transported to heaven. This is borne out by the formal similarity of the two paintings. The attitude of Hyacinthus, with one arm raised and the other grasping a fold of drapery, virtually duplicates (though in reverse) that of Ganymede; each youth, moreover, turns his head in order to look at his abductor. Equally significant is the fact that Apollo carries the lyre (cf. *Metam.* x, 205). For the sublime harmony of this instrument, in juxtaposition to the earthly music of Polyphemus' reed-pipe, serves to emphasize once more the contrast between divine love and carnal desire.

As might be expected, this fresco also contains a cryptic allusion to the Farnese. For Ovid describes the flower that sprang up from Hyacinthus' blood as taking the form of the lily (*Metam.* x, 212).

V. THE TRIUMPH OF DIVINE LOVE

The program reaches its climax with the three *quadri riportati* which occupy the center of the vault. These are the *Triumph of Bacchus and Ariadne*—the largest paint-

---

[126] The medal is by Alessandro Cesati, called Il Grechetto. See G. F. Hill, *The Gustave Dreyfus Collection, Renaissance Medals*, Ox-ford, 1931, p. 175, no. 366, pl. LXXXV.

[127] Waleys, *op.cit.*, fol. 82: "ipsum phebus in celestem floram mutavit."

ing of the cycle—and the two octagonal frescoes on either side representing *Pan and Diana* and *Paris and Mercury*. The gilt frames of the two latter pictures are unusually ornate. At each corner sits a sphinx with a tall basket of fruit on her head, and between the sphinxes at top and bottom is a cartouche formed of the aegis of Athena and crossed cornucopias.

PAN AND DIANA (FIG. 65)

The episode illustrated here has its origin in Virgil, *Georgics* III, 391-393: " 'Twas with gift of such snowy wool, if we may trust the tale, that Pan, Arcadia's god, charmed and beguiled thee, O Moon, calling thee to the depths of the woods; nor didst thou scorn his call."[128] Standing beside a pine tree in which he has hung his reed-pipe, the goat-legged god lifts up a mass of white wool in his right hand. A goatskin mantle is flung over one shoulder and his left hand holds the shepherd's crook. A wreath of bristling pine branches encircles his head, recalling Ovid's description: "pinuque caput praecinctus acuta" (*Metam.* I, 699). There is another literary allusion in the pan-pipe suspended from a branch of the tree, which surely echoes a line of Virgil's seventh *Eclogue*: "Hic arguta sacra pendebit fistula pinu" (Here from the sacred pine shall my shrill reed-pipe hang). The goat at Pan's side looks up at his master affectionately. Diana, recognizable by the lunar crescent in her hair and by the bow which she carries, flies down from heaven, her garments fluttering behind her. Seeing the gleaming wool that Pan offers to her, she smiles with pleasure and makes a gesture of surprise. Calvesi has remarked that the attitude of Pan is strikingly similar to that of the standing youth in Marcantonio's engraving, the *Old Man and the Man with the Anchor* (B. 367).[129] The resemblance is particularly close in the treatment of the arms and back.

Pan in the act of offering the wool to the moon-goddess was represented by Jacopo Zucchi in the ceiling fresco of the Palazzo Ruspoli;[130] and he also found a place in the frescoes painted by Taddeo Zuccari in the bedroom of Cardinal Alessandro Farnese at Caprarola. For the latter we have Annibal Caro's letter to the artist, specifying how the subject is to be represented: "The figure of Pan is very well known. Put a syrinx at his neck, and let him hold up with both hands a skein of white wool toward the moon, with which they say he won her love."[131]

MERCURY AND PARIS (FIG. 66)

In the corresponding panel, on the right of *Bacchus and Ariadne*, Mercury delivers the golden apple to Paris. This is the moment preceding the Judgment of Paris, when, as Apuleius describes in the *Golden Ass* (x, 30), the three goddesses have not yet appeared on the scene. The herald of the gods, his body seen at a foreshortened angle that is worthy of Tintoretto, swoops down head first to present the golden prize to

[128] Transl. by H. R. Fairclough, Loeb Classical Library.

[129] M. Calvesi, in *Commentari*, VII, 1956, p. 274, fig. 26.

[130] Saxl, *Antike Götter in der Spätrenaissance*, p. 25, pl. II.

[131] Caro, *Lettere familiari*, II, p. 347.

Paris; in his other hand he holds a trumpet. The shepherd, who is seated on a rock at the right side grasping his staff, reaches out to take the apple of Discord. In front of him a truculent dog raises his head to look at Mercury as the god makes his unexpected appearance.

The fact that Mercury holds a trumpet rather than his usual attribute, the caduceus, recalls Raphael's fresco in the Villa Farnesina, where the god likewise carries a trumpet as he announces the wedding of Cupid and Psyche. Annibale's purpose in introducing this martial instrument, Bellori suggests, was "to indicate that the golden apple would be a cause of war, not peace."[132] The attitude of the dog, seated and with head sharply upturned, is reminiscent of the animal in the antique marble group of *Ganymede and the Eagle* in the Vatican Museum.

The two octagonal frescoes are complementary in every sense. Each represents a heavenly being descending toward an earthly one (a shepherd in each instance) who is accompanied by an animal. The compositional structure of each painting is virtually duplicated in the other, but in the opposite sense, so that the tree on the left in *Pan and Diana* is echoed in the tree on the right in *Paris and Mercury*, and so forth. But it is only gradually that the observer perceives how numerous are the subtle contrasts and variations that Annibale has introduced into this pair of frescoes. There is, for example, the contrast between male and female in the heavenly apparitions, and between human and half-human in the earthly figures. Diana, fully clad, flies in a composed, upright position, whereas Mercury, who is nude except for his mantle, plunges down head foremost at a startling and precipitous angle. Pan is standing and holds the shepherd's *pedum* with the crook uppermost; Paris, who holds the staff upside down, is seated, and the position of his arms is reversed. The essential action of each picture is similarly inverted in the other: Pan's upward gesture as he offers the wool to Diana is contrasted to the downward motion with which Mercury delivers the apple to Paris. The variations extend even to the animals. The goat (like Pan himself) is standing; he takes a position close to the satyr god and looks at him. The dog, on the other hand, though he follows the example of Paris in sitting down, is at some distance from him, and gazes not at his master but at Mercury.

THE TRIUMPH OF BACCHUS AND ARIADNE (FIG. 69)

This is the grandest composition of the Farnese ceiling and as such makes a fitting culmination of the cycle. Since Bellori's description of the painting would be hard to surpass I quote it here:

> Bacchus, returning victorious from India, discovered Ariadne abandoned by Theseus, and being smitten by her beauty chose her as his bride; the painting invites us to behold her now in her triumphal marriage [Fig. 70]. Bacchus, wearing a wreath of vine leaves, is seated in a golden chariot as victor over the Indians;

[132] Bellori, *Vite*, p. 53.

in his lowered right hand he grasps the thyrsus after the manner of a scepter, and raises his left so as to display some ripe red grapes. But so delicate and soft is he that he seems barely able to hold up his arm, and beneath it there appears the head of a faun who is supporting it. His splendid chariot opens in the form of an oval throne and is so contrived that it conceals from view no part of the beautiful nude body, which is girt with an Hyrcanian skin from the left shoulder to the opposite side, knotted across the breast and with the tiger's head marking the right shoulder. The beauty of the figure is enhanced by the variety of the pose. For though Bacchus turns his face and torso into a frontal position the thigh remains in profile; one knee is raised and the other lowered, the foot resting on the tongue of the golden car, on which are carved goats and putti among vine branches. On the left side of Bacchus and a little in front is Ariadne, riding in her silver car; she too sits upright, revealing her nude shoulder and turning her face a little toward us, no longer tearful and sad because of Theseus's infidelity, but·serene and happy in the company of her celestial lover. She places her right hand on her left knee, which is raised very sharply, and infuses so much majesty and grace into the act that she seems uplifted in herself and in her divinity; for divine she is shown to be both by her garment of azure color and by Amor, who holds above her head the crown of stars, shining resplendent in heaven for her sake. Bacchus' chariot is drawn by tigers fastened to its yoke: an infant faun, turning his back, places one arm on a tiger's back and with the other hand lifts the reins from its neck. Ariadne's car is pulled along by unbridled goats; a boy has been knocked down by them and protects himself with his hand, while further back another boy is pulling at the goats' hair in order to restrain them.

Riding upon an ass at the head of the procession [Fig. 71] is Silenus, crowned with ivy: he can be recognized by his face, his bald pate and his paunch, and by his drunken and unsteady behavior; the cup dangles from his right hand, and he rests his elbow on the shoulder of a faun, who is blowing a horn with a raucous sound. This fellow is entirely nude, with only an animal's skin tied across his chest, and he performs several actions at once: with his left hand he supports Silenus from behind while at the same time he twists himself round to the right to blow with puffed cheeks into the horn that is raised in his right hand; in all he makes a graceful and spirited figure. Just in front of him is another younger faun who supports Silenus by putting his shoulder under the old man's thigh and clasping his leg. Admirable as is Annibale's mind in devising the appropriate form for each person, in this figure he has surpassed himself by representing a lively and sturdy lad in the first vigor of adolescence. Nor is the drunken old tutor neglected on the other side, for here he leans heavily against a young man's shoulder and wraps his arm about his neck. All that is visible of this fellow is his face as it emerges from Silenus' encircling arm, the rest of his body being concealed—except that his feet can be made out in their proper place behind the nearer figures. In front a satyr guides the ass and carries a wineskin on his shoulder, as if ready to refill Silenus' cup and keep him happy; he turns round at the braying of the ass, which he leads by a strand of verdant ivy tied about its neck. The figure is partly cut off by the edge of the picture. Between Silenus and the satyr is a Bacchante carrying on her head the sacred basket of Bacchus, from which emerges a calf's hoof as a sign of the punishment of Pentheus; she turns her face to us, showing little more than her shoulder and bare arm as she holds the mystic basket. Behind her there is to be seen only the profile of a youth blowing a double flute, who is attuning himself to the sound and voices of the Bacchic chorus. But reclining in the extreme foreground is a half-nude woman, supporting herself with her right arm [*sic*] against a mound and with her head resting on her hand; as if roused from sleep by the raucous din she turns her face toward Silenus, who returns her gaze as he draws near. This is the Common and Earthly Venus [*Venere vulgare, e terrena*], and standing beside her is Impure Love, who leans with folded arms against her shoulder; her breast is uncovered and she reaches to the ground with her left hand [*sic*] to grasp the mantle that covers the rest of her body. The figure is in a beautiful attitude, with one knee raised and the other leg extended so that the foot protrudes from the mantle, which is of clear yellow color changing to deep violet. Her turning toward Silenus denotes the correspondence between drunkenness and lust.

In the foreground on the opposite side [Fig. 70], near the wheels of Bacchus' car, reclines a satyr who is seen from the back. He puts his right arm round the neck of a goat and draws it close to him as if to kiss the animal; his left hand rests on the ground, but this and the left arm are cut off by the edge of the painting. Above the horned goat and behind Bacchus' car we see the upper part of a boy carrying a vase on his shoulder, and above him is a young Bacchante clashing the cymbals, which are formed of two little brazen shields, and turning upon us her cheerful and smiling face. At the very top there come into view an elephant and the driver sitting on his neck to guide him with his staff, as a sign of Bacchus' return from India. These two figures are likewise partly cut off by the edge of the painting.

Between the group of Bacchus and that of Silenus, where the tigers and goats are harnessed to the chariots of Bacchus and Ariadne, a view is opened up above them into the distance [Fig. 72]; but the composition is not disrupted because at this point a faun and a Bacchante have been inserted a little behind the other figures. Dancing and leaping, the rustic faun shakes his head and brandishes a twisted staff with his left hand, while with his right he grasps a fold of drapery that flutters behind him from his arm. The Bacchante, who is likewise leaping and whirling about, her breast bare and her hair and garments tossed by the wind, lifts her arms high over her head to strike the noisy tambourine.

And so the nuptial procession [Fig. 69] moves on in its frenzied way, to the

117

noisy accompaniment of the Bacchantes. . . . Overhead three amoretti are flying; the first bears on his head a vat of grapes, the second has a cup in his hands, and the third carries a vase on his shoulder.[133]

The *Bacchanal*, surely one of Annibale's most masterly inventions, can be read simultaneously in three ways: as a frieze-like procession, confined essentially to one plane like a sarcophagus relief, with the addition of figures in each corner to serve as *repoussoirs*; as two symmetrically balanced halves, the gap between them being bridged by the dancing figures of the faun and maenad; or as a single monumental group arranged in depth according to an arc moving inward from the left corner to its deepest point at the center and returning to the foreground once more on the right. The inventive genius of Carracci is nowhere more apparent than in the beautiful rhythmic sequence which, through a series of subtly varied postures, carries the eye from the reclining satyr in the left foreground to the radiant form of Bacchus, thence to the complementary figure of Ariadne (so much admired by Bellori), and finally to the dancing faun near the center. At this point there is a caesura, after which the rhythmic pattern resumes in the right half of the composition. Over this lively *cortège* four amoretti fly in an undulating course that lends still more variety and movement to the scene. And yet, despite its complexity, the composition gives an impression of monumental unity.

To what sources did Annibale turn for inspiration? Bellori says that he made several drawings after antique marbles while composing the *Bacchanal*.[134] Even without the evidence of the surviving preparatory drawings, the markedly classical character of the fresco would suffice to show with what thoroughness the artist had studied the reliefs of Dionysiac sarcophagi. Nevertheless it must be emphasized that the primary inspiration for this monumental composition was found, not in antique sculpture, but in a drawing by Perino del Vaga (Louvre 593, Fig. 281).

This famous drawing, representing a *Triumph of Bacchus*, is one of the preparatory designs ordered by Cardinal Alessandro Farnese for the so-called Farnese Casket, now in Naples, which contains (among other forms of decoration) six carved crystals of oval shape by Giovanni Bernardi da Castelbolognese.[135] Bernardi's *Triumph of Bacchus*,[136] although plainly copied from Perino's design, presents a drastically simplified version of the composition, omitting altogether the elephant and the figure of Ariadne. Perino's drawing was copied not only in Bernardi's crystal but also—and with much greater fidelity—in an otherwise uninteresting engraving by Giorgio Ghisi (B. 46). It has recently been suggested that Annibale used Ghisi's print as the model for his fresco.[137]

[133] *Ibid.*, pp. 48-51.
[134] *Vite*, p. 51.
[135] A. de Rinaldis, "Il Cofanetto Farnesiano del Museo di Napoli," *Bollettino d'Arte*, 2nd ser., III, 1923-1924, pp. 145 ff.
[136] *Ibid.*, fig. on p. 161.

[137] M. Calvesi, in *Commentari*, VII, 1956, pp. 272 ff. Through an oversight Calvesi has not perceived the relationship of Ghisi's print to the drawing by Perino del Vaga, but follows Bartsch in connecting it with a supposed drawing by Giulio Romano.

But this must be regarded as unlikely. In the first place, the fresco corresponds more closely to the drawing than to the engraving. Thus, to take one example, the hooked staff held by the elephant-driver in Annibale's painting finds a counterpart only in Perino's drawing; in the engraving by Ghisi this detail has been misunderstood and the staff omitted. What is more important, however, is the fact that Perino's drawing, having been made for Cardinal Alessandro Farnese, formed part of the family collection, where Carracci could not have failed to know it.

It may be asked, in view of Annibale's generally anti-Mannerist attitude, why he should have turned for inspiration to an artist so dedicated to the *maniera* as Perino del Vaga. The answer may be that the Triumph of Bacchus had become a traditional theme in Farnese iconography and that Perino's drawing was therefore set before Annibale by Fulvio Orsini as a guide to be followed in fashioning his own work. Whatever he may have thought of its style, there can be no doubt that Carracci found in the drawing a convenient synthesis of authentic motives from antique Bacchic reliefs. Specifically, Perino's design combines elements from three main sarcophagus types: the Bacchanalian procession, the triumph of Bacchus, and the finding of Ariadne.

The first type, the Bacchanalian procession, may be exemplified by a sarcophagus in Woburn Abbey.[138] From a relief of this sort Perino derived the following figures: the Bacchus seated in his chariot, one leg drawn up, the right arm resting on his head and the left placed around the neck of a girl; the Cupid with the lyre sitting on the lion's back; the drunken Silenus on the ass, holding a wreath and a cup and supported by two satyrs; the panther reclining beneath him; and the maenad with a basket on her head. Several of the lesser figures may also have been taken from the same source (compare the leaping satyr at the right side of the drawing to the similar Pan in the middle of the sarcophagus frieze).

The elephant, however, comes from the second type of Bacchic relief—the Indian triumph of Dionysus. Perino's drawing, it will be observed, includes not only the elephant but the *mahout* with his staff, a feature that can be found in several sarcophagi.[139]

There remains the sleeping Ariadne, whose garment is lifted up by a Cupid so that her beauty may be revealed to the god. This is a well-known motive in sarcophagus reliefs of the third type—those representing the finding of Ariadne.[140]

[138] *Outline Engravings and Descriptions of the Woburn Abbey Marbles*, London, 1822, pl. XII. A. Michaelis, *Ancient Marbles in Great Britain*, Cambridge, 1882, pp. 724 f., no. 61.

[139] K. Lehmann-Hartleben and E. C. Olsen, *Dionysiac Sarcophagi in Baltimore*, Baltimore, 1942, pp. 12 f., fig. 7.

[140] Cf. the sarcophagus in the Cortile del Belvedere of the Vatican (W. Amelung, *Die Sculpturen des Vaticanischen Museums*, II, Berlin, 1908, pp. 88 ff., no. 37, pl. 9). Calvesi (*op.cit.*, p. 273) rightly stresses the resemblance of Ghisi's (i.e. Perino's) Ariadne to the *Sleeping Ariadne* in the Vatican Museum, reproduced as "Cleopatra" in an engraving by Marcantonio (B. 199). The more likely source for Perino's figure, however, is a sarcophagus relief of the type described above, where Ariadne appears within an appropriate Dionysian setting.

We know that Carracci's fresco of the *Bacchanal* (Fig. 69) took shape slowly through a series of preliminary studies, and that the definitive composition was arrived at only after several tentative solutions had been tried and then modified or discarded. Nevertheless the final result, as we see it in the Farnese Gallery, still depends to a surprising degree on Perino del Vaga's conception.

Although Annibale's first idea seems to have been to represent Bacchus as intoxicated (cf. Fig. 159),[141] he returns in the end to a majestic attitude that is much closer to Perino's figure; even the little faun who supports his left arm is plainly related to the nymph embraced by the god in the drawing. There is another echo of Perino's Bacchus in the legs of Ariadne seated in her car. The tigers harnessed to the god's chariot are comparable to the lions of the drawing and wear a similar yoke about their necks. In the upper left corner we recognize the elephant and the driver with his hooked staff. Likewise adopted from Perino is the group of Silenus and his attendants, which Annibale has enriched by adding another figure—a boy faun who supports Silenus' leg, thus leaving his older colleague free to blow a trumpet. Other figures from the same source are the satyr guiding the ass, the girl with the basket on her head, the faun behind her playing a double flute, and, of course, the reclining woman with a cupid in the right foreground.

But this is not to say that Annibale looked only at Perino's drawing. It is inconceivable that he should have composed a subject such as this without consulting ancient monuments, if only in order to give new life to images derived from antiquity through the *maniera* of Perino del Vaga. The idea of Ariadne riding in her own car was surely drawn from an ancient source: this is a characteristic feature of one class of Dionysiac sarcophagi, of which there is an example in the Lateran.[142] The inclusion of the goats in the Bacchic procession may likewise have been suggested by a sarcophagus relief;[143] but it is of course possible that in this detail we have to do with an influence from another source, perhaps an engraving.

The importance of engravings for the Farnese frescoes has been stressed by Calvesi. He observes, for instance, that the braying donkey on which Silenus rides seemingly derives from a print attributed to Marco Dente (B. XIV, 222).[144] Another engraving that might be cited in this connection is the *Vintage* by Marcantonio (B. 306). Here is to be seen the familiar motive of the young woman bearing a basket on her head (already known to us from the Perino drawing and ancient sarcophagi) but with this difference: the girl is shown in full face, as in Annibale's fresco, rather than in the more usual profile. It is worth noting too that the attitude of the little boy at the extreme left of

---

[141] This is confirmed by Bellori, *Vite*, p. 51.

[142] Reproduced in J. M. C. Toynbee, *The Hadrianic School*, Cambridge, 1934, pl. 40, 1; see also Lehmann-Hartleben and Olsen, *op.cit.*, pp. 52, 77, fig. 44.

[143] On a sarcophagus in the Capitoline Museum Bacchus rides on a panther's back, and a girl (perhaps Ariadne) on a goat (H. Stuart Jones, ed., *A Catalogue of the Ancient Sculptures preserved in the Municipal Collections of Rome, The Sculptures of the Museo Capitolino*, Oxford, 1912, pp. 216 f., no. 86, pl. 53).

[144] Calvesi, *op.cit.*, p. 272, fig. 21.

the engraving is virtually reproduced in the infant faun holding the tiger's reins in the Farnese *Bacchanal*.

Raphael's *Galatea* in the Villa Farnesina, the importance of which for Agostino's *Glaucus and Scylla* is so obvious, may also have been in Annibale's mind when he composed the *Bacchanal*. The beautiful contrapposto of Ariadne has a distinctly Raphaelesque flavor: the upper part of the body may in fact contain a reminiscence of Galatea herself, the figure being turned from a frontal into a profile pose. The faun who blows a trumpet while helping to support Silenus recalls in several respects the trumpeting sea deity on the right side of Raphael's fresco, the influence of which is perhaps also to be detected in the rhythmically placed amoretti of the *Bacchanal*. Likewise Raphaelesque in origin is the ecstatic maenad with the tambourine, whose attitude was suggested by the central figure of the three *Horae* strewing blossoms over the guests in the *Wedding of Cupid and Psyche*. But no recounting of Annibale's sources can explain the grand effect of the whole, an effect summed up by Wittkower as "a flowing and floating movement, a richness and exuberance which one would seek in vain either in antiquity or in the High Renaissance."[145]

The fresco also contains a few recollections—minor ones to be sure—of a group of Bacchic subjects which occupied Annibale's attention during the nineties. The relief ornamentation of Bacchus' chariot, which shows children gathering grapes (cf. Fig. 70), may be compared to Annibale's engraving on the Tazza Farnese, the silver dish made for Cardinal Odoardo; the putto at the left who is clambering among the branches of the vine is almost identical to one of the figures in the border of the dish.[146] The same putto reappears in Annibale's panel in London, *Silenus gathering Grapes*.[147] The satyr guiding Silenus' donkey at the extreme right of the fresco (Fig. 71) derives in a general way, as we have seen, from Perino's drawing. But a still closer parallel can be found in the Farnese Dish, where there is a kneeling satyr carrying a wineskin on his shoulder and turning his head, with its unusually prominent horns, in exactly the same manner.

It was Annibale's practice in making his definitive figure studies to pose living models in the attitudes that he had decided upon in preliminary sketches. If Bellori can be believed, Agostino served as the model for Silenus, his corpulence being such that Annibale was able to portray him in this guise "con poca alteratione." Comparison with the engraved likeness of Agostino in Bellori's *Vite* suggests that the anecdote may indeed be true.[148]

How are we to interpret the three *quadri riportati* that crown the Farnese Gallery? Bellori's exegesis is oversimplified, and need not detain us for long: "The white wool

[145] R. Wittkower, *Art and Architecture in Italy, 1600 to 1750*, Baltimore, 1958, p. 37.

[146] O. Kurz, "Engravings on Silver by Annibale Carracci," *Burlington Magazine*, XCVII,

1955, pp. 282 ff., fig. 13.

[147] *Ibid.*, fig. 20.

[148] Bellori, *Vite*, pp. 101, 113.

that Diana receives from the god Pan and the golden apple given to Paris by Mercury are the gifts with which Love masters human minds and the discords caused by beauty; the Bacchanal is a symbol of drunkenness, which is the mother of impure desires."[149] He would have us believe, that is to say, that the culmination of the entire cycle is simply an illustration of the more reprehensible aspects of love. Something of these connotations may indeed be present in the complex iconography of the frescoes, but to maintain that they have no other significance is manifestly unreasonable. Such an explanation is not even consistent with Bellori's own definition of the argument of the cycle, which is, as he puts it, "human love regulated by heavenly love."

The theme of the central fresco can only be divine love. The mortal Ariadne is deified by the love of the god and the crown of stars above her head is the visible sign of her apotheosis; Bellori himself recognizes her divinity. The circumstances of her deification are told by Ovid (*Fasti* III, 459-516): "Meantime Liber had conquered the straight-haired Indians and returned, loaded with treasure, from the eastern world. . . . Long time had Liber heard [Ariadne's] plaint, for as it chanced he followed close behind. He put his arms about her, with kisses dried her tears, and 'Let us fare together,' quoth he, 'to heaven's height. . . . And I will see to it that with thee there shall be a memorial of thy crown, that crown which Vulcan gave to Venus, and she to thee.' He did as he had said and changed the nine jewels of her crown into fires. Now the golden crown doth sparkle with nine stars."[150] In another description of the same scene (*Ars Amatoria* I, 525-564) Ovid dwells at greater length on the Bacchic retinue: the frenzied beating of drums and cymbals, the satyrs, the Bacchantes with their hair streaming in the wind, and drunken old Silenus seated precariously on the ass; Bacchus' chariot, we read, is covered with clusters of grapes and drawn by yoked tigers:

> *Iam deus in curru, quem summum texerat uvis,*
> *Tigribus adiunctis aurea lora dabat.*
> (*Ibid.*, 549-50)

That Bacchus, god of wine and revelry, should have been selected to represent divine love may seem (to say the least) inappropriate; Tietze found it equally unthinkable that Ariadne could ever have ideal significance.[151] The paradox is easily resolved if we bear in mind some of the meanings, religious and philosophical, which have been attached to the myth of Dionysus. In the Bacchic cults of antiquity the revelry of the god's followers typified the symposium of the blessed in the after-life. Roman sarcophagi of the second and third centuries of our era represent Bacchus under the guise of a saviour-god who awakens Ariadne from the sleep of death in order to conduct her to everlasting bliss.[152] These meanings did not die with the passing of

---

[149] *Vite*, p. 65.
[150] Transl. by J. G. Frazer, Loeb Classical Library.
[151] Tietze, p. 114, note 1.

[152] Lehmann-Hartleben and Olsen, *op.cit.*, pp. 37 ff. F. Cumont, *Recherches sur le symbolisme funéraire des Romains*, Paris, 1942, pp. 372 f., 420 ff.

paganism but lived on in the moralizing literature of the Christian Middle Ages. The *Moralized Ovid*, which characteristically offers both favorable and unfavorable allegories of Bacchus, explains that the wine may signify "the grace of God or the ardor of the spirit."[153] Cesare Ripa, describing the image of Divine Grace (who is to be pictured holding a glass of wine) employs a similar metaphor: "Whoever is in God's grace is continually intoxicated with the sweetness of his love, for this intoxication is so strong and potent that it drives away the thirst for worldly things."[154] From Bacchus, according to Renaissance Neoplatonism, comes one of the divine madnesses—the *furor mysterialis*, or mystical frenzy, which, like the *furor amatorius*, raises the soul to a state of bliss.[155]

Bellori's notion that the reclining figure in the right foreground is to be identified as the Earthly Venus accompanied by her son deserves further consideration.[156] The reference, once again, is to Plato's two Venuses and their corresponding Cupids, one representing heavenly and the other earthly love. (Bellori is not accurate in naming the son of the Earthly Venus "Impure Love.") In mankind, however, there are not merely two but three kinds of love, and these in turn are related to the three modes of life—the contemplative, the active, and the voluptuous. "All love," writes Marsilio Ficino, "begins with sight. But the love of the contemplative man ascends from sight to the mind. That of the voluptuous man sinks from sight to touch, whereas that of the active man remains visual. . . . The love of the contemplative man is called divine, that of the active man human, that of the voluptuous man bestial."[157]

This Neoplatonic concept of threefold love is given visible form in Carracci's fresco. Bacchus represents *amor divinus*, through which Ariadne is raised to a supersensory state of contemplation; she is, in Ripa's words, so intoxicated with the sweetness of the god's love that she no longer thirsts for worldly things. But the picture also illustrates how divine love transcends both human and bestial love. At one side are the Earthly Venus and her son, who together preside over *amor humanus*; in the opposite corner the satyr with the goat exemplifies *amor ferinus* (to Bellori this group signified "brutish appetites").[158] The terrestrial nature and inferior status of these figures are emphasized by their reclining postures.

[153] Waleys, *Metamorphosis Ovidiana*, fol. 15 (*De Baccho*): "Vel dic in bono quod vinum est gratia dei vel fervor spiritus." Cf. also *ibid.*, fol. 36 v.: "Per Bacchum qui inebriat: intelligitur vera fides qui fervore devotionis inebriat servos Christi."

[154] Ripa, *Iconologia*, s.v. "Gratia divina": "Chi è in gratia di Dio, sempre sta ebrio delle dolcezze dello amore suo, perciochè questa imbriachezza è si gagliarda, & potente, che fa scordar la sete delle cose mondane."

[155] Ficino, *Comm. in Convivium Platonis*, VII, 14 (ed. Marcel, pp. 258 ff.).

[156] *Vite*, p. 50. Opposed to this is Tietze's belief that the figure has only a compositional function.

[157] Ficino, *op.cit.*, VI, 8 (ed. Marcel, p. 212): "Amor itaque omnis incipit ab aspectu. Sed contemplativi hominis amor ab aspectu ascendit in mentem. Voluptuosi, ab aspectu descendit in tactum. Activi remanet in aspectu. . . . Contemplativi hominis amor divinus, activi, humanus, voluptuosi ferinus cognominatur."

[158] *Argomento* (in Malvasia, *Felsina*, I, p. 440).

The same Neoplatonic interpretation can be seen to apply with equal force to the two octagonal panels on either side. Whereas the main subject extols divine love, in these, by contrast, we are to see allegorical expressions of human and bestial love. That Paris, on the right side (Fig. 66), stands for *amor humanus* does not perhaps require lengthy explanation. He is, plainly, the man of action, and as such does not ascend to the supreme height of contemplation, but is content with the visual experience of beauty. The Neoplatonic writer Sallustius defines his shortcomings in precisely these terms: "The soul that lives in accordance with sense-perception [κατ' αἴσθησιν] (for that is Paris), seeing beauty alone and not the other powers in the universe, says that the apple is Aphrodite's."[159] Because his love does not rise from the level of sensual perception to that of intellectual contemplation he finds the Earthly Venus to be the most beautiful. For there can be no doubt that it is *Venus Vulgaris*, not *Venus Coelestis*, to whom Paris awards the prize.[160] It is not by chance that she appears with her son, *Amor Vulgaris*, in the adjacent corner of the *Bacchanal*, thereby confirming the relation between the two subjects.

The scene of *Pan and Diana* (Fig. 65), signifying bestial love, is likewise linked iconographically with the *Triumph of Bacchus and Ariadne*. Ficino remarks that bestial love is a sort of insanity as a result of which "man degenerates from the human species, and from being human becomes in some measure a brute."[161] Pan, half man and half goat, notable for his concupiscence, answers perfectly to this description. The reed-pipe hanging on the tree beside him is a familiar sign of depravity, for the music which it utters arouses base passions. In order to satisfy his lust Pan resorts to deceitful measures, disguising his monstrous ugliness by a mass of white wool of gleaming purity. So cunning is his ruse that he succeeds in tempting even the chaste Diana to come to him. (As a scene of temptation the fresco resembles in more than one respect Tintoretto's *Christ tempted by Satan* in the Scuola di San Rocco at Venice.) Pan as the image of bestial love is echoed in the satyr embracing a goat in the *Bacchanal*; in much the same way the Earthly Venus on the opposite side establishes a link with the human love of Paris.

We cannot leave the Triumph of Bacchus and Ariadne without taking note of another iconographical component. Interwoven with the dominant theme of love is that of military glory.

[159] Sallustius, *De diis et mundo* IV (transl. by A. D. Nock, Cambridge, 1926, p. 7). I am indebted to Prof. Panofsky for directing my attention to this passage.

[160] This interpretation of the Judgment of Paris is at variance with that of Fulgentius, *Mythologiae* II, 1, who says that the three goddesses, Minerva, Juno, and Venus, exemplify respectively the contemplative, active, and voluptuous life (on this see Chapter 3 above). But if we were to assume, with Ful-

gentius, that Paris elected the voluptuous life, he would necessarily (according to the Ficinian theory) illustrate bestial love. This is obviously not the intention of Carracci's fresco, where Paris stands for human, but not subhuman, limitations.

[161] Ficino, *op.cit.* (ed. Marcel, p. 245): "Insanie morbo infra hominis spetiem homo deicitur et ex homine brutum quodammodo redditur."

That Bacchus was the first to hold a triumph was a well-established tradition even in antiquity.[162] In the sixteenth century, with the increasing emphasis on the glorification of princely families, the Triumph of Bacchus became a favorite subject of palace decoration. It appears, to cite two well-known examples, in Perino del Vaga's fresco cycle in the Palazzo Doria in Genoa,[163] and, in Rome, among the frescoes by Daniele da Volterra in the Palazzo Farnese itself.[164] Carracci's fresco, to the degree that it celebrates martial prowess (and this of course is not its primary meaning), can only refer to Odoardo's father, Alessandro Farnese, third Duke of Parma. It will be remembered that Odoardo's first idea was that the *sala grande* of the palace should be decorated with paintings of the heroic exploits of the late duke. That project, initially postponed until after the completion of the Gallery, was eventually abandoned altogether. But it requires no effort of the imagination to believe that the achievements of the great captain might be alluded to, even if cryptically, in the Farnese Gallery.

It has already been remarked that Alessandro's brilliant generalship under King Philip II invited comparison with his namesake Alexander the Great, son of Philip of Macedon.[165] The siege and capture of Antwerp in 1585 made it possible to draw an even more exact parallel: as Alexander of Macedon captured Tyre, so has Alexander of Parma taken Antwerp.[166] But the comparison did not stop there. The historians recalled that Alexander the Great had likened himself to the god Bacchus, conqueror of India and legendary inventor of the triumphal procession.[167] Thus it was that in the sixteenth century the persons of Bacchus and Alexander became virtually interchangeable as Triumphators. Taddeo Zuccari's fresco cycle of the life of Alexander the Great in the Castello Orsini at Bracciano includes a triumphal procession which is so Dionysian in character that the conqueror is even accompanied by an Ariadne-like young woman.[168] The dual reference to Bacchus and Alexander the Great is already present in Perino del Vaga's design for the Farnese casket (Fig. 281), where the triumphal theme is to be understood as a glorification of Cardinal Alessandro Farnese.

The opportunity of alluding simultaneously to Alexander the Great and to Bacchus was not one to be overlooked by the panegyrists of the Duke of Parma; for the metaphorical imagery became even more apt when applied to one who followed the profession of arms. We can see an instance of this in the triumphal procession that

---

[162] E.g., Diodorus Siculus IV, 3, 2; Pliny, *Hist. Nat.* VII, 56, 1.

[163] P. Askew, "Perino del Vaga's Decorations for the Palazzo Doria, Genoa," *Burlington Magazine*, XCVIII, 1956, pp. 46 ff., fig. 28.

[164] M. L. Mez, "Una decorazione di Daniele da Volterra nel Palazzo Farnese a Roma," *Rivista d'arte*, XVI, 1934, pp. 276 ff., fig. 4.

[165] Even before he became duke, coins were being minted at Parma having on one side the bust of Alessandro Farnese (with the inscription *A. F. Speculator*) and on the other that of Alexander the Great (inscribed *A. M. Spec-*

ulum). Cf. *Corpus Nummorum Italicorum*, vol. IX, Emilia, parte 1, Rome, 1925, pp. 468 ff., pl. XXX, 13, 14, 15.

[166] Cf. Famiano Strada, *De Bello Belgico*, Rome, 1648, Decas II, pp. 336 f.

[167] The chief ancient sources are: Arrian, *Anabasis Alexandri* V, 1 and 2; VI, 28; Pliny, *Hist. Nat.* XVI, 62; Q. Curtius Rufus, *De rebus gestis Alexandri Magni* III, 12, 18.

[168] H. Voss, *Die Malerei der Spätrenaissance in Rom und Florenz*, Berlin, 1920, II, p. 442, fig. 168.

followed the taking of Antwerp, in which Farnese's victorious troops were festooned with branches and foliage; observers were reminded (we are told) of the soldiers of Alexander the Great when, after the capture of Nysa, they held a lengthy celebration in honor of Bacchus, decking themselves with leaves of grape vine and ivy.[169] As the deeds of Cardinal Alessandro were commemorated in Perino's design for the Farnese casket, so did Annibale's *Triumph of Bacchus* recall to the observer the renowned victories of the Duke Alessandro Farnese.

But if we admit this symbolism to be part of the meaning of the fresco, what are we to say of Ariadne? This is perhaps not an insoluble problem. The marriage of Bacchus and Ariadne might very well allude to the wedding of Alessandro Farnese and the Princess Maria of Portugal in 1565. A medal struck in honor of that event shows the prince mounted on horseback and receiving a crown from Venus,[170] a motive not without analogy to the coronation of Ariadne by Cupid.

Even the satyr in the lower left corner, who is a symbol of bestial love, may carry a secondary meaning which connects him with the history of the Duke Alessandro. A medal struck in 1585 during the siege of Antwerp (Fig. 282) shows Alexander the Great seated in his tent and reaching out to grasp a satyr, beneath whom is the word SATYROΣ. In the distance appears the city of Antwerp with the "Farnese bridge" spanning the River Scheldt. The motto reads: *Concipe certas spes*.[171] Plutarch relates that during the siege of Tyre a satyr appeared to Alexander in a dream, and for a long time eluded his attempts to seize him; eventually, however, the king succeeded in catching him. Asked to interpret the dream, the soothsayers divided the word *satyros* into two parts and assured Alexander that Tyre would be his.[172] The parallel is obvious: as the city of Tyre, after a lengthy siege, at last capitulated to Alexander of Macedon, so must Antwerp fall to Alexander Farnese. It is possible that Carracci's fresco contains a reference to this anecdote in the seated satyr who looks up as the conqueror passes by in his triumphal chariot.

[169] Strada, *op.cit.*, pp. 380 f. For the Bacchic revels by the army of Alexander the Great see Curtius, *op.cit.*, VIII, 10, 10-17.

[170] Pompeo Litta, *Famiglie celebri italiane*, Farnesi Duchi di Parma. Medaglie Farnesiane, pl. III, 3.

[171] G. van Loon, *Histoire métallique des xvii provinces des Pays-Bas . . . , traduite du hollandais*, The Hague, 1732, I, pp. 349 f. Litta, *op.cit.*, pl. III, 6.

[172] Plutarch, *Life of Alexander*.

CHAPTER 7 · THE ICONOGRAPHY
OF THE WALLS

THE paintings which adorn the walls of the Gallery, unlike those of the vault, were not the product of a single, concentrated campaign, but were executed over a protracted period, during which time, moreover, the members of Annibale's workshop gradually assumed full responsibility for the work. Although these frescoes, aesthetically speaking, are generally inferior to those of the ceiling, they are not to be dismissed as of little importance. In the first place, all of them were carried out in accordance with Annibale's plans and with the aid of his drawings. And in the second place they pose some iconographical problems of unusual interest.

I. THE VIRTUES

At the ends of the long walls of the Gallery are four Virtues, each personified as a seated female figure within an oval (cf. Figs. 32-33). Owing to the contraction of the final bay at the northern end the ovals here are noticeably narrower than those at the south. The Virtues on the entrance wall are in right profile; the two opposite face front. The background of each oval is light green. *Fortitude* (Fig. 73) rests her arm against a pedestal and carries a column as a symbol of strength; with her left hand she caresses a lion seated at her feet. *Temperance* (Fig. 74), whose attitude resembles that of Isaiah on the Sistine ceiling, holds a bridle in her hands. *Justice* (Fig. 75) has for her attributes a balance and fasces. The last personification is that of *Charity* (Fig. 76), who suckles two infants at her breasts.

We are immediately struck by an anomaly. This is not the conventional group of four cardinal virtues, as they are seen, for example, in the Camerino (Figs. 25-28), but a mixture of two orders: the cardinal virtues of Fortitude, Temperance and Justice are present; but in the place of Prudence there appears Charity, chief of the theological virtues. To explain this curious substitution it may be useful to recall the speculations of the Neoplatonists on the nature of the virtues. Marsilio Ficino, here depending on Aristotle, delineates two kinds of virtues: moral and intellectual. Justice, Fortitude, and Temperance belong to the first category, Prudence to the second.[1] The fact that Prudence, the intellectual virtue, has been supplanted by Charity may remind us of the words of St. Paul: "Though I have the gift of prophecy, and understand all mysteries, and all knowledge . . . and have not charity, I am nothing" (I Cor. 13, 2). The mention of the apostle is not inappropriate here. Kristeller has shown that Ficino actually identifies the Pauline concept of Charity with the Neoplatonic concept of divine love, and even uses both terms in-

[1] *Commentarium in Convivium Platonis*, VI, 18 (ed. R. Marcel, p. 237).

terchangeably.[2] Like Paul, Ficino stresses the superiority of Charity over Knowledge. "Caritas magis valet quam scientia," he writes; and again, "Quod ergo nos celo restituit non dei cognitio est, sed amor."[3] The three remaining figures represent the moral virtues, by means of which souls may ascend to God "as if by three paths." "Some return to their creator," says Ficino, "by practicing Fortitude, others by practicing Justice, and others by practicing Temperance."[4] But greater than these is Charity, or Love, which has the power to lead souls back to heaven.[5]

It is true that the four Virtues are not part of the original scheme of decoration; on the contrary, having been in all probability executed by Domenichino in 1607-1608, they must be among the latest frescoes in the Galleria Farnese. Yet they have an integral place in the iconography of the Gallery and serve to confirm its essentially spiritual meaning. The inclusion of Charity is particularly significant, because this virtue is the only specifically Christian motive in the entire cycle.

II. THE PERSEUS FRESCOES

In 1604, not long before the onset of his critical illness, Annibale commenced work on the large paintings on the end walls of the Gallery illustrating the story of Perseus and Andromeda (*Metam.* IV, 668-764; V, 1-235). We shall follow here the narrative sequence, even though the frescoes were actually painted in reverse order.

PERSEUS AND ANDROMEDA (FIG. 77)

Over the doors at the south end of the Gallery stands the *Liberation of Andromeda*. A great rock of irregular shape rises in the middle of the scene and to this Andromeda is chained by her wrists. She is nude except for a veil that partly covers her body. Despite her confining bonds Andromeda's attitude is energetic and full of movement. She is seated, but leans back with an agonized expression as she strains to look over her shoulder; the right foot almost touches the lower edge of the picture and the fingers of the left hand graze the frame at the top. Behind her, furiously churning the waves, is the gray-green sea monster; its head is raised toward Perseus who, with golden mantle fluttering, rides through the air on Pegasus and holds out the Gorgon's head that will turn the monster to stone. Standing on the shore at the right and easily distinguished by their crowns are Andromeda's parents, who have promised her to Perseus if he will save her. King Cepheus wraps his hand in his orange-red mantle and presses it to his face, while extending the other hand to the side in a gesture of helplessness. His queen, Cassiopea, conscious that she herself is the cause of this unhappy situation, throws up her hands in horror and runs toward the water as she watches the sea monster nearing Andromeda; she wears a pale yellow dress

[2] P. O. Kristeller, *The Philosophy of Marsilio Ficino*, New York, 1943, pp. 277 f.

[3] *Comm. in Convivium*, IV, 6 (ed. Marcel, p. 176).

[4] *Ibid.*, IV, 5 (ed. Marcel, p. 174): "Alii per

fortitudinis, alii per iustitie, alii per temperantie officia suum repetant auctorem."

[5] *Ibid.*, IV, 6 (ed. Marcel, p. 176): "Amor animas reducit in celum."

(changing to violet in the shadows) and a rose mantle. Behind the royal pair a kneeling girl hides her face in her hands, and farther back along the shore a crowd of spectators looks intently at the encounter between the hero and the sea creature.

Notwithstanding the elegance of the principal figure this is one of Annibale's least successful frescoes. It is not only that the execution, especially of the right side, betrays the intervention of an assistant. The field is obviously much too large for the subject, with the result that the composition is lacking in coherence and gives an impression of vacuousness. Whether because his powers of invention had begun to flag or because he considered the problem to be really insoluble, the artist apparently took as his model the illustration of the fable by Bernard Salomon which appeared in Simeoni's edition of the *Metamorphoses* in 1559 (Fig. 284).[6] In the woodcut, as in the fresco, Andromeda is chained to a tall rock in the middle of the scene; at the left Perseus, mounted on Pegasus, attacks the sea monster, which lifts its head at his.approach; and a group of onlookers watches the encounter from the shore at the right. Annibale follows Salomon's illustration in representing Perseus riding upon Pegasus, thereby departing from the text of the fable as it is told in the *Metamorphoses*. For Ovid makes it clear that the hero flies only by means of the wings bound to his feet and that he slays the beast with his hooked sword. Annibale introduces a further peculiarity in making Perseus use the Gorgon's head, perhaps in order to reinforce the connection between this scene and its sequel.

THE COMBAT OF PERSEUS AND PHINEUS (FIG. 78)

Unlike the *Liberation of Andromeda*, the *Fight of Perseus against Phineus and his companions* depends very closely on Ovid. Cepheus' brother Phineus, who had earlier been betrothed to Andromeda, is enraged at his loss. He and his followers break into the wedding feast and attack Perseus and the guests until they are finally repulsed and turned to stone by the Gorgon's head (*Metam.* v, 1-235).

Annibale represents the climax of the action. Tables have been overturned in the struggle and the floor is littered with gold vessels; others stand still neatly racked on a table at the left. Perseus, who has been almost overwhelmed by his attackers, is at last compelled to resort to the petrifying power of the Gorgon's head. Still clutching the sword in his right hand,[7] he holds out the hideous head of Medusa before

---

[6] *La vita et Metamorfoseo d' Ovidio, figurato & abbreuiato in forma d'epigrammi da M. Gabriello Symeoni*, Lyons, 1559, p. 73. The French edition was published at Lyons in 1557. Cf. M. D. Henkel, "Illustrierte Ausgaben von Ovids Metamorphosen im xv., xvi. und xvii. Jahrhundert," *Vorträge der Bibliothek Warburg*, 1926-1927, pp. 117 f., Abb. 56. It may also be true that Annibale recalled Cellini's bronze relief of this subject on the base of his statue of Perseus, as was suggested by Navenne (*Rome et le palais Farnèse*, i, p. 79).

[7] It is assumed by Navenne (*ibid.*, i, p. 79) that the sword is superfluous, having been thoughtlessly copied by Carracci from Benvenuto Cellini's famous bronze statue in Florence. But Ovid says specifically that the hero used his sword until forced to produce the Gorgon's head. The resemblance to Cellini's *Perseus* is purely fortuitous. It is worth noting that in Salomon's illustration of this scene Perseus likewise holds both the sword and

his enemies, his face and attitude expressing the tension of the moment. He wears the winged cap and sandals, and a dark blue mantle is fastened at his shoulder. Behind him three of his companions, obedient to his command, hide their faces in their hands. Opposite the hero stands Thescelus (not Phineus, as Tietze[8] and others after him have thought), poised in readiness to hurl the javelin but already immobilized into a marble statue:

> . . . *utque manu iaculum fatale parabat*
> *mittere, in hoc haesit signum de marmore gestu.*
> (*Metam.* v, 182-183)

Another assailant, perhaps Eryx,[9] who has been rushing toward Perseus with a spear, is suddenly halted and hardened into stone in the very act of striding over a fallen comrade. At the extreme right a warrior holding a shield, possibly one of Perseus' friends, raises his sword to strike an unseen opponent. Phineus himself,[10] the author of all this strife (*belli temerarius auctor*), is seen at the left in the grip of a soldier who has seized him by the hair. Phineus kneels to beg for mercy, as Ovid describes, but in vain, for Perseus has already turned upon him the Gorgon-head. By a startling tour de force Annibale illustrates the very process of transformation: the white face and torso are rigid and marble-like, and the eyes are sightless, but the legs still retain some flexibility and show by their fading flesh-color that the conversion into stone is not yet complete.

Annibale's characteristic use of antique models is particularly evident in this fresco. Phineus, for example, assumes a half-kneeling, half-crouching position that combines features both from the Belvedere Torso and from the Borghese Warrior; but the striding soldier who grasps him by the hair was evidently suggested by the central figure of the *Battle of Ostia* in Raphael's Stanza dell'Incendio. The attitude of Perseus, whose mantle is draped over his extended left arm, is adapted from the Apollo Belvedere—not, as some have thought, from Cellini's bronze statue. As the sun god follows with his eye the course of the arrow he has loosed from his bow, so does Perseus watch the effects of the Gorgon's face on his foes. The fallen warrior at the right side, lying supine with the left arm bent above the head and the short sword resting in the relaxed left hand, reproduces exactly, though in the reverse sense, the so-called *Dead Giant* from the Farnese collection now in Naples. On the wall behind Perseus, and partly concealed by the overturned table, is a relief illustrating a scene of sacrifice, very like that in the Conservatori Museum showing Marcus

the Gorgon-head (Simeoni, *Vita et Metamorfoseo d' Ovidio*, p. 76).

[8] Tietze, p. 86. For the correct interpretation see Bellori, *Vite*, p. 62. This figure was especially admired by Albani, who planned to reproduce it in a treatise on painting (Malvasia, *Felsina*, ii, pp. 243 f.).

[9] Cf. *Metam.* v, 194-199: "incursurus erat:

tenuit vestigia tellus, / inmotusque silex armataque mansit imago."

[10] To refer to this figure merely as "one of the attackers," as does Tietze (p. 86), is to miss the point of the story. Once again Bellori provides the proper explanation (*Vite*, p. 63).

Aurelius sacrificing.[11] A bull is being led toward the officiating priest by several attendants, one of whom carries an axe over his shoulder. This is surely an allusion to Perseus' piety in making sacrifices to the gods; Ovid tells how, after slaying the sea monster, the hero built three altars and offered a calf to Mercury, a cow to Minerva, and a bull to Jupiter (*Metam.* IV, 753-756).

Bellori's explanation of the Perseus frescoes may be summarized as follows: Andromeda is the soul, bound by the senses and a prey to vice until freed by Perseus, who is reason and love of righteousness; the petrifaction of Phineus and his companions signifies the victory of reason over lust.[12] This interpretation, framed as it is in general terms, is undoubtedly correct. Some significance, however, should be attached to the fact that these frescoes stand directly beneath the scenes of Polyphemus: it would seem that the intention was to draw a contrast between the lust of the Cyclops and the pure love of Perseus, who delivers Andromeda both from the jaws of the sea monster and from the jealous rage of Phineus. Perseus, it might be said, owes his strength to his piety and virtue: himself the son of Jupiter, he enjoys the divine aid of Minerva and Mercury and does not neglect to offer sacrifices to all three. His opponent Phineus, on the other hand, resembles Polyphemus not only in his jealousy but also in his impious and defiant attitude toward the gods, as is evident from his challenge to Perseus: "Your wings will not save you from me, nor Jupiter, changed into false gold."[13] It is instructive, in this connection, to read what the Neoplatonist Marsilio Ficino has to say concerning piety in his Commentary on Plato's Symposium: "An actual man and the idea of man are the same. Therefore whoever of us on earth is separated from God is not a true man, because he is disjoined from his idea and form. To this [idea and form] we are led by divine love and piety."[14] Phineus and Polyphemus (to adopt Ficino's terminology) are not true men because, having no love for God, they are estranged from him. Neither resembles God in both idea and form, one being of inhuman shape and the other being reduced to a lifeless image.

The relationship between the Polyphemus and Perseus subjects is subtly reinforced in other ways. The rock to which Andromeda is chained resembles that on which Polyphemus, in the scene above, is seated as he sings his serenade to Galatea.

[11] H. Stuart Jones (ed.), *Catalogue of the Ancient Sculptures preserved in the Municipal Collections of Rome, The Sculptures of the Palazzo dei Conservatori*, Oxford, 1926, pp. 22-25, pl. 12 and fig. 1.

[12] *Vite*, pp. 65 f. Bellori's explanation bears some resemblance to that of the *Moralized Ovid*, where Andromeda is the human soul bound by the chains of sin; Perseus, who is Christ, delivers her from the monster, which is the devil (cf. Waleys, *Metamorphosis Ovidiana*, fol. 47).

[13] *Metam.* V, 11-12: "nec mihi te pennae nec falsum versus in aurum / Iuppiter eripiet!" The reference is to Perseus' mother Danaë, impregnated by Jupiter under the guise of a shower of gold.

[14] *Comm. in Convivium*, VI, 19 (ed. Marcel, p. 239): "Verus autem homo et idea hominis idem. Ideo quisque nostrum in terris a deo separatus, non verus est homo, cum a sui idea sit formaque disiunctus. Ad eam nos divinus amor pietasque perducet."

At the other end of the Gallery the just punishment allotted by Perseus forms a striking contrast to the murderous rage of the Cyclops.

III. THE IMPRESE

The visitor to the Gallery is not likely to pay much attention to the four emblematic devices, or *imprese*, which are enclosed within stucco cartouches on each of the long walls. They are nevertheless of some interest as being the personal emblems of four prominent members of the Farnese family: Odoardo's great-uncle, Cardinal Alessandro (1520-1589); his father, the Duke Alessandro (1545-1592); Cardinal Odoardo himself; and his brother Ranuccio, reigning Duke of Parma.

Traditionally such *imprese* were placed in the corners of vaulted ceilings.[15] That this was Annibale's original intention we may surmise from the drawing No. 50 (Fig. 155), which includes in the right corner a shield with the device of Cardinal Odoardo Farnese—three lilies with a scroll. At a later stage, probably in order to avoid duplicating the set of *imprese* already planned for the walls, it was decided that this space should be occupied instead by the Contest of the Twin Loves.

CARDINAL ALESSANDRO FARNESE (FIG. 85)

This famous emblem was invented, according to Paolo Giovio,[16] by the poet Francesco Molza. It depicts an arrow embedded in a shield hanging from the branch of a tree; the fluttering scroll that winds about the arrow is blank, but ought to bear the Greek motto βάλλ' οὕτως, as in the example illustrated in Figure 285. The words are from the *Iliad* (VIII, 282), where Agamemnon praises the skillful archery of Teucer in the fight against the Trojans: βάλλ' οὕτως, αἴ κέν τι φόως Δαναοῖσι γένηαι (Shoot on in this wise, if perchance you may become the splendor of the Greeks).

An exhaustive analysis of the *impresa* is to be found in the emblem book of Girolamo Ruscelli.[17] The author connects it with those sports in which the aim is to drive an arrow or spear into a suspended shield: if the target is not struck precisely in the center it will turn and so deflect the shaft. Such a shield, he observes, may be set up in various ways, on a wall, on a post, on a tree, or even on a herm, as in a drawing by Michelangelo[18] from which his own illustration (Fig. 285) is copied. Ruscelli rightly maintains that the *impresa* is fundamentally an illustration of the doctrine of the Mean, and in support of this interpretation he quotes the following passage from Aristotle (*Ethics*

[15] Cf. for example Perino del Vaga's ceiling of the Sala Paolina in the Castel Sant'Angelo.

[16] *Dialogo dell'imprese militari et amorose di Monsignor Giovio* . . . , Venice, 1556, p. 73.

[17] *Le imprese illustri con espositioni, et discorsi del S.or Ieronimo Ruscelli* . . . , Venice, 1572. fols. 42 v. ff.

[18] This is the famous drawing of *Archers shooting at a Herm*, which was in the pos-

session of Cardinal Alessandro Farnese. See A. E. Popham and J. Wilde, *Italian Drawings of the XV and XVI Centuries at Windsor Castle*, London, 1949, no. 424, pp. 248 f., pl. 20. On the meaning of the subject and its probable relation to our *impresa*, see especially Panofsky, *Studies in Iconology*, pp. 225 ff.

II, 6): "It is easy to miss the mark, but hard to hit it: and for these reasons therefore both the excess and defect belong to Vice, and the mean state to Virtue."

The shield too may have meaning: Homer tells how Teucer took cover beneath the shield of Ajax while he shot his arrows. In the present instance, Ruscelli says, the shield might signify "virtue, diligence, care, innocence, or some other quality such as might be appropriate to one who makes war on vice; or perhaps also the protection of his uncle the Pope [Paul III]; or prudence and wisdom, for the ancients attributed the shield to Minerva, goddess of wisdom."[19] He concludes by denying that the *impresa* was invented by Molza, preferring to believe that the author can only have been Cardinal Alessandro himself.

DUKE ALESSANDRO FARNESE (FIG. 86)

In the foreground four cannon are firing against a besieged city, from which rise columns of smoke; fires are also visible at the sides. Above is a scroll with the motto: INVITVS INVITOS.

The device alludes to the siege and capture of the Dutch city of Maastricht by Alessandro Farnese in 1579. Filled with admiration for the heroism of the defenders, Farnese called upon them to surrender. When they refused, he reluctantly ordered the assault to proceed, and the city was sacked by the Spanish troops. This is the explanation of the motto, *Invitus invitos* [*debellavi*]: "I vanquished them against my will and against theirs." Alexander of Parma, we are to understand, is essentially a man of peace, who wages war only because heresy must be suppressed.[20]

The *impresa* first makes its appearance, to my knowledge, on a medal by Giuliano Giannini (Fig. 283) which shows the besieged city with the garbled inscription MÆSTREHC.[21] Unlike the fresco, however, this is no mere conventional city-view, but a topographical record, based no doubt on a campaign map.[22] The town is seen in panoramic fashion from the high ground to the south where the Spanish batteries are deployed. On the right side is the River Maas, with the bridge that connects the town to the suburb of Wijk; on the left, in the western part of the city, can be seen the Sint Servaaskerk. Above is the motto *Invitus invitos*. The painter, who must have used the medal for his design, has made no attempt to reproduce its specific features, though the tower in the middle of the town has a distinctly northern appearance.

[19] Ruscelli, *op.cit.*, fols. 45 v.-46 r.

[20] Joannes Bochius uses a similar phrase to describe the capture of Antwerp: "INVITVS *premit* INVITAM" (*Panegyrici in Antverpiam sibi et regi obsidione restitutam*, Antwerp, 1587, p. 73).

[21] G. van Loon, *Histoire métallique des XVII provinces des Pays-Bas*, I, p. 265. P. Litta, *Famiglie celebri italiane*, Farnesi Duchi di Parma, Medaglie Farnesiane, pl. III, 4. Van

Loon points out that the medal cannot be earlier than 1586, since on the obverse Farnese is already styled "third Duke," a title to which he succeeded only after his father's death in that year. Giuliano Giannini, a Florentine medallist who signed himself Iuliano F. F., worked entirely in the Netherlands.

[22] Cf. the maps of Maastricht reproduced in L. van der Essen, *Alexandre Farnèse, Prince de Parme*, II, Brussels, 1934, pls. VII-VIII.

CARDINAL ODOARDO FARNESE (FIG. 87)

The third device, which also figures in the Camerino (Fig. 16), is that of the master of the palace. It shows three purple lilies with the motto θεόθεν αὐξάνομαι (I grow by God's aid) and was invented for Odoardo by Fulvio Orsini. By including it in this series the cardinal symbolically takes his place in the line of Farnese princes.

DUKE RANUCCIO FARNESE (FIG. 88)

Odoardo's brother Ranuccio became fourth Duke of Parma and Piacenza in 1592, on the death of their father Alessandro. Ranuccio's *impresa* shows a wind god blowing a gust of air. The motto reads: PELLIT ET ATTRAHIT.

The device appears on coins of Ranuccio minted at Piacenza from 1592 onward.[23] It is probably to be understood as a description of the ideal prince: *Pellit [malum] et [bonum] attrahit* (He expels evil and attracts good), the two actions being nicely expressed by the wind god who alternately exhales and inhales.

The four *imprese* are arranged in chronological order on each wall, with the two deceased on the left and the two living on the right. They also present an alternation of spiritual and temporal, for the sequence runs: Cardinal, Duke, Cardinal, Duke, thus emphasizing the continuing leadership of the Farnese in both the active and contemplative realms. A similar alternation may be discovered in the mottoes, those of the Cardinals being in Greek and those of the Dukes (less learned perhaps) in Latin.

THE VIRGIN WITH THE UNICORN (FIG. 89)

Over the doorway on the inner wall Domenichino painted the *Virgin with the Unicorn*. This is an emblem, not of an individual, but of the Farnese family in general, and as such it completes the series of *imprese* on the walls of the Gallery. The Virgin and the Unicorn also figure prominently in the fresco decoration of the Sala di Perseo in the Castel Sant'Angelo, executed for Pope Paul III by Perino del Vaga and his assistants.

In Domenichino's fresco the maiden is seated beneath a tree at the left, wearing a pensive and abstracted air as she gently embraces the unicorn, who has placed his forelegs in her lap and laid his head against her breast. The mythical creature has exactly the same appearance as those in Perino's frieze in the Castel Sant'Angelo: he is a small pure-white animal of equine form, but with the beard and cloven hoofs of a goat; the horn projecting from his brow has the usual spiral grooves.[24] Behind and to the right of the figures there opens a pleasant and spacious landscape, in which appears a water-spring.

[23] *Corpus Nummorum Italicorum*, IX, Emilia, parte 1, pp. 622 ff., pl. XXXIX, 8, 9 and 12.

[24] On the various forms of the unicorn, and indeed on all matters relating to this creature, see Odell Shepard, *The Lore of the Unicorn*, Boston-New York, 1930. Further information of interest is contained in G. Schönberger, "Narwal-Einhorn. Studien über einen seltenen Werkstoff," *Städel-Jahrbuch*, IX, 1935-1936, pp. 167 ff.

Two aspects of the unicorn legend are combined in this picture. One is the story of his capture by a virgin, and the other concerns his power to purify water. In the Greek *Physiologus* and its offspring, the mediaeval Bestiary, the virgin-capture is presented as an allegory of Christ's Incarnation. The *Physiologus* describes the unicorn as a small animal of such ferocity and swiftness that he cannot be caught by huntsmen. But if a virgin comes alone to a place frequented by him he will run to her lap and allow himself to be taken. The unicorn thus signifies Christ, who descended into the Virgin's womb in order to assume human form.[25] In the Renaissance, as may be seen in the illustrations of Petrarch's *Trionfi*, the unicorn became also an accepted emblem of chastity.[26] This is surely the primary sense of the fresco: in the purity and chastity of the unicorn we may perceive yet another allusion to that divine love which is the principal theme of the Farnese cycle.

Another, though related, meaning is suggested by Annibal Caro, who, in a letter of 1563 describing the *imprese* of the Farnese family, gives the following explanation: "This device, of the Virgin with the Unicorn, seems to me to be the most ancient; the motto that I have seen with it is this: VIRTUS SECURITATEM PARIT. As I believe, it means that, as innocence or chastity protect the virgin from the ferocity of that beast, so do purity and honesty of life protect him who wears this device from every adversity. . . ."[27] This interpretation (which seems to imply that the maiden would be slain by the unicorn if she were not chaste) can also be found in the emblem books.[28] The ferocious unicorn loves chastity so dearly that in the presence of a virgin he becomes docile and hastens to her embrace. It is in such a way, then, that "virtue begets security."

The second trait of the unicorn is his ability to cleanse venomous water by immersing his horn in it, so that other animals may safely drink. This also was made the subject of an *impresa* for the Farnese. On a medal of Pier Luigi Farnese, first Duke of Parma and Piacenza, the unicorn plunges his horn into a stream from which serpents are escaping, while a bull and a she-wolf stand waiting to drink. The motto reads: IN VIRTUTE TUA SERVATI SUMUS. This device is interpreted by Ireneo Affò as follows: "The unicorn is a symbol of the beneficent prince who prepares a happy state for his subjects; for Pierio Valeriano says (*Hierogl.* Lib. 2) that this animal has in its horn the virtue of purifying waters of every poison and infection. The bull signifies the city and people of Parma, the she-wolf indicates the city and people of Piacenza, which cities have these two animals in their coats of arms. Altogether this emblem is meant to allude to the

[25] F. Lauchert, *Geschichte des Physiologus*, Strasbourg, 1889, pp. 254 f. See also M. R. James (ed.), *The Bestiary*, Oxford, 1928, p. 50.

[26] Representations of the *Trionfo della Pudicizia* show Chastity's car drawn by unicorns. See Prince d'Essling and Eugène Müntz, *Pétrarque, ses études d'art, son influence sur les artistes, ses portraits et ceux de Laure, l'illustration de ses écrits*, Paris, 1902, p. 121, plates opp. pp. 148, 150, 158. Cf. also Ripa, *Iconologia*, s.v. "Carro della Castità."

[27] *Delle lettere familiari del Commendatore Annibal Caro* . . . , Padua, 1742, II, p. 364.

[28] Cf. for example Joachim Camerarius, *Symbolorum et Emblematum . . . Centuriae Quattuor*, Frankfurt, 1654, Centuria II, Emblems XII and XIII.

useful advantage enjoyed by these subjects through having acquired such a ruler."[29]

Although its principal subject is the virgin with the unicorn the fresco also includes a flowing stream as a sign of his power to cleanse poisonous waters. We may thus regard the painting both as a symbol of divine love and as an emblem of the ideal prince. In each case the key word is *Virtus*, referring both to the virtue of chastity and to the protection afforded to his subjects by the virtuous ruler.

IV. THE LESSER MYTHOLOGICAL SUBJECTS

Just below the cornice on each of the long walls are four little rectangular panels with mythological scenes in fresco. Although the designs for these subjects were made by Annibale before his breakdown, they were not actually executed in fresco until 1608, at which time Domenichino assumed general supervision of the work. It has been suggested above that he and another artist, who is perhaps to be identified as Antonio Carracci, painted the four scenes on the inner wall, and that those on the opposite side were carried out by the two Parmese painters, Sisto Badalocchio and Giovanni Lanfranco.

Bellori, who makes only brief mention of these *altre figurine picciole*, says that they have *la medesima moralità* as the subjects of the ceiling.[30] For him, that is, they are simply appendages to the main cycle and are therefore to be understood as exemplifying "human love regulated by heavenly love." But our commentator cannot have been wholly satisfied with this explanation. It is difficult, for example, to see how the *Fall of Icarus* (Fig. 92) or *Mercury and Apollo* (Fig. 95) can have anything to do with divine love. If there is one thing that is clear about these eight little pictures, it is that they are meant to be looked at, not in connection with the vault but with the emblematic devices—the *imprese*—of the Farnese family. The close association of the two is made still more evident by the fact that the "arms" which project downward from each panel seem almost to enclose the accompanying emblem (cf. Fig. 38).

DAEDALUS AND ICARUS (FIG. 92)

We may begin on the inner wall with the *Fall of Icarus* (*Metam.* VIII, 183 ff.). While Daedalus pursues a middle course across the sky, his son has ventured too high and thus comes to grief: his wings disintegrate in the heat of the sun and he falls headlong toward the sea. The event is witnessed by two fishermen in a boat and a nude youth reclining on the shore, all of whom look up in astonishment.

Bellori's explanation,[31] which is that the scene represents "the fall of the rash," is too summary. To arrive at the full meaning we have only to glance at the *impresa* of Cardinal Alessandro Farnese directly below (Fig. 85), which expresses symbolically

---

[29] Affò, *La Zecca e moneta parmigiana*, p. 167, n. 104, tav. I, no. II. (For the reference to Valeriano, see Giovanni Pierio Valeriano, *Hieroglyphica*, Lyons, 1610, II, 22.) See also Armand, *Les médailleurs italiens*, I, p. 222, no. 8.

[30] *Vite*, p. 66.

[31] *Vite*, p. 66.

the doctrine of the Mean. It is at once obvious that the fable of Daedalus and Icarus carries the same significance: before setting out on the journey Daedalus explicitly warns his son to keep to a medium level, going neither too low nor too high (*Metam.* VIII, 203-5). For a typical translation of the myth into allegorical language we may turn to the *Moralized Ovid*: "Whoever therefore seeks to fly, either in a spiritual sense through virtuous works or in a temporal sense through worldly power, must keep to the middle and not deviate from the mean of temperance."[32]

DIANA AND CALLISTO (FIG. 93)

The second panel stands over the emblem of the Duke Alessandro. Diana and her nymphs are bathing in a woodland pool, into which water flows from a fountain at the left. Seated on a bank with her arm resting on the rim of the basin the goddess orders the expulsion of Callisto, whose pregnancy has just been revealed by the nymphs who have forcibly disrobed her.

As in the previous instance, a parallel is intended between the fable and the accompanying *impresa* (Fig. 86): as Alessandro Farnese was reluctantly compelled to make war on the Dutch (*invitus invitos*) in order that heresy might be suppressed, so is Diana obliged to expel Callisto from the sacred pool, although the latter is in reality innocent. It is significant that Ovid uses the same word "*invitus*" to describe Callisto's ill-fortune: *invito est pectore passa Iovem*—"Against her will Jove ravished her" (*Fasti* II, 178).

THE TRANSFORMATION OF CALLISTO (FIG. 94)

Angered by Jupiter's infidelity Juno takes her revenge by changing Callisto into a she-bear; the goddess, attended by her peacock, points to the luckless Callisto, already transformed into a bear, while Diana, leaning gracefully against the fountain, indicates the sacred pool from which the nymph was driven.

In the ursine form of Callisto Bellori thought to see an allusion to "the deformity of error."[33] But if the fable is followed to its conclusion it becomes evident that quite another meaning was intended. In order to protect Callisto from being slain as a wild beast Jupiter raised her to the sky, where she became the constellation of the Great Bear. Ovid makes Juno exclaim bitterly at this final triumph of her rival: "She whom I deprived of human form is now made a goddess!" (*Metam.* II, 521: *esse hominem vetui: facta est dea!*). It is in this sense, as an allegory of apotheosis, that the tale of Callisto's transformation must be read so as to bring it into harmony with the emblematic device just below (Fig. 87). For Odoardo's motto, "I grow with God's aid," is likewise relevant to the nymph who rises through adversity to the stars.[34]

---

[32] Waleys, *op.cit.,* fol. 69: "Qui igitur vult volare vel spiritualiter per opera virtuosa: vel temporaliter per potentiam secularem medium tenere debet nec a mediocritate temperantie devitare." See also Alciati, *Emblematum liber*, Embl. CIII (CIV).

[33] *Vite*, p. 66.

[34] Cf. the interpretation of the myth of Callisto in Waleys, *op.cit.*, fol. 29 v.

MERCURY AND APOLLO (FIG. 95)

The fourth and final subject on the inner wall, which is coupled with the *impresa* of Ranuccio, represents Mercury giving the Lyre to Apollo. Mercury, having stolen Apollo's flocks and been discovered, offered him as a gift to the lyre which he had invented; the instrument so delighted Apollo that he forgave the thief, and the two gods made a pact of friendship.[35] Apollo sits on a tree stump over which his mantle is draped; he wears a laurel wreath, and a shepherd's staff rests against his shoulder. The lyre is given to him by Mercury, who is standing with the caduceus held in his left hand. A domical building appears behind the trees at the left.

The scene may be said to illustrate Apollo's wisdom in turning a bad situation into a happy one. He is the watchful herdsman, who not only detects Mercury's theft but in so doing acquires the lyre, the instrument of celestial harmony. Like the wind god of Ranuccio's *impresa* (Fig. 88), "he banishes evil and attracts good."

ARION AND THE DOLPHIN (FIG. 96)

A parallel set of four mythological subjects accompanies the Farnese emblems on the window wall. Above the *impresa* of Cardinal Alessandro is the fable of *Arion and the Dolphin*. Learning that the sailors of the ship in which he was traveling were about to murder him for his wealth, the musician Arion begged to be allowed to sing and play the lyre for the last time. Having concluded his song, he then threw himself into the sea. The sound of the lyre had attracted many music-loving dolphins to the scene, and one of them, taking Arion on his back, bore him safely to shore. When the ship docked, the crew were confronted by the musician and put to death. Apollo later set both the lyre and the dolphin among the stars.[36] Arion, firmly grasping his lyre, is seen riding upon the back of the dolphin, which is followed by a school of others. The musician wears a laurel wreath and looks back to the ship from which he has escaped.

Since the picture surmounts Cardinal Alessandro's *impresa* of the arrow in the shield (Fig. 85), it must be presumed to exemplify—like the fable of Daedalus and Icarus—the principle of the Mean. And it is true that Arion, like Daedalus, avoids the dangers that threaten him on either side through foresight and presence of mind. By taking thought he selects the one course that can deliver him from certain death: he calls upon the dolphins to save him. Just as a steady aim is required to hit the target in the center, so is a clear purpose needed to escape evil.

It has been noted that certain subjects in the Gallery were apparently chosen because of their previous association with the Farnese. The fresco of Arion affords another such instance. For Arion on the dolphin appears on a coin of Ottavio Farnese,

[35] *Homeric Hymn to Hermes*, 1 ff. A painting of the same subject by Francesco Albani is now in Fontainebleau (repr. in the catalogue *L'ideale classico del Seicento in Italia*, no. 47). See also the drawing by Claude in the "Liber Veritatis" (repr. in M. Röthlisberger, *Claude Lorrain, the Paintings*, New Haven, 1961, fig. 312).

[36] Herodotus, 1, 24; Servius on Virgil's *Eclogue* VIII, 55.

second Duke of Parma, with the cryptic motto QVID NON.[37] The words (which serve only as a key to unlock the meaning) are from the *Ars poetica* of Horace; the whole passage reads: "Though I myself write nothing, I will teach the poet's duty and office; whence comes his wealth; what nourishes and forms him; what is fitting and what is not; whither virtue leads and whither error."[38] Here we recognize once again the idea of virtue as the middle way between extremes. A little further on the same theme is developed by the poet in metaphors that are directly relevant to the images both of the musician and of the archer: "For the string does not always yield the sound which hand and mind intend . . . nor does the bow always hit whatever mark is threatened."[39] It is difficult to resist the conclusion that the subjects were chosen with this very passage in mind.

MINERVA AND PROMETHEUS (FIG. 97)

The bearded Prometheus, clad in a short tunic, stands with his back to the observer and places one hand on the figure which he has just fashioned of clay. His head is turned toward Minerva, who appears before a columned portico; the goddess, wearing helmet and aegis and carrying a spear, points up to heaven. A temple is visible among the trees in the distance.

Servius relates that after he had shaped men Prometheus ascended to heaven with the aid of Minerva and stole fire from the chariot of the sun, which he then brought to mankind.[40] The story is retold in more elaborate form by Boccaccio, according to whom the fire stolen from heaven is the "clarity of knowledge which is infused into the breast of the ignorant." The subsequent punishment of the Titan on Mt. Caucasus signifies the torture of the speculative mind which seeks to uncover the secrets of nature.[41] It is evident that some such meaning must be looked for both in this scene and in its sequel, *Hercules freeing Prometheus* (Fig. 99). The goddess Minerva, while offering to assist Prometheus so that the light of reason may be instilled in mankind, nevertheless does so reluctantly, knowing that the divine spark will bring not happiness but torment. The idea that certain disagreeable consequences must be accepted in the pursuit of noble ends is also implicit in the accompanying *impresa* of the Duke Alessandro (cf. Fig. 86).

[37] Affò, *op.cit.*, p. 188, pl. VI, no. 82. The figure is here erroneously described as Amphion, but is certainly Arion.

[38] *Ars Poetica* 306-308: "munus et officium, nil scribens ipse, docebo, / unde parentur opes, quid alat formetque poetam, / quid deceat, quid non, quo virtus, quo ferat error."

[39] *Ibid.*, 348-350: "nam neque chorda sonum reddit, quem volt manus et mens, / poscentique gravem persaepe remittit acutum; / nec semper feriet quodcumque minabitur arcus."

[40] Servius on Virgil's *Eclogue* VI, 42. For the many interpretations of the fable see O. Raggio, "The Myth of Prometheus," *Journal of the Warburg and Courtauld Institutes*, XXI, 1958, pp. 44 ff.

[41] Boccaccio, *Genealogia Deorum*, IV, 44. The conception of Prometheus as a symbol of the contemplative mind is further developed by Marsilio Ficino, notably in his *Quaestiones quinque de mente* (*Opera omnia*, Basel, 1576, p. 680).

THE FARNESE GALLERY

HERCULES AND THE DRAGON (FIG. 98)

The scene takes place in the garden of the Hesperides, which is pictured as a fenced enclosure. Brandishing his club over his head Hercules is about to slay the dragon which guards the tree bearing the golden apples. The hero's feat is observed by Jupiter, who looks down approvingly from the sky.

It is hardly necessary to remark how aptly the scene corresponds to Odoardo's device (cf. Fig. 87), with its implication of advancement in virtue. Gyraldus explains that the golden apples won by Hercules have a virtuous significance: specifically they represent the suppression of anger, of avarice and of lust.[42] Nor should we overlook the analogy to the myth of Callisto (Fig. 94): under divine patronage both Hercules and Callisto overcome danger and hardship and are at last deified.

HERCULES FREEING PROMETHEUS (FIG. 99)

The final scene may be regarded as a sequel to the two preceding pictures, *Minerva and Prometheus* (Fig. 97) and *Hercules and the Dragon* (Fig. 98). Because of his theft of fire from heaven Prometheus was chained to the Caucasus, where an eagle perpetually gnawed at his liver. Hyginus relates[43] that Hercules, having been sent by Eurystheus to fetch the apples of the Hesperides, had to ask Prometheus where to find them; returning later with the apples the hero showed his gratitude by slaying the eagle and freeing the Titan from his bonds. In the fresco Hercules, still holding his bow, has begun to loosen the chains that fasten Prometheus to the mountain; on the ground at his feet are his club, the three golden apples, and a quiver of arrows. The eagle lies at the left, pierced by Hercules' arrow. In thus releasing a benefactor of mankind from cruel torment Hercules may be said to symbolize the enlightened ruler. The reference is of course to the Duke Ranuccio, whose device proclaims that "he banishes evil and attracts good" (cf. Fig. 88).

The fresco, attributable to Lanfranco, follows Annibale's preparatory sketch very faithfully (No. 147; Fig. 266). In the dramatically foreshortened figure of Prometheus, whose feet are placed higher than his head, there are echoes of two famous conceptions of a related subject—the Torture of Tityus. The first is Michelangelo's drawing in Windsor, which was undoubtedly known to Annibale since it had formed part of the collection of Cardinal Alessandro Farnese.[44] The second—even more important for Annibale's picture—is the painting by Titian in the Prado. Titian's composition was copied in an engraving by Cornelis Cort, who transformed the tortured figure of Tityus into a Prometheus;[45] it was plainly this print that suggested to Carracci not only the agonized attitude of the bound hero but the effective detail of the outstretched leg straining against the chain.

[42] L. G. Gyraldus, *Opera omnia*, Leyden, 1696, p. 571 E-F.
[43] Hyginus, *Poet. Astron.* II, 15.
[44] Popham and Wilde, *Italian Drawings of the XV and XVI Centuries at Windsor Castle*, pp. 252 f., no. 429, pl. 21.
[45] Raggio, *op.cit.*, pp. 57 f., pl. 9c.

140

In this miniature cycle of eight pictures, then, the observer was expected to see exemplified in mythological guise the moral themes of the emblematic devices. Yet, although this is certainly their primary significance, it is not necessary to conclude that they can be interpreted in no other way. A moment's reflection on the choice of subjects may lead us to suspect that other meanings were also intended. It can hardly be due to mere accident that allusions to art and its divine origin are so conspicuous throughout the series. Daedalus and Prometheus, for example, will be recognized as legendary archetypes of the artist, whose struggles and achievements are in some sense an echo of theirs.[46] The intriguing possibility thus arises that in these little scenes Annibale may have been able to inject a somewhat more personal note into the otherwise official iconography of the Galleria Farnese.

With this in mind let us review the series once more, beginning this time with *Mercury and Apollo* (Fig. 95). Apollo with the lyre traditionally symbolizes poetic inspiration, which in accordance with the doctrine *ut pictura poesis* applies to painting as well as to poetry.[47] The fact that the instrument is presented to Apollo by Mercury may be taken to allude to the dual aspect of art, which combines the eloquence of Mercury and the wisdom of Apollo.

Directly opposite this scene is the fresco of *Arion and the Dolphin* (Fig. 96). The divinely inspired artist, though cruelly mistreated by men, is able through his music to arouse admiration and sympathy in brutes. Here may be detected a reference to the tribulations of the artist, a theme that recurs in other scenes of this cycle. In the end, however, the artist prevails over his enemies and detractors: out of his love for Arion Apollo assigns both the lyre and the dolphin a place among the stars.[48]

Daedalus (Fig. 92), imprisoned against his will in Crete and constrained to make his escape by air, likewise typifies the artist whose superhuman power enables him to triumph over adversity. In the same manner the Prometheus episodes (Figs. 97 and 99) illustrate the troubles visited upon the artist whose divine gift arouses the envy of the gods themselves.

The conception of Prometheus as the archetype of the creative artist was evidently a familiar one in the Carracci circle. The story of the Titan who stole fire from heaven figured among the emblematic pictures painted in grisaille for Agostino's funeral in Bologna in 1603. The painting in question, which was the work of Alessandro Albini, is known to us from the engraving by Guido Reni (Fig. 280, no. 4, upper right) and from the description by Benedetto Morello: ". . . in the fourth place [was represented] the fable of Prometheus who, while descending from heaven with the fire taken from the wheels of the sun in order to give spirit and life to the statue of Pandora which he had made, was accompanied by Pallas who came with him to earth where the newly

---

[46] Cf. E. Kris and O. Kurz, *Die Legende vom Künstler. Ein geschichtlicher Versuch*, Vienna, 1934, pp. 69 ff.

[47] See R. W. Lee, "*Ut pictura pocsis*: the

Humanistic Theory of Painting," *Art Bulletin*, XXII, 1940, pp. 197-269.

[48] See note 36 above.

formed figure was to be seen; and with it was the motto SVNT COMMERCIA COELI, to signify . . . that Agostino, accompanied by profound wisdom, gave spirit and force to his works through superhuman virtue."[49] The motto is from Ovid's *Ars Amatoria* (III, 549 f.), where the poet says (in words that apply beautifully to the Farnese pictures under discussion): "There is a god in us; we are in touch with heaven: from celestial places comes our inspiration."[50]

Albini's painting commemorating Agostino leaves little room for doubt that a similar meaning attaches to the Prometheus scenes in the Farnese Gallery: the Titan exemplifies both the divine powers and the tribulations of the artist. Once this symbolism is understood, it is easy to explain why the story of Hercules is interwoven with that of Prometheus. In one scene (Fig. 98) Hercules, signifying Odoardo Farnese himself, slays the dragon; in the next (Fig. 99) the hero releases the Titan from his ordeal. The inference to be drawn is that the virtuous prince must protect the artist from mistreatment.

But the deeper significance of this miniature cycle can only be penetrated through a closer examination of the Callisto episodes (Figs 93-94), which flank the central door on the inner wall. For in these pictures Annibale seems not merely to refer to "the artist" in general, but to be making a cryptic allusion to himself: there is perceptible here an autobiographical note, expressed in veiled, emblematic terms.

In an age which delighted in conceits of this kind it is not surprising to learn that the Carracci had their own emblem. The device was prominently displayed among the decorations prepared for the funeral of Agostino in 1603. On the walls of the church, we are told, "were hung shields with the arms of the Carracci family, which are the seven stars of the celestial car [*carro celeste*] which appear in our sky at the north pole."[51] The seven stars are those that make up the constellation of the Great Bear, under which name it commemorates Jupiter's action in placing the wronged nymph Callisto among the stars; the constellation is also known in Italian as *Il Carro*, and in English as Charles's Wain, or the Dipper. As might be expected, this heraldic device was Agostino's invention. Lucio Faberio, in his funeral eulogy of the artist, connects it with Agostino's interest in astronomy: "He sought to know the celestial images, one of which, the Great Bear, commonly called the *Carro*, is the emblem of the Carracci family."[52] Bellori, on the other hand, maintains in his life of Agostino that the artist invented the *impresa* solely for reasons of prestige. "In order to rise above his humble state," he writes, "Agostino ennobled the name of the Carracci by the device of the *Carro celeste*, which is the seven stars of the Great Bear, and which he made into the emblem and arms of his family."[53]

[49] *Il funerale d'Agostin Carraccio*, p. 15 (reprinted in Malvasia, *Felsina*, I, p. 414).

[50] "Est deus in nobis: et sunt commercia caeli: / sedibus aetheriis spiritus ille venit."

[51] *Il funerale*, p. 7 (reprinted in Malvasia, *Felsina*, I, p. 411).

[52] *Ibid.*, p. 35 (reprinted in Malvasia, *Felsina*, I, p. 428).

[53] Bellori, *Vite*, p. 114.

Whatever Annibale may have thought of his brother's social aspirations, he did not disdain to make use of the emblem, one very striking example of which has not hitherto been noticed. In the frescoed vault of the Cerasi Chapel in Santa Maria del Popolo, painted from Annibale's design by Innocenzo Tacconi, the scene of the *Vision of St. Paul* contains in the upper right corner the seven stars of the Great Bear; they serve not only to place the scene in the third heaven but also to record Carracci's authorship.[54]

Agostino's *impresa*, which has for its motto the word *Immortale*, is admirably complex and rich in allusions. As a pictorial device it can take the form of the constellation of the Great Bear, of the "celestial chariot,"[55] or of the figure of the bear itself. Each of these three images, moreover, has overtones of meaning which contribute to the richness of the *impresa* as a whole. It is, for instance, an important characteristic of the constellation of the Great Bear that it never sets, which makes it especially apt as the badge of an illustrious name. Equally felicitous is the notion of the "celestial chariot," because of the play on the words *Carro celeste* and *Carracci*. But not to be overlooked is the emblematic representation of the bear itself.

A drawing by Agostino at Windsor contains, as Wittkower has shown, several designs for an emblematic bear (Fig. 286).[56] In the small sketch (center right) the bear stands upon an ornamental base, which seems to indicate that the work was to be executed as a small sculpture. The animal has been attacked by hunters, who have stuck darts into its flesh. A larger sketch represents the bear rising on its hind legs and with teeth bared, as if to confront its tormentors; beside this Agostino has written the motto *Inmortale*, and elsewhere on the sheet he has added the names of certain members of the Carracci family: his brother Annibale, his son Antonio, and his nephew Francesco, or Franceschino. In choosing the bear as a painter's emblem Agostino may also have had in mind the famous *impresa* of Titian, showing a she-bear licking her unformed cubs into shape, with the motto *Natura potentior ars*.[57] But of course the primary reference is to the story of Callisto: virtue triumphs over adversity and at length achieves immortality.

If we now compare Agostino's drawing with the fresco of the *Transformation of Callisto* (Fig. 94) we observe a striking similarity in the rendering of the she-bears: the animal in the painting, with its head turned back and one foreleg raised, is virtually a replica of the bear mounted on a stand in Agostino's sketch. It is evident, in short, that Annibale had before him his brother's drawing (or perhaps even the

---

[54] On the Cerasi Chapel see L. Steinberg, in *Art Bulletin*, XLI, 1959, pp. 183-190; the *Vision of St. Paul* is reproduced as fig. 5.

[55] One of the pictures made for Agostino's funeral (Fig. 280, no. 1) showed "un carro spezzato nell'aria" in allusion to the death of the artist (*Il funerale*, p. 14; in Malvasia, *Felsina*, I, p. 414). The image of the "broken chariot" recurs in a poem by Cesare Rinaldi

lamenting Agostino's death (Malvasia, *Felsina*, I, p. 434).

[56] Wittkower, *Carracci Drawings*, p. 121, no. 158, pl. 39.

[57] See B. Pittoni, *Imprese nobili, et ingegniose di diversi Prencipi, et d'altri personaggi illustri nell' arme et nelle lettere . . .*, Venice, 1583.

sculptured bear) when he designed the fresco. Nor can there be any doubt about his intention. Callisto changed into a bear can in this set of pictures have only one meaning: the immortal name of the Carracci. In setting the pictures of Callisto on either side of the principal entrance to the Gallery Annibale was, in effect, placing his signature on the great work.

If it is true that these two subjects introduce a note of autobiography into the frescoes of the Gallery, the question arises whether Annibale may not also have intended to make a concealed criticism of his patron, Cardinal Farnese. This is not so improbable as it sounds. There seems to be no doubt that Odoardo's ungenerous treatment of the artist a few years earlier left Annibale deeply embittered and depressed, and it would not have been unnatural if, as the great project at last neared completion, the painter sought in this way to express his feelings of resentment. It is, of course, very unlikely that the cycle of eight mythological scenes was invented by Annibale himself. On the contrary there is a subtle allusiveness about these subjects (particularly in their relation to the *imprese*) that reveals the intervention of an experienced humanist.

Who was this *letterato*? It was surely not Fulvio Orsini, for he had died in 1600, before the final details of the decoration of the side walls had been decided upon. The possibility is therefore worth considering that in the selection of subjects for this series of eight pictures Annibale was aided by Giovanni Battista Agucchi. As a close friend and devoted admirer of the artist, Agucchi might have welcomed the opportunity to devise a set of subjects which should not only form a suitable accompaniment to the Farnese emblematic devices but which should at the same time secretly intimate that Annibale was not receiving the recognition that he deserved.[58] Did a rumor of such collaboration reach Bellori's ears? This might account for his mistaken notion that the monsignor had acted as Annibale's literary adviser in the Camerino.

Let it be added that the ideas expressed in this cycle of pictures are by no means foreign to Agucchi's way of thinking. We may cite as an example his discourse *Del Mezzo*, which was written in 1611 with the help of Galileo,[59] and in which Agucchi expounds at length the doctrine of the Mean as a universal principle. After an extended discussion of "mediocrity" and "centrality," he turns at last to an *impresa* that he has invented for himself—an *impresa* representing the planet Jupiter in the midst of its four satellites (discovered in 1610 by Galileo), with the motto *Medii*

---

[58] Agucchi makes this very statement in his *Trattato* (reprinted in Mahon, *Studies*, p. 258 and note 42). Here of course he is not referring to Cardinal Farnese but to those unenlightened princes who did not see fit to patronize Annibale.

[59] Florence, Bibl. Naz., MSS Gal., Discepoli,

Tom. 136, fols. 95-110. The discourse is analyzed by E. Panofsky, *Galileo as a Critic of the Arts*, The Hague, 1954, pp. 38-41. I am indebted to Professor Panofsky for generously permitting me to make use of his transcript of the document.

cuppedine victae (Swayed by the desire for the middle).[60] In searching for a device to embody the idea of "excellent mediocrity," Agucchi may well have remembered the *impresa* of Cardinal Alessandro Farnese with an arrow embedded in a shield (Fig. 85), especially since he employs the image of the archer and the target to exemplify the difficulty of striking the mean.[61] It is interesting, too, that he adduces the fable of Daedalus and Icarus (cf. Fig. 92), among others, to illustrate the danger of straying from the middle course.[62] Evidence may one day come to light which will tell us more of Annibale's relations with Agucchi during the final stages of the Farnese Gallery. For the time being Agucchi's role as adviser must remain hypothetical.

[60] Agucchi, *op.cit.*, fols. 107 v.-108 r. Panofsky, *op.cit.*, pp. 40 f., fig. 16.

[61] Agucchi, *op.cit.*, fol. 99 v.

[62] *Ibid.*, fols. 96 r.-96 v.

CHAPTER 8 · THE FARNESE GALLERY
AND THE BAROQUE

THE impact of Carracci's frescoes on his contemporaries, accustomed to the competent but insipid *maniera* of artists such as the Cavaliere d'Arpino, can hardly be exaggerated. The sensuousness, the exuberance, the rich inventiveness and inexhaustible variety of the Galleria Farnese were seen as heralding the advent of a new age. From the few accounts that have come down to us from the period immediately following the unveiling of the vault we may still sense something of the reaction brought about by this stupendous achievement. It seems to have been recognized at once that amid the prevailing mediocrity of fresco-painting Annibale's cycle merited comparison only with the great masterworks of the High Renaissance: this was clearly implied by Lucio Faberio when he called the Gallery an addition to the beauties of Rome; its unique character was also emphasized by Carel van Mander who (though he was merely repeating what he had heard from Rome) said that it was painted in a "manner surpassing those of all other masters."[1] These were not merely expressions of a momentary enthusiasm, to be forgotten when the novelty had worn off. Some fifteen years later Giulio Mancini, surveying the Farnese Gallery and other works by Annibale, judiciously concluded that "after Raphael there have been few, or none, who can be called his equal."[2] Giovanni Pietro Bellori voiced much the same idea in 1672 when he said that Annibale had renewed "the golden age of painting" in Rome. It was safe to predict, Bellori felt, that his fame would never die.[3]

Whether Annibale himself gave much thought to fame we shall probably never know. But there is no doubt that his brother considered it a matter of some importance. It was not lost upon Agostino, when he chose the sign of the Great Bear as a family emblem (Fig. 286), that that constellation never sets, and in adding the motto *Immortale* he was only reiterating his belief—or his hope—that the name of the Carracci would enjoy eternal renown. Agostino's prophecy held true for almost two centuries, during which time the star of the Carracci shone with undiminished brilliance. Then, as the damaging notion of "eclecticism" gradually fastened itself upon critical opinion, their reputation suffered a severe decline from which it has only recently recovered.[4]

The rehabilitation of the Carracci in our own day is a phenomenon hardly less remarkable than the revulsion of taste that earlier threw them into eclipse. The

---

[1] *Il funerale d'Agostin Carraccio*, p. 40 (reprinted in Malvasia, *Felsina*, 1, p. 431); Van Mander, *Het Schilderboeck*, fols. 190 v-191 r.

[2] Mancini, *Considerazioni sulla pittura*, 1, p. 220.

[3] Bellori, *Vite*, pp. 64, 79.

[4] Mahon, *Studies*, pp. 195 ff.; *idem*, "Eclecticism and the Carracci: Further Reflections on the Validity of a Label," *Journal of the Warburg and Courtauld Institutes*, XVI, 1953, pp. 303 ff.

change has been especially pronounced in the case of Annibale. This artist, once reduced in the estimation of influential critics to the level of an assiduous but uninspired imitator, is now accorded a secure place among the leading painters of the post-Renaissance era. A century and a half ago Henry Fuseli could describe the frescoes of the Galleria Farnese as "a chaotic series of trite fable and bacchanalian revelry, without allegory, void of allusion, [painted] merely to gratify the puerile ostentation of dauntless execution and academic vigour."[5] Today it is not considered an exaggeration to speak of these paintings as "an artistic and intellectual achievement of the highest order."[6] That Carracci's Gallery was of seminal importance to the art of the Seicento is taken for granted. The names of Rubens and Bernini are invoked in order to illustrate how the Farnese cycle prepared the way for the High Baroque, while almost in the same breath Poussin's praise of the Gallery is cited as evidence that these same frescoes contributed to the flowering of seventeenth-century classicism.

The idea is not new, but was already being expressed (though naturally in different terms) in the seventeenth century. Agucchi, for example, considered it noteworthy that Annibale had sought to unite in his art Roman *Disegno* and "Lombard" *Colore*.[7] Although such phrases generally have more to do with theory than with practice, there is no denying that Agucchi's statement contains a kernel of truth. It is worth remembering, in this connection, that Annibale's workshop actually nourished future champions of the two opposed principles: if Domenichino can be regarded as an exponent of *Disegno*, his rival Lanfranco is certainly entitled to be called a representative of *Colore*. Even more to the point is the fact that throughout the controversy which divided Roman artists of the seventeenth century into two camps[8] the Galleria Farnese continued to offer to adherents of both sides an unfailing source of inspiration. It might be said that in the eyes of Seicento observers Annibale's fresco cycle wore two different aspects: while seeming to the upholders of classicism to exemplify the virtues of rationalism, conservatism, and traditionalism, at the same time it appeared to the apologists for the High Baroque to vindicate the role of imagination, the appeal to the senses, and even, to a degree, the use of illusionism. What were the ingredients that satisfied such divergent tastes and thus ensured the authority of the Galleria in the leading artistic circles of seventeenth-century Rome?

It is evident, to begin with, that the decorative system of the ceiling was not one of the features that contributed to its popularity. For the fact is that the complicated structural organism devised by Annibale—a synthesis, as we have attempted to show, of three systems of decoration—inspired few imitators. This should not surprise us. To many observers the extensive use of *quadri riportati*, the multiple centers of

[5] H. Fuseli, *Lectures on Painting delivered at the Royal Academy, March 1801*, London, 1801, p. 84.
[6] Wittkower, *Carracci Drawings*, p. 14.
[7] G. B. Agucchi, *Trattato* (in Mahon, Studies, p. 257). Cf. also Bellori, *Vite*, p. 79.
[8] M. Missirini, *Memorie per servire alla storia della Romana Accademia di S. Luca fino alla morte di Antonio Canova*, Rome, 1823, pp. 111 ff.

interest and the intricate relationship of parts probably seemed old-fashioned. In the sophisticated ingenuities of the Farnese ceiling there is still a lingering flavor of Mannerism, which doubtless explains why the decorative system left no progeny.

More than anything else, we must conclude, it was the peculiar quality of Annibale's classicism that so impressed the younger generation of artists working in Rome. In the Farnese cycle Annibale had taken as his masters Michelangelo, Raphael, and the antique. Yet the image of classical antiquity that Carracci's frescoes presented was informed with far greater sensuousness and vitality than would ever be met with in Greco-Roman statuary or in the art of the High Renaissance. This was clearly understood by Bellori (who was careful however to omit the name of Raphael): "What statues by Agasias or Glycon will you find that are superior to those feigned statues painted by him in chiaroscuro, the Termini of the Galleria Farnese? What Hercules, or giants if you like, by Michelangelo will you choose in preference to the Hercules and Polyphemuses painted by him?"[9] Now it is significant that those artists, classic and baroque alike, on whom the Gallery produced the greatest effect were also those who were most concerned to recapture in their work the spirit of antiquity. To a large degree the Farnese frescoes owed their unique power to the fact that in them Annibale had opened up a new approach to the antique. It was an approach that was to prove especially fruitful in the seventeenth century.

Second only in importance to Annibale's classicism was his successful revival of the Renaissance tradition of history painting. This meant, above all, renewed attention to the subject of expression. The rendering of human passions by means of gesture and facial features, which Raphael had developed to so eloquent a pitch in the Cartoons, had been of comparatively little interest to the Mannerists, whose genius lay in quite another direction. But Annibale's orientation was unequivocally humanistic, and in his art the *affetti* had accordingly become once more a matter of central concern. To be sure, it was not only in the Gallery that he demonstrated his mastery of expression: the *Almsgiving of St. Roch* (Dresden), which was engraved by the young Guido Reni, was much admired in the Seicento for its insight into human nature; and it would be difficult to imagine a more lucid exposition of the *concetto della mente* (to use Leonardo's phrase) than that offered by the *Choice of Hercules* in the Camerino. But what made the Galleria especially impressive was that here the artist had concentrated upon some of the strongest human passions: love, desire, rapture, jealousy, and rage were represented in a vivid and sensuous fashion that appealed directly to the new taste for naturalistic expression.

Not to be overlooked, finally, is the provocative interweaving of real and imaginary to which we have drawn attention in the frescoes of the vault. The secret of Annibale's decorative fantasy is that it is believable: even the most extravagant imagery is governed by a strongly naturalistic sense. His illusionism does not take the form of exciting vistas into infinite space, but rather of a continuous play on levels of

9 Bellori, *Vite*, p. 79.

reality. And this conception of the role of naturalism lies at the very core of Baroque art.

I. THE FARNESE GALLERY AND THE HIGH BAROQUE

Modern criticism, in an effort to sharpen the distinction between "classic" and "baroque" in Seicento art, has tended to widen the gap between Annibale Carracci and painters such as Giovanni Lanfranco. Partly because the very name of Lanfranco conjures up an idea of painterly freedom and expansive illusionism (and also because he was a bitter enemy of the classicist Domenichino), we are apt to underestimate the importance of this artist's training in Annibale's Roman workshop. Yet it is very doubtful if Lanfranco, who after all looked on himself as a Carracci pupil, was aware of any irreconcilable conflict between his own "coloristic" leanings and the admittedly different aims of his master. In 1607, it will be remembered, he and Badalocchio gave a tangible sign of their esteem by presenting to Annibale their engravings of Raphael's Loggie; in the accompanying letter of dedication the two Parmese artists spoke with deep appreciation of Carracci's teaching and his "truly paternal regard" for his pupils.[10] Annibale, for his part, evidently thought well of Lanfranco, because in addition to allotting him a share in various collaborative projects such as the Herrera Chapel he permitted his youthful disciple to carry out a totally independent fresco cycle in the Camerino degli Eremiti in the grounds of the Farnese palace. In the Galleria Lanfranco probably executed, from Annibale's designs, two of the little mythological subjects on the window wall. It might be noted in passing that one of these, the *Arion* (Fig. 96), was taken as a model by Giovanni Francesco Romanelli for his ceiling painting in the Palazzo Costaguti.

The nature of the young Lanfranco's highly individual interpretation of Annibale's late style is nicely illustrated by his *Separation of SS. Peter and Paul* (Louvre), which must be of about the same date as his frescoes in the Galleria Farnese. It is at once apparent that the architectural setting, with its castellated walls and towers and its arched gateway, is based on Annibale's *Martyrdom of St. Stephen* (Louvre).[11] What is perhaps less obvious is the fact that for the distant spectators gathered on the bank at the upper right Lanfranco has adapted the group of persons watching Perseus' battle with the sea monster in Carracci's fresco, the *Perseus and Andromeda* (Fig. 77).[12] In spite of the characteristically looser and more animated construction of the figures there is no mistaking their derivation: the bearded old man with arm extended, the boy standing beside him, and the nude youth seated on the bank all

[10] *Ibid.*, pp. 96 ff. Bellori speaks elsewhere (p. 74) of Annibale's skill as a teacher.

[11] As was noted by A. Emiliani in the catalogue of the exhibition *L'ideale classico del Seicento*, pp. 318 ff., no. 123. The painting by Annibale is reproduced in the catalogue of the *Mostra dei Carracci*, no. 111.

[12] This was pointed out to me by Richard Spear. It may further be noted in Lanfranco's canvas that the stance of the soldier who is seen from the back grasping Peter's drapery is also derived from Annibale; cf. in particular the figure of Thescelus in the *Combat of Perseus and Phineus* (Fig. 78).

find their prototypes in the Farnese fresco, which Lanfranco himself must have seen being painted.

In the field of monumental decoration Lanfranco was by no means as eager to shake off the effects of his training under Annibale as is sometimes assumed. His fresco of *Joseph and the Wife of Potiphar* in the Palazzo Mattei (1615) may serve as an example of his continuing indebtedness to his late master. The swift and sudden changes in direction, particularly evident in the lively handling of the drapery, do not long conceal the fundamentally classical basis of the design, originating as it does in Raphael's fresco of this subject in the Loggie (engraved, it so happens, by Lanfranco himself; cf. Bartsch XVIII, 16). Closer study reveals, moreover, that both figures are modeled after inventions by Annibale: the striding form of Joseph derives from the Christ carrying the cross in the *Domine, quo vadis?* (London),[13] and the agitated pose of Potiphar's wife clearly owes its inspiration to the amorous father of the gods in the scene of *Jupiter and Juno* on the Farnese ceiling (Fig. 43). Bellori was not far from the truth when he said of Lanfranco that "la sua maniera ritiene li principij, e l'educatione della scuola de' Carracci."[14]

In 1616 Lanfranco worked under Agostino Tassi's direction on the frieze of the Sala Regia in the Quirinal Palace, where according to Bellori he was assigned responsibility for some of the ovals with scenes of Moses.[15] Was it perhaps he who proposed that the grouping of the decorative figures around these ovals should follow the example of the Farnese frieze?

Lanfranco's fresco decoration of the loggia in the Villa Borghese, painted in 1624-1625, marks a decisive step toward High Baroque illusionism.[16] In place of Carracci's multiple centers of interest, each one competing with the next for the spectator's attention, Lanfranco's ceiling is dominated by a single *quadro riportato*, which can in addition be interpreted as an opening in the vault through which the open sky is visible, with the gods of Olympus deployed on clouds. Yet, while rejecting his predecessor's intricate and crowded structural system, Lanfranco nevertheless found it expedient to adopt certain motives employed by Annibale a quarter of a century before. The stone-colored nudes who with visible effort sustain the feigned entablature were manifestly designed in imitation of the Farnese atlantes; and the intriguing glimpses of blue sky through the illusory openings of the coving were likewise suggested by the narrow apertures in the corners of the Carracci ceiling. Further reminiscences of the Farnese are to be seen in the little monochrome frescoes of the Borghese loggia: the medallion of a satyr pursuing a nymph, for instance, is quite clearly an imitation of Annibale's *Pan and Syrinx* (Fig. 51). The chiaroscuro panel

---

[13] Lanfranco imitated this figure even more closely in his large canvas *Norandino and Lucina* (Rome, Gall. Borghese).

[14] Bellori, *Vite*, p. 381.

[15] *Ibid.*, p. 369. See G. Briganti, *Il Palazzo del Quirinale*, Rome, 1962.

[16] H. Hibbard, "The Date of Lanfranco's Fresco in the Villa Borghese and other Chronological Problems," *Miscellanea Bibliothecae Hertzianae*, Munich, 1961, pp. 355 ff.

representing Aurora and Cephalus over one of the windows is based on Agostino's fresco of this subject in the Galleria.[17]

In his *Historia Augusta*, published in 1641, the collector and antiquarian Francesco Angeloni speaks of the Carracci as the restorers of painting, and at once goes on to remark that the Cavaliere Giovanni Lanfranco is one of their followers.[18] The reason for this seemingly gratuitous mention of the Parmese master becomes evident when we turn to the title-page of Angeloni's volume, which was in fact designed by Lanfranco himself (Fig. 287). For the decorative panel enframing the title exactly copies the section of the Farnese ceiling showing the medallion of *Pan and Syrinx* (Fig. 51), as if Lanfranco had chosen this cryptic way of acknowledging that he was indeed a disciple of Annibale.

One of the artists on whom the Farnese vault had a genuinely liberating effect was Pietro da Cortona; it may be said of him—as of Rubens—that it was the nascent Baroque elements in Annibale's ceiling that stimulated the development of his own dynamic style. Cortona was too young to have studied under Carracci, and in any event did not arrive in Rome until several years after the latter's death. By the twenties, when he began to paint his first important frescoes, High Baroque illusionism had already made a dramatic appearance in the ceiling paintings of Guercino and Lanfranco. Yet Cortona did not at once hurl himself into the production of illusionistic extravaganzas. Instead (and in this respect he may remind us of certain artists of our day who before embarking upon a contemporary abstract idiom have found it useful to begin in a more representational manner) he first took care to ground himself in the principles of the Carracci-Domenichino tradition, thus recapitulating, as it were, the stylistic evolution from the Early Baroque to the full-blown High Baroque. The starting-point of this evolution, at least as far as monumental art was concerned, was the Galleria Farnese. There was another element in Cortona's nature that impelled him to turn to the Farnese cycle, and that was his passion for classical antiquity. Annibale's rejuvenation of the antique undoubtedly struck a sympathetic chord in the younger artist.

Cortona made no secret of his indebtedness to the Farnese ceiling in the decoration of the gallery at Castel Fusano (1627-1629), which displays a fictive architectonic framework supported by herms; a series of *quadri riportati* resting on the cornice or spanning the center of the vault; and illusionistic openings at the corners where putti with coats of arms are seen against the sky. In the frescoes of the Villa del Pigneto, executed a few years later and now known to us only through engravings, Cortona acknowledged his study not merely of the Farnese but also of Domenichino's Camera di Diana. Only in the increased concern with effects of spatial continuity could the Pigneto ceiling be said to look forward to the High Baroque. From these essentially

[17] P. della Pergola, *Villa Borghese*, Rome, 1962, figs. 193 and 196.

[18] F. Angeloni, *La Historia Augusta da* *Giulio Cesare insino à Costantino il Magno, illustrata con la verità delle Antiche Medaglie,* Rome, 1641, p. 251.

derivative schemes it is admittedly a long step to Cortona's great masterpiece, the Barberini ceiling (1633-1639), of which the scale alone renders comparison with the Farnese Gallery difficult. In contrast to Annibale's restless, semi-Mannerist solution, where the eye must dart from one detail to the next, here the observer is treated to a single spectacular vision embracing almost the whole of the huge vault. When one thinks of prototypes it is not so much the example of Carracci that comes to mind as those of Correggio and Veronese, especially the latter's *Triumph of Venice* in the Palazzo Ducale.

Nevertheless the form of the Barberini ceiling was not determined solely by North Italian influences, potent though these undeniably were. In Rome, despite the passage of time, it was still the Farnese Gallery that set the highest standard of monumental palace decoration. Annibale's fresco cycle, it is true, was over thirty years old when Cortona began work on the Barberini project, but (like Mount Everest) "it was there," and by its very presence offered to ambitious fresco-painters a challenge that could not be ignored. And that the Galleria did in fact at this late date command Cortona's attention is, I think, indisputable.[19] The most significant link with Annibale's solution is to be seen in the retention of the architectural framework which, though fictitious, actually conforms to the shape of the vault. Moreover the fact that that framework is not an ideal or perfect architecture but is subject to damage and the erosion of time (as in the section showing *Minerva and the Giants*) is a conceit that can perhaps be traced to the provocative "breakages" in the Farnese frescoes. Cortona has also followed Carracci's example by incorporating in his structure statues which are so animated that they threaten to participate in the histories.

The illusionistic framework of the Barberini ceiling is so constructed that the entire field is subdivided into five separate areas. Despite the uniform expanse of sky which serves to bind all five sections into one, in the end it remains true that each of these requires to be viewed as an independent picture. In one sense, therefore, the *quadro riportato* still survives,[20] although the process of mutation which began with Lanfranco's Borghese ceiling has been carried further by the unimpeded movement of figures in front of, as well as behind, the framing members.[21] What is more, in placing the most active scenes of the cycle (*Pallas attacking the Giants* and *Hercules driving out the Harpies*) in the coving at the ends of the Salone, Pietro shows that he has taken

---

[19] The relationship of the Barberini ceiling to the Farnese has recently been underscored by G. Briganti, *Pietro da Cortona o della pittura barocca*, Florence, 1962, pp. 82 ff.

[20] One proof of this is to be seen in the frescoes of the Cabinet de la Reine in the Louvre painted by Cortona's pupil Romanelli: although the system of decoration is directly based on that of the Barberini ceiling (where Romanelli had been employed as assistant), the illusionistic principle has

been discarded and the five main divisions of the vault have thus reverted (so to speak) to the category of framed pictures.

[21] H. Posse cites a drawing in Munich as proving that Cortona originally planned to place a framed picture at the end of the vault after the manner of the Farnese ceiling (*Jahrbuch der Preussischen Kunstsammlungen*, XL, 1919, p. 168, Abb. 26). But I am not at all sure that the drawing in question is an original study by Cortona.

note of the analogous situation of the Polyphemus frescoes in the Galleria Farnese; it can hardly be fortuitous that the energetic pose of Hercules wielding his club resembles that of the Cyclops who is about to hurl the rock at Acis.

Among the various fables of the Farnese cycle Cortona did not overlook the *Bacchanal*, echoes of which may be detected not only in the mythological canvases painted for the Sacchetti (such as the *Triumph of Bacchus* and the *Rape of the Sabines*), but also in the scene of *Religion and Faith triumphing over Lust* on the Barberini ceiling, in which the recumbent Venus and the drunken Silenus were directly inspired by the similar pair in Annibale's fresco.[22] The battling pairs of Cupids in the same subject are surely related to the struggles of Heavenly and Earthly Love in the corners of the Carracci ceiling.

It should not surprise us to find that in the decoration of the state apartment of the Palazzo Pitti, where he worked in the 1640's, Cortona now and then drew upon the store of motives in the Galleria Farnese. The principle of superimposition, which is used so effectively in the stuccoes of the Sala d'Apollo, may well have been suggested by the illusion of overlapping planes in Carracci's frescoes. There are other details in this room that may strike us as familiar. It will be noticed, for instance, that the framed paintings in the coving have rectangular projections at the lower corners very like those of the little pictures on the Farnese walls (cf. Fig. 37), the resemblance being heightened by the presence of the stucco figures on either side.[23]

To establish the significance of the Galleria Farnese for Peter Paul Rubens is a more difficult task. The chief reason is that he was not a fresco-painter, but executed even his most monumental ceiling commissions in oil on canvas. Nevertheless the problem of his relation to the Farnese cycle is plainly one that deserves investigation. Rubens had the advantage, which Pietro da Cortona did not, of being in Rome while Annibale was still alive, and we may be certain that the Gallery, the most important work then in progress, did not escape his notice. The fact that his teacher, Otto van Veen, had been court painter to the Duke Alessandro Farnese in Flanders may have given him another motive for visiting the great Roman palace. It is probable that Rubens saw the frescoes of the ceiling as early as 1601 or 1602, when he was in Rome painting the altarpieces for Santa Croce in Gerusalemme. The vault had been completed, but work had not yet begun on the walls, and it appears from Waldstein's diary that the room was being shown to visitors at this very time. Rubens must also have returned to the Gallery during his second stay in Rome from 1606 to 1608 when, as we know from his correspondence, he was eager to see everything of importance in the city: on December 2, 1606, he wrote to the secretary of the Duke of Mantua that he had spent the whole summer "ne i studij dell'arte."

[22] An even more explicit reference to Carracci's Earthly Venus is to be seen in the beautiful reclining figure in Cortona's fresco, the *Age of Silver*, in the Sala della Stufa of the Pitti palace.

[23] This was pointed out by M. Campbell in an unpublished dissertation (Princeton University, 1961).

The scope of these "studies" may be judged from the incomparable breadth of Rubens' interests. While familiarizing himself with the sublime masterpieces of the High Renaissance, he was at the same time systematically making himself an authority on classical art and culture; if his imagination was fired by Michelangelo and Titian, he was also capable of recognizing the merits of contemporaries such as Caravaggio and Elsheimer; and even in the work of an artist of feeble powers his eye could be caught by an effective passage. The Galleria Farnese was obviously only one of a multitude of Roman works, both ancient and modern, that claimed his attention. This is not to say, however, that Rubens looked at the frescoes in a merely perfunctory fashion or that he failed to grasp their relevance to current artistic problems. On the contrary it is not difficult to imagine the exhilaration felt by the young Flemish painter, tentatively groping his way toward what was to become his mature Baroque style, when he perceived that the path had already been opened by Annibale Carracci. For the Farnese cycle was a dazzling demonstration of the fact that it was possible for an artist of vision and intellect, through diligent study of the antique and of the High Renaissance, to shake off the fetters of Mannerist artificiality and bring into being a new and original style which, though undeniably modern in its sensuous naturalism, could yet take its place in the monumental tradition. To achieve such a synthesis was Rubens' aim no less than Carracci's, and the sight of the Farnese Gallery can only have strengthened his resolve.

Rubens' mythological subjects tell us something of the impression made on him by the Farnese *favole*. He was of course familiar with the various Cinquecento interpretations of the Dionysiac theme, including the *Bacchanals* of Titian, which were then in Rome; but not even in Titian had he seen the Bacchic rout invested with such sheer animal vigor and sensuousness as in the dense group of figures pressing noisily round the drunken Silenus in Annibale's great fresco of the *Triumph of Bacchus and Ariadne* (Fig. 69). It is an unforgettable image of pagan revelry, and Rubens' own *Bacchanals* are full of reverberations of it. The *Procession of Silenus* (Munich) provides an apt example: the contrast of the corpulent Silenus and the crouching Panisca suckling her infants may well depend, as Evers has noted,[24] on the relationship between Silenus and the Earthly Venus in the Farnese fresco. Another such reminiscence may be seen in Rubens' *Drunken Hercules* (Dresden), where the staggering hero is supported by a male and a female Pan, and even the lively crisscross pattern of the legs resembles that in Carracci's *Bacchanal*.

The love scenes of the Farnese frieze have similarly left their mark on a number of erotic subjects by Rubens. Among these may be mentioned the curious *Hercules and Omphale* (Louvre), painted while the artist was still in Italy, which betrays an acquaintance both with Annibale's *Hercules and Iole* (Fig. 45) and with his *Jupiter and Juno* (Fig. 43), especially as regards the posture of the male figure. The same may

[24] H. G. Evers, *Rubens und sein Werk, Neue Forschungen*, Brussels, 1943, pp. 239 ff.

be said of the brilliant *Samson and Delilah* (Cologne, Neuerburg collection), in which the analogy to the Iole fresco is particularly striking: in both paintings the temptress, her head in gem-like profile, is seated at the left as she places her hand on the shoulder of the hero whose strength she has subdued. On occasion it was an individual figure that caught Rubens' attention. In the early *Ganymede* in Vienna, for example, the position of the youth's legs can be seen to depend on the Cyclops in *Polyphemus and Galatea* (Fig. 63) rather than on the *Laocoön* from which Annibale's figure is in fact derived.[25] Rubens appears in this instance to have looked at antiquity through the eyes of Annibale. Among other borrowings we may cite the soldier grasping a kneeling captive in the *Funeral of Decius Mus* (Liechtenstein collection), whose attitude recalls the warrior standing over Phineus in the fresco of *Perseus and Phineus* (Fig. 78).

The ornamentation of the frieze, with its Baroque profusion of figures of flesh and stone, reliefs, masks, garlands, and the like, may have proved quite as stimulating to Rubens as the fables themselves. The chief document of his interest in the decorative, as distinct from the narrative, aspects of the cycle is a drawing in the Victoria and Albert Museum (Fig. 288) reproducing a section of the frieze near the medallion of *Apollo and Marsyas* (cf. Fig. 47) but showing in place of that subject *Leda and the Swan*.[26] The discrepancy cannot be accounted for by the supposition that the copy was made from a now lost preparatory drawing by Annibale rather than from the fresco itself; for, as our analysis of the graphic material for the Gallery makes clear, it was not Annibale's practice to make such detailed studies of whole segments of the ceiling (see Chapter 11). This is unquestionably, then, a drawing after the fresco—a drawing later repaired and restored by Rubens.[27] In its original state it consisted of a sketch in black chalk, most of which is still visible; the *Punishment of Marsyas* was probably indicated, though only lightly, within the roundel. That this underlying sketch is by the hand of Rubens is perhaps doubtful.[28] The sheet was subsequently damaged, a large wedge-shaped section (including most of the medallion) being torn from the lower left corner; the missing part was in time replaced by a second piece of paper. It was only then, after the sheet had been thus repaired, that Rubens' brush drawing was made. Over most of the original surface he had simply to follow the black chalk sketch, but he was seemingly unable to interpret correctly the fragmentary design in

[25] H. G. Evers, *Peter Paul Rubens*, Munich, 1942, p. 488, note 91, Abb. 48. Rubens unquestionably perceived the derivation from the *Laocoön*, but the foreshortening of the left thigh and the placing of the feet of his figure leave no doubt of its primary indebtedness to Annibale's Polyphemus.

[26] J. Q. van Regteren Altena, in *Burlington Magazine*, LXXVI, 1940, p. 200, pl. 2c. See also D. Mahon and D. Sutton in the catalogue of the exhibition *Artists in 17th Century Rome*, London, 1955, pp. 84 f., no. 69; and L. Bur-

chard and R.-A. d'Hulst, in the exhibition catalogue, *Tekeningen van P. P. Rubens*, Antwerp, 1956, pp. 97 f., no. 116, pl. LII.

[27] This was observed by M. Jaffé, in *Burlington Magazine*, XCVIII, 1956, p. 317.

[28] Jaffé (*loc.cit.*) accepts Rubens' responsibility for the entire sheet, including the underdrawing. J. Held maintains however that the black chalk sketch is not the work of the master (*Rubens, Selected Drawings*, London, 1959, I, p. 59).

the remaining portion of the medallion. Perhaps he actually misread it as *Leda and the Swan,* or perhaps that subject merely seemed to him to be appropriate to the cycle. However that may be, he metamorphosed the head and shoulders of Apollo into a seated Leda, inserted a swan in place of the satyr tied to the tree, and completed the whole medallion accordingly. Even though he was probably not the author of the initial chalk sketch, the drawing as reworked by Rubens testifies not only to the artist's interest in the Farnese fresco but also to his keen recollection of the original. For it is noteworthy that in the modeling of the accessory figures (which in the original sketch are only drawn in outline) he has been careful to represent the light as coming from the lower right, precisely as in the Gallery.

Mention should also be made here of a chalk drawing in the collection of Walter C. Baker. It represents a young man with arms extended to the side in a manner that distinctly recalls certain termini of the Farnese vault: there is a marked resemblance, in particular, to the right-hand figure of the pair of atlantes at the left of *Polyphemus and Acis* (Fig. 42).[29]

In the light of this evidence the possibility is worth considering that some of Rubens' own decorative schemes may have been inspired by the *ornamenti* of the frieze. Let us take as an example the oil sketch of the *Battle of Coutras* (Liechtenstein collection), which is one of the *modelli* for the Galerie Henri IV. It has in fact been suggested that the decorative figures arranged symmetrically round the cartouche with the battle scene may be derived from those surrounding the bronze medallions of the Farnese vault.[30] A like observation may be made of Rubens' design for the title-page of the works of Justus Lipsius,[31] where the placing of two seated figures in front of herms, which in turn form part of an architectural setting, similarly echoes the grouping of the accessory figures in Annibale's frieze.

Rubens was in his twenties when he saw the Farnese ceiling. The sculptor Gian Lorenzo Bernini became acquainted with it at an even more impressionable age. Bernini, who was brought to Rome as a child about 1605, seems to have known Annibale personally (though he was not yet eleven when the latter died in the summer of 1609). The deep admiration that he felt for Carracci's Gallery never left him, as is evident from the numerous complimentary references to it which are interspersed throughout the diary kept by the Sieur de Chantelou during the artist's visit to France in 1665.[32] Grateful though we must be for such direct verbal testimony—sadly lacking in Rubens' correspondence—it is nevertheless true that Bernini's praise is couched in

[29] C. Virch, *Master Drawings in the Collection of Walter C. Baker,* 1962, pp. 33 f., no. 44, ill. The drawing is dated *c.* 1612-1615 by J. Goris and J. Held, *Rubens in America,* New York, 1947, p. 44.

[30] Mahon remarks (*Studies,* p. 202) that this suggestion was made by Dr. F. Grossmann.

[31] Repr. in G. Glück and F. M. Haberditzl, *Die Handzeichnungen von Peter Paul Rubens,* Berlin, 1928, p. 59, no. 214.

[32] M. de Chantelou, *Journal du voyage du Cavalier Bernin en France* (ed. L. Lalanne), Paris, 1885. For Bernini's meeting with Annibale see p. 34.

very general and conventional terms. Thanks however to Wittkower's perceptive analysis,[33] it is now possible to see that the Farnese frescoes played a definite part in shaping Bernini's early sculptural style.

The *Rape of Proserpina* (Borghese Gallery) may serve as an illustration. In so exploiting the contrast between the slender grace of the smooth female nude and the powerful muscularity of the abductor Bernini reveals how much he has profited from the study of such subjects as *Jupiter and Juno* (Fig. 43) or even, for that matter, of Agostino's *Glaucus and Scylla* (Fig. 60).[34]

The suggestion has been made above that what attracted most artists of the early Seicento to the Farnese Gallery was that it offered a way out of the Mannerist dilemma through a fresh and imaginative re-creation of the antique. To an artist like Bernini, whose instincts were fundamentally classical, this was a lesson of paramount importance, and Annibale's infusion of a new immediacy into the grand imagery of antiquity and the Renaissance can have been nothing less than a revelation. In the impassioned form of *Polyphemus serenading Galatea* (Fig. 63) Bernini would not have missed the allusion to the *Laocoön*; yet he would also have appreciated that its realism and urgency were anything but pedantic or imitative. It is surely significant that Bernini's own working procedure was closely akin to Annibale's: as Wittkower has demonstrated, he frequently selected a classical figure as a point of departure, later modifying it freely as the work took shape under his hands. The attitude of the early *David* is ultimately based on the Borghese Warrior; but the threatening mien and unresolved action which give the figure a wholly new significance reflect the impression made on the sculptor by the raging Cyclops in Annibale's *Polyphemus and Acis* (Fig. 64).

It should not be forgotten, finally, that Bernini viewed the Farnese cycle differently than, say, Pietro da Cortona, who looked upon it first of all as a masterly exercise in ceiling decoration, or than Rubens, who admired its abundance of figurative and ornamental motives. As a sculptor Bernini cannot have been insensitive to the curious spell cast over the Gallery by the decorative figures of the frieze; it seems likely indeed that he found the drama of these silent forms even more poignant than the brilliantly colored fables. Annibale's power to eliminate the barrier between the observer and the work of art is nowhere more vividly manifested than in the feigned marble termini, who in defiance of their stony and truncated shape seem to project an extraordinary psychic energy. Among all the venerated antiquities of Rome there was nothing that could compare with them for sheer presence. The author of the *David*, the *Scipione Borghese*, and the *Costanza Buonarelli* was not blind to the possibilities that they held for the art of sculpture.

---

[33] R. Wittkower, *Gian Lorenzo Bernini the Sculptor of the Roman Baroque*, London, 1955, pp. 5 ff.

[34] The influence of Agostino's fresco is perhaps also perceptible in the *Neptune and Triton* (Victoria and Albert Museum).

II. THE FARNESE GALLERY AND BAROQUE CLASSICISM

It is not to be wondered at that the fresco projects carried out by artists of the Bolognese circle in Rome during the decade following Annibale's death are, in the main, dependent on the Farnese Gallery.[35] They do not, it is true, exhibit the complex crowding and reduplication of parts that give the Farnese vault its characteristic flavor, but are noticeably simpler and more purely classical in organization. The *quadro riportato* is the preferred vehicle for narrative scenes, and the ornamental details are not permitted to detract from its authority. An early specimen is Domenichino's ceiling of the Camera di Diana (1609) in the Palazzo Giustiniani at Bassano di Sutri, which may be regarded as typical both for its liberal use of motives from the Farnese cycle and for its avoidance of the overlappings and bewildering contrasts of materials employed so effectively by Carracci. The story of Diana is set forth in five panels arranged in the familiar cross-pattern, and in the corners of the vault cupids are seen in flight against a painted sky. Two subjects, *Diana and Endymion* and *Pan and Diana*, are virtually copied from Annibale's frescoes, and the four sphinxes likewise imitate those of the Farnese. Inevitably, there are echoes of Domenichino's own contributions to the Galleria: the *Diana and Actaeon* has many points of resemblance to the little fresco of *Diana and Callisto*, and the central scene of *Latona with her Children Diana and Apollo* is closely related to the oval of *Charity*. In its classical severity, however, the Camera di Diana harks back to the solutions employed by Raphael and Tibaldi.[36] An extreme instance of the trend toward simplification is to be seen in the isolation of a single *quadro riportato* on the ceiling, as in Guido Reni's famous *Aurora* of 1613, which itself owes much to Annibale's *Triumph of Bacchus and Ariadne*.

Domenichino reached his most classical moment in the St. Cecilia cycle in San Luigi dei Francesi (1612-1614), where he attempted, not unsuccessfully, to marry the style of Raphael to that of Annibale.[37] The third decade of the century however found him moving toward a more dynamic, more "baroque" form of expression in frescoes such as those in the apse of Sant' Andrea della Valle (1624-1628). Yet it is noteworthy that Domenichino did not go so far as to sacrifice the integrity of the architectural surface for illusionistic effects: the scenes of the life of St. Andrew are treated unequivocally as *quadri riportati*, and no attempt has been made to loosen or dissolve the architectonic structure within which they are fixed. In addition, a direct link with the Farnese Gallery may be discovered in the pairs of seated nudes surmounting the first window on either side of the choir, which are plainly derived from Carracci's *ignudi*.

It is less easy to assess the effects of Annibale's monumental style on the art of

[35] On this subject see H. Posse, in *Jahrbuch der Preussischen Kunstsammlungen*, XL, 1919; and Wittkower, *Art and Architecture in Italy, 1600-1750*, pp. 46 ff.

[36] M. V. Brugnoli, in *Bollettino d'Arte*, XLII, 1957, pp. 274 ff.; J. R. Martin, in *Bollettino*

d'Arte, XLIV, 1959, pp. 43 ff.

[37] E. Borea, in *Bollettino d'Arte*, XLVI, 1961, pp. 237 ff. The *Condemnation of St. Cecilia* may reflect the influence both of Raphael and of Annibale's fresco of *Ulysses and Circe* in the Camerino (Fig. 17).

Francesco Albani.[38] Though he served as Annibale's lieutenant in the Herrera Chapel he does not seem to have participated in the decoration of the Farnese Gallery. It may have been partly for this reason that when he himself was given the opportunity to fresco a sizable ceiling in the Giustiniani palace at Bassano di Sutri (1609) he rejected Carracci's solution and boldly tried to bring the entire field within the compass of a single illusionistic view.[39] Some years later, however, in the ceiling of the Palazzo Verospi, Albani turned for inspiration to sources of a more classical kind. The principal subject (*Apollo and the Four Seasons*) occupies a large compartment in the middle of the vault, and the spandrels are filled by single figures—a scheme obviously suggested by Raphael's Loggia di Psiche in the Villa Farnesina. In addition there are certain allusions to Annibale's ceiling of the Galleria, the most pointed being the placing of two frescoed ovals at either end of the central rectangle, after the fashion of the octagonal panels of the Farnese. The reclining figure of Summer in the scene of *Apollo and the Seasons* plainly imitates the Earthly Venus in Carracci's *Bacchanal* in posture and dress as well as in compositional function; and the goddess Diana in one of the spandrels owes a good deal to Annibale's conception of that deity in the fable of *Pan and Diana*. In the Verospi ceiling, then, Albani was seeking to achieve a blend of the Carraccesque and the Raphaelesque, which as it happens was precisely what Domenichino was endeavoring to do at this same moment in the St. Cecilia frescoes in San Luigi dei Francesi.

Yet, though he worked with distinction on a number of fresco projects, Albani was undoubtedly at his best in the smaller scale of easel-painting. In the lyrical mythological canvases of the 1620's it is more often the influence of Domenichino than of Carracci that one feels: the *Diana and Actaeon* in the Louvre,[40] for example, reveals a debt to Domenichino's fresco of this subject in the Camera di Diana at Bassano (though there is also present here something of the twilight poetry of Annibale's *Actaeon* in Brussels). Such reminiscences of the Farnese Gallery as make their appearance in Albani's paintings generally have to do not with the heroic fables of the ceiling but with the miniature panels on the walls executed by members of the Carracci school. It can readily be seen, for example, that the two principal figures in his *Apollo guarding the flocks of Admetus* (Fontainebleau)[41] are related to the Farnese fresco of *Mercury and Apollo* (Fig. 95); in addition the flying attitude of Mercury suggests that Albani may also have consulted Annibale's first study for this subject (No. 142; Fig. 261).

Those artists who, like Andrea Sacchi, deplored the rise of illusionistic ceiling decoration looked to the Gallery of the Carracci, with its architectonic structure, its isolation of the histories as individually framed pictures, and its firmly enclosed space,

[38] Mention has been made above of Albani's borrowing from the Camerino fresco of *Hercules with the Globe* (see note 31 of Chapter 3).

[39] Brugnoli, in *Bollettino d'Arte*, XLII, 1957, pp. 266 ff., fig. 1.

[40] Repr. in the catalogue *L'ideale classico del Seicento*, no. 38.

[41] *Ibid.*, no. 47.

as a reaffirmation of classical propriety. The objection might be made, to be sure, that Sacchi's own ceiling painting in the Palazzo Barberini representing Divine Wisdom, though conceived essentially as an easel-painting, shows no influence whatever of the Farnese vault, but is better described as an attempt to translate Raphael's mural style into a contemporary Baroque idiom. It must be remembered, however, that Sacchi's ceiling has nothing in common with the Farnese either in iconography or in the size and shape of the space to be decorated. When, on the other hand, it was a question of decorating a vault with a steep cove like that of the Galleria, Sacchi did not hesitate to turn to Annibale's solution. The project to which we refer was, it seems, never executed, nor has it ever been identified, but we may nevertheless gain some idea of the proposed decoration from a group of preparatory drawings at Windsor Castle.[42] The vault was penetrated by windows, around which were to be clustered a number of decorative figures after the manner of the *partimenti* of the Farnese Gallery. The largest of these drawings, a study in red chalk,[43] makes the derivation particularly clear: the seated *ignudo* whose head is turned round sharply as he glances upward is a recurrent type on Carracci's ceiling, as is the atlas-herm behind him with one arm raised to his head (cf. Figs. 47-48). The putti above the window bring to mind those reclining on the medallions of the Farnese frieze; and the standing male figure (perhaps a feigned statue) similarly recalls the full-length caryatids who assist the termini to support the architrave (cf. Fig. 52).

If (as seems probable) Sacchi was introduced to the Farnese cycle by his master Albani, it was doubtless Domenichino who recommended to Nicolas Poussin that he make these frescoes an object of study. Unlike Domenichino, Poussin had no ambition to become a fresco-painter; yet there is abundant evidence that Carracci's Gallery made a deep and lasting impression on him. Bellori quotes him as saying of it "that Annibale, having excelled all the painters of the past in these *partimenti*, even outdid himself, because painting had never offered to human eyes a more stupendous set of ornaments; and that the *favole* had achieved the unique distinction of being the best compositions since Raphael."[44]

It is apparent from these remarks that Poussin admired the *favole* of the Farnese ceiling not merely as components of a program of fresco decoration but as models of history painting proper. He conceived of the Gallery, that is to say, as a *pinacotheca*. Although one must be careful not to overestimate the importance of the Farnese paintings for the young Poussin, it is at the same time undeniable that they played a

---

[42] H. Posse, *Der römische Maler Andrea Sacchi*, Leipzig, 1925, pp. 89 f.; Blunt and Cooke, *Roman Drawings of the XVII and XVIII Centuries at Windsor*, pp. 98 f., nos. 789-820.

[43] Posse, *op.cit.*, Abb. 28; Blunt and Cooke, *op.cit.*, pl. 27.

[44] Bellori, *Vite*, pp. 80 f.: "Nicolò Pussino

[diceva] che Annibale in questi partimenti hauendo superato tutti li pittori passati, auanzò anche se stesso, non hauendo mai la pittura proposto a gli occhi oggetto più stupendo d'ornamenti; e che le fauole conseguiscono l'vnica lode di essere li migliori componimenti dopo Rafaelle."

considerable part in shaping the secular compositions of the first Roman period. Among these must be counted the *Choice of Hercules* (Stourhead), which may well strike the observer as a paraphrase, in more classical language, of Annibale's original text in the Camerino (Fig. 9).[45] Nor should the possibility be overlooked that in the Dulwich *Rinaldo and Armida* Poussin had in mind the compact grouping of the goddess and the sleeping mortal in Carracci's *Diana and Endymion* (Fig. 44). The drawing of Venus, Cupid and Pan (Windsor) exhibits distinct points of similarity to the frescoed medallion of Cupid overcoming Pan (Fig. 48).[46] And in the London *Cephalus and Aurora* the attempt of Cephalus to free himself from the goddess's embrace recalls Agostino's fresco (Fig. 59).

The stimulus of Annibale's *Triumph of Bacchus and Ariadne* may frequently be detected, even in those canvases of the 1620's and 1630's in which Poussin drew heavily upon the art of Titian. Among the earliest of these are the two *Bacchanals of Children* in gouache (Rome, Collection Incisa della Rocchetta) which Bellori, in his life of the artist, rightly connected with Poussin's study of the Titian *Bacchanals*, then in the Aldobrandini collection.[47] Further confirmation may be found in the fact that the larger of the two pictures (the one showing two herms) includes a putto taken directly from Titian's *Bacchanal of the Andrians*. But Titian was not the only source of inspiration: another figure is borrowed from Michelangelo's drawing of a *Bacchanal of Children* at Windsor; and the infant with the satyr mask is a motive known on ancient sarcophagi. It should be added, finally, that the left-hand putto of the reclining pair in the foreground closely copies the little fellow in the center of Annibale's *Bacchanal* who has fallen in front of the goats that draw Ariadne's chariot and throws up his arm to protect himself (Fig. 72). In the smaller gouache by Poussin the putto seen from the back as he tugs at the goat's reins may have been suggested by the boy faun guiding the harnessed tigers in the Carracci *Triumph*; the turn of the head in *profil perdu* is strikingly similar. But above all it was the compositional principle of the Farnese *Bacchanal*, with its fluent sequence of rhythmical repeats and variations, that attracted Poussin's attention; how tellingly he made use of it may be seen in such works as the *Realm of Flora* in Dresden. The Louvre *Triumph of Flora*, despite its evident borrowings from the *Andrians* of Titian, may also owe its vigorous, march-like movement to the great Farnese fresco; the stationary figures in the first plane, though shifted somewhat toward the center, have much the same relation to the animated procession passing before them as the corresponding figures in Annibale's painting;

[45] Panofsky, *Hercules am Scheidewege*, pp. 140 ff. It is interesting that Poussin should include the figure of Cupid, who also appeared in Annibale's preparatory drafts (Nos. 9-10; Figs. 111-112) but was suppressed in the final redaction.

[46] W. Friedlaender and A. Blunt, *The Drawings of Nicolas Poussin*, III, London,

1953, p. 32, no. 210, pl. 161. It is of course possible that Poussin knew Agostino's engraving *Omnia vincit Amor*, which copies Annibale's design.

[47] Bellori, *Vite*, p. 412. For the modern bibliography see A. Blunt in the catalogue of the exhibition *Nicolas Poussin*, Paris, 1960, pp. 44 f., nos. 5-6.

and both the putto crowning Flora and the nymph carrying a basket on her head recall comparable motives in the *Bacchus and Ariadne*. Among Poussin's drawings of this period there is one in Windsor representing the *Indian Triumph of Bacchus*,[48] which in the diagonal placing of the procession as well as in such details as the Silenus group so nearly resembles Annibale's first study for the fresco in the Gallery (No. 54; Fig. 159) that one is tempted to suppose that Poussin may have known it.[49]

The growing influence of Raphael in Poussin's works of the mid thirties does not mean that henceforth the artist lost all interest in the Farnese Gallery. The *Triumph of Neptune and Amphitrite* in Philadelphia, for instance, is heavily impregnated with Raphaelesque elements; but this should not blind us to the fact that the central feature of Amphitrite flanked by two companions is derived, not from Raphael, but from Annibale's fresco of *Polyphemus and Galatea* (Fig. 63). Like Galatea, moreover, Amphitrite is made to grasp her veil with one hand while with the other she assists the nymph on her right to hold the dolphins' reins. It may also be pointed out that the Triton trumpeter seen at the right of the central group is an adaptation of the faun in Carracci's *Bacchanal* who blows a horn while supporting Silenus (Fig. 71). Another work in the Raphaelesque manner is the *Triumph of Pan* in the Morrison collection (one of the Richelieu Bacchanals), which has been shown to be based on a composition by Giulio Romano engraved by the Master of the Die.[50] Here again however Poussin has introduced a reminiscence of Annibale's *Bacchus and Ariadne* in the figure of the half-nude bacchante holding a tambourine over her head (cf. Fig. 72).

Poussin's enthusiastic praise of the *partimenti* of the Farnese ceiling, as reported by Bellori,[51] is of special interest because it is confirmed by what we know of his plans for the Grande Galerie of the Louvre.[52] On his arrival in Paris late in the year 1640 Poussin found himself involved in this vast project, in which he was to encounter so many obstacles (and which he eventually abandoned by returning to Rome). In a letter addressed to Sublet de Noyers he made it clear that in his designs for the vault of the Long Gallery he rejected any scheme of Baroque illusionism and instead proposed to employ a strictly architectonic system, affirming rather than denying the fact of enclosure. "Everything that I have placed on this vault," he wrote, "is to be understood as being attached to it in the manner of a relief, without pretending that there is any object which breaks through, or which lies beyond and at a greater distance than, the surface of the vault, but that everything follows its curvature and shape."[53]

[48] A. Blunt, *The French Drawings in the Collection of His Majesty the King at Windsor Castle*, Oxford-London, 1945, p. 41, no. 199 r., pl. 48.

[49] At this time Carracci's drawing cannot yet have been in Bellori's possession.

[50] Friedlaender and Blunt, *The Drawings of Nicolas Poussin*, III, p. 24.

[51] *Vite*, p. 80.

[52] The fundamental study of this subject is A. Blunt's article, "Poussin's Decoration of the Long Gallery in the Louvre," *Burlington Magazine*, XCIII, 1951, pp. 369-376.

[53] C. Jouanny (ed.), *Correspondance de Nicolas Poussin*, Paris, 1911, p. 144: "Tout ce que j'ay disposé dans cette voûte doit estre considéré comme y estant attaché et en plaque, sans prétendre qu' il y ait aucun corps qui rompe ou qui soit au-delà et plus enfoncé que la superficie de la voûte, mais que le tout

On another occasion Poussin explained his dislike of *trompe-l'œil* effects as being based on rational grounds. The Englishman Richard Symonds gave this report of a conversation with the artist in Rome: "And for Scorcij above, unles they be Quadri rapportati tis likely theyle be too licentious & improper perche non siamo avezzati vedere persone in Aria as Monsr Poussin sd to Sig^r G. A. [Canini] & I, Upon the like discourse."[54]

The ceiling of the Grande Galerie comprised two zones, one along the crown, and one above the cornice on either side; each zone was decorated with panels in stucco or in imitation of relief. The vault was also subdivided transversely by ribs which were in effect continuations of the wall pilasters. There can be no doubt that in devising this structural system Poussin took as his model the Farnese Gallery, omitting however the *quadri riportati* and the few illusionistic touches that enliven and give variety to that cycle. But it is in the lowest section of the ceiling that his indebtedness to Annibale's solution becomes especially clear. Over each window was a medallion flanked by two atlas herms, the derivation from the *partimenti* of the Farnese frieze being made all the more evident by the form and attitudes of the herms (painted in chiaroscuro so as to resemble sculpture), the bas-reliefs represented on the roundels, and the method of lighting from below. In order to visualize these various details it is necessary to examine the preparatory designs made for this project by Poussin and members of his studio. A single example may perhaps suffice. At Windsor there is a finished drawing, by an assistant, for *Hercules and the Erymanthian Boar* (Fig. 289), which presents a really striking similarity to certain medallions in Carracci's Gallery, such as that with *Apollo and Marsyas* (Fig. 47).[55]

The iconographical theme of the Grande Galerie was the life of Hercules, a complimentary allusion to Louis XIII. In preparing his designs for the vault Poussin no doubt remembered Annibale's paintings of this mythological hero in the Farnese palace. We know from a sheet of studies by Poussin in the Louvre, and from a studio drawing in Windsor,[56] that one of the ceiling panels of the Grande Galerie was to represent Hercules bearing the globe, a subject to which Annibale had given a prominent place in the Camerino (Fig. 10). Another sketch on the Louvre sheet is a study for Hercules freeing Prometheus, which may be compared to the little fresco of this episode in the Galleria Farnese (Fig. 99).

Poussin did not remain in Paris to see the great project brought to fulfillment, but set out for Rome late in 1642. Thereafter successive attempts were made to carry on

fait également son cintre et sa figure."

[54] Brit. Mus. Egerton ms 1636, fol. 87. Cited by Blunt, *op.cit.*, p. 375, and O. Millar, *Rubens, the Whitehall Ceiling*, London, 1958, p. 24.

[55] Blunt, *French Drawings at Windsor Castle*, p. 51, no. 255, pl. 57. On the various categories of drawings connected with this project (originals, studio drawings, and copies) see W. Friedlaender and A. Blunt, *The Drawings of Nicolas Poussin*, IV, London, 1963, pp. 11 ff.

[56] Blunt, "Poussin's Decoration of the Long Gallery," fig. 2 (Louvre, erroneously cited as in Bayonne); *idem, French Drawings at Windsor Castle*, p. 51, no. 256.

the decoration of the Long Gallery; but the results were never wholly satisfactory, and in the eighteenth century the whole interior was stripped of its ornamentation and turned into a museum. The Grande Galerie had, notwithstanding, a considerable influence in France and may be regarded as a forerunner of the monumental products undertaken a generation later by Charles Le Brun and his school.

After Poussin's return from Paris in 1642 French artists in Rome increasingly turned their attention to the Farnese Gallery. The practice of making copies after the frescoes, which was to become so important a part of the training of students of the French Academy in Rome, had its beginning about this time. Charles Le Brun, no doubt at the urging of Poussin, is known to have drawn up large cartoons after Carracci's frescoes,[57] and copies were likewise made by Pierre Mignard, a number of whose drawings after the decorative elements of the Gallery are today in the Louvre.[58] French artists also evinced an interest in Annibale's preparatory drawings for the Farnese frescoes. Charles Errard, who was later appointed first Director of the French Academy in Rome, made copies of some of the drawings in Francesco Angeloni's collection;[59] that same collection was later acquired by Mignard after Angeloni's death in 1652 and taken to France. When Jabach, about 1666, conceived the idea of reproducing in engravings the best drawings of his collection, even the most unpretentious pen sketches by Annibale were thought worthy of inclusion.[60]

To say that the Farnese Gallery had a preponderant influence on the development of the Louis XIV style would be an exaggeration. It has been rightly pointed out that the principal source of the decorative programs carried out by Le Brun at Vaux-le-Vicomte, at the Louvre (the Galerie d'Apollon), and at Versailles is to be found in the opulent combination of stucco and painting employed by Pietro da Cortona in the grand-ducal apartment of the Palazzo Pitti.[61] Yet the contribution of Annibale's Gallery to these ornate French interiors was not wholly negligible: it might be said to have supplied the classicizing ingredient that was needed to temper the exuberance of the High Baroque.

The credit for preparing the formula best suited to French taste belongs to an Italian artist. Giovanni Francesco Romanelli (*c.* 1610-1662) cannot be called a painter of great originality; but as a former pupil both of Domenichino and of

[57] H. Jouin, *Charles Le Brun et les arts sous Louis XIV*, Paris, 1889, pp. 730, 737. See also the illuminating article by Jennifer Montagu, "The Early Ceiling Decorations of Charles Le Brun," *Burlington Magazine*, September 1963, pp. 395-408.

[58] J. Guiffrey and P. Marcel, *Inventaire général des dessins du Musée du Louvre . . . , Ecole française*, x, pp. 92 ff., nos. 10258-10275. Mignard is said to have made copies for Cardinal Alphonse du Plessis (Mazière de Monville, *La vie de Pierre Mignard*, Amsterdam, 1731, p. 18).

[59] Vittoria, *Osservazioni*, p. 54. For Angeloni's collection of drawings see Chapter 9.

[60] Six of Annibale's sketches for the little mythological scenes below the cornice of the Gallery were among those reproduced (*Recueil de 283 Estampes . . . d'après les Desseins des Grands Maîtres que possedoit autrefois M. Jabach*, Paris, 1754, nos. 7A, 7B, 7C, 7D, 7F and 8D).

[61] A. Blunt, *Art and Architecture in France, 1500 to 1700*, Baltimore, 1954, pp. 159, 173, 253.

Pietro da Cortona he was uniquely qualified to effect a compromise of classic and baroque. Romanelli paid two visits to Paris. In 1646-1647 he painted the gallery of the Hôtel Mazarin, now part of the Bibliothèque Nationale. On the second visit, in 1655-1657, he decorated the summer apartment of the Queen Mother in the Louvre, where he was assisted by the sculptor Michel Anguier.[62] Of the several rooms of this apartment we may select the so-called Salle des Saisons as offering the clearest idea of Romanelli's method.

The treatment of the vaulted ceiling, with its combination of stucco and painting, bespeaks close study of Cortona's decorations in the Palazzo Pitti: certain stucco details, such as the satyrs standing on scrolls, are surely derived from the Sala di Apollo. Yet the ceiling as a whole lacks the abundant fluency of the authentic Cortonesque style, being decidedly drier in manner and simpler in organization. In part, of course, this somewhat anemic quality is simply due to Romanelli's artistic limitations. At the same time there is also perceptible here a shift in the direction of classical severity—a retrogression, one is tempted to call it—from the High Baroque to the Early Baroque of Carracci and Domenichino.

Closer examination serves to substantiate this impression. For in its basic scheme Romanelli's Salle des Saisons can be seen to be a direct descendant of Domenichino's Camera di Diana at Bassano di Sutri.[63] Not only does the subdivision of the vault into five main panels exactly duplicate that employed by Domenichino but even the subject matter—the story of Diana and Apollo—shows an evident reliance on the earlier cycle; two subjects, *Diana and Actaeon* and *Diana and Endymion*, are in fact common to both. For the ornamental sphinxes and for the illusionistic openings at the corners parallels may be found in both the Camera di Diana and the Farnese Gallery. It was also from the Farnese ceiling that Romanelli took the motive of paired atlas herms enclosing a medallion.

In the two great galleries decorated for Louis XIV—the Galerie d'Apollon in the Louvre and the Galerie des Glaces at Versailles—Le Brun drew heavily upon Romanelli's modified version of the Cortonesque Baroque, as well as upon Poussin's classicizing solution for the Grande Galerie. Doubtless this accounts for their characteristic blend of ostentation and restraint: the painted panels are large and simple in shape; illusionism is used sparingly; the ornament, both in stucco and in paint, suggests regal splendor but avoids an effect of extravagance or overabundance. In these monumental works of Le Brun one can easily single out passages derived from the Farnese ceiling, the most conspicuous being the combination of a medallion with atlantes as a unit of the frieze. It is less easy to determine whether such features are direct borrowings from Annibale's fresco, which was of course familiar to Le Brun;

[62] L. Hautecoeur, *L'Histoire des Châteaux du Louvre et des Tuileries . . . sous le règne de Louis XIV*, Paris, 1927, pp. 36 ff.

[63] Certain details may also reflect the influence of Cortona's ceiling in the Villa del Pigneto, the Domenichinesque character of which has been mentioned above.

for they might equally well have been adopted from an intermediate source such as Poussin's Long Gallery. A more explicit quotation from the Carracci cycle may be discovered in the decoration of the Salon de Vénus at Versailles, the ceiling of which was painted by Le Brun's pupil Houasse. In the cove over each wall a framed painting has been placed in front of a simulated relief plaque, so that only the protruding ends of the latter are visible. Of the origin of this conceit there can be no doubt. It is taken from the Farnese ceiling, where the *quadri riportati* are similarly made to overlap the "relief" panels of the frieze (cf. Fig. 37).

Despite these and other evidences of approbation, however, the truth is that by the last quarter of the seventeenth century the Galleria Farnese had finally lost the power to influence the course of contemporary art. Every line had been reproduced in drawings and engravings,[64] and Annibale's great work could now take its place in the canon of officially recognized masterpieces, as a monument to be venerated and studied but one no longer relevant to the artistic problems of the day. The surest sign of its new status was the approval bestowed upon the Gallery by the French Academy in Rome, the Directors of which continued for over a century to send their charges to "dessiner d'après la belle gallerie du Carache au palais Farnèse."[65] One of Errard's first tasks as Director was, as we have seen, to instruct four of his *pensionnaires* to copy the frescoes on canvases which were subsequently taken to Paris and installed in the Tuileries. Thereafter generations of students, armed with pencil and sketchbook, regularly took up their station beneath Annibale's frescoed ceiling in order to extract from it the principles of drawing.

[64] Carlo Cesio's engravings, with Bellori's commentary, were issued in 1657. Some years later (1674) followed those by Pietro Aquila, who also produced a set on the Camerino. French artists who made engravings after the Gallery included Nicolas Mignard and Jacques Belly.

[65] *Correspondance des Directeurs de l'Académie de France à Rome*, x, p. 371 (Natoire to Vandières, March 1, 1752).

PART III

THE DRAWINGS

CHAPTER 9 · INTRODUCTION

BEFORE we begin an analysis of the graphic material for the Camerino and the Gallery, it may be useful to devote some space to the vicissitudes of Annibale's drawings for these two fresco cycles, and to add some speculation concerning losses and survivals.

The largest collections of Carracci drawings are in the Cabinet des Dessins of the Louvre and in the Royal Library at Windsor Castle. It is therefore not surprising that the bulk of the Farnese drawings (i.e. drawings for both the Camerino and the Gallery) should be concentrated in these two great treasuries: the Louvre has some sixty-nine sheets, and Windsor twenty-nine. Smaller groups are in the Musée des Beaux-Arts at Besançon (twenty drawings), in the Biblioteca Reale at Turin (seven), in the Albertina in Vienna (four), and in the collection of the Earl of Ellesmere (three). There are single drawings, or pairs of drawings, in many museums and private collections in Europe and Great Britain; two have recently been acquired by the Metropolitan Museum of Art in New York.[1]

It has been estimated that Annibale Carracci must have made over a thousand drawings for the Farnese Gallery.[2] In addition, those for the Camerino certainly numbered several hundred. Only a fraction of that material survives today—probably not much more than a tenth. A few studies may still be expected to come to light, but it is obvious that the great mass of Farnese drawings is irretrievably lost. How did this immense loss occur?

It is generally supposed that virtually the entire corpus of drawings was still extant in the seventeenth century; subsequently, as the original collections were broken up and the drawings began to change hands, their numbers (so it is said) were heavily depleted until at last they were reduced to the pathetically small total that we know today. I find it difficult to accept this explanation. In my opinion what is much more likely is that large quantities of drawings were simply destroyed or thrown away by Annibale and his associates as soon as they had served their immediate purpose. The Carracci were notoriously careless of their drawings: Malvasia tells of seeing a pen sketch by Agostino on which Mastelletta had written, "I tore this drawing from the hand of Agostino Carracci, who was about to wipe a frying-pan and light the fire with it."[3] As might be expected, it was the most beautiful and most interesting of the Farnese drawings that were preserved, and these selected examples, probably amounting to several hundreds in all, quickly found a place in the cabinets of connoisseurs.

---

[1] On the history of the principal collections of drawings by the Carracci, see Wittkower, *Carracci Drawings*, pp. 9-22; P. A. Tomory, *The Ellesmere Collection of Old Master Drawings*, Leicester, 1954, pp. 3-6; Mahon, *Disegni*, pp. 7-15; R. Bacou, *Dessins des Carrache*,

XXVIIIe Exposition du Cabinet des Dessins, Musée du Louvre, Paris, 1961, pp. 9-12 (hereinafter cited as Bacou, *Dessins*).

[2] Wittkower, *Carracci Drawings*, p. 16.

[3] Malvasia, *Felsina*, I, p. 467.

One of the earliest such collections of which we have record was that formed by Annibale's pupil Domenichino, which is known to have included a number of Farnese designs. Domenichino's huge store of drawings was bequeathed to his pupil Francesco Raspantino,[4] from whom it passed, through Carlo Maratti, into the Albani collection and thence, in 1762, into the library of King George III. Inevitably Domenichino's bequest suffered depletions over the years: for example, many of the cartoons and decorative pieces described in the Raspantino inventory are not now to be found among the drawings at Windsor Castle. Nevertheless it seems to be true that the principal *disegni* from Domenichino's collection—and these include the studies by Carracci for the Farnese cycles—are still intact in the Royal Library.[5]

The belief that a vast quantity of Farnese designs, now lost, existed in the seventeenth century (a belief that still haunts students of the period) appears to be founded on a statement by the Roman collector Francesco Angeloni. In his *Historia Augusta* (1641) he remarked that the 600 Carracci drawings in his possession were "for the greatest part" studies for the Gallery.[6] It soon becomes evident, as one reviews the literature on this subject, not only that too much weight has been attached to Angeloni's words, but also that they have generally been taken to mean that *all* of his 600 drawings were related to the Gallery. Now as it happens the history of Angeloni's drawings is fairly well known. After his death in 1652 they were acquired in Rome by the painter Pierre Mignard (1612-1695), who brought them to France and arranged them in several volumes, all but one of which were purchased by Pierre Crozat (1665-1740).[7] The remaining volume appears to have come into the possession of Charles Coypel, who in 1752 donated it to the royal collection.[8] From Mariette's summary description (1741) we learn that Crozat's cabinet included 128 drawings for the Farnese Gallery and 21 for the Camerino[9]—a mere fourth of the supposed original total of nearly 600. Even when allowance is made for the existence of some additional Farnese drawings in the Angeloni-Mignard volume owned by Coypel, this represents a rate of shrinkage that is quite beyond belief. The problem can be readily solved, however, if we do not take Angeloni's casual remark too literally: it is, in a word, very doubtful that of his 600 Carracci drawings more than 200 were studies for the Galleria Farnese. This is not to say of course that many important drawings have

[4] An inventory of Raspantino's collection was made in 1664 (A. Bertolotti, *Artisti bolognesi, ferraresi ed alcuni altri del già Stato Pontificio in Roma nei secoli XV, XVI e XVII*, Bologna, 1885, pp. 168-176).

[5] Pope-Hennessy, *Domenichino Drawings*, p. 11; Wittkower, *Carracci Drawings*, p. 21.

[6] Francesco Angeloni, *La Historia Augusta da Giulio Cesare insino à Costantino il Magno, illustrata con la verità delle Antiche Medaglie*, Rome, 1641, p. 251: "Si può etiandio comprendere la finezza dell'ingegno, e la profondità del sapere di Annibale suddetto in

seicento vari disegni di lui appresso di me, inuentati la maggior parte per ornarne, con Pittura, la celebre Galleria Farnesiana."

[7] P. J. Mariette, *Description sommaire des desseins des grands maistres d'Italie, des Pays-Bas et de France du cabinet de feu M. Crozat . . .*, Paris, 1741, p. 51.

[8] F. Reiset, *Notice des dessins, cartons, pastels . . . exposés . . . au Musée Impérial du Louvre, Première partie: Ecoles d'Italie*, Paris, 1866, p. xxxiv.

[9] Mariette, *op.cit.*, p. 50, lots 462-475.

not been lost or destroyed: accounts of early collections tell of numerous individual pieces that can no longer be traced. But at the same time it is apparent that the magnitude of these losses has been greatly exaggerated.

At least some of the Angeloni drawings can now be identified. As Roseline Bacou has shown, they bear as their sole distinguishing mark a number written in ink in an easily recognizable hand (see, for example, Nos. 44, 98, 99 and 120: Figs. 148, 210, 211 and 235).[10] The numbering system was presumably devised for the volumes made up by Mignard; since the same numeral sometimes occurs on two or more leaves, Bacou has suggested that the contents of each volume were numbered separately. Most of the pieces that can be identified in this way are in the Louvre; a smaller group is in Besançon; they include some sixty sheets with authentic studies for the Camerino and the Galleria.

A rough survey of the identifiable Angeloni drawings discloses two important facts. Firstly, not all of them are designs for the Farnese frescoes: there are in addition studies for such works as the Louvre *Birth of the Virgin*[11] and the fresco of the *Coronation of the Virgin* in Santa Maria del Popolo.[12] Secondly, even among those drawings which can be connected with the Gallery there are sheets that are manifestly not preparatory studies by Annibale himself but are merely designs by pupils who were given, as part of their training, the task of developing independently some of the master's ideas.[13] The presence of these students' exercises, most of which have to do with motives derived from the decorative system of the ceiling, is only another indication that the proportion of original studies for the Farnese cycles in Angeloni's collection was by no means as high as has been supposed.

We can no longer hope to trace the movement of individual pieces from the Angeloni-Mignard volumes after their arrival in France. Those in the single volume owned by Coypel are known to have gone directly into the "Cabinet du Roi" in 1752. The remaining volumes were acquired, as we have seen, by Crozat. From Mariette's annotated copy of the Crozat catalogue (now in the Cabinet des Dessins) we learn that of the 149 drawings classified as "Etudes d'Annibal Carrache pour les tableaux de la Gallerie Farnese" (these included 21 studies for the Camerino) 132 were acquired by Mariette himself.[14] Unfortunately Mariette failed, for some reason, to place his usual collector's mark on them. This same group of drawings reappears in the catalogue of the Mariette sale of 1775, where it is described as "un Porte-Feuille, contenant plus de 100 feuilles d'Etudes de Figures, Plafonds & Ornements divers, faits au bistre, à la sanguine & pierre noire, connues dans plusieurs Tableaux

---

[10] Bacou, *Dessins*, p. 10.

[11] Louvre Inv. 7307 and 7313 (numbered *26* and *63* respectively).

[12] Louvre Inv. 7169 and 7400 (numbered *12* and *38* respectively).

[13] The following drawings (none by Annibale himself but all bearing numbers that

identify them as belonging to the Angeloni-Mignard volumes) may be cited as examples: Louvre Inv. 7417, 7424 and 7425, Besançon D. 1401.

[14] Mariette, *op.cit.*, p. 50, lots 462-473. Lots 474 and 475, comprising seventeen drawings for the Camerino, went to other buyers.

de ce Maître, du Triomphe de Bacchus, de Galatée, de Polipheme, &c."[15] At the time of the sale only twenty of these pieces were purchased by Lempereur for the "Cabinet du Roi," the rest being "détaillé à diverses personnes."[16] Some found their way, through the Gigoux collection, into the Museum of Besançon;[17] others were later absorbed through various channels into the Louvre; one (No. 124; Fig. 238) is in the Boymans Museum at Rotterdam.

Angeloni's famous collection early attracted the attention of copyists. Even before Mignard purchased them, the drawings were being studied and copied by the young Charles Errard (1606-1689), who was later to become director of the Académie de France à Rome.[18] Errard's copies have disappeared, as is true of virtually the whole of his graphic oeuvre. Only recently, however, another set of copies was discovered by Roseline Bacou in the Cabinet des Dessins of the Louvre.[19] They are contained in a bound volume of drawings bearing an erroneous attribution to François Perrier. From various particulars it may be deduced that they are the work of a French artist of the third quarter of the seventeenth century; they were made, that is, after the arrival of the Angeloni drawings in Paris. The unknown copyist was particularly interested in the decorative designs, many of which he reproduced with painstaking fidelity in pen and in pen and wash; he seems to have paid no attention to the figure drawings for the mythological subjects. Included in the album are copies of three of the most important and fundamental studies by Annibale for the Farnese ceiling: No. 44 (Fig. 148) and No. 46 (Fig. 151) on fol. 53; and No. 50 (Fig. 155) on fol. 82; another detail from the last-named appears on fol. 57. There are in addition copies of No. 43 (Fig. 145) on fol. 56 and of No. 41 (Fig. 144) on fol. 29. The draughtsman did not limit himself to reproducing original studies by Annibale, but also made copies after some of the numerous pupils' drawings in the Angeloni-Mignard volumes, especially those which are elaborations of motives from the Farnese vault. For example, several details on fol. 56 are copied from the Louvre drawings 7424 and 7425, both of which are studio pieces.

The greatest of all the collections of Carracci drawings formed in the seventeenth century was unquestionably that of Everhard Jabach (*c.* 1610-1695). It is curious that of the hundreds of authentic designs by Annibale in his possession no more than five (Nos. 144-148) were studies for the Galleria Farnese. Small groups of drawings for the Camerino and the Galleria passed at an early date into the hands of English collectors:

---

[15] F. Basan, *Catalogue raisonné des différens objets de curiosités dans les sciences et arts, qui composoient le Cabinet de feu Mr. Mariette . . .*, Paris, 1775, p. 50.

[16] *Ibid.* (annotated copy in the Cabinet des Dessins).

[17] Cf. our Nos. 24, 59, 77, 81, 94, 96 and 128, all bearing "Angeloni" numbers and all known to have been in Mariette's possession.

[18] Vittoria, *Osservazioni*, p. 54.

[19] Inv. R. F. 879-1060, 182 folios. The volume contains copies after frescoes, engravings and architectural details as well as those after the Angeloni drawings. Mlle. Bacou, who has given a preliminary account of the album in the catalogue *Dessins des Carrache* (p. 39), promises to make it the object of a fuller study.

Sir Peter Lely (1618-1680) owned three (Nos. 42, 51 and 55); five (Nos. 9, 10, 64, 72, and 103) were in the collection of Lord Somers (1650-1716); others came to England through the activities of collectors such as the Earl of Spencer (Nos. 28 and 67) and Sir Thomas Lawrence (Nos. 93 and 104). The collection of the great connoisseur Pierre-Jean Mariette (1694-1774) included a small number of Farnese drawings in addition to those in the Angeloni-Mignard-Crozat volumes. Four of these are studies for the *Bacchanal* (Nos. 55-58), and are now in the Albertina; a fifth sheet (No. 127) is in the Ellesmere collection.

One of the difficulties in tracing the ownership of individual pieces arises from the fact that many early collectors placed no distinguishing marks on their drawings. Of the drawings owned by Bellori, for instance, only one (No. 54) can now be identified with certainty. But even in more recent literature there are references to drawings that can no longer be traced. Thus, to take one example, the catalogue of the Prakhov collection of old master drawings (St. Petersburg, 1906) describes five studies of heads in black chalk said to be preparatory designs for the Farnese ceiling.[20] Unfortunately there is no way of determining whether they are originals or copies. For the drawings in question are not illustrated, nor is their present whereabouts known.

[20] *Collection Adrien Prachoff,* i. *Dessins originaux des maîtres anciens,* St. Petersburg, 1906, pp. 28 f., 52, nos. 70-74. Two of the drawings are identified as studies for the *Triumph of Bacchus and Ariadne,* one as the head of Polyphemus in the fresco of *Polyphemus and Acis,* and another as the head of Cephalus in *Aurora and Cephalus.*

CHAPTER 10 · THE DRAWINGS FOR
THE CAMERINO

BY the time he began work on the Camerino Annibale had perfected that elaborate system of preparatory drawings which we associate principally with the Farnese Gallery. It is important to realize that this working method did not evolve during the planning for the Gallery but was already fully developed when the artist arrived in Rome. There is abundant evidence to show that the Camerino cycle was carried out with the same thoroughness, and with the same extensive use of preliminary studies, that the artist was to use in the Gallery. We know from two accounts, for example, that Annibale made more than twenty drawings of a single kneeling figure (Hercules bearing the globe) in order to find the most effective posture; and it is apparent that other figures in the cycle required, if not as many drawings, at least comparable care in preparation.

The greater part of Annibale's drawings for the Camerino must be presumed to be lost. But it is remarkable that for each of the principal scenes of the ceiling at least one preparatory study can be identified, and for some there are as many as six or seven drawings still extant. It is probably true that the proportion of surviving drawings for the Camerino is as large as that for the Gallery. The reason is that, like the drawings for the Gallery, they were assiduously taken up by seventeenth-century collectors: Vittoria, writing in 1679, mentions various drawings and cartoons for the Camerino in the cabinets of such connoisseurs as Bellori, Angeloni, Maratti, and Vittoria himself.[1] Some of the cartoons, one suspects, may still be lying in closets, forgotten but intact.

Despite extensive lacunae, the Camerino drawings are sufficiently numerous that we can follow Annibale's working procedure in some detail. First he laid out the plan of the composition in a series of sketches, the earliest of which were drawn very rapidly, either in pen and ink (Fig. 122) or in chalk (Fig. 113). Later, as his ideas began to crystallize, he would make more careful drafts in chalk (Fig. 115), in pen and wash (Fig. 111), or even in a mixture of the two (Fig. 137). He next sought to fix the attitudes of the chief figures, a process that might require a number of sketches for each (Figs. 100-101, 114, 116-117). This done and the necessary adjustments made in the compositional scheme, Annibale set about making definitive studies from the life. Such drawings, for which the models were posed in the attitudes previously established, are invariably in chalk. At this stage he frequently found it necessary, in order to clarify his conception, to make separate studies of parts of the body, especially of the legs (Figs. 121 and 141). Lastly, the results of all these studies had to be consolidated either in a final design or, more frequently perhaps, in the cartoon from which the fresco was to be executed (Figs. 107-108, and 131). Although these were the suc-

---

[1] *Osservazioni*, pp. 51 f.

cessive steps by which Annibale customarily developed and refined his pictorial ideas, it must not be thought that they constituted a rigid and unvarying sequence from which the artist could not depart. In practice changes might be introduced at any stage in the evolution of the design, and it was by no means unusual for Annibale to make revisions even after the cartoon was completed.

It is remarkable that the preparatory graphic material includes no drawings by Agostino, a fact that lends weight to the conclusion that he had no share in the Camerino.

DRAWINGS FOR THE DECORATIVE SCHEME

A sheet of studies in the Ashmolean Museum at Oxford (No. 1) is of particular importance as recording some of Annibale's first ideas for the ceiling of the Camerino. On one side (Fig. 101) there appears among other sketches a schematic drawing in red chalk of the entire ceiling (cp. text fig. 2, page 22). Here are indicated all the principal compartments—the central rectangle, the oval panels, the lunettes and the triangular spandrels—and the structural network which binds them together; even the two medallions for the *impresa* are included.

On the other side of the Ashmolean drawing (Fig. 100) are further studies, most of which have to do with Hercules supporting the globe. In the middle of the sheet is a faint sketch in red chalk for one of the triangular compartments of the ceiling, one side of which shows an ornamental molding of ivy leaves. A very similar chalk sketch for one of the compartments is found on a sheet of studies in the Louvre (No. 21 verso; Fig. 128, left side), where again there is a border of ivy; here the framework of the ceiling has been expanded to include the medallion for the *impresa* (near the center of the sheet), together with a rough indication of another lunette along the top. The ivy pattern seen in these early sketches is perhaps to be connected with Cardinal Farnese's letter of August 22, 1595, to Fulvio Orsini, in which he proposes that the foliate borders in the Camerino take the form of "vine, palm or olive."[2] In the end, however, the Cardinal's suggestion does not seem to have been followed: the gilt stucco moldings of the Camerino bear little resemblance to those projected in the preliminary drawings.

A drawing in Windsor Castle presents a more detailed design for the ceiling (No. 2; Fig. 102). Like the Ashmolean sketch it provides for the central rectangle, the ovals which flank it, the spandrels and the lunettes, all articulated by broad bands of stucco; the medallion even contains a rapid pen sketch of the lily device. The spaces reserved for the mythological subjects are left blank; Annibale's concern in this drawing is with the grisaille decoration of the compartments. The section at the left containing a putto, a faun and a satyr is already close to the work actually executed; the goat-legged satyr, in particular, adopts the same posture in both drawing and fresco (cf. Fig. 8). The foliate ornament, on the other hand, has not reached the definitive stage, and

[2] See note 102 to Chapter 3.

there is as yet no sign of the Hercules medallion. The adjoining compartment in the drawing contains a female satyr quite like the corresponding figure in fresco (cf. Fig. 4). The space below her, which is to be understood as the angle of the vault, is occupied by a shield with Odoardo's *impresa* of the lily plant. It was later decided that this emblem should be transferred to the medallion (as is indicated by the rough sketch in pen and ink), and that the four Cardinal Virtues should appear in the corners. Beneath the shield are two putti seated astride branches of the foliage. Figures similar to these were later employed in the fresco as supporters for the allegorical figures in the triangular spandrels along the side (cf. Fig. 21). One of the spandrels is left empty in the drawing. The other (at the end of the ceiling) features a putto grasping a scroll; he seems to prefigure the pair of putti holding cornucopias who, with two sirens, serve to frame the gilt oval in the spandrels at either end of the room (cf. Fig. 19).

Some of Annibale's ideas for the grisaille ornament of the vault are to be seen on a sheet of sketches in the Metropolitan Museum of New York (No. 30 verso; Fig. 103). The notations are fragmentary, because the sheet has been cut down to the shape of the drawing on the other side (cf. Fig. 133). The largest of these sketches represents a putto (the face heavily shaded) holding an apple in his hand. This figure, which has been set down with a marvellously facile line, is evidently an early study for one of the boys in the compartments surrounding the *Choice of Hercules* (cf. Figs. 5-8). Beside him is a second figure, of which however not enough remains to permit identification—though the pose has some resemblance to that of *Honor* in an adjoining part of the ceiling (cf. Fig. 13). The remaining sketches are to be understood as designs for the L-shaped compartments beneath the oval frescoes (Figs. 10-11); the sheet must be turned upside down in order to make the relationship clear. At the lower left (upper right when the drawing is inverted) Annibale has indicated a section of the compartment, which may be recognized both by its peculiar shape and by the presence of a large foliate motif at the angle. The narrow vertical arm of the compartment contains a satyr herm holding a basket on his head. The sketch in the opposite corner shows that Annibale also considered a sphinx with a basket on her head as an alternative to the satyr—an interesting anticipation of the sphinxes on the ceiling of the Farnese Gallery. In the final realization in fresco, however, the artist decided not to use figures in this narrow space and the design was made up instead of rinceaux.

A chalk drawing in the Louvre, which has not hitherto been correctly identified (No. 3; Fig. 105), is a study from the life for one of the fauns in grisaille who lean in a twisted attitude against the oval compartments (cf. Fig. 8).[3] The posture is virtually identical to that seen in the fresco; it should also be compared to the preliminary idea for this figure in the Windsor design, No. 2 (Fig. 102). The oval frame of the adjoining

[3] The drawing has previously been interpreted as a first idea for the satyr in the lower left-hand corner of the *Triumph of Bacchus and Ariadne* in the Farnese Gallery. (See Bacou, *Dessins*, p. 42, no. 63.) There is a drawing in Windsor of a male nude in a similar pose (Wittkower, *Carracci Drawings*, p. 133, Cat. 284). But this seems to me to be a studio work.

scene is lightly indicated behind the figure, and a *pentimento* correcting the position of the left arm is also visible. The legs are not shown in the drawing.

In the Royal Library at Windsor are two fragments of cartoons which have been recognized by Wittkower as belonging to the grisaille decoration of the vault. One represents a putto with a cornucopia (No. 4; Fig. 107) and the other an armless siren (No. 5; Fig. 108); originally they must have been joined together as part of a larger cartoon. Figures corresponding to these are to be seen in the triangular spandrels at the ends of the room (Figs. 19-20), where they form the decorative framing of the gilt ovals with allegorical figures. There is not exact agreement in every detail. In the fresco, for example, the cornucopias are intertwined so that each putto grasps that belonging to his neighbor, a feature that does not appear in the cartoon. There is also a marked difference in the gilt oval, for which the artist originally planned an irregular cartouche-like shape.

Beneath the siren (Fig. 108) is still another fragment of a cartoon, drawn on a separate piece of paper and joined to the larger sheet. It shows the head of a putto with a cornucopia from which fruit is pouring out; the outlines have been pricked. Figures exactly like this are to be seen in the narrow corners of the triangles over the lunettes of the side walls (Figs. 3-4, 21-22). When the cartoon had served its purpose Annibale simply used it to piece out the cartoon with the siren; this is confirmed by the fact that part of the siren is actually drawn over the smaller sheet attached below.

These cartoons were originally owned by Domenichino, who bequeathed them (together with the entire contents of his studio) to his pupil Raspantino. The sheet with the putto (Fig. 107) is to be identified with that described in the Raspantino inventory of 1664 as "un chartone d'un putto con fogliami."[4] Although the inventory makes no mention of the second fragment we may be certain that it too was in the Raspantino collection. Both cartoon sections passed into the hands of the painter Carlo Maratti: Vincenzo Vittoria, describing certain Carracci drawings in Maratti's collection, speaks of "un pezzo di cartone di una sirena della nave di Ulisse, & un altro di un putto, che si vede negli ornamenti."[5] Despite the mistaken identification of the cartoon with the siren, there can be no doubt that the fragments described by Vittoria are the same as those now in Windsor.

Maratti's interest in this cycle is further reflected in a group of three red chalk drawings at Windsor, not hitherto identified, which are in fact copies after allegorical figures in the Camerino. The drawings in question were perhaps not executed by Maratti himself, but certainly issued from his studio.[6]

Only one drawing has thus far been discovered for the allegorical figures set within ovals. Denis Mahon first drew attention to the large chalk study in the Louvre for *Securitas* (No. 6; Fig. 104), which is strikingly close to the figure executed in fresco

[4] Bertolotti, *Artisti bolognesi*, p. 175.
[5] *Osservazioni*, p. 52.
[6] See A. Blunt and H. L. Cooke, *The Roman Drawings of the XVII & XVIII Centuries in* the *Collection of Her Majesty the Queen at Windsor Castle*, London, 1960, p. 68, nos. 507-509. No. 507 copies *Prudence*, no. 508 *Temperance*, and no. 509 *Honor*.

(Fig. 21). There are a few *pentimenti*: the right hip has been noticeably thickened, and the column shifted a little to the right. At the top of the sheet there is a suggestion of the oval which encloses the figure. We have already seen that Annibale's *Securitas* owes much to Marcantonio's engraving of *Fortitude*.

Also to be connected with the preparatory material for the Camerino is a sheet of pen studies in the Louvre (No. 7; Fig. 106). The vigorously drawn male nude at the right side is a study for Hercules on the funeral pyre, which is painted on the lintel of one of the windows (Fig. 13). The only difference in attitude between the two is that in the fresco the head has been turned in the opposite direction; the change was perhaps made when it was decided to place the figure over the left window rather than over the right. The sheet contains various other studies—a river landscape, an architectural perspective construction, grasshoppers, etc.—which have no relation to the Camerino; but it is possible that the perspective diagram at the lower right is to be read as a view of the window embrasure *dal di sotto in su*.

DRAWINGS FOR THE CHOICE OF HERCULES (FIG. 9)

Among the several drawings on the sheet in the Ashmolean Museum, already referred to, there is a sketch in black chalk for an oval figure-subject enclosed in an ornamental frame of rectangular shape (No. 1 verso; Fig. 101, upper left). Although it is utterly different from the final conception this must represent Annibale's first idea for the *Choice of Hercules*. One difference—an unimportant one—is the oval shape, which was soon discarded so that the composition might occupy the whole rectangle. What is more important is that the three persons are not deployed symmetrically, with Hercules in the middle between Virtue and Vice; instead the hero sits in profile at the right, facing the two women. The explanation seems to be that in this first draft Annibale has instinctively adopted the compositional scheme of a related subject—the Judgment of Paris. This becomes clear if the sketch is compared with the famous engraving by Marcantonio: Virtue and Vice stand before the seated Hercules in much the same way that the goddesses pose before Paris. Yet even in this preliminary draft, which seems so unrelated to the completed painting, Annibale has established certain fundamental relationships. Vice, who is seen from the back, is on Hercules' left. At his right is Virtue, facing the spectator and raising her arm as she points to the mountain in the distance.

Stimulated, perhaps, by the sight of an antique relief such as *Hercules and the Hesperides*, Annibale shortly abandoned his first idea and decided upon a more formal and symmetrical scheme. The early stages of the new plan cannot be traced in detail. It is not certain, for example, whether the artist first intended Virtue to stand on the left (as might be expected) or on the right. Denis Mahon has put forward the hypothesis that the drawing of a woman in Besançon (No. 8; Fig. 110) may be an early study for the figure of Virtue.[7] The drawing is in black chalk, heightened with white,

---

[7] Mahon, *Disegni*, p. 99, no. 130.

on gray paper; the book lying on the ground at the right is in red chalk. If this hypothesis is correct (as I believe it to be) Annibale must have imagined a composition in which Virtue stood on Hercules' left, thereby contradicting the customary symbolism of right and left. Pointing upward with her right hand and gathering up her mantle with her left, the woman inclines her head as if addressing someone seated beside her; she carries no sword, but her hair, like that of *Virtus* in the Naples canvas, is somewhat dishevelled. But what makes the identification virtually certain is the large volume lying open on the ground, which is surely to be connected with the book held by the poet in the final redaction of the scene. This drawing, belonging to a passing phase, must soon have been set aside as Annibale continued his search for a more workable solution.

A later stage in the evolution of the figure-group is documented by an elegant pen and wash drawing in the Louvre (No. 9; Fig. 111). It represents only Hercules and Vice, who is here accompanied by Cupid; the left side of the composition has been lost, but unquestionably included the figure of Virtue now assigned to her proper station on Hercules' right. The attitude of the young hero, whose right leg is raised on a ledge of rock, is already close to that in the painting, but the position of the arms is reversed and the head leans a little too obviously toward the side of Virtue. Another important feature is the palm tree which appears directly behind Hercules. Vice, on his left side, is obviously thought of as Venus, since she is attended by Cupid (another link with ·the Judgment of Paris). She is clad in the fluttering, transparent garment that she wears in the Naples canvas; but instead of being seen from behind she walks toward the spectator, indicating with her left hand the attributes of frivolity and sensual delights on the ground—two masks, a tambourine, and flutes. In her right hand Vice holds an unidentifiable object. It is not altogether clear whether she is tugging at Hercules' cloak (as is suggested by the crescent-shaped area of wash connecting the two figures) or whether she is simply dangling some lure before his eyes. Cupid, for his part, points along the path leading into the grove of trees. Stylistically, the drawing gives hardly any hint of the statuesque quality with which the final version will be invested. The figures lean freely to one side and the other, their bodies bent in graceful arcs and their heads inclined. The draughtsmanship is remarkably pictorial in character: the broken and varied contours are full of movement, and the modeling in broad patches of wash suggests the play of light over the forms.

Another study for the same part of the composition, but lacking almost all of the figure of Hercules, is in the Museum at Dijon (No. 10; Fig. 112). It is executed in wash over red chalk; a few contours have been strengthened with pen and ink. The drawing is evidently later than the Louvre sheet just described (No. 9; Fig. 111), because the uncertainties in the action of *Voluptas* have here been resolved. The figure still faces the observer and is still accompanied by Cupid; but the position of the arms, both swung energetically to the side,[8] is strikingly close to the final conception. The

[8] It is very likely that we have to do here with the influence of Sadeler's engraving (after F.

next step, obviously, was to turn the figure about. In this revision we may again detect the influence of Marcantonio's *Judgment of Paris*: the central figure of that engraving was certainly in Annibale's mind when he fashioned the definitive pose of *Voluptas*.

The Dijon drawing also retains the Cupid and the pile of masks and musical instruments in the right foreground. In the final conception Annibale suppressed the Cupid and inserted in his place the "altar" on which rest the masks and a book of music. A similar adjustment was made on the other side of the picture, where the poet holding the book was added; in an early study for *Virtus* (No. 8; Fig. 110) the book was shown simply lying on the ground.

The final study for the poet is in the Louvre (No. 11; Fig. 109). Like other drawings of this class it is done in black chalk, heightened with white, on gray-blue paper (in this instance faded to gray). It was drawn from the model, and the resemblance to the figure in the painting is extremely close.

Bellori owned two drawings for the *Choice of Hercules*,[9] but unluckily we have no description of them. It is possible that they might be the studies for *Voluptas* now in the Louvre and Dijon (Nos. 9 and 10; Figs. 111-112), which were formerly together in the collections of Lord Somers and His de la Salle.

DRAWINGS FOR HERCULES BEARING THE GLOBE (FIG. 10)

In describing Annibale's inventive genius Bellori speaks of the ease with which the artist was able to solve the most difficult problems. "Yet sometimes," he writes, "even he had to proceed more slowly, because he was unable to realize at once in his work the perfect conception which he had in his mind, as can be seen in his repeated studies for the figure of Hercules supporting the globe with the constellations, which is derived from another Hercules, namely the antique marble in the Farnese palace. In order to find the perfect pose Annibale made many different drawings and sketches, of which we have seen upwards of twenty."[10] Vincenzo Vittoria likewise mentions more than twenty drawings for this figure, adding that they were in the possession of Francesco Angeloni.[11] It is a fact that there are more extant drawings for *Hercules bearing the globe* than for any other scene in the Camerino cycle, and six of these (Nos. 12, 14-18) bear numbers that show them to be from the Angeloni collection. The original group of some twenty studies for the principal figure alone is no longer complete, but enough have survived to substantiate Bellori's statement that Annibale took special care to make the kneeling Hercules, bowing beneath the weight of the heavens, as effective an image as possible.

A very early drawing for this subject is in the Royal Library at Turin (No. 36 verso; Fig. 113). It is a hurried composition sketch in red chalk, the oval shape being roughly

Sustris) of the *Choice of Hercules*, in which *Voluptas* adopts a remarkably similar attitude (reproduced in Panofsky, *Hercules am Scheidewege*, Abb. 57).

[9] Vittoria, *Osservazioni*, p. 52.

[10] *Vite*, p. 81. The marble "Hercules" is of course the Farnese Atlas.

[11] *Osservazioni*, p. 52. Vittoria's informant was Carlo Maratti.

indicated. Later, when the sheet was re-used to make the drawing on the other side, part of it was cut away, with the result that the astronomer at the left is missing. Annibale has centered his attention on the figure of Hercules, whose attitude is manifestly that of the Farnese Atlas, but in mirror reversal. The hero kneels with the left knee resting on the ground and the head turned to one side; the arms are raised symmetrically to support the sphere. But already a problem arises. The globe borne by the marble Atlas is small enough that it can be grasped securely with both hands raised, whereas Annibale, in order to gain greater monumentality, has so enlarged the sphere that it can no longer be satisfactorily sustained with the arms in this position but seems in imminent danger of falling backwards to the ground.

How seriously Annibale grappled with this problem is evident from the page of drawings in the Ashmolean Museum at Oxford, which contains a whole series of studies for the figure in question. On one side of the sheet (No. 1 verso; Fig. 101), in addition to a sketch of the *Choice of Hercules* and a plan of the entire ceiling, there is a pen drawing of Hercules and the globe, with an indication of the oval frame. Though the sphere has become even larger than in the Turin sketch, the hero is still represented as supporting it with both arms raised above his head. Annibale has experienced particular difficulty with the left arm, the position of which is obviously unsatisfactory; only later will he hit upon the idea of placing it underneath the sphere. At the left is a separate drawing of the head, also in pen and ink.

On the other side of the Oxford sheet (No. 1 recto; Fig. 100) the artist continued his efforts to find an acceptable solution. The sketch at the right represents Hercules in virtually the same attitude as the study on the reverse, the only appreciable difference being that the sphere has been lowered somewhat so as to rest not on his neck but on his shoulders. Turned upside down, the sheet displays three more sketches for the same figure. At the top is a pen study for the legs, now fixed in the definitive pose. The larger drawing at the extreme right, showing the torso, the head and the right arm balancing the sphere, belongs to a later stage; we shall return to this shortly. In the lowermost sketch Annibale makes a significant advance toward the ultimate solution: the huge globe is still further lowered so that its weight is borne by Hercules' back, as in the fresco; and, what is more important, the left arm is moved down and back to help to sustain the load.

This last sketch finds an almost exact correspondence in a chalk drawing in the Royal Library at Turin, which is a study for the upper part of the figure (No. 13; Fig. 114). The attitude seen in both drawings is close to the final conception, although the position of the right arm is not yet fixed and the head is set lower than in the fresco. Both of these details are finally adjusted in the adjoining pen drawing on the Oxford sheet (Fig. 100, at the extreme right when the sheet is inverted). Closely associated with this sketch is a chalk study in the Louvre, which likewise shows the head and right arm in the definitive position (No. 14; Fig. 116). Indeed the Louvre drawing has no other purpose than to consolidate the pose of the elevated arm: the legs are left incomplete and the other arm is omitted altogether.

No drawing of the left arm alone is extant, but for the legs there exists a splendid chalk study in Besançon (No. 15; Fig. 117). In the rhythmic sureness of the contours, in the placing of light and shade, and in the indication of the ground line and cast shadows the drawing stands in a particularly close relationship to the fresco, and must accordingly be one of the latest studies in the extensive series of preparatory designs for this figure.

The graphic material for the two astronomers is much less abundant. The early red chalk sketch in Turin (No. 36 verso; Fig. 113) makes it clear that Annibale planned from the first to place the kneeling Hercules between two reclining figures; at this preliminary stage, however, no effort has yet been made to define their attitudes exactly.

A drawing in the Louvre of a reclining male figure (No. 16; Fig. 120) may perhaps be regarded as an early study from the life for the recumbent Euclid at the right side of the composition.[12] Although the identification is by no means certain it is tempting to conclude, from the position of the raised right arm, that the figure is represented pointing to the heavenly sphere borne by Hercules. The face was originally shown looking out at the observer, but the head has been redrawn so that it is turned in the direction of the outstretched arm.

To see how the whole design has progressed we may compare the early sketch in Turin (No. 36 verso; Fig. 113) with the more detailed study for the composition in the Louvre (No. 12; Fig. 115). To judge from the posture of the principal figure the latter drawing must fall between the Turin study for Hercules (No. 13; Fig. 114) and that in the Louvre (No. 14; Fig. 116); the position of the hero's head is not far from the final redaction, but the right arm still accords with the earlier solution in being at some distance from the head. The two astronomers are disposed in attitudes which are analogous, though not yet identical, to those in the fresco, one being seen from the back and the other from the front. They have also been given their proper attributes. The posture of Ptolemy, on the left, is plainly that of an antique river god.[13] He differs from his counterpart in the fresco chiefly in that he has a bald pate and carries the armillary sphere in his left hand rather than in the right. On the opposite side Euclid holds his compasses and tablet, the latter bearing geometrical figures on its surface.

Also in the Louvre are individual studies for the two seers. In the drawing of the astronomer Ptolemy (No. 17; Fig. 118) Annibale is mainly concerned with the rendering of the back. Despite its look of finish and its pronouncedly sculptural character, this cannot be the final design for the figure. The subject adopts a somewhat more upright posture than that seen in the fresco; he holds the sphere in his left hand (as in

[12] Mahon (*Disegni*, p. 105) suggests tentatively that this might be a study for the reclining Polyphemus in the *Catanian Brothers* (Fig. 24). One objection to this hypothesis is that the figure in the fresco faces in the opposite direction.

[13] Calvesi points out a resemblance, in the reverse sense, to a river god in an engraving by Caraglio of *Apollo and Daphne*, B. 18 (in *Commentari*, VII, 1956, p. 271, figs. 12-13).

the composition study, No. 12; Fig. 115); and the right arm hangs loosely at the side, the hand grasping a pair of compasses. The shaded segment in the upper right corner may be taken to indicate the celestial sphere. The second drawing bears three studies for the figure of Euclid (No. 18; Fig. 119). The largest study in the center of the sheet represents him in what is virtually the definitive attitude, looking up at the heavenly globe as he inscribes a geometrical design on his tablet. Only the left leg and the drapery that covers it are studied in detail, the remainder being merely sketched in roughly. Below, in the right corner, is a drawing of the nude upper part of the body. And at the top left is a study of the foot in foreshortening, correcting the position shown in the sketch just beneath. The sheet has faded badly through having been left too long in the light.

The cartoon for the fresco is known to have been in the collection of Francesco Raspantino and later in that of Carlo Maratti, but no trace of it remains today.[14] A red chalk drawing in Windsor is a copy by Maratti, or one of his pupils, after the figure of Euclid. In all probability this was made from the cartoon rather than from the fresco.[15]

DRAWINGS FOR HERCULES RESTING (FIG. 11)

In striking contrast to the relatively numerous preparatory drawings that have been preserved for the fresco of *Hercules bearing the globe* is the paucity of material relating to the complementary scene of *Hercules resting*. Some years ago I wrote that no drawings were extant for this subject.[16] Although some evidence has since come to light, it is still not possible to trace in detail the growth of Annibale's ideas through the medium of drawings.

We learn from Vincenzo Vittoria that the painter Carlo Maratti owned a cartoon for this subject which, though it had been put to use on the ceiling, nevertheless differed in appearance from the fresco actually executed there.[17] The inference is that at the last moment Annibale decided to revise his composition and therefore prepared a fresh set of drawings and a new cartoon. The rejected design owned by Maratti has undoubtedly been lost. Recently, however, Maria Vittoria Brugnoli has published a photograph of what appears to be a copy, probably by Maratti himself, of Annibale's first cartoon for the fresco (Fig. 268).[18] The composition is similar to that of the

[14] Bertolotti, *Artisti bolognesi*, p. 175: "Un Chartone di un Hercole che tiene il mondo." Maratti's ownership of the cartoon is recorded by Vittoria, *Osservazioni*, p. 52: "Nello studio del Signor Carlo Maratta stà il cartone dell'Ercole, che regge il globo del mondo."

[15] The drawing is erroneously connected with Maratti's *Flight into Egypt* (Siena, Chigi collection) by Blunt and Cooke, *Roman Drawings at Windsor*, p. 59, no. 304. As examples of the many copies after the figure of Hercules bearing the globe it may suffice to mention a drawing in the Uffizi, Inv. 12411 F, and an-

other from the Skippe coll. (Sale, Christie's, Nov. 20-21, 1958).

[16] J. R. Martin, in *Art Bulletin*, xxxviii, 1956, p. 97.

[17] *Osservazioni*, p. 52: "Conserva il medesimo Signor Maratta un'altro cartone finitissimo, e bellissimo dell'Ercole, che riposa dalle fatiche; il quale si conosce essere stato calcato su la colla del muro, e messo in opera da Annibale, e poi mutato, essendo differente dall'altro, che resta di sua mano dipinto."

[18] M. V. Brugnoli, "Note alla Mostra dei Carracci," *Bollettino d'Arte*, xLI, 1956, pp.

existing painting except that it is reversed, Hercules being on the left and the sphinx on the right. The chief difference is in the position of the hero, who rests his head against his left hand, supporting the left elbow on his knee. The attitude is fundamentally that of Adam on the Sistine ceiling, but the motive of the head propped against the hand is taken from the Orsini gem (Fig. 278). In the final, revised conception a new pose was invented for Hercules.

We hear nothing in the early literature of Annibale's second cartoon, nor of any other preparatory drawings for *Hercules resting*. But at least one study for this subject can be identified. A hitherto unnoticed drawing in the Louvre proves to be, as comparison with the fresco makes plain, a study for the left leg of Hercules in the final position (No. 19; Fig. 121). In order to suggest the hero's superhuman strength the artist found it necessary to thicken somewhat the muscles of the calf.

DRAWINGS FOR ULYSSES AND CIRCE (FIG. 17)

No fewer than three composition studies are preserved for the Circe fresco; all are in the Cabinet des Dessins of the Louvre.

The hurried pen sketch (No. 20; Fig. 122) may well be the first idea for the subject. Summary though it is, the drawing nevertheless contains most of the essential features of the design. A few strokes of the pen describe the architectural setting as an arcaded loggia, one corner of which is indicated (as in the fresco) between Circe and Ulysses. The sorceress is seated on a high throne in an attitude very close to the final conception. But for the figures of Ulysses and Mercury Annibale has not yet found a satisfactory solution. The former stands irresolutely poised on one foot, turning his head away from the woman as though to avoid her bewitching glance. Mercury is so placed that his head intervenes between Circe and Ulysses, an obviously unsuitable position since it destroys the illusion of his being hidden from her view. How the composition was to be completed on the right we do not know, because the drawing is a fragment, showing little more than half of the lunette.

Annibale's second idea, as recorded in a large chalk study (No. 21 recto; Fig. 123), introduces several important modifications. Ulysses and Mercury have been shifted to the right, so that the middle of the picture is left vacant. Ulysses, whose stance is now virtually the definitive one, receives the cup in his right hand and turns his head to look at Circe. The god has withdrawn to a place of concealment behind the hero and reaches over his shoulder to put the moly in the cup. Circe's posture is changed sharply: she is seated in a more upright attitude and twists her body beguilingly as she proffers the cup. Behind her is a large jar such as appears in the finished painting. The setting is likewise altered, the entire right half being open, with a glimpse of Ulysses' shipmates transformed into swine beyond a low parapet.

358 f., fig. 3. The drawing was formerly in a private collection in Rome; its present whereabouts is unknown. That Maratti made a copy of Annibale's cartoon is attested by the inventories of his possessions.

The third study, an equally elaborate drawing in chalk (No. 22; Fig. 124), approaches the final conception. For the posture of Circe Annibale reverts to his first idea (No. 20; Fig. 122), rejecting the variant pose seen in the previous study. Ulysses stands once more on the axis of the composition, though in other respects his posture is not as close to the finished work as that in the second drawing. The god Mercury, hovering in the air behind him, needs only to be lowered to the ground in order to arrive at the definitive attitude. An important addition to the scene is the swine-headed man in the lower right, who, as the preliminary sketch indicates, was originally intended to be somewhat nearer the middle.

The final redaction, as we see it in the fresco, is a synthesis incorporating the best features of all three preparatory studies. The figure of Ulysses, for example, derives rather from the second stage (Fig. 123) than from the third (Fig. 124); and the architectural setting in the fresco is actually closer to the first idea (Fig. 122) than to the later drawings.[19]

The next task was to prepare detailed studies from the life. Three such drawings are extant: only the figure of Ulysses is lacking.

The beautiful drawing of Circe in Windsor (No. 23; Fig. 125)[20] is similar to the painting, the only noticeable difference being that in the latter the left hand holding the cup is raised a little higher. But even this minor change is prefigured in the drawing by a *pentimento* which places the hand in a slightly more elevated position. For the god Mercury, partly hidden behind Ulysses, there is a study from the nude in Besançon (No. 24; Fig. 126), formerly in the possession of Mariette. The finished modeling in light and shade is confined to the upper part of the body, the legs being drawn only summarily. The attitude agrees precisely with the fresco. The last drawing of the series is the impressive study in the Louvre for Ulysses' companion at the right side of the fresco (No. 25; Fig. 127).[21] Annibale has not attempted in this study from the life to portray the swine's head.

DRAWINGS FOR ULYSSES AND THE SIRENS (FIG. 18)

Among the many drawings for the Camerino now in the Louvre there is one of unusual interest, No. 21. The recto (Fig. 123) bears an important design for the Circe scene. On the verso (Fig. 128) are three studies for other parts of the ceiling. The head of an old man at the right is a study for the father in the *Catanian Brothers*. On

---

[19] There exists no final design for the fresco. The drawing in the National Gallery of Scotland (formerly in the Royal Scottish Academy), cited by Navenne (*Rome et le palais Farnèse*, I, p. 74) and Tietze (p. 69, note 1), is merely a copy after the fresco.

[20] It is conceivable that this might be the drawing owned by Bellori, which Vittoria describes as "Circe, che porge la bevanda ad Ulisse" (*Osservazioni*, p. 52). But the descrip-

tion might apply equally well to a study for the entire composition. There was also a drawing for this fresco in the collection of Lempereur (*Catalogue d'une riche collection de tableaux, de peintures . . . , de desseins . . . , d'estampes . . . , du Cabinet de M * * **, Paris, 1773, p. 41, no. 152).

[21] A red chalk drawing of this figure, also in the Louvre (Inv. 7579), is a copy after the fresco.

the left half of the page is a sketch for a section of the decorative framework of the vault. Drawn over this is an early study for *Ulysses and the Sirens*, showing the oarsmen in the bow of the galley. Since this is an action study, intended to fix the poses of the men plying the oars, the ship is only roughly indicated. The attitude of the leading rower, whose head is turned to look at the Sirens, has already been effectively resolved and requires little modification; the legs do not appear, however, in the final realization.

The definitive attitudes of the oarsmen are established by a vigorous chalk study, drawn from the life, in the Louvre (No. 26; Fig. 129). The right-hand rower braces himself by putting his foot against a thwart; this realistic detail is suppressed in the fresco.

Also in the Louvre is a drawing of great fluency for the steersman at the right (No. 27; Fig. 130). A few modifications, chiefly having to do with the turn of the head and the position of the arms grasping the oar, remain to be made before the final redaction.

The importance of these changes in imparting greater movement and energy to the pose can be appreciated by comparing the drawing with the cartoon for the same figure, which is in the British Museum (No. 28; Fig. 131). To the left of the steersman can be seen an earlier drawing of his head and shoulders, from which it would appear that the artist had originally planned to space his design somewhat differently. At the lower right he has indicated rather sketchily the figure of Neptune which forms part of the relief decoration of the ship. The arc which cuts across the upper right corner must mark the original border of the cartoon; another fragment of the cartoon has been added here, seemingly for no other reason than to fill out the rectangular shape.

A preparatory drawing for the three Sirens is preserved in the Royal Library at Windsor (No. 29; Fig. 132). The grouping is similar to that in the fresco, but instead of singing they are represented playing flutes. The lack of balance in the placing of the figures indicates that the drawing has been cropped on the left.

Vittoria owned a drawing of Ulysses tied to the mast—*una figura stupendissima*—but this is unfortunately lost.[22]

DRAWINGS FOR PERSEUS AND MEDUSA (FIG. 23)

An important drawing for this subject was recently acquired by the Metropolitan Museum of Art (No. 30 recto; Fig. 133). It is a composition study in pen and wash, in which the main actions of the story have already been settled. Yet the drawing is plainly an early one. The figures, with their small heads and over-tall proportions,

---

[22] *Osservazioni*, p. 52. Vittoria also speaks of "un pezzo di cartone di una sirena della nave di Ulisse" in Maratti's possession. But Maratti's cartoon, as Wittkower has observed (*Carracci Drawings*, p. 133), is undoubtedly the fragment now in Windsor (No. 5; Fig. 108) which is for a siren in one of the compartments of the ceiling. The two figures are in some respects similar. Two further drawings were adduced by Bodmer as studies for *Ulysses and the Sirens* (in *Pantheon*, XIX, 1937, p. 147). The first (Louvre 7333), a man propelling a boat by means of a pole, is in reality a preparatory study by Domenichino for a *Landscape with Figures* (Collection Denis Mahon). The other, a drawing of a helmsman (Venice, Accad., 289), is in my opinion not by Annibale.

are strangely Mannerist in appearance, especially the rather willowy Minerva. The pen lines drawn over part of the sheet are impossible to decipher: perhaps they are related to the studies on the verso (cf. Fig. 103). Annibale has still to adjust the spacing of the figures within the lunette, the left half of which is overweighted. Minerva will be made to assume a more vigorous pose, lifting her shield from the ground so that its reflecting surface may be more easily seen by Perseus. Medusa, instead of kneeling on the rock, will be shown in a half-reclining posture, as if suddenly aroused from sleep; the attitudes of her slumbering sisters will likewise be restudied.

These and other revisions were carried out in a series of definitive figure studies, of which there are three in the Louvre.

The first is a vivid study for Medusa (No. 31; Fig. 134) in the attitude which she assumes in the fresco. The artist has concentrated his attention on the violent gestures and the agonized twist of the neck, omitting the legs altogether. The sculptural treatment of the mask testifies to the study of antique marbles, especially the Niobid figures.[23]

Likewise in Paris are two studies for the figure of Mercury. One represents the helmeted head of the god as he gazes at the polished shield (No. 32; Fig. 136); the diagonal stroke at the lower left serves to indicate the staff of the caduceus.[24] The resemblance to the painting is unquestionably close, but the features have a classicizing quality that has somehow been lost in the fresco. The other (No. 33; Fig. 135) is a fine chalk study for the legs of Mercury, which in the fresco are almost concealed behind those of Perseus.[25] It can nevertheless be seen that the drawing agrees in every particular with the final realization.

No studies have yet been discovered for the figures of Perseus and Minerva. Bellori is said to have possessed a drawing for this fresco,[26] which one would like to think might be the work now in the Metropolitan Museum.

DRAWINGS FOR THE CATANIAN BROTHERS (FIG. 24)

An interesting set of drawings can be assembled for this lunette. Most of them have to do with the central group of Amphinomus carrying his father.

[23] Cf., for example, the drawing in Windsor, Cat. 365 (Wittkower, *Carracci Drawings*, pl. 55).

[24] Mahon (*Disegni*, p. 103) understandably relates the drawing to the Circe fresco (Fig. 17), where the head of Mercury appears in a not dissimilar pose. But comparison reveals that the drawing belongs without question to the Perseus lunette.

[25] Previously identified by Bacou (*Dessins*, p. 48, no. 84) as a study for the legs of Perseus in the *Combat of Perseus and Phineus* in the Galleria Farnese. It is to be noted that in his drawings for the Gallery Annibale largely gave up the practice, still followed in the Camerino, of making separate studies of arms and legs.

[26] Vittoria, *Osservazioni*, p. 52. Two drawings were erroneously associated with the figures of Perseus and Minerva by Bodmer (*op.cit.*, p. 148). The drawing in Windsor showing Perseus with the Gorgon's head is a study for the Gallery, not the Camerino (see No. 137; Fig. 250). The second drawing, Louvre 7355, representing a helmeted warrior leaning on a spear, is not (as Bodmer supposes) a study for the figure of Minerva, to which it bears only a superficial resemblance.

As the composition was first planned, however, there was to have been no central group. This may be deduced from an early sketch in Windsor for the left half of the lunette (No. 34; Fig. 137), in which the father and son are placed well to the left of the center line; the group of the mother and second son may thus be thought of as providing a balance in the right half of the scene. (A similar uncertainty regarding the placing of the principal figures has been noticed in the drawings for *Ulysses and Circe*.) The Windsor drawing presents an unusually brilliant appearance, being executed in pen and brown ink, red chalk and red wash. The youth is represented walking diagonally to the left, whereas in the painting he is shown *en face*, moving directly toward the spectator. Otherwise his attitude and the manner in which he supports the old man—one arm holding his thigh and the other encircling his arm—are remarkably close to the final solution. In the background can be seen the erupting volcano, but the reclining figure of Polyphemus is not yet included.[27] This is almost certainly the drawing which Vittoria saw in the collection of Carlo Maratti.[28]

A chalk sketch in Montpellier (No. 35; Fig. 139) is devoted to the group of father and son. After some initial uncertainties regarding the position of the young man's right leg, Annibale decided upon a frontal view, causing him to advance directly toward the observer. The drawing has been squared as if for enlargement; this is somewhat puzzling, for the draughtsmanship alone is sufficient to show that we are dealing here with a preliminary draft and not a finished design.

Having established the general postures of the central pair, the artist had next to prepare detailed studies from the life. The task was made more difficult by the complicated interlacement of the two figures. It has not previously been recognized that the chalk drawing in Turin of a half-length male nude (No. 36 recto; Fig. 140) is a study for the youth who carries his father.[29] In the fresco the left hand will be brought closer to the shoulder and the tilt of the head will be slightly modified. Annibale has been at pains to illustrate the forward thrust of the right shoulder which results from the twisting of the arm to the rear. The drawing also exhibits his characteristic thoroughness in the placing of the highlights and shadows, which are almost exactly duplicated in the painting.

Closely associated with this work is another study, hitherto unnoticed, for the legs of the father (No. 37; Fig. 141). The drawing, which is in the Louvre, can be under-

---

[27] I find it difficult to agree with Mahon's suggestion (*Disegni*, p. 105) that drawing No. 16 (Fig. 120) might be an early study for Polyphemus. See note 12 above.

[28] *Osservazioni*, p. 52. The fact that Vittoria mentions both groups of figures may mean either that the drawing had not yet been cut down to its present size, or perhaps that he was merely identifying what he knew to be the subject.

[29] A. Bertini (in *Commentari*, II, 1951, pp. 40 f.) interprets the figure as a study for one of the *ignudi* of the Galleria. Mahon, on the other hand (*Disegni*, pp. 99 f., no. 131), sees it as a study for Hercules bearing the sphere, no doubt because the verso (Fig. 113) has a sketch of that subject.

stood as interlocking with the preceding study for the son. It so happens that in the final redaction the leg on the right side is almost completely concealed, but Annibale has not for that reason neglected to draw it.

For the father's head there is, finally, the impressive life-size drawing in the Louvre (No. 21 verso; Fig. 128, at the right), which appears on a sheet with other studies for the Camerino. The affinity to the fresco is particularly marked in the lighting: both show the face in shadow, with strong highlights on the cheekbone and on the beard along the jaw.

Annibale likewise made separate figure studies for the second group, the mother being carried by her son. These are today in the Louvre. In the drawing of Anapius (No. 38; Fig. 143) the artist was chiefly concerned with the left arm as it encircled the mother's legs. The model does not appear, from his stance, to be supporting a heavy burden. Annibale was evidently aware of this fault and corrected it in the fresco by lowering the youth's head and by causing the left leg to bend more noticeably under the weight.

The complementary drawing of the frightened mother (No. 39; Fig. 142) shows only the upper part of the figure. In its concentration on gesture and facial expression it is comparable to the study for Medusa in the adjoining scene (Fig. 134).

THE DRAWING OF BELLEROPHON AND THE CHIMERA

To the list of drawings for the Camerino there must be added, finally, the sheet in the Louvre with *Bellerophon and the Chimera* (No. 40; Fig. 138). It is one of a group of four sizable drawings in that collection, the other three being the study for *Hercules bearing the globe* (No. 12; Fig. 115), and the two studies for *Ulysses and Circe* (Nos. 21 recto and 22; Figs. 123-124). Mariette, perceiving their similarity in style and format, correctly identified all four as belonging to the Camerino project; they are described as follows in his catalogue of the drawings in the Crozat collection: "Quatre Desseins pour les tableaux du Cabinet Farnese; sçavoir le Bellerophon, l'Atlas, & deux pensées differentes pour la Circé."[30] All four drawings, as Mahon has remarked, were purchased by Mariette for his own collection.

The fable of *Bellerophon and the Chimera*, as I have endeavored to show above, was originally meant to occupy one of the lunettes on the side opposite the windows. Later, when it seemed politic to find some subject which should honor the Duke Ranuccio as well as Odoardo, Fulvio Orsini must have hit upon the story of the *Catanian Brothers*, and Annibale's design for *Bellerophon* was therefore discarded.

As work on the Camerino progressed, Annibale began to make the first tentative drafts for the more formidable project which Cardinal Farnese now desired him to undertake—the decoration of the Galleria. To these drawings we turn in the following chapter.

[30] Mariette, *Description sommaire*, p. 50, no. 473 (cited by Mahon, *Disegni*, p. 105).

CHAPTER 11 · THE DRAWINGS FOR
THE GALLERY

CARRACCI'S systematic working method, already fully developed in the Camerino, underwent no fundamental change in the Galleria. The drawings that have been preserved show him following the same deliberate sequence of graphic preparation, from preliminary sketches to final studies from the life. As regards quality of draughtsmanship, however, the designs for the Farnese ceiling are unquestionably superior. Here it is pertinent to recall Mariette's judgment: "Ces Desseins sont faits sçavamment, & avec encore plus fermeté, que tout ce qu' Annibal avoit fait précedemment, lorsqu' il n'avoit pas encore vû les Statuës antiques, & les peintures de Raphaël & de Michel-Ange."[1] It is no doubt true that his prolonged residence in Rome, amid the most celebrated works of antiquity and the High Renaissance, contributed materially to the artist's command of the discipline of form. Certainly there is nothing among the Camerino drawings that can match the magnificent series of *ignudi* and atlantes, which have been set down with such practiced ease and assurance (cf. No. 98; Fig. 210).

The charm of such works lies in the firm, incisive draughtsmanship, the satisfying arabesque of the contours, the sensitive spacing on the sheet, and in the soft, even texture of the chalk medium which lies over the form like a transparent veil. But there also speaks through these drawings an intense feeling for nature. Even when Annibale is concerned with a technical problem of posture or of foreshortening, as in the study of an atlas herm (No. 115; Fig. 229), we are conscious of the sympathetic humanity of the artist, and this imparts to the drawing a quality of life that is deeply moving. To compare the figure studies with the final realization in fresco is to gain a fuller awareness of the importance of the drawing in his art. That importance is due not only to its purely mechanical function in fixing posture and the like, but also to the fact that it was through the drawing that the contact with life was transmitted to the fresco. The vivid psychological atmosphere of the Galleria, as it is manifested for instance in the decorative figures of the frieze, was to a considerable degree made possible by the experience of physical and psychic presence which the artist first captured in his studies from the model. It is an interesting fact that these final studies were not made in advance, but were only worked up as needed. Throughout, the drawing remained an integral part of the creative process.

I. DRAWINGS FOR THE DECORATIVE SYSTEM

It is no easy matter to identify the earliest designs for the Farnese ceiling. Several of the drawings which have been accepted as Annibale's first studies for this project exhibit none of the distinctive features of the Gallery and thus might conceivably have been made for some other purpose.

[1] P. J. Mariette, *Description sommaire des desseins*, p. 51.

One such drawing is the sketch in the Louvre for a painted frieze (No. 41; Fig. 144) which Tietze interpreted as an early study for the lower zone of the vault.[2] The artist is chiefly concerned with the three figures of the *partimento* between the framed pictures of the frieze—an atlas herm supporting an architrave and two nude youths seated back to back and holding garlands. If this is indeed a study for the Gallery (and I am inclined to think it is), then it is evident that Annibale's thinking at this primary stage was still dominated by the recollection of the great frieze in the Palazzo Magnani. The solution propounded in this drawing is applicable only to the coving; there is no indication how the upper part of the vault is to be treated.

A related study, showing some variation in the elements, is in the Ecole des Beaux-Arts at Paris (No. 42 recto; Fig. 146). The two *ignudi* are still present, though now pictured as captives with arms bound behind their backs, but in place of the atlas herm there appears a round-headed niche containing a statue of Hercules; in making this substitution Annibale probably intended to echo the series of statues standing in the niches along the walls of the Gallery, but in the end the idea was abandoned. There is perhaps a fleeting anticipation of the ultimate system of the frieze in the indication of a large medallion at the right side of the sheet. The verso (Fig. 147) is covered with various architectural and figure sketches, the most interesting of which represents a damaged antique statue in a niche.[3]

The most problematical of this group of drawings is a study in the Louvre for the end of a vaulted ceiling (No. 43; Fig. 145), of which there is also a copy in the "Perrier" album (fol. 56). The central feature is a *quadro riportato* with oddly tapered sides, beneath which are two sphinxes and two putti supporting a shield. The picture is flanked by two energetic *ignudi*, somewhat like those in the preceding drawings, and surmounted by a pair of reclining female figures. The sculptured bust set within a circular recess recalls those seen on the side walls of the Gallery. A folded curtain hung with masks serves to mark off the entire field. The fruit garland summarily indicated at the upper left was probably repeated on the other side, where a large part of the sheet has been torn away. In spite of certain points of resemblance to the frescoed ceiling (such as the framed picture flanked by *ignudi*) it is clear that this can only have been a tentative solution. It is difficult to see how a design of such sharply triangular shape could have been adapted to the curvature of the vault of the Gallery and even more difficult to grasp how it was to have been coordinated with the continuous frieze along the sides.

If, as the foregoing drawings suggest, Annibale first conceived of the decorative system of the ceiling largely in terms of a frieze of narrative pictures punctuated and enlivened by groups of figures, he must at the same time have been aware that it would be necessary to invent a more comprehensive scheme with which to span the central area of the vault. The scheme that he eventually adopted was derived, as

[2] Tietze, pp. 96 f. There is a copy in the Louvre, on fol. 29 of the so-called Perrier album.

[3] It seems to me unlikely that the drawing in the Uffizi cited by Tietze (pp. 105 f., fig. 36) can have been intended for the Farnese ceiling.

we have seen, from Pellegrino Tibaldi's ceiling of the Sala d'Ulisse in the Palazzo Poggi (Fig. 275). Annibale's solution, in a word, was to make a synthesis of Tibaldi's system—with its cruciform disposition of *quadri riportati* and its illusionistically treated corners—and the system of the continuous mural frieze.

The first drawing in which the artist can be seen exploring the possibility of such a synthesis is in the Louvre (No. 44 recto; Fig. 148). He is here mainly preoccupied with the corner of the vault, surely the most troublesome part of the entire complex. The little pen sketch near the top left corner (see text fig. 4B below) presents a simplified plan of the ceiling which, as Tietze observed,[4] roughly follows Tibaldi's system of nine compartments: there are five panels (three rectangular and two oval) and four corners which are seemingly left "open." A second sketch (cf. text fig. 4A) along the upper edge of the sheet further elaborates the scheme. It represents one of the side walls of the Gallery with its pilasters, and, above, the frieze in the coving of the vault (compare the engraving by Giovanni Volpato, Fig. 32). The frieze can be seen to consist of three units: a large *quadro riportato* in the middle, flanked by two square panels; the corners are to be painted illusionistically with balustrades seen in foreshortening from below, as in Tibaldi's ceiling. The central area of the vault is merely hinted at by a few strokes, but from these it can be perceived that the principal compartments are already provided for. The obvious dependence on Tibaldi's fresco lends color to Malvasia's report that "before beginning work on the Farnese Gallery Annibale had a sketch sent to him of this rich and well-ordered ceiling."[5]

The principal drawing on this sheet is a study for the angle of the ceiling, which is here viewed from below as if it were relatively flat. Seated on the balustrade is a youth with fluttering draperies, plainly a reminiscence of Tibaldi's Ulysses cycle. The corner of the balustrade supports a Marzocco. The adjoining panels are framed by caryatid herms carrying baskets on their heads. They are the forerunners of the pairs of herms who, in the final conception, will entwine their arms at the junctures of the side and end walls. The purely experimental nature of the present solution is apparent from the fact that the two herms are of unequal height, an unsatisfactory feature that Annibale would not long have tolerated. At the upper right, finally, is a detailed study of the balustrade.

The verso of this sheet (Fig. 149) bears a number of architectural details, chiefly of moldings, all of which seem to relate to the balustrade at the angle. Partly obscured by these sketches is a winged putto, who is perhaps intended as an alternative to the lion with the shield on the reverse.

In the Louvre is another drawing for this part of the ceiling (No. 45; Fig. 150). Two figures are seated on a balustrade over which a putto is clambering. The resemblance to Tibaldi's fresco is particularly striking. The rough pen sketch at the

---

[4] Tietze, p. 100. The drawing was copied on fol. 53 of the "Perrier" volume.

[5] Malvasia, *Felsina*, I, pp. 193 and 466.

left illustrates the juncture of the upright picture at the end of the vault and the octagonal fresco on the crown.

The most advanced drawing belonging to this early stage is No. 46 (Fig. 151), which represents a little more than half of the total area of the vault (cf. the photograph of the entire ceiling, Fig. 36).[6] The structural system projected here is a direct

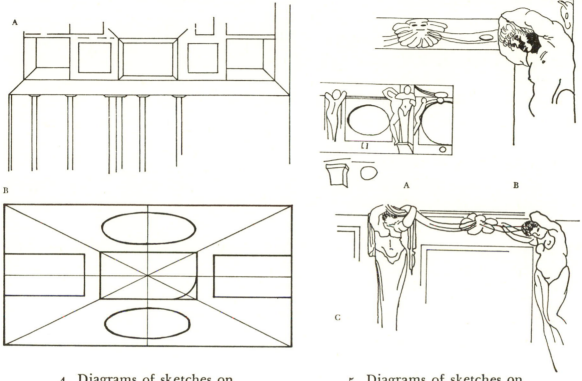

4. Diagrams of sketches on
drawing No. 44 recto

5. Diagrams of sketches on
drawing No. 48

outgrowth of the sketch on No. 44 recto (Fig. 148 and text fig. 4A). Once again we recognize the large rectangular opening at the corner with a balustrade on which youths are seated; an alternative is provided in the corner at the upper left, where a winged figure holds a wreath over a rearing horse. The main *quadri riportati* have now been assigned their final places in the middle zone of the ceiling: these are the large center panel flanked by octagons (here given an oval shape), and the upright panels at the ends of the vault: compare the preceding drawing (No. 45; Fig. 150). There is one significant addition: the seated youths are no longer confined to the balustrade at the corner but are placed on pedestals which are themselves extensions of the wall pilasters. At a still later stage the youths will be co-ordinated with the herms—a solution already adumbrated in the early study No. 41 (Fig. 144). The frieze comprises three main units, as in the previous project (No. 44 recto; Fig. 148), a large oblong picture in the middle and a smaller square panel on either side

[6] There is a copy on fol. 53 of the "Perrier" album.

of it; these are linked together by an intermediate unit for which the artist proposes two tentative solutions: in the section at the right he has imagined a kind of apselike recess or exedra in which are set niches with statues (an echo, perhaps, of the ornamentation planned for the Gallery itself); in the left-hand section the inserted unit takes the form of a round-headed niche before which are two standing figures, a motive that again recalls the early study No. 42 (Fig. 146). Although Annibale has seemingly not yet hit upon the idea of employing medallions in alternation with the square panels, it is already obvious that they can be incorporated into the scheme without difficulty. When this step has been taken, the awkward open spaces at the corners (which are in fact unsuited to a ceiling of this form) will be drastically reduced in size.

Surprisingly, the situation of the main subjects has still not been firmly established. There is, for example, no indication that the *Bacchanal* is to occupy the central place. On the contrary, part of that subject, showing Bacchus riding in his chariot, appears in the square panel of the frieze along the right side.

A pen drawing in Windsor (No. 47; Fig. 152) must belong to the same stage as No. 46. It is a rapidly executed sketch for the large picture in the middle of the frieze, complete with its elaborate frame and adjacent decorative figures. The episode represented is the Finding of Ariadne, another proof that the decision has not yet been taken to place the *Bacchanal* in the center of the vault. Annibale has still not inserted the medallions into the frieze, but continues instead to experiment with the cluster of decorative figures seen at the left of the picture.

The first drawing to set forth the fully developed system of the frieze is at Windsor Castle (No. 48; Fig. 154). Covered as it is with overlapping studies, the sheet is difficult to interpret; but with careful scrutiny it is possible to distinguish several independent sketches. The first extends across the middle of the drawing (cf. text fig. 5A above). It is a design for a section of the frieze, with a square picture (altered to an oval) and a medallion, a segment of which is cut off by the frame of the large panel over the center of the wall. The seated youths are omitted,[7] so that Annibale may concentrate his attention upon the upright figures. These, it will be observed, already conform very closely to the ones actually executed in fresco (cf. Fig. 45): the square picture is flanked by herms, and on its right there stands also the full-length atlas whose function is to aid in supporting the structural framework. There is even an indication of the putto reclining against the medallion. Below the frieze are two objects which may represent the capital of a pilaster and one of the circular niches of the wall (or perhaps the pedestal at the base of a herm and the mask centered beneath the painted panel).

The second study on the sheet (cf. text fig. 5C) illustrates, on a larger scale, the figures flanking the square panel: a herm on the left and a human atlas with one arm

[7] We know from a previous drawing (No. 46; Fig. 151) that the *ignudi* had already become an integral part of the system.

resting on the garland at the right. Two further studies for the latter figure are to be seen at the right edge of the drawing. In this reduplication of decorative figures we may be reminded of the frieze of the Palazzo Magnani, which was surely in Annibale's mind while he worked on this part of the ceiling.

In the center of the sheet is a still larger study for the caryatid (cf. text fig. 5B), here unaccountably transformed into a herm. Annibale later decided, however, to restore the fully human form so as to avoid the juxtaposition of two herms. In the angle above the man's shoulder can be seen the goat mask to which one end of the garland is fastened.

The remaining sketches on the sheet have no connection with the Galleria. On the larger of the two geometrical constructions in perspective the letter "I" appears twice: the same hand has written along the thigh of the central atlas: *Innocencio fe.* Is it possible, as Mahon has suggested, that this might be the signature of Annibale's pupil Innocenzo Tacconi?[8] Perhaps it was he who drew the geometric designs on this sheet. And perhaps he should also be credited with some of the studio exercises to which we have drawn attention among the Angeloni drawings.

An unpublished drawing in the Louvre (No. 49; Fig. 153) may be identified as an early idea for the decoration of the frame enclosing the frescoes of *Pan and Diana* and *Paris and Mercury*. In this hastily executed pen sketch Annibale imagines the triangular corner of the frame as being occupied by a lion confronting a crawling putto who holds a mask before his face; but this motive (derived from ancient sarcophagi) was subsequently rejected and a sedate sphinx introduced in its place. The inserted chalk drawing of a child's head appears to have no relation to the Farnese cycle.

The most advanced project for the structural system of the ceiling is a drawing in the Louvre (No. 50; Fig. 155), in which Annibale addresses himself particularly to the problem of the ends of the vault.[9] But the sheet also contains several quick sketches relating to other sections of the work. Near the center, for example, can be seen a rough sketch in red chalk for one of the sphinxes in the ornamental frames of *Pan and Diana* and *Paris and Mercury*; this solution supersedes the tentative idea recorded in the preceding drawing (Fig. 153). (For a finished study of a sphinx, see No. 78; Fig. 186.) Among the earliest notations on this sheet must be the faint red chalk sketches along the lower edge. The one at the left is a schematic rendering of the frieze like that in No. 48 (Fig. 154), but with an indication also of the large panels on the crown of the vault. The second sketch, in the lower right corner, is even more summary; it is a perspective view of the corner of the vaulting, in which the artist has sought to visualize the transition from the long to the short wall of the Gallery. A third chalk sketch, barely visible under the pen drawings at the top of the sheet, illustrates the sequence of compartments along the center of the vault.

The principal drawing on the sheet is a surprisingly detailed rendering of the

---

[8] Mahon, *Disegni*, p. 112, no. 148.
[9] There is a copy on fol. 82 of the "Perrier" album.

north end of the ceiling, with the large framed picture corresponding to *Polyphemus and Acis* and the smaller picture of *Ganymede and the Eagle* above it (cf. Fig. 62). The source of light, as in the completed fresco, is on the left. (The system is repeated, in schematic form, in the miniature pen sketch directly over the Ganymede panel.) Annibale gives no indication of the Polyphemus subject which is to fill the *quadro riportato*; but for the smaller picture, the *Rape of Ganymede*, he has set down three separate sketches. Protruding from behind the frame of the Polyphemus painting is a medallion on which may be discerned two figures, one seated and one standing.

The grouping of the various accessory figures has now begun to approach the final solution. This marks the first appearance in a drawing of the satyr perched on the console of the large framed picture; the closest parallel to this figure is to be found in the satyr at the upper right corner of *Polyphemus and Galatea* (Fig. 67), i.e., at the opposite end of the Gallery. And similarly the *ignudo* in the drawing with his back to us resembles to some degree the youth sitting at the right of that fresco. The atlas herm above him does not correspond to any of those existing in fresco; his companion at the corner is lightly indicated in chalk. Although they seem to be quite independent of each other, the hand resting on the shoulder of the left-hand herm proves that Annibale is already thinking of the corner atlantes as embracing. On the balustrade at the angle stands an amoretto supporting a shield. This figure has been drawn in ink over an earlier sketch of two putti holding a shield on which can be perceived the *impresa* of Cardinal Odoardo Farnese—three lilies with a scroll (cf. Fig. 16). A similar feature appears in one of the earliest projects for the ceiling (No. 44 recto; Fig. 148), where a lion holds the shield at the corner. It is apparent from these drawings that Annibale, in accordance with the traditional method, first intended to place the four *imprese* at the angles of the vault. Later, however, it was decided that the corners should be occupied by Heavenly and Earthly Love, and the *imprese*, thus displaced, were assigned to their present positions along the walls.

Because the Twin Loves do not appear in the preliminary drawings, Tietze argued that they are not essential to the meaning of the cycle, and owe their existence solely to decorative considerations.[10] Yet if decoration was really to be the deciding factor, it would surely have been more reasonable to adhere to the original scheme with putti supporting shields at the corners, and not to introduce the *Amori* at all. The fact that they *were* introduced is proof of their significance in the cycle.

It might be thought that Annibale's next step, after he had determined the structural system of the vault, its subdivision into compartments, the organization of the frieze and so forth, would be to draw up a final design, or set of designs, for the whole ceiling. No such *modello* exists, and it is virtually certain that none was ever made. Annibale's method was to clarify the organization of the ceiling in drawings such as Nos. 48 (Fig. 154) and 50 (Fig. 155), which are in no sense detailed designs,

[10] Tietze, pp. 89 f. and 104.

and then to proceed directly to studies for the individual scenes and for the decorative figures. Drawings which show whole sections of the ceiling in the definitive state invariably prove to be copies after the fresco.[11]

The importance of the remarkable project in the Louvre (No. 50; Fig. 155) does not lie solely in what it reveals about the design of the ceiling. In addition it demonstrates conclusively that even at this relatively late stage Annibale had still made no provision for the Perseus scenes on the end walls of the room. The section of the wall visible below the cornice in this study is, surprisingly enough, articulated in the same fashion as the side walls, namely by Corinthian pilasters between which circular niches containing sculptured busts alternate with rectangular panels in fresco. Yet it is obvious that this would never have been a satisfactory solution. In the first place, two of the pilasters would unavoidably have come into collision with the doorways (cf. Fig. 35), and, to make matters worse, the middle pilaster would have stood on the axis of the Gallery—an unclassical feature that would surely have been found unacceptable. Secondly, the alternation of round niche and rectangular panel would have posed an equally insoluble problem: there being four bays between the pilasters, it would have been impossible to produce a sequence at once alternating and symmetrical. It must therefore be concluded that Annibale was merely experimenting with the possibility of making the end walls match the sides; finding it to be unfeasible, he abandoned the idea. Ultimately, as we know, he solved the problem by a bold expedient: a single large framed picture was made to span the width of the Gallery, its weight sustained by the lintels of the doors and by three crouching caryatids.

A drawing at Chatsworth may give a hint of the intermediate stage leading to the final solution (No. 51; Fig. 156). It is a pen sketch of a seated woman, the purpose of which is unknown. As an afterthought, perhaps, Annibale added an architectural setting, which can be recognized as a carelessly drawn view of the interior of the Farnese Gallery (compare the engraving by Volpato, Fig. 34). The vault is not shown, nor are we given any details of what must be the window wall at the left side. But the main features of the long inner wall are unquestionably reproduced at the right, though not with complete accuracy. For here we see the narrow bays framed by

[11] Copies after the decorative system of the Galleria are numerous, and some have been thought to be original studies by Annibale. A few such drawings are listed here.

1. Albertina Sc. B. 195. Copy in pen and ink after part of the frieze. F. Wickhoff, "Die italienischen Handzeichnungen der Albertina," *Jahrbuch der kunsthistorischen Sammlungen,* XII, 1891, p. CCXCII.

2. Besançon D. 1495. Copies in pen and ink after parts of the ceiling and walls of the Gallery.

3. Windsor Inv. 1572 and 1588. Two drawings in sanguine after sections of the ceiling,

by Domenichino or a pupil. Pope-Hennessy, *Domenichino Drawings,* p. 124, Cat. 1754 and 1755.

4. Windsor Inv. 4393. Copy in sanguine by Carlo Maratti after part of the ceiling. Blunt and Cooke, *Roman Drawings of the XVII and XVIII Centuries at Windsor,* p. 67, Cat. 484.

5. Louvre Inv. 7424. Free copy in sanguine, by a pupil, of part of the decoration of the ceiling.

6. Louvre Inv. 7585. Copy after a section of the frieze.

pilasters and the niches with their full-length statues; at the top of one niche is a circular recess containing a bust, and in the next a panel with the characteristic projections at the lower corners. The end wall is of particular interest: the artist has indicated the two doors (incorrectly shown as being no higher than the dado of the adjoining side wall), and above them he has imagined a row of pilasters with niches containing statues in the intercolumniations. It will be observed that the system tallies with that in No. 50 (Fig. 155) in placing a pilaster in the middle. But there is one fundamental difference: the entire upper section of the wall is screened by a large picture with a heavy frame composed of human figures, masks, scrolls and other ornamental features.

What is the significance of the Chatsworth sheet? I think it unlikely that this is a drawing made after the completion of the Gallery, because the end wall in fact looks very different from what is seen here. On the other hand the presence of the seated figure proves that this is not a formal study in the sense that the term may be applied to a drawing such as No. 50 (Fig. 155). The best explanation, it seems to me, is that Annibale dashed off this rough sketch before he had fully resolved the system of decoration which was to be employed on the walls. Realizing that his earlier plan— of continuing the architectural system of the long walls across the ends—was unworkable, he decided to mask the troublesome upper half of the pilasters with a framed picture. The next step, plainly, was to enlarge that picture so as to eliminate the pilasters altogether. The Chatsworth drawing, summary though it is, thus marks a measurable advance toward the definitive treatment of the short walls of the Gallery.

Bernini related an anecdote concerning the Farnese Gallery, according to which Annibale at first decided to leave to his brother Agostino the responsibility for the compartments of the vault. Agostino produced a design in which everything was to be seen from one point of view. When this proved unacceptable, he became angry and would have nothing more to do with the lay-out of the ceiling. Annibale therefore executed the ceiling as it now appears, using not one but multiple points of view.[12]

Bernini's story is not corroborated by any other source and should therefore perhaps be treated with suspicion. It is of course conceivable that Agostino, with his interest in geometry and perspective, might have drawn up a design in the *quadratura* tradition represented by such Bolognese ceilings as Pellegrino Tibaldi's Sala di Fetonte and that by Tommaso Laureti in the Palazzo Vizzani, which are intended to be seen from a single point of view.[13] Such a system, however effective it might have been in a room of normal proportions, would not have been at all suitable to a long, narrow ceiling like that of the Farnese Gallery, and we can readily imagine that Annibale would not have approved it. On the other hand it is difficult to believe that Annibale would have entrusted to anyone—even to his brother—a task as impor-

[12] Chantelou, *Journal du voyage du Cavalier Bernin*, pp. 68 f.

[13] F. Würtenberger, in *Römisches Jahrbuch für Kunstgeschichte*, IV, 1940, pp. 74 f., fig. 31, and pp. 89 ff., fig. 41.

tant and fundamental as that of preparing the structural framework of the ceiling; and for this reason I believe that Bernini's anecdote must be dismissed as fanciful. The whole story sounds rather like an attempt to account for the disagreement known to have arisen between the two brothers.

Agostino's part in the planning of the Gallery is difficult to assess. The number of drawings by his hand that can be connected with the project is admittedly small; yet it is surely unlikely that during a period of nearly three years he was occupied only with his own two frescoes. An analogous situation is perhaps to be discovered in the decoration of the Palazzo Magnani, which was a collaborative enterprise carried out by all three Carracci. Agostino's participation in the narrative part of that cycle, as in the *favole* of the Farnese ceiling, was a very limited one: only one scene, the *Asylum on the Capitol,* appears to have been painted by him. But Agostino may have been given other tasks in the Sala Magnani: there is for example a study by him in the Albertina for some of the grotesque masks,[14] which suggests that he may have been responsible for the decorative elements of the frieze. Since his fame as an artist rested to a considerable degree on his inventiveness in designing ornaments, it is reasonable to suppose that he was also called upon to draw some of the masks, cartouches, and the like that enliven the frescoes of the Farnese Gallery. It is unfortunate that, as far as the vault is concerned, there are no extant drawings by Agostino to substantiate this hypothesis.

We are, however, not completely in the dark about Agostino's share in the ornamentation of the Gallery. Some important evidence, heretofore overlooked, is provided by a sheet of studies in the Louvre (No. 53 verso; Fig. 188), which bears several drawings by Agostino.[15] The female figure in the center of the sheet is a study for Aurora in the fresco of *Aurora and Cephalus.* At the upper right are two cartouches, which may be identified as preliminary designs for the Farnese coats of arms carved in stucco at the extremities of the longs walls (cf. Figs. 32-33 and 38). Another pen drawing by Agostino shows further studies of this sort (No. 52 verso; Fig. 157); the coat of arms at the left, with the *gigli* emblazoned on the shield and the cardinal's hat above, is quite like that of Cardinal Farnese as it appears in the Gallery.

The existence of such drawings for the Farnese *stemmi* may cause us to speculate whether at an early stage Agostino intended to shoulder even more of the ornamental work of the Gallery. It appears probable that in the original plan the design of all the stucco-work was to be left to him, and that only his abrupt departure in 1600 made it necessary to allot this task to someone else.

---

[14] A. Stix and A. Spitzmüller, *Beschreibender Katalog der Handzeichnungen in der Staatlichen Graphischen Sammlung Albertina, Die Schulen von Ferrara, Bologna,* etc., Vienna, 1941, p. 12, no. 84.

[15] Agostino made these sketches on the back of a discarded study by Annibale for the *Bacchanal* (Fig. 158).

II. DRAWINGS FOR THE PRINCIPAL SUBJECTS OF THE VAULT

DRAWINGS FOR THE TRIUMPH OF BACCHUS AND ARIADNE (FIGS. 69-72)

It can readily be understood that the *Bacchanal*, as the chief subject of the ceiling, was meant from the beginning to form part of the cycle. Two drawings, both belonging to an early stage of the planning, prove that even while Annibale was working out the fundamental structure of the ceiling he was already thinking of the Bacchic procession. Surprisingly, however, it does not seem to have been his original intention to place the *Bacchanal* in the center; instead, as the drawings indicate, he first conceived of it as being incorporated in the frieze along the coving of the vault.

The first of the drawings in question is the study in the Louvre (No. 46; Fig. 151), which establishes the positions of the principal *quadri riportati*. Only one of these compartments contains a suggestion of subject, and that is the square panel in the right-hand zone (corresponding to the picture of *Jupiter and Juno* in the Gallery itself). Unmistakably represented within it, as Tietze was the first to observe,[16] is a section of the Bacchanalian *cortège*. The god sits in his chariot, which is drawn by lions or panthers (only partly visible); his mantle flutters behind him, and in his left hand he holds a lyre. He is accompanied by a satyr and a figure carrying a spear or thyrsus. The fragmentary nature of the scene suggests that the procession was to be continued in the succeeding panel, although that space has been left blank in the drawing.

Evidence to support this idea is provided by the second drawing (No. 47; Fig. 152), which is a design for the middle section of the frieze, corresponding to the stage of No. 46. Within the heavily ornate frame is a pen sketch for a picture which, despite its cursory execution, can only represent the Finding of Ariadne.[17] The corpulent nude figure at the left is Silenus, riding sideways on an ass. He is preceded by two attendants, one of whom is seen from the back with one arm raised as if playing cymbals. Ariadne is represented nude at the right side in the conventional attitude of sleep, the left arm supporting the head and the right lying in a relaxed position along her side. She appears to have been discovered by the person in the center of the picture who points to her and turns his head toward Silenus. A background of trees is indicated behind Ariadne.

At this point we may consider a rather puzzling drawing in the Louvre (No. 53 recto; Fig. 158). It is a vigorous pen sketch representing the vanguard of the Bacchic train; Ariadne, Silenus, and the god himself are not included. The drawing is difficult to place in the sequence of studies for the *Bacchanal*. Tietze conceived of it—perhaps rightly—as belonging to a distinctly later phase: for him this was simply Annibale's attempt to improve on the head of the procession as it appears in a study

---

[16] Tietze, pp. 101 f.   [17] *Ibid.*, p. 108.

such as No. 54 (Fig. 159).[18] But the group of frenzied Bacchantes seen here is too numerous to be merely part of that composition; furthermore the border enclosing the scene strongly suggests that it is to be regarded as a separate picture. Later, when the drawing was discarded, it was turned over to Agostino, who made the sketches on the reverse (No. 53 verso; Fig. 188).

Carracci's original intention, it thus appears, was to treat the *Bacchanal* as three successive scenes in the frieze: the first (cf. Fig. 151) was to show Bacchus in his chariot; the second (cf. Fig. 152) would represent the Finding of Ariadne; and the third scene (cf. Fig. 158) would be devoted to the leading figures of the Bacchic retinue. It is hardly necessary to emphasize the point that these are merely preliminary drawings, made before Annibale had seriously begun to consider the disposition of subjects upon the ceiling. He would not long have been satisfied with an arrangement such as this, which had the obvious disadvantage of breaking up the Bacchic procession into three disconnected episodes; that disconnectedness, moreover, would only have been increased by the insertion of the medallions into the frieze. Very soon, therefore, it must have been decided that the *Bacchanal* should become the principal subject of the entire cycle, and as such should take its place as a single, consolidated composition at the crown of the vault.

The development of that composition, which can be traced through a considerable number of preparatory drawings, was to be a slow and complex process, with frequent changes of plan. For no other subject in the Farnese cycle have so many drawings been preserved. They have an interesting story to tell. The *Triumph of Bacchus and Ariadne*, for all its look of easy grace and fluency, did not spring from a sudden happy inspiration, but was perfected only after lengthy study and experiment.

Bellori's collection of drawings included, as he himself informs us, Annibale's first idea for the composition, which showed "Bacchus intoxicated and supported by fauns upon his car amid Bacchantes"; he adds that the artist subsequently changed the god's attitude into a more majestic one, reserving the drunken state for Silenus.[19] The same drawing is mentioned as being in Bellori's possession by Vittoria, who says further that it was executed in pen and ink, heightened with white, on tinted paper.[20] Tietze proposed that Bellori's drawing should be identified with the large preparatory study which is now in the Albertina in Vienna (No. 54; Fig. 159), but which at the time was known to him only through an aquatint copy by W. W. Ryland.[21] This identification is now generally accepted. The Vienna drawing is executed in pen and wash heightened with white over black chalk, on paper pre-

[18] *Ibid.*, p. 112.

[19] Bellori, *Vite*, p. 51: "si conserva ne' nostri libri, la prima inventione con Bacco ubbriaco sostentato da fauni sù'l carro frà Baccanti, che egli mutò, formandolo in maestà, ed attribuendo più convenevolmente l'ebrietà à Sileno."

[20] Vittoria, *Osservazioni*, pp. 54 f.: "Veggan-si nell'altro studio del Sig. Bellori la prima invenzione di tutto l'istesso Baccanale a tratti di penna, e biacca in carta tinta."

[21] Tietze, pp. 109, f., fig. 38. Ryland's aquatint was published by Charles Rogers, *A Collection of Prints in Imitation of Drawings*, London, 1778.

pared with a yellowish wash; Bacchus is undeniably pictured as drunken and, like Silenus, has to be held up by his attendants.

Calvesi has remarked on Annibale's indebtedness—even in this first draft—to Perino del Vaga's *Triumph of Bacchus* (Fig. 281).[22] The sleeping Ariadne has been shifted from the right to the left foreground, where she has not yet been discovered by the god (although the faun at his side has evidently just caught sight of her); in keeping with this change, the chariot is made to advance diagonally toward the right foreground. These modifications have in turn created a difficult problem at the right side of the composition, a problem which has not been successfully resolved. The foreground space remains painfully empty, no doubt because anything placed there would lie in the path of Bacchus' chariot. And the two drunken figures seated on the ground in the second plane are obviously out of place in a processional scene. Despite these revisions and the loosening of the dense compositional structure, Annibale has in the main followed Perino closely. The car of the wine-god is drawn by a pair of yoked lions on whose backs sit *amorini*, one holding a lyre. For the drunken Bacchus supported by two fauns (which might seem at first glance to be a totally new feature) Carracci has copied almost exactly the grouping used by Perino for Silenus and his two attendants. Among other elements borrowed from the latter we recognize the maenad with the basket and the faun playing the double flute; there is even a hint of a fluttering pennant at the upper right corner.

Incompletely realized though it is, the Albertina sheet yet announces certain features which will appear in the final redaction (Fig. 69). The Silenus group, for example, will undergo little modification: already Annibale has inserted here the little satyr whose task is to support the old man's leg. Silenus' attitude is virtually the definitive one; and the girl with the basket has already taken her place near him. Her companion balancing a wine jar on her head will ultimately be moved to the left side, just behind Bacchus' head. In the center of the drawing the maenad twisting round as she clashes the cymbals clearly foretells the analogous figure in the fresco who strikes a tambourine. And lastly there is the cupid flying over the company, who will be joined by three others in the final version.

It is evident that Annibale regarded this *prima invenzione* as a work of some importance: it is a large drawing, measuring nearly seventeen inches in length, and it contains almost no *pentimenti*. Indeed its rather formal character (and in this respect too it resembles Perino's design for the Farnese Casket) suggests that we have to do with a *modello*—a drawing submitted for approval to Cardinal Farnese and, in all probability, to Fulvio Orsini.

A beautiful pen and wash drawing in the Louvre (No. 55; Fig. 160) must follow soon after the *prima idea*. It is a study of Bacchus and the group around his chariot, and seems to be an attempt to resolve some of the difficulties posed by the preceding

---

[22] Calvesi, in *Commentari*, VII, 1956, p. 272. In fact the author refers to Giorgio Ghisi's engraving, but this we have shown to be merely a copy after Perino's drawing.

drawing. The diagonal placement of the chariot has been discarded, and the god, no longer intoxicated, is now seen in the conventional profile view. In making these changes Annibale has once again consulted Perino's design (Fig. 281), from which he has also appropriated the seated posture of Bacchus. At the same time, however, the drawing also proves that the idea of representing the Finding of Ariadne has already been given up. The lower left corner is left blank: it is as if, having deleted the figure of Ariadne, the artist had not found a suitable replacement.[23] We have here, then, evidence of a major change in plan. In Tietze's opinion the change was dictated largely by compositional reasons: Annibale, finding that his first idea was incompatible with the frieze-like procession required by the long, narrow shape of the ceiling picture, was compelled to devise a new scheme, suppressing the discovery of Ariadne.[24] While it is undoubtedly true that he was not wholly satisfied with his first plan, there is no reason whatever to think that the artist could not have adjusted his composition without making a fundamental alteration in iconography. Such a revision, affecting as it does the meaning of the principal subject of the cycle, must rather reflect the intervention of Orsini, who may have proposed to the artist that Ariadne be represented as exalted, and not (as in the *modello*) forlorn and abandoned.

Annibale's solution, preserved in a pen and wash drawing in the Albertina (No. 56; Fig. 161), was to place Ariadne in her own chariot alongside of that of Bacchus. What is more, by a flash of intuition he has found for her the definitive pose. Two goats, held in check by a putto, are harnessed to her car, and Amor displays the crown above her head. The elephant at the left side is, of course, taken from Perino's design; the camel beside him appears only in this drawing and will not be used in the fresco. In the lower left corner Annibale has added another essential feature of the final redaction—a faun embracing a goat. The compositional function of this figure, as a form of *repoussoir* balancing the Earthly Venus on the other side, is too obvious to require demonstration; at the same time it reveals something more of the gradual enrichment of the iconographical program through the collaboration of artist and literary adviser. For the next step will be to change the faun into a goat-legged satyr, and thereby to establish a link with the adjacent scene of *Pan and Diana*.

A puzzling feature of this drawing, which in most respects is so advanced, is the lolling attitude of Bacchus. This can only be construed as a reversion to the initial conception (No. 54; Fig. 159), where he is similarly held up by his followers; Annibale may have felt that the pose of the god should not too closely resemble that of Ariadne. But whatever the explanation, the figure was soon to be recast.

The definitive posture of Bacchus seems to be established, as Tietze observed,[25] by another drawing in the Albertina (No. 57; Fig. 162). The sheet contains several studies, the most important of which pictures the god seated upright as in the fresco,

[23] There is a faint chalk sketch here of a crouching lioness almost exactly like that ornamenting Bacchus' chariot in the preceding drawing (No. 54; Fig. 159).

[24] Tietze, p. 112.

[25] *Ibid.*, p. 117.

the left arm raised and supported by an attendant, the right knee elevated, and the face turned toward the observer. The position of the right arm has been shifted several times, and the *pentimenti* in this passage also prove that Annibale was slow to discard the nearer of the two supporting figures. The winged putto drawn in pen and gray wash in the upper center of the sheet is clearly a study for the boy restraining the goats of Ariadne's car. The rough pen sketch at the right is more difficult to interpret, but is probably an early idea for the obese figure of Silenus.

Still another clarifying sketch in the Albertina (No. 58; Fig. 163) is devoted to the figure of Ariadne, already fixed in the final pose by No. 56 (Fig. 161). The prancing satyr and putto beside her are reminiscent of a similar pair in the first idea (No. 54; Fig. 159); they will in time be replaced by the dancing faun carrying a staff.

Through these drawings, four of which (Nos. 55-58) belonged to Mariette, we have been able to follow the development of the composition in all essential features. It now remains to examine the studies of individual figures, which are more widely dispersed: though the majority are in the Louvre, others are found in Windsor, Besançon, Florence, Budapest, and Turin. In the description that follows we shall begin with the left side of the composition.

Three drawings have been preserved for the lower left corner (cf. Fig. 70). The first, in the Museum at Besançon, is a study for the reclining satyr (No. 59; Fig. 164). Like most of these studies it is in black chalk with heightening in white; a few strokes of the pen have been added along the spine and on the arms. The torso is considerably slimmer and more attenuated than that in the fresco, but the pose is identical. The raised right arm, drawn in foreshortening, is to be understood as encircling the goat's neck; in an alternative sketch at the right, however, the satyr grasps the animal by one of its horns.

Also in Besançon is a large chalk study from the life for the head of the goat (No. 60 recto; Fig. 165).[26] There are several cancelled sketches of unidentifiable objects around the animal's mouth and beard.

For the putto directly above the goat, who is carrying an amphora on his shoulder, there is a rapid chalk sketch in the Uffizi (No. 69 verso; Fig. 167), which is intended primarily to fix the position of the boy's right arm. Slight though the drawing is, its relation to the completed figure is unmistakable.[27]

The light sketch of a man's head (No. 60 verso; Fig. 166) on the reverse of the drawing of the goat's head is a preliminary study for the Bacchus.[28] The head has the same thick, curly hair and the same classicizing character as that of Bacchus in the painting. The long curving strokes beneath the head do not, as might at first

[26] Mahon connects the drawing with the goat in the fresco of *Pan and Diana* (*Disegni*, p. 119, no. 162). But this must be a slip, for the resemblance to the animal in the *Bacchanal* is too close to permit any other identification.

[27] The figure is understandably described as female by Mahon (*ibid.*, p. 118, no. 159). Only when the drawing and the boy in the fresco are actually confronted does the relationship become clear.

[28] Mahon regards this identification as questionable (*ibid.*, p. 119, no. 162).

appear to be the case, delineate the neck of the figure, but mark the ribbons which are tied behind the head and fall forward over the shoulders. Looked at in this way, it can be seen that the neck is set at much the same angle as that of the god in the fresco. For the entire figure of Bacchus, unluckily, no finished study has yet come to light. Since this must have been one of the most handsome of all the Farnese drawings, it is not likely to have been destroyed or carelessly tossed aside; perhaps it will one day be rediscovered.

For the companion figure, that of Ariadne, there is a brilliant study in the Gernsheim Collection (No. 61; Fig. 168). The nude model has been posed in the attitude already established in previous drawings (cf. Figs. 161 and 163), and Annibale now proceeds to adjust the contours and to determine the light and shade (see particularly the highlights on the shoulders and right elbow). For the head he has not yet found the definitive position (in this respect the earlier drawings are closer to the fresco); presumably the set of the head was corrected in a subsequent study.[29] Another last-minute alteration was made in the position of the left arm, which is here shown in full length: in the fresco the elbow rests on the rim of the chariot and the forearm is bent sharply upward.

Likewise from the life is the study in the Louvre (No. 62; Fig. 170) for the dancing youth brandishing a staff in front of Ariadne's car (cf. Fig. 72). The pose of this figure, one of Annibale's happiest inventions, is foreshadowed in the preliminary pen sketch No. 53 recto (Fig. 158).

Some uncertainty must still be felt regarding a sheet at Windsor (No. 63; Fig. 169), the sketches on which have been described as "almost certainly preparatory studies from nature for the goats which draw Ariadne's car."[30] This would seem to be confirmed by the glimpse of wooded landscape in the upper half of the sheet, which is very like that in the fresco. But there is a possibility that the drawing may be for another subject altogether, especially since both pairs of goats seem to be butting one another. We have already taken note of a study for the boy restraining the goats (No. 57; Fig. 162).

The detailed studies for the right half of the *Bacchanal* are almost as numerous as those for the left. Among the Italian drawings in the National Museum at Budapest there has recently come to light an impressive study for the ecstatic maenad striking the tambourine (No. 64; Fig. 171). A *pentimento* in the position of the right arm makes the correspondence with the fresco almost perfect.[31]

[29] I find myself unable to agree with Michael Jaffé that the drawing of a woman's head in the Boymans Museum (Koenigs V. 4 v., attributed to Rubens) is a study for Ariadne (*Paragone*, no. 83, Nov. 1956, pp. 12 ff., pl. 6b). Not only would it be unusual for Annibale to use gray rather than gray-blue paper for a Farnese study in chalk, but the severity of the expression, and in particular the frowning brows, are quite inappropriate for Ariadne in her moment of apotheosis. Her face, in the fresco, is remarkable for its look of serenity and composure.

[30] Wittkower, *Carracci Drawings*, p. 138, no. 305.

[31] In the eighteenth century the drawing formed part of the collection of Jonathan Richardson Sr. This must be the work cited

In the Louvre there is a large study from the life for the adjacent figure—the faun who blows a horn while supporting Silenus (No. 65; Fig. 172). The tentative notations of alternative positions for the legs were not followed in the fresco. The portion cut away near the left shoulder is to be understood as being concealed behind Silenus.

Closely connected with this is a drawing in sanguine at Turin (No. 66; Fig. 173), which is a study for Silenus and the attendant on his left (cf. Fig. 71). It is interesting to see in how many respects even so finished a drawing as this differs from the group actually realized in fresco. In the painting, for instance, the old man's eyes are wide open as he looks down intently at Venus, and his effort to remain seated on the ass is vividly conveyed by a certain tenseness in his posture. In the Turin drawing, by contrast, his attitude is more helpless and somnolent. The eyes are closed, and the right arm, instead of resting on the trumpeter's shoulder, hangs limply behind him; the face, however, is corrected by the sketch (inverted) at the bottom of the sheet, which shows the eyes open. The left arm, which in the painting is tightly wrapped around his companion's neck, here lies loosely across his shoulders; the right leg similarly rests in a relaxed position with the foot advanced, whereas in the final version it is bent downward more sharply at the knee. The adolescent faun who grasps Silenus' leg is only hinted at.

Near Silenus is the nymph carrying a basket on her head, for whom there exists a fine drawing in the Louvre (No. 67; Fig. 174). It is a study from the nude model and as is often true shows considerably more of the figure than is visible in the fresco.

The reclining attitude of the Earthly Venus follows in a general way that of Ariadne in Perino's drawing (Fig. 281). It was pointed out by Tietze[32] that before preparing his definitive study of this figure Annibale first made use of a male model, probably a *garzone* from his studio, as is recorded in a drawing in the Louvre (No. 68; Fig. 176). Having thus clarified the pose to his satisfaction the artist then made the final study from the female nude. This drawing, which is in the Uffizi (No. 69 recto; Fig. 177), is very close to the figure in the fresco both in attitude and in the arrangement of drapery.

A beautiful chalk drawing of an *amoretto* at Budapest (No. 70; Fig. 175) has recently been identified as a study for the Cupid standing beside the Earthly Venus.[33]

Annibale's next task was to combine all these studies and, using the composition sketches as a guide, to determine the proper spacing of the figures both on the plane and in depth. The result was then transferred to the cartoon. Happily there is preserved in the Galleria Nazionale at Urbino a large section of the cartoon of the *Bacchanal*, showing the entire right half of the composition (No. 71; Fig. 178). This

by the younger Richardson: ". . . an Admirable Figure (very near as much as is seen of it in the Picture) 'tis in the *Bacchanale* on the Cieling. My Father has this Drawing" (*An Account*, pp. 143 f.).

[32] Tietze, p. 118.

[33] A drawing of a putto at Windsor, cited by Tietze (p. 118) as a study for one of the *amoretti* flying over the procession, is a copy after the fresco, probably by Domenichino. Cf. Pope-Hennessy, *Domenichino Drawings*, p. 114, no. 1539A; and Wittkower, *Carracci Drawings*, p. 161.

huge drawing is amply documented, so that the history of its ownership can easily be traced. It belonged to Domenichino, who bequeathed it to his pupil Francesco Raspantino; an inventory of 1664 mentions it among the drawings then in Raspantino's studio.[34] It is next reported by Bellori and Vittoria as being in the collection of the painter Carlo Maratti; the cartoon was then already fragmentary, for both writers specify that only the right half of the composition was represented.[35] Maratti in turn sold the cartoon, together with most of his other drawings, to Pope Clement XI Albani. It remained in the Albani Collection until 1915, when it was acquired by the Galleria Nazionale of Urbino.[36]

The cartoon, being carried out on the same scale as the fresco itself, is more than eleven feet high. It is a work of superb draughtsmanship, and exhibits the same incisiveness and elasticity of contour that are found in the best preliminary studies. The design is set down in black chalk and is remarkably close to the corresponding section of the fresco, not only in the detailed rendering of each figure, but in the subtle intervals and overlappings that give the work its rhythmic force. One major *pentimento* may be pointed out. Silenus' right leg originally extended further to the right, its position being exactly similar to that seen in the preparatory study in Turin (No. 66; Fig. 173). This part of the figure was later crossed out and the leg redrawn in its present and final position. It is important to realize that this change (which also affects the boy at Silenus' side) was not taken care of in a preliminary drawing, but was carried out at the last minute on the cartoon itself.

Two problematical drawings have still to be considered in connection with this scene. The first is the large pen and wash drawing in the Louvre (Inv. 7184; Fig. 272),[37] which Jonathan Richardson, Jr. saw in the royal collection in Paris: *"Bacchus* upon an Elephant, and *Ariadne* standing at a distance on a Chariot: Several of the Figures the same as in this Story in the *Farnese."*[38] The triumphal procession consists of three parts: at the left is Ariadne in her chariot; in the center Bacchus is shown riding on an elephant; and the right side is occupied by Silenus and his attendants. The left-hand and middle parts of the composition are derived from an antique sarcophagus relief showing the Triumph of Bacchus.[39] The person of the god, wearing a long garment and standing in his chariot at the left of the scene, has been metamorphosed into that of Ariadne, and in like manner the captive barbarian riding on an elephant with his arms bound behind him has, rather ludicrously, become Bacchus himself.

[34] A. Bertolotti, *Artisti bolognesi,* p. 175: "Un Chartone della Baccanaria di Fernese."

[35] M. Piacentini (ed.), *Le vite inedite del Bellori,* I, Rome, 1942, p. 122 (Vita di Carlo Maratti): "L'altro Cartone è il Baccanale della Galleria Farnese, cioè il Sileno con i Baccanti, studio mirabile per la forza del più sublime disegno." Vittoria, *Osservazioni,* p. 54: "Veggasi l'ammirabile cartone grande del Baccanale dalla parte del Sileno nello studio del Sig. Maratta, il quale lo conserva, come unico te-

soro dell'arte."

[36] L. Serra, *Il Palazzo Ducale e la Galleria Nazionale di Urbino,* Rome, 1930, pp. 121 f. Tietze, writing in 1906, was unaware that the cartoon still existed.

[37] Tietze, p. 113, fig. 41.

[38] Richardson, *An Account,* p. 19.

[39] See for example K. Lehmann-Hartleben and E. C. Olsen, *Dionysiac Sarcophagi in Baltimore,* Baltimore, 1942, fig. 7.

Although Tietze accepted the drawing as original, Bacou is surely correct in arguing that it is too weak in execution to be by the hand of Annibale.[40] She thinks it possible that the sheet may be a copy after a lost original. But if on the one hand the evidence of style suffices to prove that this is not an autograph study by the master, the evidence of iconography on the other hand may be used to show that this bizarre solution was not even invented by Annibale. As a compositional study a work such as this would be understandable only if it could be shown to belong to a very early stage; yet it is obvious that the draughtsman was in fact acquainted with the final version of the design, from which he appropriated a number of details: these include the dancing youth with the staff, the maenad with the tambourine (whose attitude is actually closer to the figure in the fresco than to the definitive study, No. 64; Fig. 171), the group of Silenus and his colleagues, the Earthly Venus and her son, and the three *amorini* disposed in flight overhead. The Louvre drawing is thus not a copy after a lost original, but a pupil's ingenious attempt to fuse various figures taken from Annibale's *Bacchanal* with elements derived from an antique Dionysiac relief. It is, in short, only one of the studio exercises that Annibale frequently set for his pupils.

A large drawing of the *Bacchanal* at Windsor (Cat. 305A) poses an even more vexing problem (Fig. 270). Its history can be traced with reasonable certainty. The inventory of the Bonfiglioli collection in Bologna, drawn up in 1696, lists "a very large drawing of the Triumph of Bacchus, by the hand of Annibale."[41] Jonathan Richardson, Jr., who saw the drawing there some years later, gives a more complete description of it: "The Design for the Triumph of *Bacchus*, sketch'd, and shadow'd with Bl. Ch. and the Outline mark'd with a large Pen; five Foot long."[42] Although some of the Bonfiglioli drawings were known to have passed to the Royal Collection at Windsor Castle it was long believed that this monumental drawing had been lost. A few years ago, however, it was discovered by Wittkower at Windsor, where despite its large size it had lain unrecognized. He has described it as "perhaps the grandest surviving example of a final design into which all the preliminary studies of single figures were incorporated and which was used as a guide for work on the cartoon."[43] It is drawn in black chalk, and pen and brown ink, which agrees with Richardson's description; the sheet has been cut away a little on the right, and now measures something less than four feet in length. Richardson may have included the frame in his estimate of size, but in any event his "five Foot long" need not be taken too literally. There is, I believe, no reason to doubt that this is the drawing formerly in the Bonfiglioli collection.

A drawing such as this, showing the whole composition in developed form, must inevitably come under suspicion as being perhaps a copy after the fresco, or even after an engraving. Yet if we compare the Windsor drawing with a known copy such as Uffizi 770E we perceive that, whereas the latter follows the fresco slavishly, the

[40] Bacou, *Dessins*, p. 40, under no. 58.

[41] "Un dissegno assai grande col Trionfo di Bacco di mano d'Annibale" (cited by Witt-

kower, *Carracci Drawings*, p. 170, no. 305A).

[42] Richardson, *An Account*, p. 32.

[43] Wittkower, *Carracci Drawings*, pp. 170 f.

Windsor sheet contains certain features which have no counterpart in the painting. One of these discrepancies occurs in the lower left corner of the composition: in the fresco (Fig. 70) the seated satyr in the foreground encircles the goat's neck with his right arm; in the drawing, however, his right hand grasps the animal by its horn. This is no copyist's blunder, but an authentic alternative invented by Annibale himself. Indeed both gestures are represented in the study for the satyr in Besançon (No. 59; Fig. 164): in the principal drawing at the left he embraces the goat, but in the lighter sketch at the right he takes hold of its horn. The exact repetition of the latter gesture in the Windsor drawing effectively rules out the possibility that this sheet is only a copy after the finished painting.

But this is not to say that it is necessarily Annibale's final design. Not only does the style of the drawing militate against that conclusion, but there is also evidence to prove that it did not precede, but rather followed, the making of the cartoon. That evidence has to do with the placing of the right leg of Silenus. In the cartoon, it will be recalled (Fig. 178), Annibale first represented the leg in the diagonal position which he had earlier visualized in his preparatory drawing (No. 66; Fig. 173); then, revising his intention directly on the cartoon, he shifted the leg to a more vertical position. Now it would be only logical to expect that the final design, as the forerunner of the cartoon, would represent the leg in the original, uncorrected position. In point of fact, however, the Windsor drawing follows the later, revised attitude. That it can be the consolidated design from which the cartoon was fashioned is thus virtually out of the question.

How are we to explain this monumental drawing, which, though evidently posterior to the cartoon, yet does not appear to have been copied from the fresco? The answer must be that it is a copy after the cartoon; doubtless it was made with the purpose of preserving a record of that fragile document before it should wholly disintegrate. Since the entire left half of the cartoon is lost, this hypothesis can never be completely substantiated; for it involves the assumption that the missing portion contained the same discrepancies with respect to the fresco that we have observed in the Windsor drawing. But we must not overlook one further detail which lends support to this conclusion. The pine tree at the extreme right of the Windsor sheet is identical to that in the cartoon; in the fresco, however (Fig. 71), the tree is given a different shape, and the double flute played by a Bacchante in the background does not overlap its trunk. This explanation of the Windsor drawing as a copy after the cartoon is also compatible with its rather spiritless and unadventurous draughtsmanship, which can be more easily understood as the work of an obedient copyist than of Annibale Carracci.

DRAWINGS FOR PAN AND DIANA (FIG. 65)

Annibale's first idea for the scene of *Pan and Diana* is at Chatsworth (No. 72; Fig. 179). Like the *prima invenzione* for the *Bacchanal* (No. 54; Fig. 159), it presents an unusually finished appearance, being drawn in chalk, pen and ink, and wash on paper tinted gray. Except for the obvious fact that the composition is horizontal rather than vertical, it is not fundamentally different from the final redaction. Instead of standing as he proffers the wool to Diana, Pan is seated, and the goat is similarly in a reclining rather than an upright position. The Pan-pipes hang from a branch of the tree behind the god. Diana is represented in the act of receiving the wool as she hovers in the air with her garments fluttering; the bow is held in her right hand. As in the fresco, trees and foliage fill the upper left and lower right corner. The carefully thought-out system of light and shade is already developed in the drawing. The hind quarters of the goat, for example, are fully illumined, while the head and forelegs are in the shadow cast by Pan.

In the attitude of the satyr god, who is seated on a rock with the left knee elevated, there is perhaps an echo of the figure of Pan in the marble group of *Pan and Olympus*, a work that influenced Annibale on more than one occasion.[44] A few faint strokes of chalk beneath the figure of Diana suggest that the artist has already begun to consider a more upright position for the goddess.

The Chatsworth drawing may be the *invenzione* once owned by Bellori, which Vittoria says was similar to that of the *Bacchanal*.[45] It is plainly a *modello*, and as such was no doubt submitted to Orsini for approval. At this early stage Annibale intended the octagonal panels to be viewed from the ends of the Gallery in conjunction with the Polyphemus frescoes; they would thus have been read at right angles to the *Bacchanal*. Perhaps it was Orsini who objected to this arrangement. In any event, Annibale shortly revised his composition, changing it from an oblong to an upright so that it might be viewed in the same sense as the *Bacchanal*.

A pen and wash sketch at Windsor (No. 73; Fig. 180) represents the artist's first attempt to adapt the subject to the new upright shape. As a transitional study the drawing contains elements both of the first idea at Chatsworth and of the final design. The octagonal frame is clearly indicated. In keeping with the change to a vertical composition Pan is shown standing with the shepherd's staff resting against his shoulder. The goat, however, is still in a reclining position, and Pan's foot rests on its back. The goddess appears upon a bank of clouds, the angle of her body being approximately that seen in the painting; but she is still shown as receiving Pan's gift instead of raising her arm in surprise. The spear held in her left hand and the deer that is visible behind her are features peculiar to this drawing and do not reappear in the fresco. Although several changes have yet to be made, especially in the posture of Diana, the main outlines of the composition are now settled.

The final pose of Diana is determined by a beautiful chalk drawing in the Louvre (No. 74 recto; Fig. 183). It is a study from the nude model for the upper part of the body only. The goddess holds a bow in her left hand, and extends the right in a gesture of astonishment: although the sheet is torn along this side the direction of the right arm is clearly evident. A quiver of arrows is lightly indicated behind her shoulder.

[44] Annibale copied the head of Pan from this group in a drawing now in the Louvre (Inv. 7193).

[45] Vittoria, *Osservazioni*, p. 55.

In the final conception the arm with the bow is given a more vertical position, and the quiver is omitted, perhaps because of the draperies that flutter around the goddess's shoulders.

The verso of this sheet bears several rapid sketches in pen and ink (No. 74 verso; Fig. 181); at the left is a study for the figure of Pan, improving upon that in the Windsor composition sketch (No. 73; Fig. 180). Instead of holding up the fleece with both hands, the god raises only the right arm, the left being bent back to hold the shepherd's crook. The left foot rests upon a rock, as in the fresco. Above is a separate sketch of the right arm. The eagle at the right seems to be unrelated to the Farnese cycle.[46]

The pose of Pan now settled, Annibale's next task was to make the final figure study. The resulting chalk drawing—a particularly brilliant one—is now in the Louvre (No. 75; Fig. 182). The torso and arms are drawn from the model, the goat legs and satyr's face being only roughly indicated. Since the model probably supported himself by grasping a sling suspended from the ceiling, the raised right hand is not shown; no doubt Annibale made a separate study of this detail.[47]

DRAWINGS FOR MERCURY AND PARIS (FIG. 66)

Unluckily no composition sketches have come down to us for this scene. The lack is in part compensated for by three fine drawings from the life.

One of these is the luminous chalk study in the Louvre for the seated Paris (No. 76; Fig. 185). The model has been posed in an attitude almost identical to that seen in the fresco (in which, however, the left leg has been shifted somewhat so as to bring more of the foot within the picture). The diagonal strokes in the corner of the sheet tell of Annibale's attempts to mark the approximate angle of the frame. Once again, as in the preceding study (Fig. 182), the model maintained his pose by taking hold of a sling with his hand, which was therefore omitted in the drawing; but the artist made a separate study of the hand grasping the staff at the upper left.

For the figure of Mercury in flight there exists a study in Besançon (No. 77; Fig. 184). The posture of the body, seen as it is in foreshortening, must have presented some difficulty to the artist. The model appears to have been posed in a reclining position on a platform or table, and viewed from above; the right arm extended downward beyond the edge of the platform, and the left leg and arm probably rested on some kind of support. The suggestion of fluttering drapery helps, even in the drawing, to create the illusion of a figure floating freely in the air. There are several

[46] Bacou believes that the pen sketches on the verso may be by Agostino (*Dessins*, p. 43, no. 65).

[47] Mahon has proposed (*Disegni*, p. 119, no. 161) that the drawing of a satyr in the Boymans Museum (Koenigs I. 184) might be a first idea for the figure of Pan. Despite certain similarities in the pose, it is difficult to see how the figure could suit the subject in question: the satyr seems to be plucking grapes from a vine rather than holding up the fleece. Its connection with this fresco would appear to be doubtful.

faint indications of alternative positions for the arms and legs. In the fresco the figure of Mercury becomes rather more compact: the extended left leg is bent back slightly so as to overlap the other foot and the head is tilted upward; the enclosing arcs of drapery above and below the figure contribute further to its self-contained quality.

The third drawing, also in Besançon, is a study for the dog (No. 101 verso; Fig. 187). Unfortunately the sheet has been cropped, with the result that part of the animal's head has been lost. Annibale later used the reverse of this drawing to make a study of one of the *ignudi* (Fig. 214).

For the sphinxes which appear on the frames of these two octagonal frescoes there is a study in the Louvre (No. 78; Fig. 186). An earlier sketch for a sphinx, showing its position within the structural framework, can be seen in the drawing No. 50 (Fig. 155).

AGOSTINO'S FRESCOES

The preparatory drawings for the two frescoes executed by Agostino Carracci are of particular interest in that they permit us to define more exactly the role of this artist in the Farnese cycle. These are in fact the only histories in the Gallery for which studies by Agostino can be identified with absolute certainty. Yet even here he was not given a totally free hand. For, as the drawings themselves reveal, Annibale took it upon himself as master of the workshop to edit and correct his brother's ideas before they were carried out in fresco.

DRAWINGS FOR AURORA AND CEPHALUS (FIG. 59)

Agostino made several sketches on the back of a discarded drawing by Annibale for the *Bacchanal* (No. 53 verso; Fig. 188). The drawing of a man's legs, in ink over red chalk, cannot be related to any known work and is perhaps only an exercise; sketches of this sort are common in Agostino's graphic work.[48] The sketches of a cartouche at the upper right are evidently preliminary designs for one of the Farnese coats of arms in stucco on the walls of the Gallery. The principal drawing on the sheet, a pen sketch of a kneeling woman, is a preliminary study for the Aurora in the fresco of *Aurora and Cephalus*. Her attitude is virtually the definitive one, but the fluttering drapery will be considerably altered. No doubt this pen drawing was followed by a more detailed study in chalk.

In the Louvre there exists such a study, made from the life, for the recumbent figure of Tithonus (No. 79; Fig. 189). Though executed in the manner of Annibale, it is incontestably by the hand of Agostino, whose interest in the bony frame and sagging flesh of old age are clearly apparent. Comparison with the fresco shows that a few minor changes were made in the posture of the figure: the head is raised so as to reveal a little more of the face, and the right arm is shifted toward the right. A separate sketch in

[48] E.g. Windsor Cat. nos. 131, 133, 134 and 136 (Wittkower, *Carracci Drawings*, pp. 117 ff., pls. 31 and 34, figs. 18 and 19).

brush and ink in the left corner of the Louvre sheet presents a revised view of the head as it appears in the finished work.

Agostino's cartoon for this fresco, like that for its pendant, is preserved in the National Gallery in London (No. 80; Fig. 190). Except for a large rectangular patch at the upper right the design is complete. It can be seen that the cartoon differs from the fresco in several particulars. The putto with the basket of roses appears in the former to be seated on a cloud; in the final state he is given a flying attitude. Changes were also made in the ornamentation of Aurora's chariot and in the placing of the dog's forepaws. As for Tithonus, the cartoon does not show his head in the definitive position but still follows the preparatory chalk drawing in the Louvre (No. 79; Fig. 189). This means, as Mahon has observed,[49] that the change was undertaken at the last moment, and that the corrected head drawn in ink on the Louvre sheet must be later than the cartoon. Some of these alterations are probably due to suggestions made by Annibale. He may well have objected to the inappropriate seated posture of the putto strewing roses and proposed instead the flying attitude seen in the fresco.

DRAWINGS FOR GLAUCUS AND SCYLLA (FIG. 60)

The preparatory material for this fresco, like that for *Aurora and Cephalus*, is fragmentary. There is in Besançon a chalk study for the head and shoulder of Glaucus embracing Scylla, the outlines of whose body are only lightly indicated (No. 81 verso; Fig. 192). Despite the pencilled notation "Anibal Carrache," the drawing is manifestly by the hand of Agostino.

The sheet bears on its other side a study for the rather ungainly putto with the torch in the upper right corner of the picture (No. 81 recto; Fig. 191). It is close, but not identical, to the final form; the position of the arms is different in the fresco, and the right leg is bent more sharply at the knee, with the result that his posture is very like that of the putto with the basket of roses in the *Aurora and Cephalus*.

By a stroke of good luck Agostino's cartoon for this scene is also preserved in the National Gallery in London (No. 82; Fig. 194); it is in even better condition than the other. Although the contours are pricked for transfer to the vault, the cartoon does not agree with the fresco in every detail. Many of the discrepancies are of a minor kind, but there is one that gives evidence of a drastic remodeling. The Nereid behind Scylla, who in the cartoon gazes up at her, is made in the final conception to glance downward, and the boy who appears just behind Glaucus has been omitted altogether. Scylla's nudity, unconcealed in the cartoon, is veiled by a piece of drapery in the completed work.[50] Certain other changes were made on the cartoon itself. The Nereid at the extreme left was probably first represented as entirely nude; the drapery that now covers her legs is drawn on an irregularly shaped piece of paper pasted to the cartoon. The putto riding on the dolphin was originally shown looking up at Scylla,

---

[49] Mahon, *Disegni*, pp. 54 f.
[50] Tietze (p. 124) is obviously right in main-

taining that this passage is original and not a later bowdlerization.

but his face was later redrawn so that he looks out at the spectator. The face of the swimming boy beside him has likewise been recast.

The principal figures, Glaucus and Scylla, are here shown in their definitive attitudes; to be sure, those attitudes were already fixed, at least for the upper parts of the bodies, by the preparatory study in Besançon (No. 81 verso; Fig. 192). The hand, very lightly sketched, which can be discerned resting on Glaucus' shoulder in the cartoon proves that Agostino considered an alternative position for Scylla's left arm. But it is to be emphasized that this position (so inappropriate to the situation) was not the original one: there is no trace of the girl's hand on the sea-god's shoulder in the preliminary drawing, and it is furthermore obvious that it was added to the cartoon *after* the two figures had been completed. The gesture is therefore simply an afterthought, briefly tried and then rejected.

Annibale's influence can be felt throughout this scene. The two Nereids at the left side are derived, as we have earlier observed, from Annibale's painting of *Diana and Callisto* in the Ellesmere collection. (Agostino used the same two figures in his engraving *Omnia vincit Amor*, Fig. 276.) But the most convincing demonstration of Annibale's authority is to be seen at the right side of the composition, where there occurs a notable discrepancy between cartoon and fresco. For this place (as we know from the cartoon) Agostino had invented a Triton blowing a shell-trumpet, his right arm extended in a forceful gesture. But in the fresco the Triton appears in a wholly different attitude, the body twisted in an energetic *contrapposto*, the face in *profil perdu*, and both hands raised to grasp the shell. This transformed figure depends, as Mahon has brilliantly demonstrated,[51] on a powerful chalk drawing by Annibale now in the Winter collection (No. 83; Fig. 193). Mahon's interpretation of the substitution is undoubtedly the correct one: "Annibale [he writes] felt uncomfortable about the figure, and suggested an alternative, which Agostino adopted in the fresco, though without the exuberant *brio* which is so evident in Annibale's superb study; nevertheless, in spite of the process of desiccation which the figure undergoes in the fresco, it still stands somewhat apart, amid the elegances of Agostino, by reason of its vigorous solidity combined with an air of easy naturalness of movement." Yet, impressive though Annibale's solution is, it is perhaps possible to overestimate its originality. For the fact is that Annibale's Triton, like many of the other figures in the composition, is derived from Raphael's *Galatea*: his prototype is the amorous Triton at the left of the Farnesina fresco who clasps a nymph in his arms in a robust movement that proved easily adaptable to Annibale's trumpeter.

This little incident is only another example of the firm control exercised by Annibale over the cycle. Even in the frescoes that had been assigned to him Agostino was not allowed complete autonomy. The partnership was clearly not one of equals, but of master and subordinate.

[51] In *Journal of the Warburg and Courtauld Institutes*, XVI, 1953, p. 337.

THE POLYPHEMUS FRESCOES

Annibale's drawing for the end of the vault (No. 50; Fig. 155) provides, among other things, for the little picture of the *Rape of Ganymede* and, beneath it, for the large *quadro riportato* which is to contain *Polyphemus slaying Acis*. Of this subject, however, there is no indication in the drawing, although its frame has been elaborated in some detail.

Seven preparatory drawings have been identified for the Polyphemus frescoes, but only one of these has to do with the scene of *Polyphemus and Acis*.

DRAWINGS FOR POLYPHEMUS AND GALATEA (FIG. 63)

The earliest draft for this subject must be the rapid and forceful pen sketch of Polyphemus in the Louvre (No. 84; Fig. 195). It is obviously a preliminary idea, yet Annibale has already seized upon the tortured form of the *Laocoön* as the basis of the Cyclops' attitude. Only the arms are significantly different from the fresco, the right hand being raised to grasp the shepherd's crook while the other holds the syrinx. Two diminutive figures, one of them a satyr, stand in the foreground near Polyphemus' foot. In this swiftly executed sketch the artist has not troubled to represent the light as coming from the right (as required by the situation of the fresco) but has shaded the figure in accordance with a conventional source of light on the left.

How the pose of Polyphemus evolved through successive studies we can only imagine, but at least we can see it finally perfected in the monumental chalk drawing in the Louvre (No. 85; Fig. 197): the giant now holds the Pan-pipe in both hands, and hooks both the left arm and left leg over the staff. The drawing reveals some uncertainty regarding the placing of the arms. The right hand has been omitted so as not to interfere with the rendering of the head; for this Annibale made a separate study on a larger scale near the lower right corner of the sheet. The effects of light and shade have been fully worked out to correspond with a source of light on the right, and even the shadow cast by the syrinx has been clearly indicated on the chest of the figure.

Another chalk drawing in the Louvre (No. 86; Fig. 196) represents almost the entire composition; the missing part at the right may have been cut away. The figure of Polyphemus resembles the foregoing study (Fig. 197) very closely, so closely indeed as to make it evident that the sheet under discussion must follow rather than precede that drawing. Though certain adjustments have still to be made, the group of Galatea and her companions is essentially settled. As a clarifying sketch, the work logically takes its place in the sequence of preparatory studies for the fresco. In execution, however, it is decidedly inferior to the other specimens in the series. Bacou was so struck by its weaknesses in draughtsmanship that she has suggested an attribution to Agostino.[52] This seems to me not impossible, though I am more inclined to interpret

[52] Bacou, *Dessins*, p. 44, under no. 71.

the drawing as a rather careless piece of work by Annibale, who occasionally produced equally negligent passages in drawings like the *Apollo and Hyacinthus* (No. 91; Fig. 198). Nor is it necessary to dismiss the sheet as the work of a copyist, for the *pentimenti*, particularly the one altering the position of Galatea's head, look quite natural and unrehearsed.

The composition being thus fixed, Annibale now drew up final studies for the figures at the right side of the scene. In Besançon (No. 87; Fig. 201) is a drawing of Galatea which is mainly devoted to the torso and the arm holding the veil. The head is set at a different angle from that in the fresco, but the added strokes around the neck and chin show the artist beginning to adopt the final upright position (already adumbrated in the preceding drawing, Fig. 196).

A drawing in the Louvre (No. 88; Fig. 199), first cited by Wittkower,[53] is very probably a study for the arm and hand of the Nereid holding the dolphins' reins; this seems the more likely in that the light is from the right. Annibale was however not satisfied with the gesture, and revised it in the splendid drawing of the Nereid at Windsor (No. 89 verso; Fig. 200). The girl is posed in the final attitude, the right arm being shown in the more foreshortened position seen in the fresco.

The curious red chalk drawing of Polyphemus and Galatea in the Louvre (Inv. 7198; Fig. 269), though accepted as original by Tietze and other authorities, is beyond question (as Bacou has rightly said) the work of an imitator.[54] The draughtsmanship betrays a remarkably poor grasp of form (see particularly the feeble modeling of Galatea and her companions); it is significant that an indifferent copy after this drawing in Windsor (Cat. 507) actually reveals a somewhat surer rendering of volume and foreshortening.[55] At the same time the hypothesis that this might be a copy after an original design by Annibale must be rejected. Like the strange drawing of the *Triumph of Bacchus and Ariadne* (Fig. 272), this is nothing more than a student's exercise, made after the completion of the fresco. The group at the right side comprising Galatea and her attendant Nereids unquestionably follows the final redaction of the scene (Fig. 63). The posture of Polyphemus, on the other hand, who sits with one leg crossed over the other, is simply an imitation of the boy with the syrinx in the Farnese group of *Pan and Olympus* (Naples, Museum). In both of these studio drawings the procedure is the same: the pupil seeks to achieve an effect of originality by combining motives from a Carracci fresco with details from an antique monument.[56]

---

[53] *Carracci Drawings*, p. 138, under no. 302.

[54] Tietze, p. 122 (wrongly cited as Inv. 7197). Bacou, *Dessins*, p. 44, under no. 71.

[55] Wittkower, *Carracci Drawings*, p. 162, no. 507.

[56] The pen drawing at Lille (Musée Wicar 145), published by Tietze as a preliminary study by Agostino for *Polyphemus and Galatea* (pp. 120 f., fig. 46), is a free copy after the fresco. Other copies are in the Gabinetto Nazionale delle Stampe in Rome (Inv. 127426) and in the collection of the Earl of Leicester.

DRAWINGS FOR POLYPHEMUS AND ACIS (FIG. 64)

Unfortunately only one surely identifiable drawing for this scene has come down to us. It is a large and impressive study from the life for Polyphemus hurling the rock at Acis (No. 90; Fig. 202). In the attitude and in the distribution of light and shade the figure is almost identical to that in the fresco, but as is often true the proportions are noticeably more slender. Only in Polyphemus' right shoulder is there a hint of the more muscular build which Annibale will give to the giant in the fresco. The swirling drapery and shaggy hair are indicated by a few light strokes of chalk.[57]

Mahon has drawn attention to a red chalk drawing in the Gabinetto Nazionale delle Stampe in Rome (Fondo Corsini 126846), the verso of which shows studies of two legs.[58] Although one of these admittedly bears some resemblance to the left leg of Polyphemus, it seems unlikely that the drawing might be a study for that figure: for the leg in question is wholly lacking in the sinewy hardness and tense muscularity of Annibale's Cyclops.

DRAWINGS FOR THE GANYMEDE AND HYACINTHUS FRESCOES

The sheet of studies in Paris for the end of the vault (No. 50; Fig. 155) contains three preliminary sketches of the *Rape of Ganymede*. All three versions are different, and none agrees with the final conception (Fig. 68).

The sketch in the upper center of the sheet must be the earliest of the three because it shows the picture in its proper situation. Ganymede lies across the eagle's back in an attitude that is plainly derived from the Prophet Jonah of the Sistine ceiling. It may have seemed to Annibale that the ecstatic figure of Jonah, as he falls back to contemplate the Almighty on the vault just above him, was readily adaptable to the spiritual ravishment of Ganymede. However that may be, the pose did not long satisfy the artist, as is evident from the fact that he even neglected to complete the sketch.

The second version, enclosed within a rectangular border at the lower left side of the sheet, presents a thoroughly different conception. Once again the source is to be looked for in a work by Michelangelo, in this instance a more obvious one—the famous Ganymede drawing, of which Fulvio Orsini owned a copy.[59] Despite certain modifications, the position of the youth's legs and the way in which he is supported by the eagle leave no doubt as to the derivation. At the same time the final pose is foreshadowed in several important respects, namely in the pronounced diagonal of the body, the

[57] The drawing of Polyphemus in the Uffizi, Inv. 12316 F, which Giglioli connected with this fresco (*Bollettino d'Arte*, II, 1922-1923, p. 504), has been shown to relate rather to Annibale's fresco in the Palazzo Fava in Bologna. See H. Bodmer, *Lodovico Carracci*, Burg bei Magdeburg, 1939, p. 118.

[58] Mahon, *Disegni*, pp. 129 f., no. 183. See also note 71 below.

[59] P. de Nolhac, "Les collections d'antiquités de Fulvio Orsini," *Mélanges*, IV, 1884, p. 178, no. 97. The connection with Michelangelo's drawing was noted by Tietze, p. 105.

upturned head, and the position of the arms, one extended behind the eagle's head and the other bent sharply at the elbow.

At the right of this sketch (within the framed space reserved for the Polyphemus scene) appears yet a third idea for Ganymede. It is essentially another variation of the Michelangelesque posture, in which Annibale reverses the position of the legs and experiments with an upraised arm. This too proved to be an abortive solution.

In the final conception Annibale may have been influenced by the antique group of *Ganymede and the Eagle* (now in Naples), for which a place was actually found in the Farnese Gallery itself (cf. Fig. 33). No graphic record of this stage remains. It appears unlikely that the drawing of an eagle with wings outspread, which is to be seen on a sheet of studies for the adjoining fresco of *Pan and Diana* (No. 74 verso; Fig. 181), can have anything to do with the Ganymede subject.

For the companion picture of *Apollo and Hyacinthus* (Fig. 67) there is a single drawing in the Louvre (No. 91; Fig. 198). It is a study from the model for Hyacinthus, whose attitude is very close to that in the fresco. But Annibale has not yet found a satisfactory solution for Apollo, who is awkwardly compressed, with his lyre, into the upper right corner. In the painting he will be shifted to the left, in order to fill the empty space above Hyacinthus.

III. DRAWINGS FOR THE MYTHOLOGICAL SUBJECTS OF THE FRIEZE

THE BRONZE MEDALLIONS

The graphic material relating to the frieze is disappointingly meager. It is curious, for example, that not a single study for the bronze medallions has survived. This represents the most serious lacuna in the corpus of drawings for the Farnese Gallery.

There is, however, one slight piece of evidence which should not be overlooked. In his project for the end of the vault (No. 50; Fig. 155) Annibale made a rough sketch of a figure subject on the segment of the medallion protruding from behind the Polyphemus fresco. Two persons may be distinguished: one is seated with the right arm extended toward the other, who stands facing him. Even this rapid notation suffices to identify the episode as Paris awarding the prize to Venus; indeed the two figures are strikingly similar to those in Marcantonio's engraving of the *Judgment of Paris*. In the final conception the subject was shifted from the right to the left side of the Polyphemus picture (Fig. 57), where it fits neatly within the arc of the roundel. The figure of Venus has consequently disappeared behind the overlapping frame, but the seated posture of Paris remains much the same as that in the ink sketch.

THE PAINTED PANELS OF THE FRIEZE

There are, surprisingly, only a few drawings for the square paintings of the frieze, and most of these relate to a single composition—*Juno and Jupiter* (Fig. 43).

In the Courtauld Institute of Art is a pen and wash drawing of a standing female figure (No. 92; Fig. 203). Despite its almost eighteenth-century flavor it is beyond question an early study by Annibale for the figure of Juno. She has partly disrobed and carries in her hands a heavy mass of drapery. This preliminary conception is clearly inspired by the figure of Psyche being received into the presence of the gods in Raphael's ceiling fresco of the Farnesina: the similarity is particularly evident in the stance, in the arrangement of the drapery, and in the position of the right hand and arm.

An important study in the Ellesmere Collection (No. 93; Fig. 204) represents an early attempt to settle the main features of the composition. Although her drapery has not yet been logically organized, the posture and slender proportions of Juno are close to the final version; the right knee now rests upon the bed, and the entire figure is drawn as if seen from below. The attitude of Jupiter, on the other hand, is still far from settled. The upper part of the body will require little modification, but the legs, here shown undraped, are drawn up on the bed in a rather unstable manner; the attitude is in fact taken from the figure of Diogenes reclining on the steps in Raphael's *School of Athens*. A curious feature of the drawing is that Jupiter wears around his chest the ornamented band—the girdle of Venus—which in the fresco will be worn by Juno. The eagle, carrying the thunderbolt in his beak, lurks in the shadows of the curtained bed, but the peacock has already taken his position behind the goddess at the left.

The remaining adjustments in the pose of Juno were made in a chalk study in Besançon (No. 94 recto; Fig. 205). The neck and left leg have been straightened so that the figure now assumes a firmer structural role in the composition, and the drapery has been arranged in its final form (though Juno does not yet wear the girdle of Venus). At the right is a larger study of the goddess's face, here turned in the opposite direction. The work is drawn on white paper of a coarser texture than the gray-blue paper normally used by Annibale for black chalk studies of this sort.

On the reverse of this sheet (No. 94 verso; Fig. 206) there are two studies for the figure of Jupiter. The earlier one, at the right, is a hurried posture sketch, following in the main the Raphaelesque attitude established in the composition study, No. 93 (Fig. 204), in which the left leg is drawn up on the bed. The second and more detailed sketch revises the placing of the right leg, bringing it approximately into the position it takes in the fresco.

The next step, which is recorded by a drawing in the Louvre (No. 95; Fig. 207), was to lower the left foot to the ground. In making this adjustment Annibale seems to have had in mind the attitude of the *Laocoön*. Except for the eagle, which is only roughly indicated, the resemblance of the drawing to the fresco is very marked. The drapery folds have been studied with particular care—though the artist appears to have forgotten momentarily that the lighting should come from the right and not from the left. The drawing is once again in black chalk on white paper.

In the final redaction (Fig. 43) the legs of Jupiter effectively counterbalance those of Juno. The two figures are now combined so as to form a monumental and stable triangle, within which arms and legs make a satisfying series of smaller angular patterns. It is revealing to discover that none of these relationships are present in the early composition study (No. 93; Fig. 204), but evolved, in accordance with Annibale's usual procedure, through a succession of clarifying drawings.

In the Museum at Besançon is a large study in chalks (No. 96; Fig. 208) for the figure of Iole in the fresco of *Hercules and Iole* (Fig. 45). In this drawing from the nude Annibale has been at pains to establish not only the pose (witness the careful foreshortening of the right leg) but also the system of light and shade: the shadow cast by the club, for example, is indicated both on Iole's side and on the rock on which she is seated. The face and the extended arm are left unfinished. No drawing has come to light for her companion, the enslaved Hercules.

Bellori is said to have owned an *invenzione* for the fresco of *Diana and Endymion* (Fig. 44),[60] but this has evidently been lost. The only design that can be connected with this fresco is a red chalk drawing in the Louvre (No. 97; Fig. 209), which seems to be a study for the sleeping dog. The sheet has the look of a quick sketch done from life in the studio, the landscape background having patently been added. In adapting his sketch for the fresco Annibale retained the pose, but altered the breed and markings of the animal and closed its eyes.

IV. DRAWINGS FOR THE DECORATIVE FIGURES

In order to illustrate the extreme thoroughness with which Annibale composed his paintings Malvasia tells an anecdote concerning the Farnese Gallery. Tacconi, Albani, and other pupils, he says, found it miraculous that anyone could have painted figures as beautiful and as lifelike as the atlantes of the vault. At this Annibale grew indignant, like a schoolmaster whose pupils have not learned their lesson:

> Surely you can see just how it is done. First you take care that the pose of each figure is quite different from the others, that it is beautiful, suited to the situation, pleasing and understandable. More sketches are set down, and from the nude model you draw this leg, that arm, piece by piece, in that attitude and from that point of view. Then everything is put together, and when you transfer this to the cartoon there is no need to work out the light and shade: for if the model was placed up high, in the identical situation and in the same light, doesn't that take care of it? And now don't they have to turn out right? Do they still seem to you to be miracles?[61]

[60] Vittoria, *Osservazioni*, p. 55. A drawing of *Diana and Endymion* in Munich (Staatliche Graphische Sammlung, Inv. 2844) is a free copy after the fresco.

[61] Malvasia, *Felsina*, I, p. 484: "lo vedete pur anche voi altri . . . quel che sì fà: prima si pensa all' attitudine dalle altre affatto diversa, che sia bella, propria al sito, grata, ed intelligibile: se ne metton giù più schizzi, e spogliando il modello, si disegna quella gamba, quel

Now Malvasia's anecdotes are not invariably trustworthy, and in this instance the speech attributed to Annibale, for all its air of plausibility, is almost certainly fictitious. In what can only be described as a parody, the artist is made to explain his working method as an almost mechanical process whereby a figure is built up piecemeal, *cosa per cosa*, from various detailed studies. Yet there is some truth in the story, particularly in the emphasis that is placed on Annibale's method of drawing from the life. Here we find mention of the need for variety in the poses, which must at the same time be both beautiful and intelligible. And, what is equally important, if the frescoed figure is to be viewed *di sotto in su* the artist must make his drawing from a model placed at the proper elevation, with the light coming from below and in the right direction. That these things were matters of genuine concern to Carracci is proved by the studies for the decorative figures of the Farnese ceiling.

There are some thirty-five of these drawings extant, and they include studies for every type of decorative figure on the vault. For the termini Annibale even made three-dimensional models in addition to the usual drawings, his purpose being to achieve an effect of statuary as distinct from the "living" figures such as the seated youths.[62] None of these statuettes has survived.

THE IGNUDI

In one of the earliest projects for the ceiling (No. 46; Fig. 151) Annibale represented several nude youths in whom we may recognize the predecessors of the seated *ignudi*. The postures of these figures were of course not intended to be final; nevertheless it is possible to discover certain similarities in pose among the *ignudi* actually executed in fresco. The uppermost figure on the right side of the drawing, for example, presents a distinct resemblance to the youth sitting at the left of *Hero and Leander* (Fig. 54). Another idea for an *ignudo* appears in No. 50 (Fig. 155) in the figure seated at the right of the large framed picture; it is probably not mere coincidence that a similar pose was used for the youth sitting at the right of *Polyphemus and Galatea* (Fig. 61).

Many of the drawings of individual *ignudi* are of great beauty. We may begin with the brilliant study in the Louvre (No. 98 recto; Fig. 210) for the youth seated on the left of the medallion of *Apollo and Marsyas* (Fig. 47). It is over sixteen inches high, and is executed, like most of the Farnese designs, in black chalk heightened with white on gray-blue paper, which in this instance has been yellowed through prolonged exposure to the light. The affinity between the drawing and the fresco is remarkable, even for Annibale: the only perceptible difference is that in the latter the extended left hand does not appear but is to be understood as being hidden by the mask. It is instructive to compare with this finished study Annibale's first idea

braccio, cosa per cosa, in quella attitudine, e veduta; poi tutta si pone insieme, e portandola sul cartone, quello non s'ombreggia e lumeggia, se posto in alto il modello nello stesso sito,

e al medesimo lume, non si compisce; e poi non han da far bene? e poi vi paion miracoli?"
[62] Bellori, *Vite*, p. 47.

for the figure, which is to be seen on the reverse of the sheet (Fig. 212). The pose is fundamentally the same, but the youth's head is turned so that he is looking at the observer, and the left knee is raised somewhat more than in the final drawing.

For the companion figure, the youth seated to the right of *Apollo and Marsyas* (Fig. 47), there is also a splendid drawing in the Louvre, which is frequently reproduced as an example of Annibale's draughtsmanship at its best (No. 99; Fig. 211). Here, however, there is not complete agreement with the fresco. The raised left arm is seen in bold foreshortening, the elbow being held away from the body (an echo, perhaps, of the Delphic Sibyl) and the hand covering part of the face; the right leg is extended, but the final position is also faintly indicated. A variant pose for the left arm, with the elbow lowered somewhat, appears in a separate sketch at the upper right: it will be seen that this approaches the definitive position. The final attitude of the figure, as it was realized in fresco, is still more compact. The left arm, instead of jutting out at an angle, is hugged close to the body with the hand resting on the opposite shoulder; and the left leg, which in the drawing extends in front of the figure, is now bent sharply at the knee, which adds further to the effect of self-containedness.

These two studies may be taken as typical of the drawings made from the life for the decorative figures of the vault. The models have been posed above eye-level to ensure accurate foreshortening, and the lighting has been controlled so as to strike both figures from below and from the right, which is the effect required by the position assigned to the two *ignudi* on the ceiling (cf. Fig. 47). But no description of Annibale's method of posing the model can explain the extraordinarily vivid quality of drawings such as these, which combine a forceful realism with a richly decorative effect. Even the lights and shades which model the form so naturally have been set down in a beautifully rhythmic sequence.

Another drawing in the Louvre (No. 100; Fig. 213) is a study for the seated *ignudo* at the right of the medallion with *Orpheus and Eurydice* (Fig. 50). Both in the pose and in the highlights and shadows the drawing is identical to the fresco. Only the upper part of the figure is shown: for the legs the artist no doubt made a separate study, as was occasionally his practice. At the left is a rough sketch of the left arm and shoulder, which may have served to indicate how the hand grips the edge of the seat.

In the Museum at Besançon are two studies for the seated youths who flank the medallion of *Hero and Leander* (Fig. 54). The first (No. 101 recto; Fig. 214) shows the legs and lower part of the body of the *ignudo* at the left.[63] The position of the left leg has been altered slightly in the painting. That this is not the final drawing

[63] Both Wittkower (*Carracci Drawings*, p. 138) and Mahon (*Disegni*, pp. 120 f., 139, no. 165) thought the drawing to be for the *ignudo* to the left of *Polyphemus and Galatea* (cf. Fig. 55). But the direction of the torso and the twist of the right leg below the knee make it certain that this is a study for the youth at the left of the *Leander* medallion. For the verso, see Fig. 187.

is evident from the fact that the illumination is from the upper left, not from below.

The second drawing (No. 102; Fig. 216) is for the figure on the other side of the roundel. A few changes were made in the final version: the youth in the fresco wears a kind of loin-cloth and is of a heavier and more muscular build; the turn of the head into a profile position tends to emphasize the relief-like character of the pose. The pattern of light and shade is astonishingly similar. As may be seen from the faint sketch at the left, Annibale considered an alternative position for the legs of the youth. In the end, however, he followed his original design.

Two drawings are known for the animated *ignudo* who sits (if that is the word for his posture) at the right of *Salmacis and Hermaphroditus* (Fig. 52). The earlier drawing, a vigorous pen sketch now in the Kunsthalle at Bremen (No. 103; Fig. 215), fixes the fundamental character of the pose—derived, as we have noted, from the Jonah of the Sistine ceiling. This was followed by the impressive chalk study from the life in the Ellesmere collection (No. 104; Fig. 217), which in its vibrancy and elasticity of contour is almost unmatched. Yet the Ellesmere drawing, though freely handled, is in every respect a definitive study, as comparison with the fresco makes evident. An unusual feature is that the sheet is squared for enlargement.

Lastly, there is preserved in the Louvre (No. 105; Fig. 218) a study for the nude youth seated at the right of *Polyphemus and Acis* (Fig. 62). The painted figure is a fairly accurate transcription of the preparatory drawing, but with two modifications: for the smiling face looking out at the spectator Annibale has substituted a more serious expression, at the same time turning the head so that it is almost in profile; and the right hand, instead of resting across the thigh with fingers relaxed, is made to grasp the band to which the garland of fruit is attached. The effect of these changes is to increase the resemblance of the figure to the Sistine *ignudo* from which the pose derives.[64] In the heavy strokes about the head the drawing gives a hint of the shaggy hair worn by the youth in the fresco.

THE ATLANTES

Another series of drawings is made up of studies for the stone-colored atlantes of the frieze. These, it will be remembered, are of two kinds: full-length figures of entirely human form, and atlas herms (or termini). It was for these figures, as Bellori informs us,[65] that Annibale made three-dimensional models. An early attempt to visualize both kinds of atlantes *in situ* may be seen in the Windsor drawing No. 48 (Fig. 154); several of the atlas herms at the left side of the sheet appear to have arms broken off near the shoulder.

A drawing in Besançon (No. 106; Fig. 221) of the lower part of a standing male figure can be seen to be a study for the atlas who appears immediately to the right of *Jupiter and Juno* (Fig. 43). Since this is evidently not a fragment but a detailed study

---

[64] *Viz.*, the figure on the left above Ezekiel.   [65] Bellori, *Vite*, p. 47.

(as its height of nearly sixteen inches would also indicate), there must have existed another drawing for the upper part of the figure.

As an example of a full-length figure study of this sort we may cite the fine drawing of a standing male nude in the Louvre (No. 107; Fig. 219), which is a study for the atlas at the left of *Diana and Endymion* (Fig. 44). The fresco follows the drawing very closely, except that the left leg is bent a little more sharply at the knee.

Several preparatory drawings can be connected with the atlas standing at the left of *Venus and Anchises* (Fig. 46), whose extended left arm is twisted round the garland.[66] An early idea for this motive can be seen on the sheet of studies at Windsor (No. 48; Fig. 154), which contains, among other drawings, four sketches for an atlas. In the two figures at the upper right Annibale has already found the position of the head and arms which will be used, in reverse, for the atlas beside *Venus and Anchises*. Two studies, both in Besançon, illustrate the final development of the pose. In the first (No. 108; Fig. 220), which is unusual in that it is drawn in chalk on paper prepared with an olive-green wash, we are given a view of the entire figure. The straight lines at the right mark the frame of the picture of *Venus and Anchises*. The second study, which shows only part of the figure, was drawn by Annibale on a sheet which he had already used for another drawing (No. 115 recto; Fig. 229); the sheet must be inverted in order to see the figure in question. Despite its confusing appearance, this is no preliminary idea, but a careful study which represents almost as much of the figure as is visible in the fresco itself: only the feet and the back of the youth are missing. This suggests that the drawing is actually later than the more formal full-length design (Fig. 220), and that it may have been made as a supplementary study when work on the fresco was already under way, with the specific object of clarifying the upper part of the figure. The musculature of the arms and the arrangement of the drapery about the head are in fact more clearly rendered here than in the first study; and the way in which the left arm and hand are entwined about the garland is also more plainly indicated.

In designing the atlantes Annibale's imagination was surely stimulated by the powerful muscularity of the Farnese *Hercules* which stood in the palace courtyard. Twice he used sheets of studies for the atlantes to make a sketch of the Hercules statue as seen from the back (No. 115 verso; Fig. 230, and No. 116; Fig. 228). It was perhaps from these sketches that he developed the idea for the atlas at the right of *Hercules and Iole* (Fig. 45); the figure is viewed from the same angle and the attitude is in several respects similar.

Turning now to the studies for the atlas herms, we may start with one of the most distinctive—the bearded figure at the left of *Europa and the Bull* (Fig. 53), whose right arm has been broken off near the shoulder. A drawing in Turin (No. 109; Fig. 222) of a man with both hands placed on his head is perhaps an early idea for this

[66] The pose may be traced back to the bronze boys of the Magnani frieze, for whom there is a drawing by Annibale at Windsor (Witt- kower, *Carracci Drawings*, p. 131, cat. 275 v., fig. 24).

figure, not as yet transformed into a herm. But this is admittedly uncertain, and the drawing may have been intended for another atlas altogether.[67] We are on surer ground with the drawing of an atlas herm in Windsor (No. 110 verso; Fig. 224, right side), which is almost certainly a design for the figure in question. This finds confirmation in the direction of the lighting and in the shape of the pillar where it joins the torso. The indication of a break below the elbow of the left arm proves that Annibale has already begun to think of the *rottura*. At the left side of the sheet there is a fragmentary study for the same figure, over which Annibale later drew a St. John Baptist. A still later stage in the evolution of the terminus is to be seen in an elegant study in Turin (No. 111; Fig. 223). Both arms are now elevated, as in the preliminary drawing cited above (No. 109; Fig. 222). At the lower left is a variant sketch of the head in three-quarter view. It is to be noted that Annibale has seemingly given up for the moment the idea of the *rottura*, already hinted at in the previous study. In executing the figure in fresco the artist made a few further changes, thickening the proportions and turning the head to the left, though not as much as in the alternative sketch on No. 111.

For the terminal figure at the right of *Salmacis and Hermaphroditus* (Fig. 52) there exists a preliminary drawing from the model (No. 112; Fig. 226). The process of transformation from a human figure into a herm is already perceptible in the heavy lines drawn along the thighs. Except for the fact that the head is turned downward and to the side, the attitude is identical to that in the fresco.[68] A drawing in Windsor (No. 113; Fig. 227) corresponds exactly to the finished figure. The head assumes a fully frontal position and the musculature of the torso and arms is rendered in an almost schematic manner. The drawing is accepted as authentic—though with some reservation—by the editor of the Carracci drawings at Windsor; yet there is perhaps some doubt whether this is really an original study by Annibale. It is not only that the figure resembles the fresco in every particular (this is not in itself a suspicious circumstance), but also that the draughtsmanship, even for a final study, is dry and lacking in spontaneousness. The possibility that this is a pupil's copy after the fresco (made on the back of a drawing by Annibale himself)[69] ought not to be excluded. It may be, on the other hand, that the drawing has merely been reworked.

In the Uffizi (No. 114; Fig. 225) is a study from the model for the herm with club and lion-skin at the left of *Cupid and Pan* (Fig. 48). It is drawn in black chalk, lightly touched with white, on paper prepared with a gray-green wash, and shows only the upper part of the figure. The atlas in the fresco adopts the same pose, but is noticeably more robust in physique.

It remains to consider the drawings for the paired atlantes who stand with arms

---

[67] Mahon (*Disegni*, p. 126) relates it tentatively to the herm at the left of *Pan and Syrinx* (cf. Fig. 51). But the asymmetrical placing of the arms and the fact that the lighting is from the left do not support this hypothesis.

[68] This pose is foreshadowed in the atlas stationed near the corner of the vault in the Louvre drawing No. 50 (Fig. 155).

[69] For the verso, which is surely by Annibale, see Wittkower, *Carracci Drawings*, p. 144, no. 344, fig. 44.

interlocked at the corners of the vault. In the early stages of the planning (cf. No. 44 recto; Fig. 148) Annibale thought of these figures as independent herms. It was only later that he conceived the idea of joining each pair at the corners in a kind of embrace, as a means of effecting the transition from one wall to the next; the first hint of this solution appears in No. 50 (Fig. 155). Needless to say, since the two figures do not stand in the same plane, the preparatory drawings presented special problems of visualization. There are examples for each of the four groups; these include studies both of paired atlantes and of single figures. Analysis of the drawings makes it clear that Annibale began with the atlantes at the southern extremity, that is, with the figures standing to the right and left of *Polyphemus and Galatea*. Here the artist was not wholly at ease in his attempt to combine the figures satisfactorily.

For the herms at the left of *Polyphemus and Galatea* (Fig. 40) there are two drawings, one for each herm. In Besançon is an admirable study for the right-hand figure (No. 115 recto; Fig. 229). The model, a young man with prominent ears, stands with the left arm extended, holding in his right hand the cloth that covers his loins. The effect of foreshortening is very pronounced. The only noticeable change in the fresco is that there the face is that of an older man with a disapproving frown. When this drawing had served its purpose Annibale turned the sheet upside down to make a study for another atlas, a fact which tends to confirm our belief that the principal drawing is an early one.

The study for the companion figure on the left is in the Louvre (No. 116; Fig. 228). The pose is exactly duplicated in the fresco, the sole difference being that the angle of the left leg is shifted. (It is a peculiarity of both the drawing and the fresco that the legs are not fused into a flat, pillar-like surface, but are, so to speak, merely shaved down to approximate the outline of a herm.) The drawing also makes provision for the arm of the right-hand atlas. Here however Annibale made a miscalculation which was to have its effect on the fresco: he assumed, that is, that the arm of the neighboring atlas would cross this figure at the level of the shoulder. But in the actual execution the point of intersection proved to be considerably lower, with the result that the arms of the two atlantes do not meet as they were intended to do (cf. Fig. 40). Instead of starting afresh Annibale decided to let his original designs stand. This explains the odd piece of drapery that is wrapped around the arm of the right-hand figure in the fresco, the purpose of which is simply to mask the discrepancy; without this veil there would be a disturbing gap between the two arms.[70] A second drawing on the Louvre sheet, hardly decipherable, is a sketch of the Farnese Hercules from the rear, very much like that which appears on the reverse of the preceding drawing (No. 115 verso; Fig. 230).

A drawing in Turin (No. 117; Fig. 231) is easily identifiable as a study for the

[70] Carlo Cesio, in his engraving of this detail, has sought to rationalize it by representing the left-hand atlas as grasping the drapery with his fingers, instead of merely resting his open hand upon it. Cf. *Argomento della Galeria Farnese . . . intagliata da Carlo Cesio*, Rome, 1657, pl. XVI, 2.

two atlantes at the right of *Polyphemus and Galatea* (Fig. 41). Here it is interesting to see that Annibale, being as yet unsure of the distance separating the pair, has indicated alternative positions for the hands. In the fresco, where the heads and shoulders are not as far apart, the arms are bent more than in the drawing. A drawing in Windsor (No. 118 verso; Fig. 232) may be tentatively regarded as a study for the hand of the atlas at the right which rests on his companion's shoulder; it is to be noted however that the lighting is from above rather than from below.

Whatever difficulties may have been encountered in the foregoing figures seem to have been successfully overcome in the drawings for the atlantes at the north end of the Gallery. There is in Windsor (No. 118 recto; Fig. 233) a study for the upper part of the embracing pair to the left of *Polyphemus and Acis* (Fig. 42). Although it corresponds closely enough with the fresco this is not a final design: there is, for example, some uncertainty regarding the placing of the right hand belonging to the man on the left. (The position of this hand does not seem to have been satisfactorily solved even in the fresco, though this may be due in part to clumsy restoration.) A red chalk drawing of a man's head and shoulders (Gabinetto Nazionale delle Stampe, Fondo Corsini, Inv. 126846) has been described as a later study for the atlas at the right.[71] The attitude is admittedly similar, but it is curious that in so finished a drawing the source of light should be at the upper left; in addition the soulful expression on the face is surely too strong even for Annibale's animated termini. The connection of the drawing with the Farnese ceiling cannot, in my opinion, be substantiated.

Separate drawings were made for the two atlas herms at the right of *Polyphemus and Acis* (Fig. 39). The study for the bearded figure on the left is in Besançon (No. 119; Fig. 234); to judge from the protruding ears the model may be the same as the one seen in an earlier study (No. 115; Fig. 229). The faint horizontal lines behind the head denote the entablature supported by the figure. The hand resting on the right shoulder is to be understood as belonging to the companion figure; it is less prominent in the fresco, where the tips of the fingers alone are visible.

A superb drawing in the Louvre (No. 120; Fig. 235) is a study for the right-hand atlas of this group. Oddly enough, it is drawn in red chalk, although its pendant (Fig. 234) is in the customary black chalk. The frescoed figure differs little from the preparatory study, which likewise has an indication of the entablature behind the head. In addition, the drawing includes part of the arm of the companion atlas, of which there is also a faint sketch at the bottom of the sheet.

THE SATYRS

The four satyrs who impudently sit on the corners of the large framed pictures at either end of the Gallery are, as we have seen, a relatively late enrichment of the structural system, since the first indication of their presence occurs in drawing No. 50 (Fig. 155), which belongs to an advanced stage in the planning of the ceiling.

[71] Mahon, *Disegni*, pp. 129 f., no. 183. See also note 58.

As elements of the decorative scheme they are plainly related to the satyr-figures in the grisaille sections of the Camerino ceiling (Figs. 5-8); it is likely, moreover, that the attitude used for all these goat-legged figures, each of whom sits with one leg drawn up, was suggested to Annibale by the pose of the satyr-god in the antique marble group of *Pan and Olympus* in the Farnese collection. In the drawing just cited (No. 50, Fig. 155) the satyr is seated on the frame of the picture corresponding to *Polyphemus and Acis*. In the Gallery itself, however, his attitude is most closely matched by the satyr at the opposite end of the room, i.e. the figure sitting on the upper right corner of *Polyphemus and Galatea* (Fig. 67).

A study from the life for this figure is in the Louvre (No. 121; Fig. 237); it agrees very closely with the fresco. The artist's attention has been chiefly concentrated on the torso and right arm, the goat legs and details of ornament being only hinted at. Also in the Louvre (No. 122; Fig. 236) is the definitive study for his mate, the satyr perched on the left corner of the frame.

Studies have also been preserved for the corresponding figures at the opposite end of the Gallery (Fig. 68), whose attitudes are more animated than those of the first pair. In the Louvre (No. 123; Fig. 239) is a drawing for the satyr at the right side. Annibale has tried different positions for the left hand. The egg-and-dart molding of the picture frame is described in unusual detail (cf. also No. 50; Fig. 155). For the satyr sitting on the left corner there is a study in the Boymans Museum (No. 124; Fig. 238). Although this is a final drawing, as comparison with the fresco makes clear, the handling is noticeably freer and less finished than in the other studies of this group.

It is obvious, as one inspects these four drawings, that the two first described, i.e. the studies for the satyrs above *Polyphemus and Galatea* (Figs. 236-237), are the earlier pair. The figures are in profile, the poses simple, and the areas of light and shade carefully defined. In the second pair, by contrast (Figs. 238-239), the postures are more active and the draughtsmanship more summary. Here, then, we find additional support for our conclusion that the decorative figures at the south end of the vault preceded those at the north. The definitive figure studies were not all made at once, but were drawn up as work on the frescoes progressed.

THE CUPIDS

Although they are not strictly speaking decorative figures, but (in Bellori's words) the "foundation of the entire work,"[72] it is nevertheless convenient to mention here the preparatory drawings for the four pairs of cupids in the corners of the vault. Despite their significance in the iconography of the cycle, these cupids do not appear to have had a place in the early projects for the ceiling. Even the drawing No. 50 (Fig. 155), which registers so many of the definitive features of the decorative system, makes no provision for them, but shows, instead, that each corner was to be occupied by putti holding a shield with a Farnese emblem.

[72] *Argomento della Galeria Farnese* (reprinted in Malvasia, *Felsina*, I, p. 437).

The decision to place the twin loves in the angles of the vault was only arrived at, it seems, after some experimentation. A transitional stage may be discovered in a spirited red chalk drawing in the Metropolitan Museum of Art (No. 125; Fig. 240), which, rather surprisingly, represents two cupids carrying between them a third who holds up a palm branch as if in triumph. The next step was to reduce the three cupids to two. In making this change Annibale may have been guided both by the fact that the aperture was simply too narrow to admit more than two figures and by the need to give more emphasis to the contrast between Heavenly and Earthly Love.

It is interesting to see that this preliminary idea was made to serve as the basis for the composition of the *Fight for the Palm* (Fig. 39), in which the palm branch likewise serves as the crowning feature, and for which there is a fine chalk study in the Louvre (No. 126; Fig. 242). Comparison with the preceding sketch (Fig. 240) reveals that, except for some unavoidable shifting of the arms and heads, Annibale has not fundamentally altered the positions of the two standing figures. In the final execution in fresco a few changes were made: the legs of the cupids are further apart than in the Louvre drawing, and the upper parts of their bodies are brought correspondingly closer together, so that the boy at the left now grasps his opponent's arm. Adjustments of this sort were of course necessitated by the intractable structure of the vault at the corners.

In the Ellesmere collection (No. 127; Fig. 241) is a charming sketch in pen and ink for the *Struggle under the Wreath* (Fig. 40). The oval frame and ornamental ribbon which impart such an eighteenth-century flavor to the drawing were probably added by Mariette, who frequently adorned the mounts of his drawings in this manner. Though unfinished, the sketch represents the struggling putti in attitudes almost identical to those in the fresco: the leg of the right-hand cupid is plainly intended to be hooked round his opponent's thigh, and the horizontal strokes at his ankle mark the edge of the balustrade. We may imagine this study as being followed by a final drawing in chalk.

Two studies, both in chalk, are known for the *Fight for the Torch* (Fig. 41). A drawing in Besançon shows both figures (No. 128; Fig. 244); it also includes both the balustrade and the aperture within which the group is placed (cf. also No. 126; Fig. 242). In this lively study, with its numerous *pentimenti*, Annibale is still searching for the final attitudes. A drawing at Windsor (No. 129; Fig. 245) is a study for the cupid with his back to us. The arms have here been fixed in the definitive position. But in the placing of the head and wings the preceding drawing is closer to the final version.

Two drawings have also been identified for the *Union of Sacred and Profane Love* (Fig. 42), which, as Wittkower has shown,[73] depends on the illustration of Eros and Anteros in Cartari's *Imagini* (Fig. 279). There is at Windsor a study in chalk for the cupid at the left (No. 130; Fig. 246). The influence of Cartari's illustration is even

---

[73] *Carracci Drawings*, p. 139.

plainer here than in the fresco, where the position of the arms has been altered. (The faint sketch of a male figure at the right seems to have no relation to the Farnese Gallery.) This was followed by a study in the Louvre (No. 131 verso; Fig. 247) representing both putti in the final pose. In transferring the group to the vault Annibale found it necessary to widen the space between the cupids, with the result that in the fresco their legs do not overlap. In nearly every instance we have found it to be true that the preparatory drawings do not adequately convey the distances separating adjacent figures at the corners of the vault.

THE PUTTI OVER THE MEDALLIONS

For the numerous putti who are grouped in pairs above the medallions of the frieze only one drawing has been preserved. This is the study at Windsor (No. 132; Fig. 243) for the right-hand boy above the roundel of *Cupid and Pan* (Fig. 48); it has the further distinction of being drawn in red chalk. In the final conception the figure was considerably enlarged so as to fill more of the available space. The extended right hand, which in the drawing points toward the ox-skull, is made in the fresco to pass behind it, and the gesture of pointing is accordingly transferred to the left hand.[74]

V. DRAWINGS FOR THE FRESCOES ON THE WALLS

It is not by chance that of the nineteen drawings that have been identified for the frescoes on the walls of the Gallery more than half (twelve, to be exact) are in the Royal Library in Windsor Castle. The bulk of the Carracci drawings in Windsor came from Domenichino's collection: hence the fact that so many of the later drawings for the Gallery are concentrated there tends to confirm the hypothesis that Domenichino was given increased responsibility during the final stages of the decoration. This is not meant to imply that he was the author of the drawings in question, but only that he was in a position, as Annibale's henchman, to acquire a number of them for himself. It was not until the very end of the work, when the master was virtually incapacitated, that Domenichino took it upon himself to make designs for the Virtues at the ends of the long walls.

[74] Almost every drawing cabinet has its share of copies after the decorative figures of the vault, the work of generations of students seeking to emulate Annibale's mastery of the human form. I list here some characteristic examples; many more could be added.

1. Louvre Inv. 7588. Copy in sanguine after the *ignudo* on the left of *Jupiter and Juno*.
2. Schaffhausen, Collection H. E. Bühler. Pencil drawing by Géricault after the *ignudo* on the left of *Apollo and Marsyas*. *Sammlung H. E. Bühler, Géricault 1791-1824,* *Gemälde, Aquarelle, Zeichnungen,* Winterthur, 1956, pl. 46.
3. Warsaw, Museum. Codex Bonola, pp. 46-47. Copies in sanguine by Luigi Scaramuccia after decorative figures of the frieze. M. Mrozinska, *I disegni del Codice Bonola del Museo di Varsavia,* Venice, 1959, pp. 93 f.
4. Windsor Cat. 503, 504 and 505. Copies in chalk after decorative figures of the frieze. Wittkower, *Carracci Drawings,* p. 162.

Tietze, who was convinced that the Perseus frescoes were the work of Domenichino, argued that the preparatory drawings for these subjects must also be by that artist, although there is nothing in their style to warrant such a conclusion.[75] His view has not found general acceptance. Pope-Hennessy has rejected the attribution of these drawings to Domenichino; and Annibale's authorship has recently been reaffirmed by Wittkower and Mahon.[76] It is true of course that the Perseus drawings form a group that is stylistically distinct from those made for the vault. The chalk studies for *Perseus and Phineus* possess little of the vivacity, the brilliance, and the rhythmic fluency of the best designs for the ceiling, as may be seen by comparing a drawing for one of the *ignudi* (No. 104; Fig. 217) with that of Phineus (No. 136; Fig. 249). It is evident that a considerable space of time must have elapsed between the execution of these two works. The dryness of the latter drawing is in fact characteristic of Annibale's late Roman manner; in addition there is perceptible here a momentary slackening of power, due in all probability to the artist's fatigue and nervous exhaustion in the period following the completion of the vault.

DRAWINGS FOR THE COMBAT OF PERSEUS AND PHINEUS (FIG. 78)

The first drawing to make provision for the large frescoes on the end walls is the Chatsworth sketch (No. 51; Fig. 156), which of course contains no hint of the subject matter. A surprisingly large and varied group of drawings survives for the *Combat of Perseus and Phineus*. With one exception, all are in Windsor Castle.

One of the most interesting of these is a composition study in chalk, unfortunately much rubbed (No. 133; Fig. 248). Though it is obviously a preliminary draft, it contains all the principal features of the scene. At the left side is Phineus, kneeling and in the grip of a soldier. Next are three men hiding their faces. Behind Perseus and looking over his shoulder is another of his companions (eliminated in the final version). Perseus himself is of lithe and slender physique, in contrast to the heavy-set hero in the fresco. An overturned table occupies the left foreground, and a vessel may be seen lying on the floor between Perseus' legs. Opposite the hero is the petrified form of Thescelus, here shown with his left arm held before his face and his right arm drawn back to hurl the spear; in the fresco he carries a shield and raises the spear above his head. The dramatic confrontation of Perseus and Thescelus is weakened in this early draft by the insertion of a third figure who gazes at the miraculous transformation with a gesture of astonishment. Behind Thescelus a man (probably Eryx) rushes forward with a spear, and at the extreme right there can be dis-

---

[75] Tietze, pp. 149-153.

[76] Pope-Hennessy, *Domenichino Drawings*, p. 14, note 33; Wittkower, *Carracci Drawings*, pp. 137 f., nos. 294-301; Mahon, *Disegni*, pp. 139 ff.

cerned a soldier brandishing a sword and carrying a shield, very much as in the painting; a fallen warrior is faintly visible on the floor.

Annibale's efforts to clarify and give greater force to the composition can be followed through a number of individual figure studies. We may conveniently begin with the rapid pen drawing in Windsor (No. 134; Fig. 251), which is a study for Thescelus. The pose, unlike that in the preliminary composition sketch, is very close to the final version, in that Thescelus defends himself with a shield while preparing to throw the javelin. The head was originally drawn in an upright position, but has been moved backward so as to impart more energy to the figure. The spear is a later addition by another hand: it is done in a darker ink than the rest (a few strokes of the same dark shade are visible on the left shoulder and on the buttocks) and part of it extends over the patch at the top right corner.

This sketch was followed by the fine chalk study for Thescelus in Besançon (No. 135; Fig. 252). It is a drawing from the life, in which attention has been concentrated on the musculature and on the modeling in light and shade; there is hardly any indication of the body armor and the fluttering drapery is only summarily sketched. The left arm with the shield is raised almost horizontally, as if to balance the extended right arm; but in the final conception the shield will be lowered to a position corresponding more closely to that in the pen sketch (Fig. 251).[77]

Wittkower has with good reason suggested that a drawing at Windsor (No. 89 recto; Fig. 253), representing a man with one arm raised and a look of grief or fear on his face, may be an early study for this fresco.[78] It is set down on the back of a study for a Nereid in the fresco of *Polyphemus and Galatea* (Fig. 200). Although there is nothing corresponding to this attitude in the painting, it is to be noted that Annibale's preliminary sketch for the composition (No. 133; Fig. 248) contains an idea for such a figure in the horror-stricken soldier to the left of Thescelus. But the connection of the drawing with this scene is still uncertain.

The remaining drawings for the *Combat of Perseus and Phineus* are all in Windsor. One of the most important is a study from the life for the kneeling Phineus, who is hardened into stone even while he begs for mercy (No. 136; Fig. 249). Though admittedly lacking the *brio* of many of the Farnese drawings this is unquestionably by the hand of Annibale himself. The drawing includes an alternative position for the left leg, which is in fact somewhat closer to that adopted in the fresco.

Also in the Royal Library is a full-length study in chalk for Perseus (No. 137; Fig. 250). In posing for the drawing the nude model wore neither helmet nor mantle, but Carracci has lightly indicated the sword, the Gorgon's head and the winged sandals. The attitude is virtually the definitive one; yet the figure conveys little of

---

[77] It might be argued that No. 135 is the earlier drawing, and that the pen sketch No. 134 was made afterward with the express purpose of correcting the position of the arm with the shield. But the uncertainty regarding the placing of the head in the latter drawing plainly identifies it as a preliminary draft.

[78] Wittkower, *Carracci Drawings*, p. 138, no. 300.

the dramatic power of Perseus in the fresco, where the head is pressed forward, the arms are more tensed, and the whole body is more robust and muscular.

No drawing is known for the soldier who seizes Phineus by the hair, but there are in Windsor two preparatory studies for the companions of Perseus hiding their faces in their hands. The first is a spirited drawing (No. 138; Fig. 254) for the two men at the left of this group; they are shown in three-quarter length, in attitudes that are not exactly similar to those in the fresco, where Annibale was obliged for reasons of space to compress the figures into a closer grouping. The other drawing (No. 139; Fig. 255) is a study for the man farthest right of the three covering their eyes; the pose is virtually unchanged in the painting.

DRAWINGS FOR PERSEUS AND ANDROMEDA (FIG. 77)

Only two drawings have been identified for this subject; both are studies in pen and ink for the principal figure, and both exhibit the characteristics of Annibale's late pen style about 1604. The first is in Windsor Castle (No. 140; Fig. 256). It represents Andromeda in an attitude substantially like that in the painting, the chief differences being in the position of the head and arms. It is nevertheless a preliminary study. For Annibale has not yet taken into consideration the fact that for the fresco the source of light will be on the right; here the light is represented as coming in the usual way from the left.

The second study for Andromeda, a little pen drawing in the Louvre (No. 141; Fig. 257), is even closer to the definitive posture in its adherence to the picture plane and its suppression of depth. The figure now exhibits the dramatic gestures and agonized expression seen in the fresco; the similarities are most remarkable in the turn of the head and the opened hands. In addition the light is visualized as coming from the right. The lower part of the leg is concealed by a heavily drawn clump of foliage, which is perhaps intended to obliterate an error. The drawing was undoubtedly followed by a more elaborate chalk study from the life. But this, like the several other drawings that must have been made for the fresco, no longer exists. Their loss is the more regrettable because they might have thrown some light on the authorship of the remainder of the composition. It would be interesting to know, for example, whether Cepheus and Cassiopea were painted from studies made by Annibale himself or whether the preliminary designs for these figures were by another hand.

DRAWINGS FOR THE LITTLE MYTHOLOGICAL SCENES

Annibale drew up no finished studies for the eight little mythological subjects on the side walls. Before his illness, however, he had produced a series of sketches in pen and ink, and when, in about 1607, it became obvious that the master would never resume work on the Gallery, these sketches were given to his pupils, who for their part made only minor changes in executing the designs in fresco. Most of the extant sketches belonged in the seventeenth century to Everhard Jabach, who had engravings made after them;[79] these drawings are now in the Louvre.

The largest and most finished drawing of the series is a preliminary study for *Mercury and Apollo* (Fig. 95), in which Mercury is pictured handing the lyre to Apollo while still in flight (No. 142; Fig. 261).[80] In the end, however, this scheme was rejected, perhaps because it seemed to resemble the fresco of *Mercury and Paris* (Fig. 66). Annibale's second idea for the subject appears on a drawing in Windsor (No. 143; Fig. 262), which though rendered more hastily is nevertheless much nearer the painting: Mercury now stands before Apollo, and the scene is closed by a temple at the left and a cluster of trees at the right. It was this drawing that was used by the executant of the fresco (who as we have suggested above may have been Antonio Carracci). The drawing itself, we may surmise, remained in Domenichino's hands, passing in due course to the Royal Library at Windsor.

Here we must also take notice of a drawing in the Louvre (Inv. 8005; Fig. 271), which agrees so exactly with the Windsor study as to make it evident that "one of the two is either a deliberate fake or a faithful copy commissioned by an old collector."[81] Though it is true that in most instances of this sort the Louvre drawings prove to be the originals, Wittkower is surely right in concluding that the Windsor sketch is the genuine one. Despite the effort of a remarkably skillful copyist to reproduce every line of the original, careful scrutiny of the Louvre sheet discloses certain mannerisms that are inconsistent with Annibale's vigorous and "unbeautiful" penmanship. It may suffice to point to such passages as the wings of Mercury's helmet and the left shoulder of Apollo, both of which are drawn in conventional little curving strokes; in the Windsor drawing, on the other hand, the treatment of these details is entirely characteristic of Annibale's brusque manner. The copyist also felt obliged, unconsciously perhaps, to correct the rendering of the pediment of the temple, the raking cornice of which, in the Windsor sketch, is shown as overlapping the horizontal cornice. It should be added, finally, that Louvre 8005 does not have the same provenance as most of the other drawings of this series: it was not part of the Jabach collection, but belonged in the seventeenth century to the Duke Alfonso IV d'Este, whose mark is seen in the top left corner.[82] It is, in short, an old copy.

Whereas the scene of *Mercury and Apollo* is the only one on the inner wall for which drawings have been preserved, there remains a complete set of four sketches for the frescoes on the window wall. The responsibility for executing these subjects, it will be remembered, was assigned to the Parmesan painters Lanfranco and Badalocchio. This may explain why the drawings did not enter Domenichino's collection

---

[79] *Recueil de 283 Estampes . . . d'après les Desseins des Grands Maîtres, que possedoit autrefois M. Jabach, et qui depuis ont passé au Cabinet du Roy*, Paris, 1754.

[80] Engraved in the reverse sense by Michel Corneille the Younger for the Jabach series

(*Recueil de 283 Estampes*, no. 7D).

[81] Wittkower, *Carracci Drawings*, p. 140.

[82] F. Lugt, *Les marques de collections de dessins et d'estampes*, Amsterdam, 1921, no. 106.

(from which they would in all probability have passed eventually to Windsor Castle), but found their way into the Jabach cabinet, and thence into the Louvre.

The study for *Arion and the Dolphin* (No. 144; Fig. 263)[83] is the most interesting of the series, because no other drawing differs to such a degree from the final result in fresco (cf. Fig. 96). Not only are the posture and dress of the musician different, but he carries a viol instead of a lyre; the ship is fitted with a sail, and the building and trees in the background indicate that Arion is at no very great distance from dry land. Across the upper part of the sheet is a faint correction in pale brown chalk (hardly visible in our reproduction), marking a higher horizon and a distant mountain. Lanfranco made a corresponding revision in the fresco itself, where the mountain and the uppermost strip of water have patently been painted over the original sky.

For *Minerva and Prometheus* (Fig. 97) there is also a pen and ink drawing (No. 145; Fig. 264).[84] The Titan (inscribed "prometeo") is nude except for a cloak that is worn loosely over his shoulder and fastened at the left side; the right arm of the statue is extended as if in a gesture of speech. In Badalocchio's fresco Prometheus is bearded and wears a knee-length tunic, and the statue assumes a more passive and composed attitude.

The fresco of *Hercules and the Dragon of the Hesperides* (Fig. 98) differs only slightly from Annibale's preparatory design (No. 146; Fig. 265).[85] The form of the dragon has been somewhat modified, and we are shown less of Jupiter as he looks down from the sky.

Equally close to the final execution is the study for *Prometheus freed by Hercules* (No. 147; Fig. 266).[86] The foreshortened posture of Prometheus in the fresco (Fig. 99) is virtually identical to that in the drawing, except that the right arm is bent at the elbow. There are a few other minor alterations: Hercules' club and the golden apples have been shifted to new positions, and the quiver of arrows lies on the ground at the right instead of being slung from the hero's shoulder.

Another drawing in the Louvre may be considered here (No. 148; Fig. 267). It shows Jupiter, holding a thunderbolt and followed by the eagle, in pursuit of a nymph. The fleeing girl has eluded his grasp, but Jupiter has apparently seized a fold of her drapery. At her feet appears a crayfish. The subject is difficult to identify. Perhaps it represents Jupiter pursuing Io, before the god decided to conceal himself within a cloud. I am unable to account for the crayfish. Whatever the subject, the drawing has all the marks of a preparatory study for the cycle of little mythological scenes: it is similar in size, in technique and in iconography to the examples described above,

[83] Engraved in reverse by M. Corneille (*Recueil*, no. 7C), who also made a free copy after the original (J. Guiffrey and P. Marcel, *Inventaire général des dessins du Musée du Louvre . . . , Ecole française*, III, p. 84, no. 2353). Louvre 7580 is a copy in sanguine.

[84] Engraved in reverse by M. Corneille (*Recueil*, no. 7F). See also Corneille's free copy

in pen and wash and an anonymous copy in sanguine, both in the Louvre (Guiffrey and Marcel, *op.cit.*, III, p. 88, nos. 2390 and 2391).

[85] Engraved in reverse by Corneille (*Recueil*, no. 7A).

[86] Engraved in reverse by Corneille (*ibid.*, no. 7B).

and like them was owned by Jabach, who had it engraved by Charles Massé.[87] It may be classified as a discarded project for the cycle.

DRAWINGS FOR THE FOUR VIRTUES (FIGS. 73-76)

Tietze's wholesale attribution to Domenichino of almost all the frescoes on the walls of the Gallery may cause us to look with distrust on his conclusion that the ovals with personifications of the Virtues are likewise the work of that artist.[88] No one would be tempted, admittedly, to credit their execution to Annibale; but it might seem reasonable to suppose that he at least prepared the designs, as he did for the little mythological subjects. From certain drawings at Windsor, however, it may be inferred that the responsibility for these figures was largely Domenichino's.

Two of the drawings are pen sketches by Annibale. The first (No. 149; Fig. 258) is a quick preliminary study. It represents a female figure seated on a block, facing to the right and holding a scroll in her hands (a motive which tends to confirm the derivation of the Virtues from the Sistine Prophets and Sibyls). The attitude, with the left leg slightly elevated and the left arm extended, is to some degree echoed in *Fortitude* (Fig. 73); but since the drawing does not correspond exactly to any of the four Virtues, it must have been meant chiefly to fix the pose of one of the figures in profile on the inner wall of the Gallery.

The second pen drawing at Windsor, likewise by Annibale (No. 150; Fig. 259), is an elaboration of the attitude set out in the preceding sketch. The woman, who is identifiable as Justice, rests her arm on a pedestal and holds the balance in her left hand and the fasces in her right. Oddly enough, however, the drawing was not used for *Justice* (Fig. 75), who has a frontal position, but for *Fortitude* (Fig. 73). Except for the changed attributes (the fasces being replaced by the column and the balance by the lion) the frescoed personification faithfully reproduces the main features of the drawing: *Fortitude* wears a turban, her breasts are uncovered, and the mantle which is folded over her shoulder also serves to cushion the right elbow where it rests on the pedestal. The extended left arm has been slightly lowered in order to caress the head of the lion. Faintly visible in the lower right corner is a drawing on the verso of the sheet (which has been stuck down). It represents the upper part, without the head, of a female figure seen frontally, with one arm held out as if supporting a scroll. This might be an alternative sketch for one of the Virtues; the arrangement of the draperies, falling in folds upon the breast, recalls in particular the figure of *Justice* (Fig. 75).

I know of no other study by Annibale for the four Virtues. In all probability he entrusted to an assistant the task of elaborating the remaining figures from these preliminary sketches. There is reason to believe, furthermore, that that assistant was Domenichino.

---

[87] *Ibid.*, no. 8D. The connection of Annibale's drawing with the Farnese Gallery has also been noted by Bacou, *Dessins*, p. 49, no. 88. There are copies in the Louvre (Inv. 7561) and in the Ecole des Beaux-Arts, Paris (Inv. Ancien fonds 95).

[88] Tietze, p. 153.

A third drawing at Windsor, also representing *Justice* (No. 151; Fig. 260), is described by Wittkower as a copy after the fresco, executed "by a pupil, and in a manner close to Domenichino's."[89] I am inclined to believe, on the contrary, that this is not a copy, but an original study by Domenichino himself for the figure in question. The draughtsmanship, in the first place, is entirely typical of Domenichino's early manner, as may be seen by comparing the work with his drawings for the Grottaferrata frescoes.[90] In the second place the drawing is not sufficiently close to the painting to be considered a copy. It is significant, for example, that the left knee is not drawn in foreshortening as in the fresco, but is turned in profile very much as in Carracci's preliminary sketches (Figs. 258-259). The drapery, moreover, does not at all suggest the ample fullness of that in the frescoed oval, but falls in simpler and more angular folds. Such discrepancies militate against this being the work of an imitator. Indeed an instructive comparison may be made with another drawing at Windsor (Cat. 506), which is unquestionably a copy by a pupil after the *Charity*.[91] Here the rather mechanical system of hatching lines and the painstaking imitation of drapery folds betray the hand of the copyist. The *Justice*, on the other hand, despite certain weaknesses, can be better understood as a preliminary study by Domenichino, a study in which the attitude of the figure and the disposition of the drapery have still to be settled. In all probability Domenichino also made comparable studies for the other three Virtues.

No trace remains of Annibale's cartoon for the *Virgin with the Unicorn* from which Domenichino painted the fresco over the door (Fig. 89). This was a drawing that Domenichino might have been expected to save: perhaps it was ruined in the process of transferring the design to the wall.

[89] Wittkower, *Carracci Drawings*, p. 162, no. 502. It is true that there is a copy on the verso after a figure on the vault. But this is by another hand.

[90] See particularly the drawing of St. Bartholomew, Windsor Cat. 116 (Pope-Hennessy, *Domenichino Drawings*, pl. 10).

[91] Wittkower, *Carracci Drawings*, p. 162, no. 506. It is not, however, "a free version," but an exact copy of the painting. See the reproduction in J. R. Martin, "Disegni del Domenichino," *Bollettino d'Arte*, XLIV, 1959, fig. 10. Tietze (p. 153) believed the drawing to be a study by Domenichino for the fresco.

CATALOGUE OF DRAWINGS

HERE are listed all the authentic drawings known to me for the Camerino and the Galleria Farnese. Except where otherwise stated, the drawings are considered to be the work of Annibale Carracci himself. Although I have made a careful search of the principal collections of Carracci drawings in English and European print rooms, I do not pretend to have unearthed all the surviving preparatory studies for these two cycles. On the contrary, I am quite certain that others will come to light, in public as well as in private collections.* ·

The following bibliographical abbreviations are used in the catalogue, in addition to those encountered throughout the text.

BERTINI, *Cat. Disegni*: A. Bertini, *I Disegni italiani della Biblioteca Reale di Torino*, Rome, 1958.

BERTINI, "Disegni inediti": A. Bertini, "Disegni inediti di Annibale Carracci nella Biblioteca Reale di Torino," *Commentari*, II, 1951, pp. 40-42.

BODMER, "Camerino": H. Bodmer, "Die Fresken des Annibale Carracci im Camerino des Palazzo Farnese in Rom," *Pantheon*, XIX, 1937, pp. 146-149.

BODMER, *O.M.D.*: H. Bodmer, "Drawings by the Carracci: an Aesthetic Analysis," *Old Master Drawings*, VIII, 1933-34, pp. 51-66.

CALVESI: M. Calvesi, "Note ai Carracci," *Commentari*, VII, 1956, pp. 263-276.

HOLLAND: R. Holland (ed.), *The Carracci, Drawings and Paintings*, Newcastle upon Tyne, 1961 (exhibition catalogue).

INV. A.: "Inventory A," a manuscript copy, made in 1816-17, of the original 18th-century inventory of the drawings in the Royal Library at Windsor Castle.

LUGT: F. Lugt, *Les marques de collections de dessins et d'estampes*, Amsterdam, 1921, *Supplément*, The Hague, 1956.

MARTIN: J. R. Martin, "Immagini della Virtù: the Paintings of the Camerino Farnese," *Art Bulletin*, XXXVIII, 1956, pp. 91-112.

MOREL D' ARLEUX: Manuscript inventory of drawings in the Cabinet des Dessins of the Louvre by Morel d' Arleux, Conservateur des Dessins from 1797 to 1827.

REISET: F. Reiset, *Notice des dessins, cartons, pastels, miniatures et émaux exposés dans les salles du premier et du deuxième étages au Musée Impérial du Louvre. Première partie: Ecoles d' Italie . . . ,* Paris, 1866.

STIX-SPITZMÜLLER: A. Stix and A. Spitzmüller, *Beschreibender Katalog der Handzeichnungen in der staatlichen graphischen Sammlung Albertina, Die Schulen von Ferrara, Bologna . . . ,* Vienna, 1941.

TOMORY: P. A. Tomory, *The Ellesmere Collection of Old Master Drawings*, Leicester, 1954.

* Cf. W. Vitzthum, "Two Drawings by Annibale Carracci in Madrid and a Comment on the Farnese Gallery," *Master Drawings*, II, no. 1, 1964.

1. OXFORD, ASHMOLEAN MUSEUM

Studies for the Camerino Farnese. Pen and gray ink, some gray wash; red and black chalk. 219 x 267 mm. Recto inscribed: *Annibale Caracci* in ink; the numbers *6* and *54* in ink; and *A 22903F* in pencil. The drawing was purchased in 1958.
Recto (Fig. 100):
     (a) Pen sketches of Hercules supporting the globe;
     (b) Red chalk study of ornamental border of ceiling compartment;
     (c) Drawing in gray wash of a mask *di sotto in su*;
     (d) Ink sketches of three profile heads, one in caricature style.
Verso (Fig. 101):
     (a) Black chalk composition sketch of *Choice of Hercules*;
     (b) Ink sketch of Hercules bearing the globe;
     (c) Red chalk design of ceiling showing compartments.
Lit.: Holland, no. 125, pl. xxx; Bacou, *Dessins*, p. 34, under no. 45.

2. WINDSOR CASTLE, ROYAL LIBRARY,
    INV. 2065, CAT. 280
    Fig. 102

Design for the decorative framework of the ceiling. Black chalk, some pen, heightened with white, on gray-green paper. 232 x 363 mm.
Lit.: Inv. A., p. 76; Bodmer, "Camerino," pp. 146 f.; Wittkower, *Carracci Drawings*, p. 133, no. 280, pl. 60; Martin, pp. 93, 103, fig. 29; Mahon, *Disegni*, p. 106, no. 144, pl. 70; Bacou, *Dessins*, p. 37, under no. 53.

3. PARIS, LOUVRE, INV. 7367
    Fig. 105

Faun. Black chalk heightened with white on gray-blue paper. Lower left corner repaired. 268/270 x 231/234 mm. Fragmentary inscription in ink: *10* (?) (from the Angeloni collection). Marks of the Louvre (Lugt 1899 and 2207).
Study from the model for one of the fauns in grisaille on the ceiling of the Camerino.
Lit.: Morel d' Arleux, IV, p. 118, no. 5101; Bacou, *Dessins*, p. 42, no. 63.

4. WINDSOR CASTLE, ROYAL LIBRARY,
    INV. 2024, CAT. 282
    Fig. 107

Cartoon of a putto with a cornucopia. Black chalk heightened with white on brown paper. Two sheets joined together; the right side damaged and repaired. 526 x 395 mm. With No. 5, this formed part of a larger cartoon for the grisaille decoration of the ceiling.

Lit.: Inv. A., p. 75; Wittkower, *Carracci Drawings*, p. 133, no. 282, pl. 59; Martin, p. 93; Mahon, *Disegni*, pp. 107 f., no. 146; Bacou, *Dessins*, p. 37, under no. 53.

5. WINDSOR CASTLE, ROYAL LIBRARY,
   INV. 2025, CAT. 281
   Fig. 108

Cartoon of a siren and a putto with a cornucopia. Black chalk heightened with white on brown paper. Three pieces of paper joined together; much damaged, and cut along the top. 523 x 384 mm.
With No. 4, this formed part of a larger cartoon for the grisaille decoration of the ceiling.
Lit.: Inv. A., p. 75; Wittkower, *Carracci Drawings*, p. 133, no. 281, pl. 58; Martin, p. 93; Mahon, *Disegni*, p. 107, no. 145; Holland, no. 126; Bacou, *Dessins*, p. 37, under no. 53.

6. PARIS, LOUVRE, INV. 7306
   Fig. 104

Allegorical female figure leaning on a column. Black chalk heightened with white on faded gray-blue paper. 479/483 x 273 mm. Marks of the Louvre (Lugt 1899 and 2207).
Study for the figure of *Securitas*.
Lit.: Morel d' Arleux, IV, p. 110, no. 5046; Mahon, *Disegni*, p. 106, under no. 144; Bacou, *Dessins*, p. 37, no. 53.

7. PARIS, LOUVRE, INV. 7210
   Fig. 106

Sheet of studies. Pen. 231 x 377/379 mm. Mark of the Louvre (Lugt 2207).
(a) At the left and center, three trees and a landscape sketch;
(b) In the upper center, perspective diagrams, including a church with a horseman and various persons on foot;
(c) At the right, Hercules seated, with one arm raised;
(d) At the upper right, three grasshoppers near a rock;
(e) In the lower right, perspective construction.
The figure of Hercules is a study for the *Death of Hercules*.
Lit.: Morel d' Arleux, IV, p. 107, no. 5029; Bacou, *Dessins*, p. 37, no. 54, pl. XIII; W. Vitzthum, in *Burlington Magazine*, CIV, 1962, p. 76, fig. 24.

8. BESANÇON, MUSÉE DES BEAUX-ARTS, INV. D. 1496
   Fig. 110

Woman standing and pointing upward. Black chalk heightened with white on gray paper; the book in the lower right corner drawn in red chalk. Badly stained. 263 x

158/160 mm. Marks of Jean Gigoux (Lugt 1164) and the Museum of Besançon (Lugt 238c) with the number *D. 1496* in ink.

Probably an early study for the figure of Virtue in the *Choice of Hercules*.

Lit.: Mahon, *Disegni*, p. 99, no. 130; Bacou, *Dessins*, p. 33, under no. 43.

9. PARIS, LOUVRE, INV. R.F. 609
Fig. 111

Study of Hercules and Vice, accompanied by Cupid. Pen and wash. Cut along the left side. 165 x 135/148 mm. Inscribed in ink: *h. 108* (mark of Lord Somers; Lugt 2981); mark of A. C. H. His de la Salle (Lugt 1333).

Study for the *Choice of Hercules*.

Lit.: Mahon, *Disegni*, p. 99, under no. 129; Bacou, *Dessins*, p. 33, no. 43.

10. DIJON, MUSÉE DES BEAUX-ARTS, INV. 783
Fig. 112

Study of Vice, accompanied by Cupid. Red chalk and light wash; a few touches of pen. 176 x 138 mm. Inscribed in ink: *h. 106* (mark of Lord Somers; Lugt 2981); mark of A. C. H. His de la Salle (Lugt 1333).

Study for the *Choice of Hercules*. On the verso, several figure sketches in pen and black chalk, seemingly unrelated to the Camerino.

Lit.: *Catalogue historique et descriptif du Musée de Dijon*, Dijon, 1883, p. 229, no. 783.

11. PARIS, LOUVRE, INV. 7368
Fig. 109

Poet. Black chalk heightened with white on gray-blue paper. 259/260 x 321/325 mm. Inscribed in ink: *13* (from the Angeloni collection). Marks of the Louvre (Lugt 1899 and 2207).

Study for the poet in the *Choice of Hercules*.

Lit.: Morel d' Arleux, IV, p. 118, no. 5102; Mahon, *Disegni*, pp. 98 f., no. 129; Bacou, *Dessins*, p. 34, no. 44.

12. PARIS, LOUVRE, INV. 7205
Fig. 115

Study for Hercules bearing the globe. Black chalk heightened with white on gray-blue paper. 268/270 x 412 mm. Inscribed in ink: *2* (from the Angeloni collection). Marks of the Louvre (Lugt 1899 and 2207).

Lit.: Morel d' Arleux, IV, p. 108, no. 5034; Tietze, p. 67, fig. 9; Bodmer, "Camerino," p. 147; Bertini, "Disegni inediti," p. 40; Mahon, *Disegni*, p. 100, under no. 131; Calvesi, p. 271, pl. LXXII, 12; Bacou, *Dessins*, p. 34, no. 45, pl. XII.

13. TURIN, BIBLIOTECA REALE, INV. 16074, CAT. 93
Fig. 114

Hercules with the globe. Black chalk heightened with white on gray-blue paper. 207 x 312/313 mm. Mark of the Biblioteca Reale of Turin (Lugt 2724).
Lit.: Bertini, "Disegni inediti," p. 40, pl. x, fig. 39; Mahon, *Disegni*, p. 100, no. 132; Bertini, *Cat. Disegni*, p. 22, no. 93; Bacou, *Dessins*, p. 34, under no. 45.

14. PARIS, LOUVRE, INV. 7206
    Fig. 116

Hercules with the globe. Black chalk heightened with white on gray-blue paper. 382 x 247 mm. Inscribed in ink: *6* (from the Angeloni collection). Marks of the Louvre (Lugt 1899 and 2207).
Lit.: Morel d' Arleux, iv, p. 119, no. 5109; Tietze, p. 68; Bodmer, *O.M.D.*, p. 63, pl. 57; Bodmer, "Camerino," p. 147; Mahon, *Disegni*, pp. 100 f., no. 133, pl. 63; Bacou, *Dessins*, p. 34, no. 46.

15. BESANÇON, MUSÉE DES BEAUX-ARTS, INV. D. 1539
    Fig. 117

Study for the legs of Hercules with the globe. Black chalk heightened with white on gray-blue paper. 258 x 150/165 mm. Inscribed in ink: *12* (from the Angeloni collection). Marks of Jean Gigoux (Lugt 1164) and the Museum of Besançon (Lugt 238c) with the number *D. 1539* in ink.
Lit.: Mahon, *Disegni*, p. 101, no. 134; Bacou, *Dessins*, p. 34, under no. 46.

16. PARIS, LOUVRE, INV. 7328
    Fig. 120

Seated male figure with outstretched arm. Black chalk heightened with white on gray-blue paper. 262 x 327 mm. Inscribed in ink: *18* (from the Angeloni collection). Marks of the Louvre (Lugt 1899 and 2207).
Perhaps an early study for Euclid in the fresco of *Hercules bearing the globe.*
Lit.: Morel d' Arleux, iv, p. 119, no. 5103; Reiset, pp. 55 f., no. 169; Mahon, *Disegni*, p. 105, under no. 142; Bacou, *Dessins*, p. 37, under no. 52.

17. PARIS, LOUVRE, INV. 7327
    Fig. 118

Astronomer. Black chalk heightened with white on gray-blue paper. 341 x 231/232 mm. Inscribed in ink: *23* (from the Angeloni collection). Marks of the Louvre (Lugt 1899 and 2207).
Study from the model for Ptolemy in the fresco of *Hercules bearing the globe.*
Lit.: Morel d' Arleux, iv, p. 119, no. 5108; Tietze, p. 68; Bodmer, "Camerino," p. 147; Mahon, *Disegni*, pp. 101 f., no. 135, pl. 64; Bacou, *Dessins*, p. 35, no. 47, pl. xiv.

18. PARIS, LOUVRE, INV. 7331
    Fig. 119

Studies of an astronomer. Black chalk heightened with white on yellowish-gray paper. 360/364 x 460/463 mm. Inscribed in ink: *12* (from the Angeloni collection). Marks of the Louvre (Lugt 1899 and 2207).

Studies for the figure of Euclid in *Hercules bearing the globe.*

Lit.: Morel d' Arleux, IV, p. 118, no. 5099; Reiset, p. 56, no. 172; Tietze, p. 68; Bodmer, "Camerino," p. 147; Wittkower, *Carracci Drawings*, p. 149, under no. 365; Mahon, *Disegni*, p. 100, under no. 131; Bacou, *Dessins*, p. 35, under no. 47.

19. PARIS, LOUVRE, INV. 7404
Fig. 121

Study for the leg of Hercules. Black chalk heightened with white on gray-blue paper. The upper part of the sheet cut and repaired. 185/187 x 311 mm. Inscribed in ink: *51* (52 crossed out) (from the Angeloni collection). Marks of the Louvre (Lugt 1899 and 2207).

Study from the life for the left leg of Hercules in the fresco of *Hercules resting.*

Lit.: Morel d' Arleux, IV, p. 126, no. 5163.

20. PARIS, LOUVRE, INV. 7211
Fig. 122

Study for Ulysses and Circe. Pen and gray-black ink. Cut and repaired at the top, the right side, and lower left corner. 154 x 161 mm. Marks of the Louvre (Lugt 1899 and 2207).

Lit.: Morel d' Arleux, IV, p. 115, no. 5082; Tietze, p. 69, fig. 11; Wittkower, *Carracci Drawings*, p. 133, under no. 283; Mahon, *Disegni*, p. 102, under no. 136; Bacou, *Dessins*, p. 35, under no. 49.

21. PARIS, LOUVRE, INV. 7203

Studies for the Camerino. Black chalk heightened with white on gray-blue paper. 375 x 525 mm. Inscribed in ink: *3* (from the Angeloni collection). Marks of the Louvre (Lugt 1899 and 2207).

Recto (Fig. 123): Composition study for *Ulysses and Circe.*

Verso (Fig. 128):
    (a) Study for the oarsmen in *Ulysses and the Sirens*;
    (b) Design of the compartments of the ceiling;
    (c) Study for the head of the father in the *Catanian Brothers.*

Lit.: Morel d' Arleux, IV, p. 108, no. 5035; Reiset, p. 52, no. 155; Tietze, p. 69; Wittkower, *Carracci Drawings*, p. 133, under no. 283; Mahon, *Disegni*, p. 102, under no. 136; Bacou, *Dessins*, p. 35, under no. 49.

22. PARIS, LOUVRE, INV. 7201
Fig. 124

Study for Ulysses and Circe. Black chalk heightened with white on light brown paper. 385 x 565 mm. Inscribed in ink: *23* (from the Angeloni collection). Marks of the Louvre (Lugt 1899 and 2207).
Lit.: Morel d' Arleux, IV, p. 89, no. 4898; Reiset, pp. 52 f., no. 156; Tietze, pp. 69 f., fig. 12 (cited in error as Inv. 7200); Wittkower, *Carracci Drawings*, p. 133, under no. 283; Mahon, *Disegni*, p. 102, under no. 136; Bacou, *Dessins*, pp. 35 f., no. 49.

23. WINDSOR CASTLE, ROYAL LIBRARY, INV. 2066, CAT. 283
Fig. 125

Circe. Black chalk heightened with white on gray-blue paper. 250 x 300 mm.
Final study from the model for Circe in the fresco of *Ulysses and Circe.*
Lit.: Inv. A., p. 76; Tietze, p. 69; Wittkower, *Carracci Drawings*, p. 133, no. 283, pl. 57; Mahon, *Disegni*, p. 102, no. 136, pl. 65; Holland, no. 127; Bacou, *Dessins*, p. 36, under no. 49.

24. BESANÇON, MUSÉE DES BEAUX-ARTS, INV. D. 1494
Fig. 126

Mercury. Black chalk heightened with white on gray-blue paper. 402/405 x 225/229 mm. Inscribed in ink: *15* (from the Angeloni collection). Mark of the Museum of Besançon (Lugt 238c) with the number *D. 1494* in ink. On the mount, in Mariette's handwriting: *figure de Mercure du tableau d' Ulisse devant Circé.*
Study for the figure of Mercury in the fresco of *Ulysses and Circe.*
Lit.: Mahon, *Disegni*, pp. 102 f., no. 137.

25. PARIS, LOUVRE, INV. 7337
Fig. 127

One of Ulysses' companions. Black chalk heightened with white on gray-blue paper. 276/277 x 480/482 mm. Marks of the Louvre (Lugt 1899 and 2207).
Study from the model for the companion of Ulysses in the right foreground of *Ulysses and Circe.*
Lit.: Morel d' Arleux, IV, p. 108, no. 5036; Tietze, pp. 69, 71, fig. 13; Wittkower, *Carracci Drawings*, p. 133, under no. 284; Mahon, *Disegni*, p. 103, no. 138; Bacou, *Dessins*, p. 36, no. 50.

26. PARIS, LOUVRE, INV. 7324
Fig. 129

Two oarsmen. Black chalk heightened with white on gray-blue paper. 246 x 382 mm. Marks of the Louvre (Lugt 1899 and 2207).
Study for the two rowers in the bow of the ship in *Ulysses and the Sirens.*

Lit.: Morel d' Arleux, IV, p. 109, no. 5042; Reiset, p. 55, no. 166; Tietze, p. 68; Bodmer, "Camerino," p. 147; A. E. Popham, in *Old Master Drawings*, XIV, 1939, p. 7; Wittkower, *Carracci Drawings*, p. 134, under no. 285; Mahon, *Disegni*, p. 104, no. 140, pl. 67; Bacou, *Dessins*, p. 35, no. 48.

27. PARIS, LOUVRE, INV. 7334
    Fig. 130

Helmsman. Black chalk heightened with white on gray-blue paper. 239 x 183 mm. Inscribed in ink: 5 (from the Angeloni collection). Mark of the Louvre (Lugt 1899). Study for the helmsman in *Ulysses and the Sirens*.
Lit.: Morel d' Arleux, IV, p. 109, no. 5042; Tietze, p. 68; Bodmer, "Camerino," p. 147; Popham, *op.cit.*, pp. 7 f., pl. 7; Wittkower, *Carracci Drawings*, p. 134, under no. 285; Mahon, *Disegni*, p. 104, under no. 140; Bacou, *Dessins*, p. 35, under no. 48.

28. LONDON, BRITISH MUSEUM, PAYNE KNIGHT O. O. 3-6
    Fig. 131

Cartoon of a helmsman. Black chalk on gray paper. Three sheets joined together and repaired. 443 x 459 mm. Mark of Lord Spencer (Lugt 1531).
Part of the cartoon for the fresco of *Ulysses and the Sirens*.
Lot.: Popham, *op.cit.*, pp. 7 f., pl. 6; Wittkower, *Carracci Drawings*, p. 134, under no. 285; Mahon, *Disegni*, p. 104, under no. 140; Bacou, *Dessins*, p. 35, under no. 48.

29. WINDSOR CASTLE, ROYAL LIBRARY,
    INV. 2026, CAT. 285
    Fig. 132

Three Sirens. Black chalk heightened with white on gray-green paper. 300 x 259 mm. Study for the Sirens in the fresco of *Ulysses and the Sirens*.
Lit.: Inv. A., p. 75; Tietze, p. 68; Bodmer, "Camerino," p. 147; Popham, *op.cit.*, p. 7; Wittkower, *Carracci Drawings*, pp. 133 f., no. 285, pl. 61; Martin, p. 100; Mahon, *Disegni*, pp. 103 f., no. 139, pl. 66; Bacou, *Dessins*, p. 35, under no. 48.

30. NEW YORK, METROPOLITAN MUSEUM OF ART,
    ACC. NO. 62.204.3

Studies for the Camerino. Pen and wash. Lunette, filled out to make a rectangle. 128 x 245 mm.
Recto (Fig. 133): Composition study for *Perseus and Medusa*.
Verso (Fig. 103): Sketches for the grisaille ornament of the ceiling.
Lit.: R. Bacou, "Two unpublished Drawings by Annibale Carracci for the Palazzo Farnese," *Master Drawings*, II, 1964, pp. 40 ff.

31. PARIS, LOUVRE, INV. 7371
    Fig. 134

Medusa. Black chalk heightened with white on gray-blue paper. 259 x 398/399 mm. Marks of the Louvre (Lugt 1899 and 2207).
Study for Medusa in the lunette of *Perseus and Medusa.*
Lit.: Morel d'Arleux, IV, p. 119, no. 5105; Mahon, *Disegni,* p. 106, no. 143; Bacou, *Dessins,* p. 36, no. 51.

32. PARIS, LOUVRE, INV. 7179
    Fig. 136

Head of Mercury. Black chalk heightened with white on gray-blue paper. Cut and repaired along the left and bottom. 214 x 200/201 mm. Marks of the Louvre (Lugt 1899 and 2207).
Study for the head of Mercury in the fresco of *Perseus and Medusa.*
Lit.: Morel d'Arleux, IV, p. 118, no. 5096; Mahon, *Disegni,* p. 103, under no. 137; Bacou, *Dessins,* p. 36, under nos. 49 and 51; *idem,* "Two unpublished Drawings," pp. 40 ff.

33. PARIS, LOUVRE, INV. 7405
    Fig. 135

Legs of Mercury. Black chalk heightened with white on gray-blue paper. 288/290 x 194 mm. Inscribed in ink: *50* (from the Angeloni collection). Marks of the Louvre (Lugt 1899 and 2207).
Study for the legs of Mercury in *Perseus and Medusa.*
Lit.: Morel d'Arleux, IV, p. 126, no. 5163; Bacou, p. 48, no. 84.

34. WINDSOR CASTLE, ROYAL LIBRARY,
    INV. 1850, CAT. 286
    Fig. 137

Amphinomus carrying his father. Pen, red chalk and red wash. Upper right corner torn and repaired. 151 x 155 mm.
An early study for the *Catanian Brothers.*
Lit.: Inv. A., p. 74; Tietze, p. 70; Bodmer, "Camerino," p. 148; Wittkower, *Carracci Drawings,* p. 134, no. 286, fig. 28; Martin, p. 102; Mahon, *Disegni,* p. 105, under no. 142; Bacou, *Dessins,* p. 37, under no. 52.

35. MONTPELLIER, MUSÉE ATGER, NO. 116
    Fig. 139

Amphinomus carrying his father. Black chalk heightened with white on gray (originally gray-blue?) paper. Squared in black chalk. 314/315 x 130/133 mm. Inscribed *Tintoretto,* and the number *20* in ink. Mark of the Musée Atger (Lugt 38).
Study for the central group in the *Catanian Brothers.*

Lit.: Notice des dessins . . . réunis à la Bibliothèque de la Faculté de Médecine à Montpellier, Montpellier, 1830, p. 50, no. 116; Mahon, *Disegni,* p. 105, no. 142, pl. 69; Bacou, *Dessins,* p. 37, under no. 52.

36. TURIN, BIBLIOTECA REALE, INV. 16073, CAT. 92

Studies for the Camerino. Black chalk heightened with white on gray-blue paper (recto); red chalk (verso). The upper left corner torn and repaired. 219 x 250 mm. Mark of the Biblioteca Reale of Turin (Lugt 2724).
Recto (Fig. 140): Study for *Amphinomus carrying his father.*
Verso (Fig. 113): Composition sketch of *Hercules bearing the globe.*
Lit.: Bertini, "Disegni inediti," pp. 40 f., pl. x, fig. 41; Mahon, *Disegni,* pp. 99 f., no. 131; Bertini, *Cat. Disegni,* p. 22, no. 92; Bacou, *Dessins,* p. 34, under no. 45.

37. PARIS, LOUVRE, INV. 7406
    Fig. 141

Study for the legs of Amphinomus' father. Black chalk heightened with white on gray-blue paper. 268 x 205 mm. Inscribed in ink: *28* (from the Angeloni collection). Marks of the Louvre (Lugt 1899 and 2207).
Study for the legs of the father in the *Catanian Brothers.*
Lit.: Morel d' Arleux, IV, p. 118, no. 5096.

38. PARIS, LOUVRE, INV. 7326
    Fig. 143

Anapius. Black chalk heightened with white on gray-blue paper. 399 x 186 mm. Fragmentary inscription in ink: *25 (?)* (from the Angeloni collection?). Marks of the Louvre (Lugt 1899 and 2207).
Study from the model for the *Catanian Brothers.*
Lit.: Morel d' Arleux, IV, p. 119, no. 5107; Reiset, p. 55, no. 168; Mahon, *Disegni,* p. 104, no. 141, pl. 68; Bacou, *Dessins,* pp. 36 f., no. 52.

39. PARIS, LOUVRE, INV. 7312
    Fig. 142

Study for the mother carried by Anapius. Black chalk heightened with white on gray-blue paper. 184/186 x 270 mm. Inscribed in ink: *2* (from the Angeloni collection). Marks of the Louvre (Lugt 1899 and 2207).
Lit.: Morel d' Arleux, IV, p. 119, no. 5105; Mahon, *Disegni,* p. 104, under no. 141; Bacou, *Dessins,* p. 37, under no. 52.

40. PARIS, LOUVRE, INV. 7204
    Fig. 138

Bellerophon and the Chimera. Black chalk heightened with white on gray-blue paper. 295 x 532 mm. Marks of the Louvre (Lugt 1899 and 2207).

Probably a rejected study for one of the lunettes in the Camerino.

Lit.: Morel d' Arleux, IV, p. 108, no. 5033; Bodmer, "Camerino," p. 147; Martin, p. 103, fig. 28; Mahon, *Disegni*, p. 105, under no. 142; Bacou, *Dessins*, pp. 37 f., no. 55.

DRAWINGS FOR THE FARNESE GALLERY

41. PARIS, LOUVRE, INV. 7419
    Fig. 144

Sketch for a decorative frieze. Pen and wash. 146 x 202 mm. Inscribed in ink: *66* (crossed out) and *65* (from the Angeloni collection). Marks of the Louvre (Lugt 1899 and 2207).

Perhaps an early idea for the frieze of the Farnese ceiling.

Lit.: Morel d' Arleux, IV, p. 116, no. 5087; Tietze, pp. 96 f., fig. 29; Bacou, *Dessins*, p. 39, under no. 56.

42. PARIS, ECOLE DES BEAUX-ARTS, INV. FONDS
    MASSON 2287

Studies for a decorative frieze. Pen and wash (recto); pen (verso). 270 x 242 mm. Verso inscribed in ink: *An: Carrazio. 2.3.* Marks of Sir Peter Lely (Lugt 2092), Lord Spencer (Lugt 1531), William Esdaile (Lugt 2617), J. Masson (Lugt 1494a), and the Ecole des Beaux-Arts (Lugt 829).

Recto (Fig. 146): Two bound slaves seated before a niche containing a statue of Hercules.

Verso (Fig. 147):
    (a) A fragmentary antique statue in a niche;
    (b) a seated male nude figure holding a globe;
    (c) various architectural details.

Possibly early studies for the decoration of the Gallery.

Lit.: Bacou, *Dessins*, p. 39, under no. 56; *idem*, "Two unpublished Drawings," *Master Drawings*, II, 1964, pp. 40 ff.

43. PARIS, LOUVRE, INV. 7418
    Fig. 145

Study for the decoration of a ceiling. Pen and wash over black chalk, with some touches of white, on gray-blue paper. Upper right corner torn away. 278 x 352 mm.

Perhaps an early study for the end of the Farnese ceiling.

Lit.: Morel d' Arleux, IV, p. 117, no. 5091; Tietze, pp. 97 f.; G. Rouchès, *Catalogue des dessins italiens du XVIIe siècle exposés au Château de Maisons-Lafitte, puis au Musée du Louvre, de mai à novembre 1927*, Paris, 1927, pp. 14 f., no. 6; Bacou, *Dessins*, p. 39, under no. 56.

44. PARIS, LOUVRE, INV. 7422

Studies for the Farnese ceiling. Pen, and gray and brown wash; a few touches of red chalk. 212/218 x 235/239 mm. Inscribed in ink: *46* (from the Angeloni collection). Marks of the Louvre (Lugt 1899 and 2207).
Recto (Fig. 148):
    (a) Study for the corner of the vault;
    (b) Design for a balustrade at the corner;
    (c) Various pen sketches showing the ceiling with its compartments, and the
        frieze in relation to the wall pilasters.
Verso (Fig. 149): Pen studies of a putto and various architectural details.
Lit.: Morel d' Arleux, IV, p. 117, no. 5093; Tietze, p. 100, fig. 31 (recto); G. Rouchès, *La peinture bolonaise à la fin du XVIe siècle, les Carrache*, Paris, 1913, p. 166; Wittkower, *Carracci Drawings*, pp. 135 f., under nos. 289-292 (cited as Inv. 7420); Mahon, *Disegni*, p. 111, under no. 147; Bacou, *Dessins*, p. 139, under no. 56 (cited as Inv. 6422).

45. PARIS, LOUVRE, INV. 7420

Studies for the Farnese ceiling. Pen and wash. 161/164 x 255 mm. Inscribed in ink: *45* (from the Angeloni collection). Marks of the Louvre (Lugt 1899 and 2207).
Recto (Fig. 150):
    (a) Study for the corner of the vault;
    (b) Pen sketches of the decorative framework of the ceiling.
Verso (stuck down): Studies of architectural details.
Lit.: Morel d' Arleux, IV, p. 117, no. 5091; Bacou, *Dessins*, p. 39, under no. 56.

46. PARIS, LOUVRE, INV. 8048
    Fig. 151

Design for the Farnese ceiling. Pen and wash; the sketch in the upper left corner in pen and gray ink. 241 x 286 mm. Marks of the Louvre (Lugt 1899 and 2207).
Lit.: Morel d' Arleux, II, no. 1640 (as Giovanni da Udine); Tietze, pp. 100 f., fig. 32; Rouchès, *La peinture bolonaise*, pp. 167 f.; Wittkower, *Carracci Drawings*, pp. 134 f., under nos. 287-289; Mahon, *Disegni*, p. 111, under no. 147; Bacou, *Dessins*, pp. 38 f., no. 56.

47. WINDSOR CASTLE, ROYAL LIBRARY,
    INV. 2155, CAT. 287
    Fig. 152

Design for the middle section of the frieze. Pen. Lower left corner torn. 168 x 223 mm. Inscribed in ink: *Al molto . . . , Al molto Ill.*
Lit.: Inv. A., p. 76; Tietze, pp. 103, 108, fig. 34; Wittkower, *Carracci Drawings*, pp. 134 f., no. 287, fig. 29; Mahon, *Disegni*, p. 111, under no. 147; Holland, no. 129, pl. XXXII.

48. WINDSOR CASTLE, ROYAL LIBRARY,
    INV. 2131, CAT. 293
    Fig. 154

Studies for the frieze. Black chalk, partly drawn over in pen. 282 x 343 mm. Inscribed in ink along the thigh of the central herm: *Innocencio fe.*

(a) Across the middle of the sheet, a small-scale design for a section of the frieze.

(b) Along the top, a larger study for a square panel flanked by an atlas-herm and a full-length caryatid; at the right, two further studies for the latter figure.

(c) In the center, a large study for a herm in relation to the garland with the mask.

(d) Various sketches not related to the Gallery. On the lower part of the sheet: two geometrical constructions; a figure carrying a large basket; a study for the midwife with the infant Mary in the Louvre *Nativity of the Virgin*. In the upper right corner, part of a man's face in profile.

Lit.: Inv. A., p. 76; Tietze, pp. 103 f., fig. 35; Wittkower, *Carracci Drawings*, pp. 136 f., no. 293, fig. 32; Mahon, *Disegni*, pp. 111 f., no. 148; D. Mahon, in *Gazette des Beaux-Arts*, XLIX, 1957, p. 285, note 68; Holland, no. 131; Bacou, *Dessins*, p. 39, under no. 56.

49. PARIS, LOUVRE, INV. 7421
    Fig. 153

Study for a decorative frame, and a child's head. Pen; black chalk. The chalk drawing of the child's head is on a separate piece of paper joined to the larger sheet. 97 x 127 mm. Inscribed in ink: *6; Coregio;* and *A. Correge.* Marks of the Louvre (Lugt 1866 and 2207).

An early pen study for the frame of the octagonal panels of the ceiling.

50. PARIS, LOUVRE, INV. 7416

Studies for the Farnese ceiling. Pen and red chalk. 386/388 x 263/267 mm. Inscribed in ink: *88; Francesco, annn,* and *alli.* Verso inscribed in ink: *89* (from the Angeloni collection). Marks of the Louvre (Lugt 1899 and 2207).

Recto (Fig. 155):

(a) Study for the north end of the Gallery with three ideas for the *Rape of Ganymede*;

(b) Near the center, a red chalk sketch of a sphinx;

(c) At the top and bottom of the sheet, red chalk sketches of the frieze and compartments of the ceiling;

(d) Various pen sketches of architectural details.

Verso:

(a) Pen drawing of a river landscape with houses and a bridge;

(b) Fragment of an architectural decoration.

Lit.: Morel d' Arleux, iv, p. 117, no. 5090; Tietze, pp. 104 f., pl. iv; H. Weizsäcker, *Adam Elsheimer der Maler von Frankfurt*, Berlin, 1936, 1 Teil, Tafelband, pl. 147, fig. 167; Wittkower, *Carracci Drawings*, p. 137, under no. 294; Mahon, *Disegni*, pp. 109 ff., no. 147; Bacou, *Dessins*, pp. 39 f., no. 57, pl. xvi.

51. CHATSWORTH, DEVONSHIRE COLLECTION, NO. 436
Fig. 156

Woman seated in a richly ornamented room. Pen, with a few touches of black chalk. 220 x 170 mm. Marks of Sir Peter Lely (Lugt 2092) and P. H. Lankrink (Lugt 2090). Perhaps an early idea for the treatment of the end walls of the Gallery.
Lit.: Holland, no. 81, pl. xxi; M. Jaffé, in *Burlington Magazine*, civ, 1962, pp. 29 f., fig. 34.

52. PARIS, LOUVRE, INV. 7137

Sheet of studies. Red chalk, and pen and black ink over a black chalk sketch (recto); pen and black ink (verso). 194 x 184/186 mm. Recto inscribed in ink: *29*; verso inscribed: *30* (from the Angeloni collection). Marks of the Louvre (Lugt 1899 and 2207).
Recto:
    (a) Red chalk sketch of an arm and part of a reclining figure;
    (b) Sketch in pen and black chalk of two women kneeling over an infant in a bed, perhaps a study for a *Finding of Moses*.
Verso (Fig. 157):
    (a) Pen sketches for a coat of arms, probably studies for one of the stucco cartouches in the Farnese Gallery;
    (b) A man's leg.

The drawings are by Agostino.
Lit.: Morel d' Arleux, iv, p. 115, no. 5081 (as Annibale).

53. PARIS, LOUVRE, INV. 7185

Bacchic procession; study for Aurora and Cephalus. Pen (recto); pen and red chalk (verso). 190 x 253 mm. Recto inscribed in ink: *53; Al molto mag.ᶜᵒ Francesco* . . . (illegible). Verso inscribed: *55* (from the Angeloni collection). Marks of the Louvre (Lugt 1899 and 2207).
Recto (Fig. 158):
    (a) Study for the head of the Bacchic procession;
    (b) A foot; a man's head and shoulders seen from the back; an animal's head.
Verso (Fig. 188):
    (a) Study for Aurora in the fresco of *Aurora and Cephalus*;
    (b) A man's legs;
    (c) Studies for the stucco cartouches in the corners of the Gallery.

The drawings on the recto are by Annibale; those on the verso are by Agostino.
Lit.: Morel d' Arleux, IV, p. 117, no. 5092; Tietze, pp. 112, 124, fig. 40 (recto); Mahon, *Disegni*, p. 113, under no. 149; Bacou, *Dessins*, p. 40, no. 58.

54. VIENNA, ALBERTINA, INV. 23370, CAT. B. 105
     Fig. 159

Bacchic procession. Pen and wash heightened with white over black chalk on paper prepared with a yellowish wash. 328 x 427 mm.
Probably the first idea for the *Triumph of Bacchus and Ariadne*.
Lit.: Charles Rogers, *A Collection of Prints in Imitation of Drawings*, London, 1778 (Ryland's aquatint of 1765 after the original drawing); Tietze, pp. 109 f., fig. 38 (reproduces Ryland's aquatint); A. Stix, in *Belvedere*, IX, 1930, pp. 180 f., pl. 121; Stix-Spitzmüller, p. 14, no. 105; Mahon, *Disegni*, pp. 112 f., no. 149, pl. 71; Calvesi, p. 272, fig. 18; Bacou, *Dessins*, p. 40, under no. 58.

55. PARIS, LOUVRE, INV. 7183
     Fig. 160

Bacchus in his chariot. Gray wash over black chalk, partly retraced in pen and ink. All four corners cut and repaired. 275 x 264/265 mm. Marks of Sir Peter Lely (Lugt 2092), P. J. Mariette (Lugt 1852), and of the Louvre (Lugt 1899 and 2207). Mariette's mount has a cartouche inscribed *An. Carracci*.
Lit.: Morel d' Arleux, IV, p. 108, no. 5037; Tietze, p. 111, fig. 39; Mahon, *Disegni*, p. 113, under no. 149; Bacou, *Dessins*, pp. 40 f., no. 59, pl. XVII.

56. VIENNA, ALBERTINA, INV. 2144, CAT. B. 106
     Fig. 161

Triumph of Bacchus and Ariadne. Pen and gray wash. 204 x 259 mm. Marks of P. J. Mariette (Lugt 2097) and of the Albertina (Lugt 174).
Lit.: A. Bartsch, *Catalogue raisonné des desseins originaux . . . du Cabinet de feu le Prince Charles de Ligne*, Vienna, 1794, p. 92, no. 5; F. Wickhoff, "Die italienischen Handzeichnungen der Albertina, I," *Jahrbuch der kunsthistorischen Sammlungen des Allerhöchsten Kaiserhauses*, XII, 1891, p. CCXCII, Sc.B. 190; Tietze, p. 117, pl. V; Stix-Spitzmüller, p. 14, no. 106; Mahon, *Disegni*, pp. 113 f., no. 150, pl. 72; Bacou, *Dessins*, p. 41, under no. 59.

57. VIENNA, ALBERTINA, INV. 2148, CAT. B. 108
     Fig. 162

Studies for the Triumph of Bacchus and Ariadne. Pen and gray wash over black chalk. 120 x 146 mm. Marks of P. J. Mariette (Lugt 2097) and of the Albertina (Lugt 174).
    (a) Study for Bacchus in his chariot;

(b) Study for the boy restraining the goats;

(c) Study for a male figure, perhaps Silenus.

Lit.: Wickhoff, *op.cit.*, p. CCXCII, Sc.B. 194; Tietze, p. 117, fig. 42; Stix-Spitzmüller, p. 14, no. 108; Mahon, *Disegni*, p. 114, under no. 150; Bacou, *Dessins*, p. 41, under no. 59.

58. VIENNA, ALBERTINA, INV. 2145, CAT. B. 107
      Fig. 163

Ariadne in her chariot. Pen and gray wash. 179 x 168 mm. Marks of P. J. Mariette (Lugt 2097) and of the Albertina (Lugt 174).

Lit.: Bartsch, *op.cit.*, p. 92, no. 7; Wickhoff, *op.cit.*, p. CCXCII, Sc.B. 191; Tietze, p. 117, fig. 43; Stix-Spitzmüller, p. 14, no. 107; Mahon, *Disegni*, p. 114, no. 151; Bacou, *Dessins*, p. 41, under no. 59.

59. BESANÇON, MUSÉE DES BEAUX-ARTS, INV. D. 1452

Satyr. Black chalk heightened with white on gray-blue paper; a few touches of pen. 393/407 x 505/512 mm. Inscribed in ink: *9* (from the Angeloni collection). Marks of Jean Gigoux (Lugt 1164) and the Museum of Besançon (Lugt 238c) with the number *D. 1452* in ink. On a strip of reinforcing paper, a note in Mariette's handwriting: *Faune qui est dans le grand tableau du Triomphe de Bacus et d'Arianne.*

Recto (Fig. 164): Study for the satyr with the goat in the lower left corner of the *Bacchanal.*

Verso: Studies in black chalk of a hand, a sword, and a foot, seemingly unrelated to the Farnese frescoes.

Lit.: Mahon, *Disegni*, p. 117, no. 157.

60. BESANÇON, MUSÉE DES BEAUX-ARTS, INV. D. 1501

Studies for the Triumph of Bacchus and Ariadne. Black chalk heightened with white on gray-blue paper. 415/419 x 268/278 mm. Recto inscribed in ink: *16* (from the Angeloni collection). Verso inscribed in ink: *dans le tableau du triomphe no. 13* (a reference to pl. 13 in Cesio's volume on the Gallery). Marks of Jean Gigoux (Lugt 1164) and the Museum of Besançon (Lugt 238c) with the number *D. 1501* in ink.

Recto (Fig. 165): Study for the head of the goat embraced by the satyr in the lower left corner of the *Bacchanal.*

Verso (Fig. 166): Study for the head of Bacchus in the same fresco.

Lit.: Mahon, *Disegni*, p. 119, no. 162, pl. 77 (recto).

61. FLORENCE, COLLECTION W. GERNSHEIM
      Fig. 168

Ariadne. Black chalk heightened with white on gray-blue paper. 338/393 x 270/274

mm. Inscribed in ink: *7* (from the Angeloni collection). Marks of Jean Gigoux (Lugt 1164) and Archibald G. B. Russell (Lugt 2770a).

Final study from the model for Ariadne in the *Triumph of Bacchus and Ariadne*.

Lit.: Italian Art of the Seventeenth Century, Burlington Fine Arts Club, London, 1925, p. 47, no. 5, pl. xiv; A. E. Popham, *Italian Drawings exhibited at the Royal Academy*, London, 1931, p. 79, no. 295, pl. ccxlixa; Mahon, *Disegni*, pp. 114 f., no. 152; Bacou, *Dessins*, p. 41, under no. 59.

62. PARIS, LOUVRE, INV. 7187
    Fig. 170

Dancing faun. Black chalk heightened with white on gray-blue paper. 421 x 359 mm. Inscribed in ink: *10* (from the Angeloni collection). Marks of the Louvre (Lugt 1899 and 2207).

Study from the model for the faun in front of Ariadne's car in the *Bacchanal*.

Lit.: Morel d' Arleux, iv, p. 119, no. 5104; Reiset, p. 51, no. 150; Tietze, p. 118; Mahon, *Disegni*, p. 115, no. 153; Bacou, *Dessins*, p. 40, under no. 58.

63. WINDSOR CASTLE, ROYAL LIBRARY,
    INV. 1978, CAT. 305
    Fig. 169

Studies of goats. Pen and black and brown inks. 202 x 130 mm.

Probably studies for the goats which draw Ariadne's car.

Lit.: Inv. A., p. 75; Wittkower, *Carracci Drawings*, p. 138, no. 305; Mahon, *Disegni*, p. 114, under no. 150.

64. BUDAPEST, MUSEUM OF FINE ARTS, INV. 1812
    Fig. 171

Bacchante with a tambourine. Black chalk heightened with white on gray-blue paper. 475 x 278 mm. Inscribed in ink: *h. 111* (mark of Lord Somers; Lugt 2981); marks of Jonathan Richardson (Lugt 2184), A. C. Poggi (Lugt 617), and Prince Esterházy (Lugt 1965).

Study for the bacchante with the tambourine in the *Triumph of Bacchus and Ariadne*.

Lit.: Richardson, *An Account*, pp. 143 f.; I. Fenyö, "Dessins inconnus des Carracci," *Bulletin du Musée National Hongrois des Beaux-Arts*, No. 17, 1960, pp. 36 f., fig. 30; Bacou, *Dessins*, p. 41, under no. 61.

65. PARIS, LOUVRE, INV. 7316
    Fig. 172

Faun blowing a trumpet. Black chalk heightened with white on faded gray-blue paper. 541/542 x 281 mm. Marks of the Louvre (Lugt 1899 and 2207) partly cut off.

Study for the faun who blows a trumpet while helping to support Silenus.

Lit.: Morel d' Arleux, IV, p. 90, no. 4903; Reiset, p. 53, no. 158; Tietze, p. 118; Mahon, *Disegni*, pp. 115 f., no. 154, pl. 73; Bacou, p. 41, no. 61.

66. TURIN, BIBLIOTECA REALE, INV. 16060, CAT. 98
Fig. 173

Silenus supported by a faun. Red chalk. 298 x 232 mm. Mark of the Biblioteca Reale of Turin (Lugt 2724).
Study for the Silenus group in the *Bacchanal.*
Lit.: Tietze, p. 117; Bertini, "Disegni inediti," p. 41, note 8; Mahon, *Disegni*, p. 116, no. 155, pl. 74; Bertini, *Cat. Disegni*, p. 23, no. 98; Bacou, *Dessins*, p. 41, under no. 61.

67. PARIS, LOUVRE, INV. R.F. 610
Fig. 174

Girl carrying a basket on her head. Black chalk heightened with white on gray-blue paper. 426 x 287 mm. Marks of Lord Spencer (Lugt 1531), A.C.H. His de la Salle (Lugt 1333), and of the Louvre (Lugt 1886).
Study for the girl carrying a basket on her head in the *Triumph of Bacchus and Ariadne.*
Lit.: Bodmer, *O.M.D.*, p. 63, pl. 58; Mahon, *Disegni*, pp. 116 f., no. 156, pl. 75; Bacou, *Dessins*, p. 41, no. 60, pl. xx.

68. PARIS, LOUVRE, INV. 7372
Fig. 176

Reclining male figure. Black chalk heightened with white on gray-blue paper. The lower left corner torn and repaired. 233/234 x 302/304 mm. Marks of the Louvre (Lugt 1899 and 2207).
Study from a male model for the pose which will be used for the Earthly Venus in the *Triumph of Bacchus and Ariadne* (see the following number).
Lit.: Morel d' Arleux, IV, p. 119, no. 5110; Tietze, p. 118, fig. 44; Mahon, *Disegni*, p. 117, no. 158; Calvesi, pp. 273 f.; Bacou, *Dessins*, p. 42, no. 62.

69. FLORENCE, UFFIZI, INV. 815 E

Studies for the Triumph of Bacchus and Ariadne. Black chalk on gray (originally gray-blue) paper. 313 x 486/487 mm. Recto inscribed in ink: *106*, and *D' Anibale.* Mark of the Uffizi (Lugt 930).
Recto (Fig. 177): Study for the Earthly Venus in the *Triumph of Bacchus and Ariadne* (see the preceding number).
Verso (Fig. 167): Study for the putto carrying an amphora at the left side of the same fresco.
Lit.: Tietze, p. 118; *I Disegni della R. Galleria degli Uffizi*, Florence, 1916, Serie IV, fasc. 2, no. 12 (recto); H. Leporini, *Die Stilentwicklung der Handzeichnung*, Vienna-

Leipzig, 1925, p. 65, pl. 173 (recto); Mahon, *Disegni*, pp. 117 f., no. 159; Calvesi, pp. 273 f.; Bacou, *Dessins*, p. 42, under no. 62.

70. BUDAPEST, MUSEUM OF FINE ARTS, INV. 2094
Fig. 175

Amoretto. Black chalk heightened with white on gray-blue paper. 246 x 199 mm. Inscribed in ink: *Annibal Carracci*. Marks of A. C. Poggi (Lugt 617) and Prince Esterházy (Lugt 1965).
Study for the *amoretto* beside the Earthly Venus in the *Bacchanal*.
Lit.: I. Fenyö, in *Bulletin du Musée National Hongrois des Beaux-Arts*, No. 17, 1960, pp. 37 f., fig. 32; Bacou, *Dessins*, p. 42, under no. 62.

71. URBINO, GALLERIA NAZIONALE DELLE MARCHE
Fig. 178

Part of the cartoon of the Triumph of Bacchus and Ariadne. Black chalk on brown paper. Torn and repaired along the left side; numerous holes and patches. 3.45 x 3.32 m.
This fragment forms the right half of the cartoon.
Lit.: L. Serra, *Il Palazzo Ducale e la Galleria Nazionale di Urbino*, Rome, 1930, pp. 121 f.; Wittkower, *Carracci Drawings*, p. 134; Mahon, *Disegni*, p. 114, under no. 151; Bacou, *Dessins*, p. 40, under no. 58.

72. CHATSWORTH, DEVONSHIRE COLLECTION, NO. 414
Fig. 179

Pan and Diana. Black chalk heightened with white, and pen and wash, on paper tinted gray. 285/286 x 399/403 mm. Inscribed in ink: *h. 135* (mark of Lord Somers; Lugt 2981); mark of second Duke of Devonshire (Lugt 718).
An early study for the fresco.
Lit.: Wittkower, *Carracci Drawings*, p. 138, under no. 304; Mahon, *Disegni*, p. 118, under no. 160; Calvesi, p. 274; Holland, no. 140, pl. XXXIII; M. Jaffé, in *Burlington Magazine*, CIV, 1962, p. 26, fig. 32.

73. WINDSOR CASTLE, ROYAL LIBRARY, INV. 1858, CAT. 304
Fig. 180

Pan and Diana. Pen and brown ink with gray wash. 199 x 117 mm.
Composition study for the fresco.
Lit.: Inv. A., p. 74; Tietze, p. 120, fig. 45; Wittkower, *Carracci Drawings*, p. 138, no. 304; Mahon, *Disegni*, p. 118, under no. 160; Calvesi, p. 274; Bacou, *Dessins*, p. 42, under no. 64.

74. PARIS, LOUVRE, INV. 7360

Diana. Black chalk heightened with white on gray-blue paper (recto); pen (verso). Left side of the sheet torn and repaired. 405 x 278 mm. Recto inscribed in ink: *3.* Verso inscribed: *Jacobus de Canetis . . . , Carazzi . . . Franciscus de . . . fecit,* and the number *4* (from the Angeloni collection). Marks of the Louvre (Lugt 1899 and 2207).
Recto (Fig. 183): Study from the nude for Diana in the fresco of *Pan and Diana.*
Verso (Fig. 181):
(a) Pen sketch of Pan;
(b) An arm;
(c) An eagle.
Lit.: Morel d' Arleux, IV, p. 111, no. 5054; Mahon, *Disegni,* p. 118, under no. 160; Bacou, *Dessins,* pp. 42 f., no. 65, pl. XIX.

75. PARIS, LOUVRE, INV. 7190
Fig. 182

Pan. Black chalk heightened with white on gray-blue paper. 541/542 x 313 mm. Inscribed in ink: *5* (from the Angeloni collection). Marks of the Louvre (Lugt 1899 and 2207).
Final study for the figure of Pan in the fresco of *Pan and Diana.*
Lit.: Morel d' Arleux, IV, p. 110, no. 5045; Reiset, p. 52, no. 153; Tietze, p. 120; Wittkower, *Carracci Drawings,* p. 138, under no. 304; Mahon, *Disegni,* p. 118, no. 160, pl. 76; Bacou, *Dessins,* p. 42, no. 64, pl. XVII.

76. PARIS, LOUVRE, INV. 7318
Fig. 185

Paris. Black chalk heightened with white on gray-blue paper. 502 x 362 mm. Marks of the Louvre (Lugt 1899 and 2207).
Study for the figure of Paris in the fresco of *Paris and Mercury.*
Lit.: Morel d' Arleux, IV, pp. 89-90, no. 4901; Reiset, p. 53, no. 160; Mahon, *Disegni,* p. 120, no. 163, pl. 78; Bacou, *Dessins,* p. 43, no. 66.

77. BESANÇON, MUSÉE DES BEAUX-ARTS, INV. D. 1492
Fig. 184

Mercury. Black chalk heightened with white on gray-blue paper. Upper left corner cut and repaired. 415 x 307 mm. Inscribed in ink: *22* (from the Angeloni collection). Marks of Jean Gigoux (Lugt 1164) and the Museum of Besançon (Lugt 238c) with the number *D. 1492* in ink. On the mount two notations in Mariette's handwriting: *Mercure estude p^r le tableau qui est a la galerie Farnese,* and *Mercure estude pour le tableau de Paris.*

Study for the figure of Mercury in the fresco of *Paris and Mercury*.
Lit.: Mahon, *Disegni*, p. 120, no. 164; Bacou, *Dessins*, p. 43, under no. 66.

78. PARIS, LOUVRE, INV. 7414
Fig. 186

Sphinx. Black chalk on gray-blue paper. 237/238 x 230/232 mm. Inscribed in ink: *50* (from the Angeloni collection). Marks of the Louvre (Lugt 1899 and 2207).
Study for one of the sphinxes at the corners of the frames of the frescoes of *Pan and Diana* and *Paris and Mercury*.
Lit.: Morel d' Arleux, IV, p. 118, no. 5098; Bodmer, "Camerino," p. 147 (wrongly connected with the Camerino); Martin, p. 97, note 37; Mahon, *Disegni*, p. 110, under no. 147; Bacou, *Dessins*, p. 43, no. 67.

79. PARIS, LOUVRE, INV. 7339
Fig. 189

Tithonus. Black chalk heightened with white on gray-blue paper. In the lower left corner a sketch of a head in brush and ink. 272 x 429 mm. Inscribed in ink: *20* (from the Angeloni collection). Marks of the Louvre (Lugt 1899 and 2207).
Study by Agostino for the figure of Tithonus in the fresco of *Aurora and Cephalus*.
Lit.: Morel d' Arleux, IV, p. 110, no. 5051; Wittkower, *Carracci Drawings*, p. 141, under no. 323; Mahon, *Disegni*, pp. 54 f., no. 58, pl. 29; Bacou, *Dessins*, p. 24, no. 21.

80. LONDON, NATIONAL GALLERY, NO. 147
Fig. 190

Cartoon of Aurora and Cephalus. Black chalk heightened with white on brown paper on canvas. The upper right corner damaged and repaired. 2.03 x 4.06 m.
The cartoon is the work of Agostino.
Lit.: G. F. Waagen, *Treasures of Art in Great Britain*, London, 1854-57, I, p. 336; Tietze, p. 124, pl. VIII; *National Gallery Catalogue*, 86th ed., London, 1929, p. 55, no. 147; Wittkower, *Carracci Drawings*, p. 134; Mahon, *Disegni*, p. 55, under no. 58; Bacou, *Dessins*, p. 24, under no. 21.

81. BESANÇON, MUSÉE DES BEAUX-ARTS, INV. D. 2294

Studies for Glaucus and Scylla. Black chalk lightly heightened with white on gray-blue paper. 238/242 (249 including a strip added at the top) x 359 mm.
Recto inscribed in ink: *26* (from the Angeloni collection); a notation in Mariette's handwriting: *pour le tableau du Triomphe de Venus*. Verso inscribed in pencil: *Anibal Carrache*. Marks of Jean Gigoux (Lugt 1164) and the Museum of Besançon (Lugt 238c) with the number *D. 2294* in ink.
Recto (Fig. 191): Study by Agostino for the flying cupid with a torch.

Verso (Fig. 192): Study by Agostino for the head and shoulders of Glaucus, with a
light sketch of Scylla.

Lit.: Mahon, *Disegni*, pp. 55 f., no. 59, pl. 30 (recto).

82. LONDON, NATIONAL GALLERY, NO. 148
Fig. 194

Cartoon of Glaucus and Scylla. Black chalk heightened with white on brown paper on
canvas. The lower left corner repaired. 2.04 x 4.14 m.
The cartoon is the work of Agostino.

Lit.: Waagen, *op.cit.*, I, p. 336; Tietze, p. 124, pl. VII; *National Gallery Catalogue*,
86th ed., p. 55, no. 148; Wittkower, *Carrraci Drawings*, p. 134; Mahon, *Disegni*, p. 136,
under no. 195.

83. CAMBRIDGE, COLLECTION CARL WINTER
Fig. 193

Triton. Black chalk heightened with white on gray-blue paper. 406 x 241 mm. Study
by Annibale for the Triton blowing a shell at the right side of the fresco of *Glaucus
and Scylla.* Formerly in the collection of Sir Bruce Ingram.

Lit.: D. Mahon, in *Journal of the Warburg and Courtauld Institutes*, XVI, 1953, p.
337, fig. 47; Catalogue, *Artists in 17th Century Rome*, Wildenstein Gallery, London,
1955, p. 31, no. 24; Mahon, *Disegni*, pp. 135 f., no. 195, pl. 89.

84. PARIS, LOUVRE, INV. 7196
Fig. 195

Polyphemus. Pen. 258 x 185 mm. Marks of the Louvre (Lugt 1899 and 2207). An
early study for the figure of Polyphemus in the fresco of *Polyphemus and Galatea.*

Lit.: Morel d' Arleux, IV, p. 116, no. 5088; Wittkower, *Carracci Drawings*, p. 138,
under no. 302; Mahon, *Disegni*, p. 121, no. 166, pl. 79; Bacou, *Dessins*, p. 44, no. 71.

85. PARIS, LOUVRE, INV. 7319

Polyphemus. Black chalk heightened with white on gray-blue paper. 521 x 383/386
mm. Inscribed in ink, in Mariette's handwriting: *Figure du Polipheme du tableau de
Polipheme et de Galattée*; and the number 27 (from the Angeloni collection). Marks
of the Louvre (Lugt 1899 and 2207).

Recto (Fig. 197): Final study for the figure of Polyphemus in the fresco of *Polyphemus
and Galatea.*

Verso: Studies of heads, arms and hands, seemingly unrelated to the Farnese ceiling.

Lit.: Morel d' Arleux, IV, p. 89, no. 4900; Reiset, p. 54, no. 161; Rouchès, *Catalogue
des dessins italiens*, 1927, p. 15, no. 7; Wittkower, *Carracci Drawings*, p. 138, under
no. 302; Mahon, *Disegni*, pp. 121 f., no. 167, pl. 80; Bacou, *Dessins*, pp. 44 f., no. 72.

86. PARIS, LOUVRE, INV. 7197
Fig. 196

Polyphemus and Galatea. Black chalk on gray-blue paper. 407/409 x 283/287 mm. Inscribed in ink: *94* (from the Angeloni collection). Marks of the Louvre (Lugt 1899 and 2207).
Perhaps a composition study for the fresco.
Lit.: Morel d' Arleux, IV, p. 111, no. 5057; Tietze, p. 122, fig. 47 (erroneously cited as Inv. 7193 and reproduced as if in red chalk); Wittkower, *Carracci Drawings*, p. 138, under no. 302, and p. 162, under no. 507; Mahon, *Disegni*, p. 122, under no. 167; Bacou, *Dessins*, p. 44, under no. 71.

87. BESANÇON, MUSÉE DES BEAUX-ARTS, INV. D. 2293

Galatea. Black chalk with a little heightening in white on gray-blue paper. 369/372 x 249/254 mm. Recto inscribed in ink: *28* (from the Angeloni collection). Verso inscribed in pencil: *Galattée du tableau de Polypheme. Anibal Carrache.* Marks of Jean Gigoux (Lugt 1164) and of the Museum of Besançon (Lugt 238c) with the number D. 2293 in ink.
Recto (Fig. 201): Study for Galatea in the fresco of *Polyphemus and Galatea.*
Verso: Drawing of a man's head, shoulder and raised right arm; two feet (seemingly unrelated to the Farnese ceiling).
Lit.: Wittkower, *Carracci Drawings*, p. 138, under no. 302; Mahon, *Disegni*, p. 122, no. 168; Bacou, *Dessins*, p. 45, under no. 72.

88. PARIS, LOUVRE, INV. 7303 BIS
Fig. 199

Study of an arm. Black chalk heightened with white on gray-blue paper. 157 x 90 mm. Inscribed in ink: *53* (crossed out) and *52* (from the Angeloni collection). Marks of the Louvre (Lugt 1899 and 2207).
Perhaps a study for the arm of the Nereid holding the reins of the dolphin in *Polyphemus and Galatea.*
Lit.: Morel d' Arleux, IV, p. 125, no. 5161; Wittkower, *Carracci Drawings*, p. 138, under no. 302; Mahon, *Disegni*, p. 123, under no. 169; Bacou, *Dessins*, p. 45, under no. 72.

89. WINDSOR CASTLE, ROYAL LIBRARY, INV. 2106, CAT. 300 (RECTO), CAT. 302 (VERSO)

Figure studies. Black chalk heightened with white on gray-blue paper. 339 x 232 mm.
Recto (Fig. 253): Man with arm raised, perhaps an early study for one of Perseus' companions in *Perseus and Phineus.*

Verso (Fig. 200): Study of the Nereid on the left of Galatea in *Polyphemus and Galatea*.

Lit.: Inv. A., p. 76; Wittkower, *Carracci Drawings*, p. 138, no. 300 and no. 302, pl. 66; Mahon, *Disegni*, p. 123, no. 169; Holland, no. 141, pl. XXXVII; Bacou, *Dessins*, p. 45, under no. 72.

90. WINDSOR CASTLE, ROYAL LIBRARY, INV. 1944, CAT. 303
Fig. 202

Polyphemus. Black chalk heightened with white on gray-blue paper. The lower part torn off and re-joined. 611/613 x 355 mm.
Study from the model for Polyphemus hurling the rock in *Polyphemus and Acis*.
Lit.: Inv. A., p. 74; Wittkower, *Carracci Drawings*, p. 138, no. 303, fig. 33; Mahon, *Disegni*, p. 130, under no. 183; Holland, no. 142.

91. PARIS, LOUVRE, INV. 7329

Hyacinthus. Black chalk on gray-blue paper. Upper left corner cut and repaired. 233 x 346 mm. Inscribed in ink: *6 or 9* (from the Angeloni collection). Marks of the Louvre (Lugt 1899 and 2207).
Recto (Fig. 198): Study for the figure of Hyacinthus in the fresco of *Hyacinthus and Apollo*; above, the head of Apollo.
Verso: Three studies of hands, seemingly unrelated to the Farnese Gallery.
Lit.: Morel d' Arleux, IV, p. 118, no. 5103; Reiset, p. 56, no. 170; Tietze, p. 120; Wittkower, *Carracci Drawings*, p. 138, under no. 302; Mahon, *Disegni*, p. 124, under no. 171; Bacou, *Dessins*, p. 45, no. 75.

92. LONDON, COURTAULD INSTITUTE OF ART, WITT COLLECTION, NO. 1275
Fig. 203

Juno. Pen and wash over a light sketch in black chalk. All four corners cut diagonally. 193 x 133/134 mm.
An early study for the figure of Juno in the fresco of *Jupiter and Juno*.
Lit.: Tomory, p. 22, under no. 50; Mahon, *Disegni*, p. 134, no. 192; Holland, no. 138, pl. XXXVIII; Bacou, *Dessins*, p. 47, under no. 82.

93. MERTOUN, ST. BOSWELL'S, ROXBURGHSHIRE, COLLECTION THE EARL OF ELLESMERE, NO. 50 (ON LOAN TO LEICESTER MUSEUMS AND ART GALLERY)
Fig. 204

Jupiter and Juno. Pen and black ink, and gray wash. 314 x 313 mm. Inscribed in ink: *Annibale Carracci.* Marks of Sir Thomas Lawrence (Lugt 2445) and the Earl of Ellesmere (Lugt 2710b).

Composition study for the fresco of *Jupiter and Juno.*

Lit.: (S. Woodburn), *The Lawrence Gallery, Sixth Exhibition: A Catalogue of One Hundred Original Drawings, by Ludovico, Agostino, & Annibal Carracci, collected by Sir Thomas Lawrence ...*, London, 1836, p. 27, no. 88; Tietze, p. 120; Tomory, p. 22, no. 50, pl. XVIII; Mahon, *Disegni*, p. 135, no. 194; Holland, no. 139; Bacou, *Dessins*, p. 47, under no. 82.

94. BESANÇON, MUSÉE DES BEAUX-ARTS, INV. D. 1491

Studies for Jupiter and Juno. Black chalk. 437 x 278/280 mm. Recto inscribed in ink: *29* (from the Angeloni collection). On a strip of reinforcing paper a note in Mariette's handwriting: *Du tableau de Jupiter et Junon.* Verso inscribed in ink: *Jean Gigoux.* Marks of Jean Gigoux (Lugt 1164) and the Museum of Besançon (Lugt 238c) with the number *D. 1491* in ink.

Recto (Fig. 205): Study for figure of Juno; sketch of face of Juno.

Verso (Fig. 206): Study for the right leg of Jupiter; sketch of the posture of Jupiter.

Lit.: Tomory, p. 22, under no. 50 (wrongly described as unnumbered); Mahon, *Disegni*, p. 134, no. 193; Bacou, *Dessins*, p. 47, under no. 82.

95. PARIS, LOUVRE, INV. 7403
    Fig. 207

Study for the legs of Jupiter. Black chalk. 240/242 x 239 mm. Inscribed in ink: two illegible digits (from the Angeloni collection?). Marks of the Louvre (Lugt 1899 and 2207).

Definitive study for the position of the legs of Jupiter in the fresco of *Jupiter and Juno.*

Lit.: Morel d' Arleux, IV, p. 123, no. 5141; Tietze, p. 120; Mahon, *Disegni*, p. 134, under no. 193; Bacou, *Dessins*, p. 47, no. 82.

96. BESANÇON, MUSÉE DES BEAUX-ARTS, INV. D. 3075
    Fig. 208

Iole. Black chalk heightened with white on yellowish brown paper. 386/389 x 252/255 mm. Inscribed in ink: *30* (from the Angeloni collection). On the mount an inscription in ink by Mariette: *Iole du tableau d' Hercule et Iole.* Marks of Jean Gigoux (Lugt 1164) and the Museum of Besançon (Lugt 238c) with the number *D. 3075* in ink.

Study from the model for Iole in the fresco of *Hercules and Iole.*

Lit.: Mahon, *Disegni*, p. 125, no. 174.

97. PARIS, LOUVRE, INV. 7409
    Fig. 209

Dog. Red chalk. 273 x 359 mm. Inscribed in ink; *31* (from the Angeloni collection). Marks of the Louvre (Lugt 1899 and 2207).

Probably a study for the sleeping dog in the fresco of *Diana and Endymion*.

Lit.: Morel d' Arleux, IV, p. 111, no. 5059; Mahon, *Disegni*, p. 137, under no. 196; Bacou, *Dessins*, p. 43, no. 68.

98. PARIS, LOUVRE, INV. 7322

Seated ignudo. Black chalk heightened with white on gray-blue paper. 413 x 408/410 mm. Inscribed in ink: *32* (from the Angeloni collection). Marks of the Louvre (Lugt 1899 and 2207).

Recto (Fig. 210): Study for the *ignudo* at the left of *Apollo and Marsyas*.

Verso (Fig. 212): Preliminary sketch in black chalk of the same figure (partly covered by a reinforcing strip pasted to the sheet).

Lit.: Morel d' Arleux, IV, p. 110, no. 5048; Reiset, p. 54, no. 164; Tietze, p. 108; Mahon, *Disegni*, p. 133, no. 190, pl. 87; Bacou, *Dessins*, pp. 46 f., no. 80.

99. PARIS, LOUVRE, INV. 7325
Fig. 211

Seated ignudo. Black chalk heightened with white on gray-blue paper. 495 x 384 mm. Inscribed in ink: *33* (from the Angeloni collection). Marks of the Louvre (Lugt 1899 and 2207).

Study for the *ignudo* at the right of *Apollo and Marsyas*.

Lit.: Morel d' Arleux, IV, p. 109, no. 5041; Reiset, p. 55, no. 167; J. Meder, *Die Handzeichnung*, Vienna, 1923, p. 410, pl. 168; G. Rouchès, *Dessins italiens du XVIIe siècle au Musée du Louvre*, Paris, n.d., pp. 11 f., pl. 4; Rouchès, *Catalogue des dessins italiens*, 1927, p. 15, no. 9; Bodmer, *O.M.D.*, pp. 63 f., pl. 59; Wittkower, *Carracci Drawings*, p. 139, under no. 310; Mahon, *Disegni*, pp. 133 f., no. 191, pl. 88; Bacou, *Dessins*, pp. 47 f., no. 83.

100. PARIS, LOUVRE, INV. 7369
Fig. 213

Seated ignudo. Black chalk heightened with white on gray-blue paper. 255 x 223 mm. Inscribed in ink: *14* (?) (from the Angeloni collection). Marks of the Louvre (Lugt 1899 and 2207).

Study for the *ignudo* at the right of *Orpheus and Eurydice*.

Lit.: Morel d' Arleux, IV, p. 118, no. 5102; Bacou, *Dessins*, p. 44, no. 70.

101. BESANÇON, MUSÉE DES BEAUX-ARTS, INV. D. 1538

Studies for the Farnese ceiling. Black chalk heightened with white on gray-blue paper. 216/221 x 307 mm. Marks of Jean Gigoux (Lugt 1164) and the Museum of Besançon (Lugt 238c) with the number *D. 1538* in ink.

Recto (Fig. 214): Study for the lower part of the *ignudo* at the left of *Hero and Leander*.

Verso (Fig. 187): Study for the dog in the fresco of *Mercury and Paris*.

Lit.: Wittkower, *Carracci Drawings*, p. 138, under no. 302; Mahon, *Disegni*, pp. 120 f., no. 165, and p. 139, under no. 199; Bacou, *Dessins*, p. 43, under no. 66.

102. BESANÇON, MUSÉE DES BEAUX-ARTS, INV. D. 1490
    Fig. 216

Seated ignudo. Black chalk heightened with white on gray-blue paper. 355/357 x 456/457 mm. Marks of Jean Gigoux (Lugt 1164) and the Museum of Besançon (Lugt 238c) with the number *D. 1490* in ink.

Study for the *ignudo* at the right of *Hero and Leander*.

Lit.: Wittkower, *Carracci Drawings*, p. 139, under no. 310; Mahon, *Disegni*, pp. 125 f., no. 175, pl. 83.

103. BREMEN, KUNSTHALLE, INV. 51/220
    Fig. 215

Seated ignudo. Pen. 92 x 92 mm. Inscribed in ink: *h. 131* (mark of Lord Somers; Lugt 2981); marks of Sir Joshua Reynolds (Lugt 2364) and A. C. Poggi (Lugt 617).

Study for the *ignudo* at the right of *Salmacis and Hermaphroditus*. Cf. the following number.

Lit.: G. Busch and H. Keller, *Handbuch der Kunsthalle Bremen*, 1954, p. 54; Mahon, *Disegni*, pp. 127 f., under no. 178.

104. MERTOUN, ST. BOSWELL'S, ROXBURGHSHIRE,
    COLLECTION THE EARL OF ELLESMERE, NO. 49
    (ON LOAN TO LEICESTER MUSEUMS AND
    ART GALLERY)
    Fig. 217

Seated ignudo. Black chalk lightly heightened with white on gray-blue paper, squared in black chalk. 377 x 326/328 mm. Marks of Sir Thomas Lawrence (Lugt 2445) and of the Earl of Ellesmere (Lugt 2710b).

Study for the *ignudo* at the right of *Salmacis and Hermaphroditus*. Cf. the preceding number.

Lit.: Bodmer, *O.M.D.*, pl. 60; A. E. Popham, in *Burlington Magazine*, LXXII, 1938, p. 14, pl. 1A; Wittkower, *Carracci Drawings*, p. 139, under no. 310; Tomory, p. 21, no. 49; Catalogue, *Artists in 17th Century Rome*, Wildenstein Gallery, London, 1955, p. 30, no. 23; Mahon, *Disegni*, pp. 127 f., no. 178; Holland, no. 134, pl. XXXIV.

105. PARIS, LOUVRE, INV. 7323
    Fig. 218

Seated ignudo. Black chalk heightened with white on gray-blue paper. 422/425 x 370/371 mm. Inscribed in ink: *39* (from the Angeloni collection). Marks of the Louvre (Lugt 1899 and 2207).

Study for the *ignudo* at the right of *Polyphemus and Acis.*

Lit.: Morel d' Arleux, IV, p. 110, no. 5047; Reiset, p. 55, no. 165; Tietze, p. 108; Wittkower, *Carracci Drawings*, p. 138, under no. 303; Mahon, *Disegni*, p. 132, no. 189; Bacou, *Dessins*, p. 46, no. 78.

106. BESANÇON, MUSÉE DES BEAUX-ARTS, INV. D. 1493
Fig. 221

Study for an atlas. Black chalk heightened with white on gray-blue paper. 399 x 145/147 mm. Inscribed in ink: *16* (from the Angeloni collection). Marks of Jean Gigoux (Lugt 1164) and the Museum of Besançon (Lugt 238c) with the number *D. 1493* in ink.

Study for the lower part of the atlas standing at the right of *Jupiter and Juno.*

Lit.: Mahon, *Disegni*, p. 103, under no. 137 (here cited as D. 1494), and p. 135, under no. 194.

107. PARIS, LOUVRE, INV. 7317
Fig. 219

Atlas. Black chalk heightened with white on gray-blue paper. 526 x 290/291 mm.

Study for the atlas standing at the left of *Diana and Endymion.*

Lit.: Morel d' Arleux, IV, p. 90, no. 4902; Reiset, p. 53, no. 159; Tietze, p. 108; Wittkower, *Carracci Drawings*, p. 139, under no. 310; Mahon, *Disegni*, pp. 136 f., no. 196, pl. 90; Bacou, *Dessins*, pp. 43 f., no. 69.

108. BESANÇON, MUSÉE DES BEAUX-ARTS, INV. D. 1451
Fig. 220

Atlas. Black chalk heightened with white on paper prepared with a dark green wash. 527/532 x 257/260 mm. Faintly inscribed in ink in the lower right corner: *carraccio*; and the number *44* (from the Angeloni collection). Marks of Jean Gigoux (Lugt 1164) and the Museum of Besançon (Lugt 238c) with the number *D. 1451* in ink.

Study for the atlas standing at the left of *Venus and Anchises.* Cf. No. 115.

Lit.: Wittkower, *Carracci Drawings*, p. 139, under no. 310; Mahon, *Disegni*, p. 128, no. 179.

109. TURIN, BIBLIOTECA REALE, INV. 16072, CAT. 95

Atlas herm. Black chalk on blue paper. 365 x 247/249 mm. Verso inscribed in ink: *ibal Ca fe.* Mark of the Biblioteca Reale of Turin (Lugt 2724).

Recto (Fig. 222): Perhaps an early study for the atlas herm at the left of *Europa and the Bull.*

Verso: Light sketch in black chalk of two women; not related to the Farnese ceiling.
Lit.: Bertini, "Disegni inediti," p. 41; Mahon, *Disegni*, p. 126, no. 176; Bertini, *Cat. Disegni*, p. 22, no. 95.

110. WINDSOR CASTLE, ROYAL LIBRARY, INV. 2366,
CAT. 323 (RECTO), CAT. 309 AND CAT. 338 (VERSO)

Figure studies. Black chalk heightened with white on gray-blue paper. 367 x 477/481 mm.
Recto: A recumbent nude (Cat. 323), not related to the Farnese ceiling.
Verso (Fig. 224):
    (a) Fragmentary study of an atlas herm;
    (b) St. John the Baptist (Cat. 338);
    (c) Study for the atlas herm at the left of *Europa and the Bull* (Cat. 309).
Lit.: Inv. A., p. 77; Wittkower, *Carracci Drawings*, p. 139, no. 309; p. 141, no. 323; and p. 143, no. 338, pls. 76-77; Mahon, *Disegni*, p. 137, under no. 197; Holland, nos. 132 and 157.

111. TURIN, BIBLIOTECA REALE, INV. 16076, CAT. 94

Atlas herm. Black chalk heightened with white on gray-blue paper. 472 x 363 mm.
Mark of the Biblioteca Reale of Turin (Lugt 2724).
Recto (Fig. 223): Study for the atlas herm at the left of *Europa and the Bull*; variant study for the head of this figure.
Verso: Drawings of heads, legs, etc.; not related to the Farnese ceiling.
Lit.: Bertini, "Disegni inediti," p. 41, pl. XI, fig. 45; Mahon, *Disegni*, pp. 137 f., no. 197, pl. 91; D. Mahon, in *Gazette des Beaux-Arts*, XLIX, 1957, p. 285, note 68; Bertini, *Cat. Disegni*, p. 22, no. 94.

112. TURIN, BIBLIOTECA REALE, INV. 16071, CAT. 96
    Fig. 226

Atlas herm. Black chalk on blue paper. 416/417 x 237 mm. Mark of the Biblioteca Reale of Turin (Lugt 2724).
Preliminary study for the atlas herm at the right of *Salmacis and Hermaphroditus*.
Lit.: Bertini, "Disegni inediti," p. 41, pl. X, fig. 40; Wittkower, *Carracci Drawings*, p. 139, under no. 310; Mahon, *Disegni*, p. 127, no. 177; Bertini, *Cat. Disegni*, pp. 22 f., no. 96.

113. WINDSOR CASTLE, ROYAL LIBRARY, INV. 2083,
CAT. 310 (RECTO), CAT. 344 (VERSO)

Figure studies. Black chalk heightened with white on gray-blue paper. 353 x 230 mm.
Recto (Fig. 227): Study for, or perhaps a copy after, the atlas herm at the right of *Salmacis and Hermaphroditus* (Cat. 310).

Verso: Study for a kneeling boy in the *Adoration of the Shepherds* (Dulwich Gallery) (Cat. 344).
Lit.: Inv. A., p. 76; Wittkower, *Carracci Drawings*, p. 139, no. 310; p. 144, no. 344, fig. 44; Mahon, *Disegni*, p. 127, under no. 177.

114. FLORENCE, UFFIZI, INV. 12425 F.
Fig. 225

Atlas herm with a club. Black chalk lightly heightened with white on paper prepared with a gray-green wash. 234/237 x 268/270 mm. Mark of the Uffizi (Lugt 929).
Study for the atlas herm with a club at the left of *Cupid and Pan*.
Lit.: Wittkower, *Carracci Drawings*, p. 139, under no. 310; Mahon, *Disegni*, p. 128, no. 180.

115. BESANÇON, MUSÉE DES BEAUX-ARTS, INV. D. 2297

Studies of atlantes. Black chalk heightened with white on gray-blue paper. 396/399 x 193 mm. Verso inscribed in pencil: *Anibal Carrache.* Marks of Jean Gigoux (Lugt 1164) and of the Museum of Besançon (Lugt 238c) with the number *D. 2297* in ink.
Recto (Fig. 229):
  (a) Study for the right-hand figure of the pair of atlas herms at the left of *Polyphemus and Galatea*. For the companion figure see No. 116.
  (b) Study (inverted) for the atlas standing at the left of *Venus and Anchises*. Cf. No. 108.
Verso (Fig. 230): The *Farnese Hercules* seen from the back. Cf. No. 116.
Lit.: Wittkower, *Carracci Drawings*, p. 139, under no. 308; Mahon, *Disegni*, pp. 138 f., no. 199; and p. 128, under no. 179; Bacou, *Dessins*, p. 46, under no. 76.

116. PARIS, LOUVRE, INV. 7354
Fig. 228

Atlas herm. Black chalk heightened with white on gray-blue paper. 398 x 204 mm. Inscribed in ink (illegible number; from the Angeloni collection?). Marks of the Louvre (Lugt 1899 and 2207).
Study for the left-hand figure of the pair of atlas herms at the left of *Polyphemus and Galatea*. Beneath this drawing is a faint sketch of the *Farnese Hercules*, similar to that on No. 115 verso.
Lit.: Morel d' Arleux, IV, p. 110, no. 5044; Wittkower, *Carracci Drawings*, p. 139, under no. 308; Mahon, *Disegni*, p. 138, no. 198, pl. 92; Bacou, *Dessins*, pp. 45 f., no. 76.

117. TURIN, BIBLIOTECA REALE, INV. 16075, CAT. 97

Pair of atlantes. Black chalk heightened with white on blue paper. 415 x 346/347 mm. Mark of the Biblioteca Reale of Turin (Lugt 2724).

Recto (Fig. 231): Study for the pair of atlantes at the right of *Polyphemus and Galatea*.
Verso: Pen drawing of three women and the head of an old man in profile; seemingly
    unrelated to the Farnese Gallery.
Lit.: Bertini, "Disegni inediti," pp. 40 f., pl. XI, fig. 46; Wittkower, *Carracci Drawings*,
p. 139, under no. 308; Mahon, *Disegni*, p. 124, no. 172; Bertini, *Cat. Disegni*, p. 23,
no. 97.

118. WINDSOR CASTLE, ROYAL LIBRARY, INV. 2087, CAT. 308

Pair of atlantes. Black chalk heightened with white on gray-blue paper. 218 x 332 mm.
Recto (Fig. 233): Study for the pair of atlantes at the left of *Polyphemus and Acis*.
Verso (Fig. 232): A hand, perhaps a study for the hand of the right-hand atlas of the
    pair at the right of *Polyphemus and Galatea*. Cf. No. 117.
Lit.: Inv. A., p. 76; Wittkower, *Carracci Drawings*, p. 139, no. 308, pl. 68; Mahon,
Disegni, p. 129, no. 182.

119. BESANÇON, MUSÉE DES BEAUX-ARTS, INV. D. 2296
    Fig. 234

Atlas herm. Black chalk lightly heightened with white on gray-blue paper. 397 x
208/214 mm. Marks of Jean Gigoux (Lugt 1164) and the Museum of Besançon (Lugt
238c) with the number *D. 2296* in ink.
Study for the left-hand atlas of the pair at the right of *Polyphemus and Acis*. For the
companion figure see No. 120.
Lit.: Wittkower, *Carracci Drawings*, p. 139, under no. 308; Mahon, *Disegni*, p. 131,
no. 186; Bacou, *Dessins*, p. 46, under no. 78.

120. PARIS, LOUVRE, INV. 7363
    Fig. 235

Atlas herm. Red chalk. 345 x 195/196 mm. Inscribed in ink, in Mariette's handwriting: *gravé N°. 15* (a reference to pl. 15 in Cesio's volume on the Gallery); and the
number *46* (from the Angeloni collection). Marks of the Louvre (Lugt 1899 and 2207).
Study for the right-hand figure of the pair of atlas herms at the right of *Polyphemus
and Acis*. For the companion figure see No. 119.
Lit.: Morel d' Arleux, IV, p. 91, no. 4913; Wittkower, *Carracci Drawings*, p. 139, under
no. 308; Mahon, *Disegni*, pp. 131 f., no. 187, pl. 86; Bacou, *Dessins*, p. 46, no. 79, pl.
XXI.

121. PARIS, LOUVRE, INV. 7189
    Fig. 237

Satyr. Black chalk heightened with white on gray-blue paper. 365 x 245 mm. Inscribed
in ink: *48* (from the Angeloni collection). Marks of the Louvre (Lugt 1899 and 2207).

Study for the satyr seated on the right corner of the frame of *Polyphemus and Galatea*.
Lit.: Morel d' Arleux, IV, p. 109, no. 5043; Reiset, p. 51, no. 152; Wittkower, *Carracci Drawings*, p. 138, under no. 302 (cited in error as Inv. 7389); Mahon, *Disegni*, p. 124, no. 171; Bacou, *Dessins*, p. 45, no. 73.

122. PARIS, LOUVRE, INV. 7188
Fig. 236

Satyr. Black chalk heightened with white on gray-blue paper. Torn and repaired along upper left side. 378 x 234 mm. Inscribed in ink: *49* (from the Angeloni collection). Marks of the Louvre (Lugt 1899 and 2207).
Study for the satyr seated on the left corner of the frame of *Polyphemus and Galatea*.
Lit.: Morel d' Arleux, IV, p. 109, no. 5043; Reiset, p. 51, no. 151; Mahon, *Disegni*, p. 123, no. 170, pl. 81; Bacou, *Dessins*, p. 45, no. 74.

123. PARIS, LOUVRE, INV. 7191
Fig. 239

Satyr. Black chalk heightened with white on gray-blue paper. The sheet consists of two pieces of paper, one of which is a narrow strip joined to the larger piece. 353 x 225 mm. Inscribed in ink: *45* (from the Angeloni collection). Marks of the Louvre (Lugt 1899 and 2207).
Study for the satyr seated on the right corner of the frame of *Polyphemus and Acis*.
Lit.: Morel d' Arleux, IV, p. 110, no. 5049; Reiset, p. 52, no. 154; Rouchès, *Catalogue des dessins italiens*, 1927, p. 15, no. 8; Wittkower, *Carracci Drawings*, p. 138, under no. 303; Mahon, *Disegni*, pp. 130 f., no. 185; Bacou, *Dessins*, p. 46, no. 77.

124. ROTTERDAM, MUSEUM BOYMANS-VAN BEUNINGEN, KOENIGS I. 183
Fig. 238

Satyr. Black chalk heightened with white on gray-blue paper. 336 x 221 mm. Inscribed in ink: *47* (from the Angeloni collection). Mark of E. Wauters (Lugt 911).
Study for the satyr seated on the left corner of the frame of *Polyphemus and Acis*.
Lit.: Wittkower, *Carracci Drawings*, p. 138, under no. 303; Mahon, *Disegni*, p. 130, no. 184, pl. 85; Bacou, *Dessins*, p. 46, under no. 77.

125. NEW YORK, METROPOLITAN MUSEUM OF ART, ACC. NO. 62.120.2
Fig. 240

Two cupids carrying a third. Red chalk. 220 x 155 mm. Inscribed in ink: *Annibale Caracci*. Mark of Lionel Lucas (Lugt 1733a).
An early idea for one of the groups of cupids in the corners of the Gallery.

Lit.: Holland, no. 136, pl. xxxvi; M. Jaffé, in *Burlington Magazine*, CIV, 1962, p. 26, fig. 29; J. Bean, in *Metropolitan Museum of Art Bulletin*, March 1963, p. 231.

1 2 6 .   P A R I S ,   L O U V R E ,   I N V .   7 3 0 5
    Fig. 242

Cupids fighting for a palm branch. Black chalk on gray-blue paper. 249/251 x 287/290 mm. Inscribed in ink: *87* (from the Angeloni collection). Marks of the Louvre (Lugt 1889 and 2207).
Study for the cupids fighting for the palm in the corner at the right of *Polyphemus and Acis.*
Lit.: Morel d' Arleux, IV, p. 109, no. 5039; Wittkower, *Carracci Drawings*, p. 139, under no. 307; Tomory, p. 21, under no. 47; Mahon, *Disegni*, p. 132, no. 188; Bacou, *Dessins*, p. 47, under no. 80.

1 2 7 .   M E R T O U N ,   S T .   B O S W E L L ' S ,   R O X B U R G H S H I R E ,
          C O L L E C T I O N   T H E   E A R L   O F   E L L E S M E R E ,   N O .   4 7
          (O N   L O A N   T O   L E I C E S T E R   M U S E U M S   A N D
          A R T   G A L L E R Y)

Studies for the Tazza Farnese; two cupids. Pen and wash (recto); pen (verso). 274/276 x 169 mm. Inscribed in ink in Mariette's handwriting: *T.S.V.P.* Marks of P. J. Mariette (Lugt 1852) and Sir Thomas Lawrence (Lugt 2445).
Recto: Preparatory designs for the Farnese dish.
Verso (Fig. 241): Study for the struggling cupids in the corner at the left of *Polyphemus and Galatea* (the oval frame and ribbon probably added by Mariette).
Lit.: Woodburn, *The Lawrence Gallery*, 1836, p. 23, no. 59; Tomory, pp. 20 f., no. 47, pl. XII (recto and verso); O. Kurz, in *Burlington Magazine*, XCVII, 1955, pp. 284 ff., fig. 22 (recto); Mahon, *Disegni*, pp. 87 f., no. 112, pl. 58 (recto); Holland, no. 123; Bacou, p. 47, under no. 81.

1 2 8 .   B E S A N Ç O N ,   M U S É E   D E S   B E A U X - A R T S ,   I N V .   D .   2 6 4 8
    Fig. 244

Cupids fighting for a torch. Black chalk heightened with white on light brown paper; stained. 340/342 x 264 mm. Inscribed in ink: *54* (from the Angeloni collection); and a note in Mariette's handwriting: *gravé N°. 22* (a reference to pl. 22 in Cesio's volume on the Gallery). Marks of Jean Gigoux (Lugt 1164) and the Museum of Besançon (Lugt 238c) with the number *D. 2648* in ink.
Study for the two cupids struggling for the torch in the corner at the right of *Polyphemus and Galatea.*
Lit.: Mahon, *Disegni*, pp. 124 f., no. 173, pl. 82; Bacou, *Dessins*, p. 47, under no. 81.

129. WINDSOR CASTLE, ROYAL LIBRARY,
INV. 2067, CAT. 306
Fig. 245

Cupid with a torch. Black chalk heightened with white on gray-blue paper. 336 x 228 mm.
Study for the cupid holding the torch in the corner at the right of *Polyphemus and Galatea.*
Lit.: Inv. A., p. 76; Wittkower, *Carracci Drawings,* pp. 138 f., no. 306, fig. 34; Mahon, *Disegni,* p. 125, under no. 173; Bacou, *Dessins,* p. 47, under no. 81.

130. WINDSOR CASTLE, ROYAL LIBRARY,
INV. 2089, CAT. 307
Fig. 246

Cupid. Black chalk heightened with white on blue paper. 365 x 250 mm.
Study for one of the two embracing cupids in the corner at the left of *Polyphemus and Acis.*
Lit.: Inv. A., p. 76; Wittkower, *Carracci Drawings,* p. 139, no. 307, pl. 70; Mahon, *Disegni,* pp. 128 f., no. 181, pl. 84; Holland, no. 137; Bacou, p. 47, under no. 81.

131. PARIS, LOUVRE, INV. 7395

A hand; cupids embracing. Black chalk heightened with white on gray-blue paper. 271 x 389 mm. Inscribed in ink: 55 (from the Angeloni collection). Marks of the Louvre (Lugt 1899 and 2207).
Recto: Drawing of a left hand.
Verso (Fig. 247): Study for the two cupids embracing in the corner at the left of *Polyphemus and Acis.*
Lit.: Morel d' Arleux, IV, p. 109, no. 5040; Reiset, pp. 58 f., no. 182; Wittkower, *Carracci Drawings,* p. 139, under no. 307; Mahon, *Disegni,* p. 129, under no. 181; Bacou, *Dessins,* p. 47, no. 81.

132. WINDSOR CASTLE, ROYAL LIBRARY,
INV. 2035, CAT. 311
Fig. 243

Putto. Red chalk. Lower left corner cut off and repaired. 141 x 166 mm.
Study for the right-hand putto above the medallion of *Cupid and Pan.*
Lit.: Inv. A., p. 75; Wittkower, *Carracci Drawings,* p. 140, no. 311, fig. 35; Mahon, *Disegni,* p. 129, under no. 181.

133. WINDSOR CASTLE, ROYAL LIBRARY,
INV. 2039, CAT. 294
Fig. 248

Combat of Perseus and Phineus. Black chalk heightened with a little white on gray-blue paper. Much rubbed. 261 x 413 mm.
Preliminary sketch for the fresco.
Lit.: Inv. A., p. 75; Tietze, p. 151, fig. 58 (as Domenichino); A. Foratti, *I Carracci nella teoria e nella pratica*, Città di Castello, 1913, p. 287 (as Domenichino); Pope-Hennessy, *Domenichino Drawings*, p. 14, note 33; Wittkower, *Carracci Drawings*, p. 137, no. 294, pl. 67; Mahon, *Disegni*, p. 140, under no. 201; Bacou, *Dessins*, p. 48, under no. 84.

1 3 4 . W I N D S O R C A S T L E , R O Y A L L I B R A R Y ,
        I N V . 1 9 7 3 , C A T . 2 9 6
        Fig. 251

Thescelus. Pen. Top right corner torn and repaired. 198 x 135 mm. Inscribed in ink: *87*.
Study for the figure of Thescelus in the fresco of *Perseus and Phineus*.
Lit.: Inv. A., p. 75; Tietze, p. 151, fig. 59 (as Domenichino); Foratti, *op.cit.*, p. 287 (as Agostino); Pope-Hennessy, *Domenichino Drawings*, p. 14, note 33; Wittkower, *Carracci Drawings*, p. 137, no. 296; Mahon, *Disegni*, p. 141, under no. 202; Bacou, *Dessins*, p. 48, under no. 84.

1 3 5 . B E S A N Ç O N , M U S É E D E S B E A U X - A R T S , I N V . D . 2 2 9 8
        Fig. 252

Thescelus. Black chalk heightened with white on gray-blue paper. 510/511 x 391 mm. Inscribed in ink: *17* (from the Angeloni collection). Marks of Jean Gigoux (Lugt 1164) and the Museum of Besançon (Lugt 238c) with the number *D. 2298* in ink.
Study for the figure of Thescelus in the fresco of *Perseus and Phineus*.
Lit.: Wittkower, *Carracci Drawings*, p. 137, under no. 296; Mahon, *Disegni*, pp. 140 f., no. 202, pl. 94; Bacou, *Dessins*, p. 48, under no. 84.

1 3 6 . W I N D S O R C A S T L E , R O Y A L L I B R A R Y ,
        I N V . 1 9 4 8 , C A T . 2 9 9
        Fig. 249

Phineus. Black chalk heightened with white on gray-blue paper. Most of the right side of the sheet has been cut away. Stained. 465/467 x 296 mm. Width at bottom 421 mm.
Study for the kneeling figure of Phineus in the fresco of *Perseus and Phineus*.
Lit.: Inv. A., p. 74; Tietze, p. 152 (as Domenichino); Wittkower, *Carracci Drawings*, p. 137, no. 299; Mahon, *Disegni*, p. 140, under no. 201; Bacou, *Dessins*, p. 48, under no. 84.

1 3 7 . W I N D S O R C A S T L E , R O Y A L L I B R A R Y ,
        I N V . 2 3 5 7 , C A T . 2 9 5
        Fig. 250

Perseus. Black chalk heightened with white on gray-blue paper. Two pieces of paper joined together; stained. 588 x 395 mm.

Study for the figure of Perseus holding the Gorgon's head in the fresco of *Perseus and Phineus.*

Lit.: Inv. A., p. 77; Tietze, p. 152 (as Domenichino); Bodmer, "Camerino," p. 148 (wrongly connected with the Camerino); Pope-Hennessy, *Domenichino Drawings,* p. 14, note 33; Wittkower, *Carracci Drawings,* p. 137, no. 295; Martin, p. 101, note 67; Mahon, *Disegni,* p. 140, under no. 201; Bacou, *Dessins,* p. 48, under no. 84.

138. WINDSOR CASTLE, ROYAL LIBRARY,
      INV. 2072, CAT. 297
      Fig. 254

Two of Perseus' warriors. Black chalk heightened with white on gray-blue paper. 334 x 237 mm.

Study for the two left-hand figures of the group of men hiding their faces in the fresco of *Perseus and Phineus.*

Lit.: Inv. A., p. 76; Tietze, p. 152 (as Domenichino); Pope-Hennessy, *Domenichino Drawings,* p. 14, note 33; Wittkower, *Carracci Drawings,* p. 137, no. 297, pl. 65; Mahon, *Disegni,* p. 140, no. 201; Bacou, *Dessins,* p. 48, under no. 84.

139. WINDSOR CASTLE, ROYAL LIBRARY,
      INV. 2073, CAT. 298
      Fig. 255

One of Perseus' warriors. Black chalk heightened with white on gray-blue paper. 375 x 227 mm.

Study for the right-hand figure of the group of men covering their eyes in the fresco of *Perseus and Phineus.*

Lit.: Inv. A., p. 76; Wittkower, *Carracci Drawings,* p. 137, no. 298; Mahon, *Disegni,* p. 140, under no. 201; Bacou, *Dessins,* p. 48, under no. 84.

140. WINDSOR CASTLE, ROYAL LIBRARY,
      INV. 2003, CAT. 301
      Fig. 256

Andromeda. Pen on gray-blue paper. 337 x 199 mm.

Study for the figure of Andromeda in the fresco of *Perseus and Andromeda.*

Lit.: Inv. A., p. 75; Tietze, p. 150, fig. 57 (as Domenichino); Pope-Hennessy, *Domenichino Drawings,* p. 14, note 33; Wittkower, *Carracci Drawings,* p. 138, no. 301, pl. 64; Mahon, *Disegni,* p. 139, no. 200, pl. 93; Holland, no. 144, pl. XXXIX; Bacou, *Dessins,* p. 48, under no. 85.

141. PARIS, LOUVRE, INV. 7303
      Fig. 257

Andromeda. Pen. 146 x 98 mm. Marks of the Louvre (Lugt 1899 and 2207).
Study for the figure of Andromeda in the fresco of *Perseus and Andromeda.*
Lit.: Morel d' Arleux, IV, p. 125, no. 5161; Tietze, p. 150 (as Domenichino); Pope-
Hennessy, *Domenichino Drawings*, p. 14, note 33; Wittkower, *Carracci Drawings*,
p. 138, under no. 301; Mahon, *Disegni*, p. 139, under no. 200; Bacou, *Dessins*, p. 48,
no. 85.

142. PARIS, LOUVRE, INV. 7178
     Fig. 261

Mercury and Apollo. Pen. Upper left and lower left corners torn and repaired; restorations by a later hand in gray ink. 285 x 356/357 mm. Marks of the Louvre (Lugt 1899
and 2207).
Preliminary study for the fresco of *Mercury and Apollo.*
Lit.: Morel d' Arleux, IV, p. 97, no. 4959; Tietze, p. 153; Wittkower, *Carracci Drawings*, p. 140, under no. 312; Mahon, *Disegni*, p. 141, under no. 202; Bacou, *Dessins*,
p. 49, under no. 86.

143. WINDSOR CASTLE, ROYAL LIBRARY,
     INV. 2285, CAT. 312
     Fig. 262

Mercury and Apollo. Pen. Right margin torn. 167 x 242 mm.
Sketch for the fresco of *Mercury and Apollo.*
Lit.: Inv. A., p. 77; Wittkower, *Carracci Drawings*, p. 140, no. 312, fig. 36; Mahon,
Disegni, p. 141, under no. 202; Bacou, *Dessins*, p. 49, under no. 86; catalogue of the
exhibition, *L' ideale classico del Seicento in Italia e la pittura di paesaggio*, Bologna,
1962, p. 376, no. 153.

144. PARIS, LOUVRE, INV. 7207
     Fig. 263

Arion and the Dolphin. Pen, and a faint sketch in brown chalk. 169 x 230 mm. Marks
of the Louvre (Lugt 1899 and 2207). From the Jabach collection.
Lit.: Morel d' Arleux, IV, p. 98, no. 4967; Tietze, p. 153, fig. 60; Wittkower, *Carracci
Drawings*, p. 140, under no. 312; Mahon, *Disegni*, p. 141, under no. 202; Bacou,
Dessins, p. 49, no. 87; W. Vitzthum, in *Burlington Magazine*, CIV, 1962, p. 76, fig. 28.

145. PARIS, LOUVRE, INV. 7208
     Fig. 264

Minerva and Prometheus. Pen. 179 x 218 mm. Inscribed in ink: *prometeo.* Marks
of the Louvre (Lugt 1899 and 2207). From the Jabach collection.
Lit.: Morel d' Arleux, IV, p. 98, no. 4966; Tietze, p. 153; Wittkower, *Carracci Draw-*

ings, p. 140, under no. 312; Mahon, *Disegni*, p. 141, under no. 202; Bacou, *Dessins*, p. 49, under no. 86.

146. PARIS, LOUVRE, INV. 7194
Fig. 265

Hercules and the Dragon of the Hesperides. Pen, and a faint sketch in brown chalk. 174 x 231/232 mm. Marks of the Louvre (Lugt 1899 and 2207). From the Jabach collection.

Lit.: Morel d' Arleux, IV, p. 98, no. 4968; Tietze, p. 153; Wittkower, *Carracci Drawings*, p. 140, under no. 312, and p. 154, under no. 407; Mahon, *Disegni*, p. 141, under no. 202; Bacou, *Dessins*, pp. 48 f., no. 86.

147. PARIS, LOUVRE, INV. 7195
Fig. 266

Prometheus freed by Hercules. Pen, and a faint sketch in brown chalk. 161 x 233 mm. Marks of the Louvre (Lugt 1899 and 2207). From the Jabach collection.

Lit.: Morel d' Arleux, IV, p. 98, no. 4962; Tietze, p. 153; Wittkower, *Carracci Drawings*, p. 140, under no. 312; Mahon, *Disegni*, p. 141, under no. 202; Bacou, *Dessins*, p. 49, under no. 86.

148. PARIS, LOUVRE, INV. 7177
Fig. 267

Jupiter pursuing a nymph. Pen. 180 x 222 mm. Marks of the Louvre (Lugt 1899 and 2207). From the Jabach collection.
Probably a rejected study for one of the little frescoes below the cornice.
Lit.: Morel d' Arleux, IV, p. 99, no. 4969; Bacou, *Dessins*, p. 49, no. 88; W. Vitzthum, in *Burlington Magazine*, CIV, 1962, p. 76, fig. 27.

149. WINDSOR CASTLE, ROYAL LIBRARY, INV. 1822, CAT. 314
Fig. 258

Study for one of the Virtues. Pen. Cut out as an oval. 109 x 81 mm.
Preliminary sketch by Annibale for one of the Virtues.
Lit.: Inv. A., p. 74; Wittkower, *Carracci Drawings*, p. 140, no. 314; Mahon, *Disegni*, p. 141, under no. 202; J. R. Martin, "Disegni del Domenichino per la Galleria Farnese e per la Camera di Diana nel Palazzo di Bassano di Sutri," *Bollettino d' Arte*, XLIV, 1959, pp. 41 f., fig. 6.

150. WINDSOR CASTLE, ROYAL LIBRARY, INV. 2146, CAT. 313
Fig. 259

Justice. Pen. 197 x 180 mm. Inscribed in ink: *No. 41*.

Recto: Study by Annibale for the figure of *Justice*.

Verso (stuck down): Fragmentary figure drawing.

Lit.: Inv. A., p. 76; Wittkower, *Carracci Drawings*, p. 140, no. 313; Mahon, *Disegni*, p. 141, under no. 202; Martin, "Disegni del Domenichino," pp. 41 f., fig. 5; Cat. of the exhibition, *L'ideale classico del Seicento*, p. 377, no. 154.

151. WINDSOR CASTLE, ROYAL LIBRARY,
     INV. 2037, CAT. 502
     Fig. 260

Justice. Black chalk heightened with white on paper prepared with a violet wash. 278 x 182 mm.

Recto:

    (a) Study, perhaps by Domenichino, for the figure of *Justice*;

    (b) Sketch of the upper part of a male nude (inverted).

Verso: Copy in black chalk, by another hand, after the figure of Paris in *Paris and Mercury*.

Lit.: Inv. A., p. 75; Wittkower, *Carracci Drawings*, p. 140, under no. 313, and p. 162, no. 502; Martin, "Disegni del Domenichino," pp. 42 ff., fig. 7.

BIBLIOGRAPHY

Ackerman, James S. *The Architecture of Michelangelo*. London, 1961.

Ædium Farnesiarum Tabulae ab Annibale Caraccio depictae a Carolo Cesio aeri insculptae atque a Lucio Philarchaeo explicationibus illustratae. Rome, 1753.

Affò, Ireneo. *La Zecca e moneta parmigiana illustrata*. Parma, 1788.

Alciati, Andrea. *Emblematum liber*. Augsburg, 1531.

Angeloni, Francesco. *La Historia Augusta da Giulio Cesare insino à Costantino il Magno, illustrata con la verità delle Antiche Medaglie*. Rome, 1641.

Aquila, Pietro. *Galeriae Farnesianae Icones Romae in Aedibus Sereniss. Ducis Parmensis . . . a Petro Aquila delineatae incisae*. Rome, 1674.

————. *Imagines Farnesiani Cubiculi cum ipsarum monocromatibus et ornamentis Romae in Aedibus Sereniss. Ducis Parmensis ab Annibale Carraccio aeternitati pictae à Petro Aquila delineatae incisae*. Rome, n. d.

Bacou, Roseline. *Dessins des Carrache. XXVIIIe Exposition du Cabinet des Dessins, Musée du Louvre*. Paris, 1961.

————. "Two unpublished Drawings by Annibale Carracci for the Palazzo Farnese," *Master Drawings*, II, No. 1, 1964.

Baglione, Giovanni. *Le vite de' pittori, scultori et architetti dal Pontificato di Gregorio XIII del 1572 in fino a' tempi di Papa Urbano Ottavo nel 1642*. Rome, 1642.

Basan, F. *Catalogue raisonné des différens objets de curiosités dans les sciences et arts, qui composoient le Cabinet de feu Mr. Mariette. . . .* Paris, 1775.

Baumgart, F. "La Caprarola di Ameto Orti," *Studj Romanzi*, XXV, 1935.

[Bellori, Giovanni Pietro]. *Argomento della Galeria Farnese dipinta da Annibale Carracci disegnata & intagliata da Carlo Cesio*. Rome, 1657.

Bellori, Giovanni Pietro. *Le vite de' pittori, scultori et architetti moderni*. Rome, 1672.

————. *Descrizzione delle imagini dipinte da Rafaelle d'Urbino nelle Camere del Palazzo Apostolico Vaticano*. Rome, 1695.

————. *Le vite inedite del Bellori*. Ed. by M. Piacentini. Rome, 1942.

Bertini, Aldo. "Disegni inediti di Annibale Carracci nella Biblioteca Reale di Torino," *Commentari*, II, 1951.

————. *I Disegni italiani della Biblioteca Reale di Torino*. Rome, 1958.

Bertolotti, A. *Artisti bolognesi, ferraresi ed alcuni altri del già Stato Pontificio in Roma nei secoli XV, XVI e XVII*. Bologna, 1885.

Bocchi, Achille. *Symbolicarum quaestionum de universo genere . . . libri quinque*. Bologna, 1555. Second edition, Bologna, 1574.

Bode, G. H. *Scriptores rerum mythicarum Latini tres*. Celle, 1834, 2 vols.

Bodmer, Heinrich. "Gli affreschi dei Carracci nel Palazzo Magnani ora Salem a Bologna," *Il Comune di Bologna*, XX, No. 12, 1933.

————. "Drawings by the Carracci: an Aesthetic Analysis," *Old Master Drawings*, VIII, 1933-34.

————. "Die Fresken des Annibale Carracci im Camerino des Palazzo Farnese," *Pantheon*, XIX, 1937.

————. "Die Entwicklung der Stechkunst des Agostino Carracci," *Die graphischen Künste*, N.F., V, 1940.

Boer, C. De. "Ovide moralisé. Poème du commencement du quatorzième siècle," *Ver-*

handelingen der K. Akademie van Wetenschappen, Afd. Letterkunde, new ser., XV, 1915; XXI, 1920; XXX, 1931; XXXVII, 1936; XLIII, 1938.

Bourdon, P. and Laurent-Vibert, R. "Le palais Farnèse d'après l'inventaire de 1653." *Mélanges d'archéologie et d'histoire, Ecole Française de Rome*, XXIX, 1909.

Brugnoli, Maria Vittoria. "Note alla Mostra dei Carracci," *Bollettino d'Arte*, XLI, 1956.

————. "Gli affreschi dell' Albani e del Domenichino nel palazzo di Bassano di Sutri," *Bollettino d'Arte*, XLII, 1957.

Calvesi, Maurizio. "Note ai Carracci," *Commentari*, VII, 1956.

Campori, G. *Raccolta di cataloghi ed inventarii inediti*. Modena, 1870.

Caro, Annibal. *Delle lettere familiari del Commendatore Annibal Caro . . .* , Padua, 1742, 3 vols.

Cartari, Vincenzo. *Le imagini de i dei de gli antichi*. Lyons, 1581.

Chantelou, M. de. *Journal du voyage du Cavalier Bernin en France*. Ed. by L. Lalanne. Paris, 1885.

Erizzo, Sebastiano. *Discorso sopra le medaglie de gli antichi*. Venice, 1568.

Evelyn, John. *The Diary of John Evelyn*. Ed. by E. S. de Beer. Oxford, 1955.

Félibien, A. *Entretiens sur les vies et sur les ouvrages des plus excellens peintres anciens et modernes*. Second edition, Paris, 1685-1688, 2 vols.

Ficino, Marsilio. *Opera, & quae hactenus extetêre, & quae in lucem nunc primum prodiêre omnia. . . .* Basel, 1576, 2 vols.

————. *Commentaire sur le Banquet de Platon*. Ed. by R. Marcel. Paris, 1956.

Förster, Richard. *Farnesina-Studien*. Rostock, 1880.

Foratti, Aldo. *I Carracci nella teoria e nella pratica*. Città di Castello, 1913.

————. "L'organismo decorativo del soffito nella Galleria Farnese," *Il Comune di Bologna*, XIX, 1932.

Il Funerale d'Agostin Carraccio fatto in Bologna sua patria da gl' Incaminati Academici del Disegno scritto all' Ill.ᵐᵒ et R.ᵐᵒ Sig.ʳ Cardinal Farnese. Bologna, 1603.

Giovio, Paolo. *Dialogo dell' imprese militari et amorose. . . .* Venice, 1556.

Holland, R. *The Carracci, Drawings and Paintings*. Exhibition catalogue. Newcastle upon Tyne, 1961.

L'Ideale classico del Seicento in Italia e la pittura di paesaggio. Exhibition catalogue. Bologna, 1962.

Jouanny, C. *Correspondance de Nicolas Poussin*. Paris, 1911.

Kurz, Otto. " 'Gli Amori de' Carracci': Four Forgotten Paintings by Agostino Carracci," *Journal of the Warburg and Courtauld Institutes*, XIV, 1951.

————. "Engravings on Silver by Annibale Carracci," *Burlington Magazine*, XCVII, 1955.

Lavin, Irving. "Cephalus and Procris," *Journal of the Warburg and Courtauld Institutes*, XVII, 1954.

Litta, P. *Famiglie celebri italiane*. Milan, 1819 ff., 16 vols.

Lugt, Frits. *Les marques de collections de dessins et d'estampes.* Amsterdam, 1921. *Supplément.* The Hague, 1956.

Mahon, Denis. *Studies in Seicento Art and Theory.* London, 1947.

———. "Eclecticism and the Carracci: Further Reflections on the Validity of a Label," *Journal of the Warburg and Courtauld Institutes,* XVI, 1953.

———. *Mostra dei Carracci, Disegni. Catalogo critico.* 2nd edition, Bologna, 1963.

Malaguzzi, F. "Annibale Caracci e il suo quadro di S. Rocco," *Archivio storico dell'arte,* V, 1892.

Malvasia, Carlo Cesare. *Felsina Pittrice, Vite de pittori bolognesi.* Bologna, 1678, 2 vols.

Mancini, Giulio. *Considerazioni sulla pittura.* Ed. by A. Marucchi and L. Salerno. Rome, 1956-57, 2 vols.

Mariette, Pierre-Jean. *Description sommaire des desseins des grands maistres d'Italie, des Pays-Bas et de France du cabinet de feu M. Crozat. . . .* Paris, 1741.

———. *Description sommaire des pierres gravées du cabinet de feu M. Crozat.* Paris, 1741.

———. *Traité des pierres gravées.* Paris, 1750.

Martin, John Rupert. "Immagini della Virtù: the Paintings of the Camerino Farnese," *Art Bulletin,* XXXVIII, 1956.

———. "Disegni del Domenichino per la Galleria Farnese e per la Camera di Diana nel palazzo di Bassano di Sutri," *Bollettino d'Arte,* XLIV, 1959.

Merrill, Robert V. "Eros and Anteros," *Speculum,* XIX, 1944.

Mostra dei Carracci. Catalogo critico. 3rd edition, Bologna, 1958.

Navenne, F. de. "Annibal Carrache et le Cardinal Odoardo Farnese," *Revue des Deux Mondes,* CLVIII, March, 1900.

———. *Rome, le Palais Farnèse et les Farnèse.* Paris, 1914.

———. *Rome et le Palais Farnèse pendant les trois derniers siècles.* Paris, 1923, 2 vols.

Noë, H. *Carel van Mander en Italië.* The Hague, 1954.

Nolhac, Pierre de. "Les collections d'antiquités de Fulvio Orsini," *Mélanges d'archéologie et d'histoire, Ecole Française de Rome,* IV, 1884.

———. "Une galerie de peinture au XVIe siècle: les collections de Fulvio Orsini," *Gazette des Beaux-Arts,* XXXIX, 1884.

———. *La bibliothèque de Fulvio Orsini.* Paris, 1887.

Odier, Jeanne. "Voyage en France d'un jeune gentilhomme morave en 1599 et 1600," *Mélanges d'archéologie et d'histoire, Ecole Française de Rome,* XLIII, 1926.

Orbaan, J. A. F. *Bescheiden in Italië omtrent Nederlandsche Kunstenaars en Geleerden.* The Hague, 1911.

———. *Rome onder Clemens VIII.* The Hague, 1920.

Orsini, Fulvio. *Imagines et elogia virorum illustrium et eruditor. ex antiquis lapidibus et nomismatibus expressa cum annotationib. ex bibliotheca Fulvi Ursini.* Rome, 1570.

———. *Familiae Romanae quae reperiuntur in antiquis numismatibus ab urbe condita ad tempora divi Augusti, ex bibliotheca Fulvi Ursini. Adiunctis Familiis XXX ex libro Antoni Augustini Ep. Ilerdensis.* Rome, 1577.

Ostrow, Stephen. "Note sugli affreschi con 'Storie di Giasone' in Palazzo Fava," *Arte Antica e Moderna,* No. 9, 1960.

Panofsky, Erwin. *Hercules am Scheidewege und andere antike Bildstoffe in den neueren Kunst.* Leipzig-Berlin, 1930.

Panofsky, Erwin. "Der gefesselte Eros," *Oud Holland*, L, 1933.

————. *Studies in Iconology*. New York, 1939.

————. *Galileo as a Critic of the Arts*. The Hague, 1954.

Passeri, Giovanni Battista. *Die Künstlerbiographien von G. B. Passeri*. Ed. by J. Hess. Leipzig-Vienna, 1934.

Petrucci, A. "L'incisione carraccesca," *Bollettino d'Arte*, serie IV, XXXV, 1950.

Pope-Hennessy, John. *The Drawings of Domenichino in the Collection of His Majesty the King at Windsor Castle*. New York, 1948.

Popham, A. E. and Wilde, J. *The Italian Drawings of the XV and XVI Centuries in the Collection of His Majesty the King at Windsor Castle*. London, 1949.

Posner, Donald. "Annibale Carracci and his School: the Paintings of the Herrera Chapel," *Arte Antica e Moderna*, No. 12, 1960.

Posse, H. "Das Deckenfresco des Pietro da Cortona im Palazzo Barberini und die Deckenmalerei in Rom," *Jahrbuch der Preussischen Kunstsammlungen*, XL, 1919.

Raggio, Olga, "The Myth of Prometheus," *Journal of the Warburg and Courtauld Institutes*, XXI, 1958.

Recueil de 283 Estampes . . . d'après les Desseins des Grands Maîtres, que possedoit autrefois M. Jabach, et qui depuis ont passé au Cabinet du Roy. Paris, 1754.

Reiset, F. *Notice des dessins, cartons, pastels, miniatures et émaux exposés dans les salles du premier et du deuxième étages au Musée Impérial du Louvre. Première partie: Ecoles d'Italie. . . .* Paris, 1866.

Richardson, Jonathan, Sr. and Jr. *An Account of the Statues, Bas-reliefs, Drawings and Pictures in Italy, France, &c. with Remarks*. 2nd edition, London, 1754.

Rinaldis, A. de. "Il Cofanetto Farnesiano del Museo di Napoli," *Bollettino d'Arte*, III, 1923-24.

Ripa, Cesare. *Iconologia*. Siena, 1613.

Ronchini, A. and Poggi, V. "Fulvio Orsini e sue lettere ai Farnesi," *Atti e memorie delle RR. Deputazioni di Storia Patria per le provincie dell' Emilia*, nuova serie, IV, parte II, 1880.

Ruscelli, G. *Le imprese illustri con espositioni, et discorsi. . . .* Venice, 1572.

Salerno, Luigi. "Seventeenth-Century English Literature on Painting," *Journal of the Warburg and Courtauld Institutes*, XIV, 1951.

————. "The Early Work of Giovanni Lanfranco," *Burlington Magazine*, XCIV, 1952.

————. "L'opera di Antonio Carracci," *Bollettino d'Arte*, XLI, 1956.

————. "Per Sisto Badalocchi e la cronologia del Lanfranco," *Commentari*, IX, 1958.

————. "A Domenichino Series at the National Gallery: the Frescoes from the Villa Aldobrandini," *Burlington Magazine*, CV, 1963.

Serra, L. *Domenico Zampieri detto il Domenichino*. Rome, 1909.

————. *Il Palazzo Ducale e la Galleria Nazionale di Urbino*. Rome, 1930.

Simeoni, G. *La vita et Metamorfoseo d'Ovidio, figurato & abbreuiato in forma d'epigrammi*. Lyons, 1559.

Steinberg, Leo. "Observations in the Cerasi Chapel," *Art Bulletin*, XLI, 1959.

Stix, A. and Spitzmüller, A. *Beschreibender Katalog der Handzeichnungen in der staatlichen graphischen Sammlung Albertina. Die Schulen von Ferrara, Bologna. . . .* Vienna, 1941.

Strada, Famiano. *De Bello Belgico*. Rome, 1648, 2 vols.

Tietze, Hans. "Annibale Carraccis Galerie im Palazzo Farnese und seine römische Werkstätte," *Jahrbuch der kunsthistorischen Sammlungen des allerhöchsten Kaiserhauses,* XXVI, 1906-1907.

Tomory, P. A. *The Ellesmere Collection of Old Master Drawings.* Leicester, 1954.

Valeriano, Giovanni Pierio. *Hieroglyphica, seu de sacris Aegyptiorum aliarumque gentium literis commentarii.* Lyons, 1610.

Van der Essen, L. *Alexandre Farnèse.* Brussels, 1933-37, 5 vols.

Van Loon, G. *Histoire métallique des XVII provinces des Pays-Bas. . . .* The Hague, 1732.

Van Mander, Carel. *Het Schilderboeck.* Haarlem, 1604.

Vittoria, Vincenzo. *Osservazioni sopra il libro della Felsina Pittrice.* Rome, 1703.

Vitzthum, W. "A Drawing for the Walls of the Farnese Gallery and a Comment on Annibale Carracci's 'Sala Grande,'" *Burlington Magazine,* CV, 1963.

Waleys, T. *Metamorphosis Ovidiana moraliter . . . explanata.* Paris, 1515.

Wittkower, R. *The Drawings of the Carracci in the Collection of Her Majesty the Queen at Windsor Castle.* London, 1952.

Würtenberger, F. "Die manieristische Deckenmalerei in Mittelitalien," *Römisches Jahrbuch für Kunstgeschichte,* IV, 1940.

INDEX

PLATES

1. Palazzo Farnese. Façade

2. Palazzo Farnese. Garden Façade

3. End of ceiling

4. End of ceiling

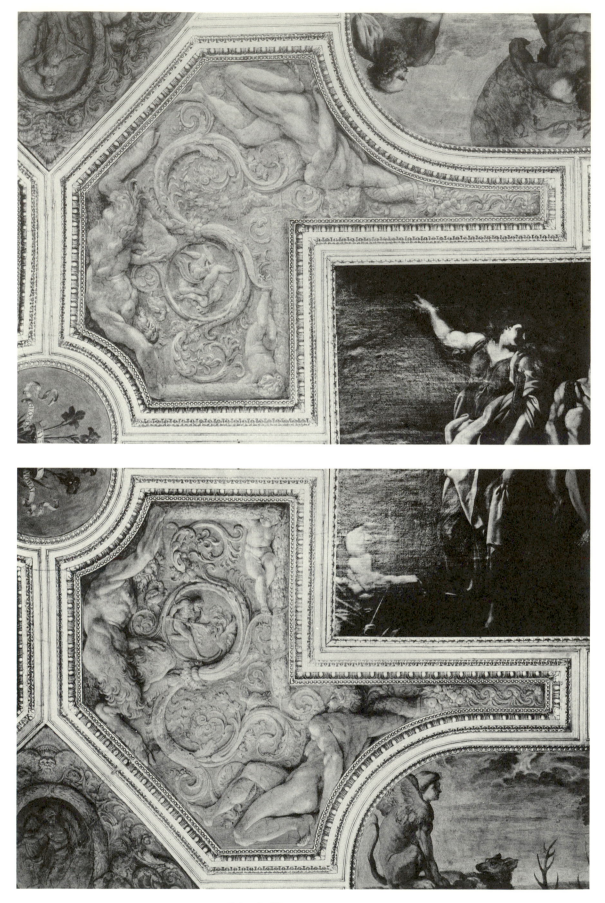

5-6. Ceiling compartments

7-8. Ceiling compartments

9. *The Choice of Hercules.* Naples, Galleria Nazionale

10. *Hercules bearing the globe*

11. *Hercules resting*

12. Lunette with Victory

13. *Honor* (spandrel); *Death of Hercules* (soffit of window)

14. Lunette with Victory

15. *Fame* (spandrel); *Infant Hercules strangling the Serpents* (soffit of window)

16. *Impresa* of Cardinal Odoardo Farnese

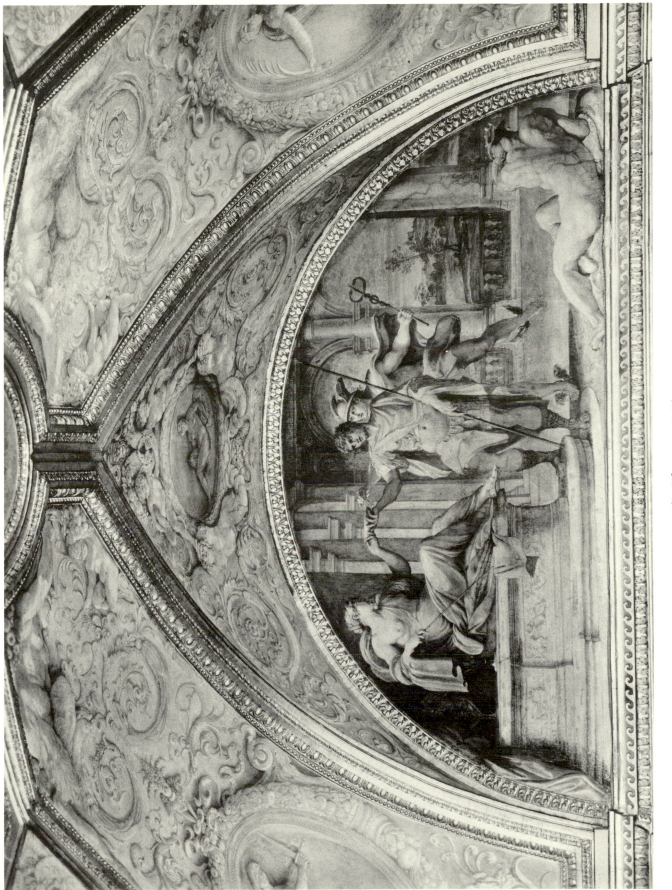

17. *Ulysses and Circe*

18. *Ulysses and the Sirens*

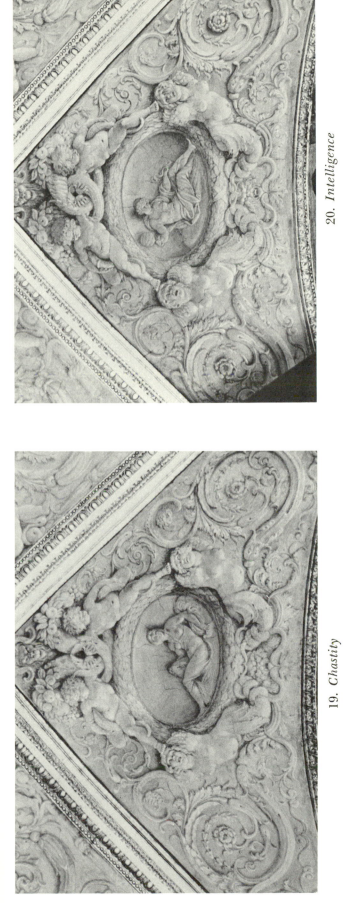

20. *Intelligence*

19. *Chastity*

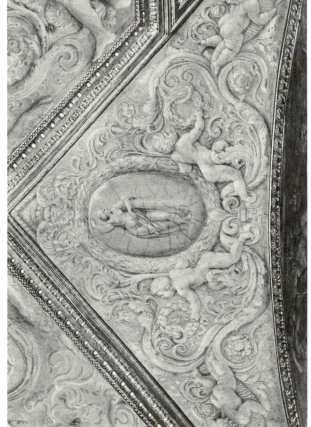

22. *Piety*

21. *Security*

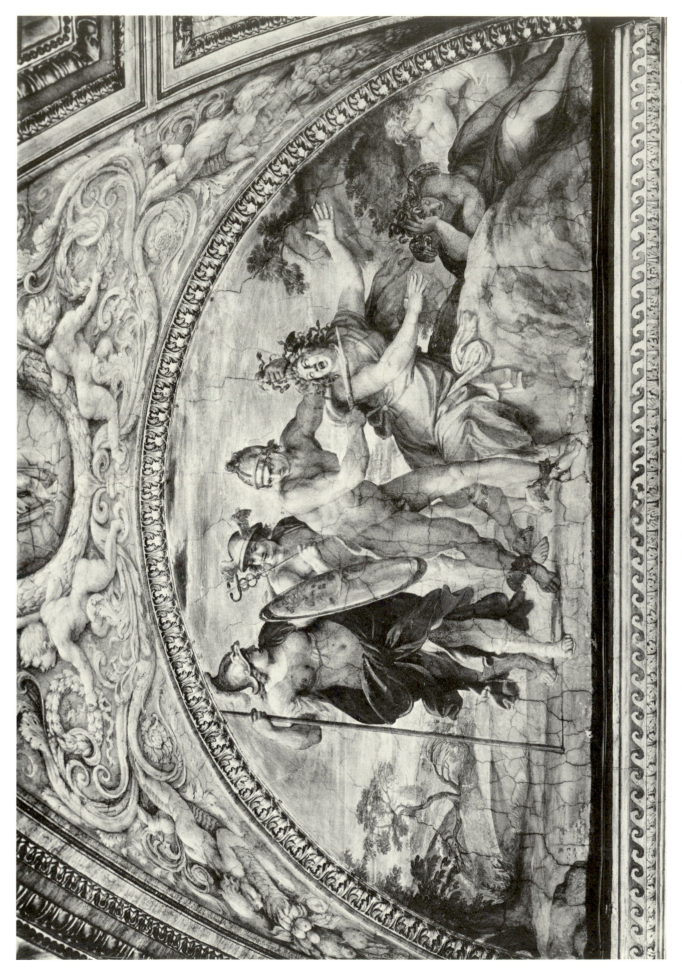

23. *Perseus and Medusa*

24. *Catanian Brothers*

25. *Justice*

26. *Temperance*

27. *Fortitude*

28. *Prudence*

29. Cherubino Alberti (attributed to), *Project for the Farnese Gallery*. Berlin-Dahlem, Kupferstichkabinett

30-31. Farnese Gallery

32. *Elevation of the Inner Wall of the Gallery.* Engraving by Giovanni Volpato

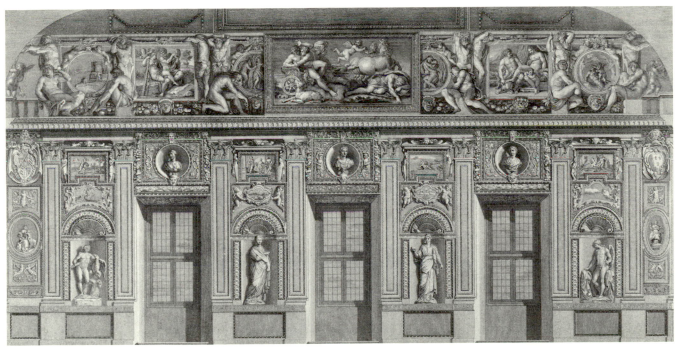

33. *Elevation of the Window Wall of the Gallery.* Engraving by Giovanni Volpato

34. *Farnese Gallery.* Engraving by Giovanni Volpato

35. *Elevation of the North End of the Gallery.* Engraving by Giovanni Volpato

36. Ceiling of the Farnese Gallery

37. Farnese Gallery. Detail of ceiling, showing decoration of wall

38. Farnese Gallery. End of ceiling

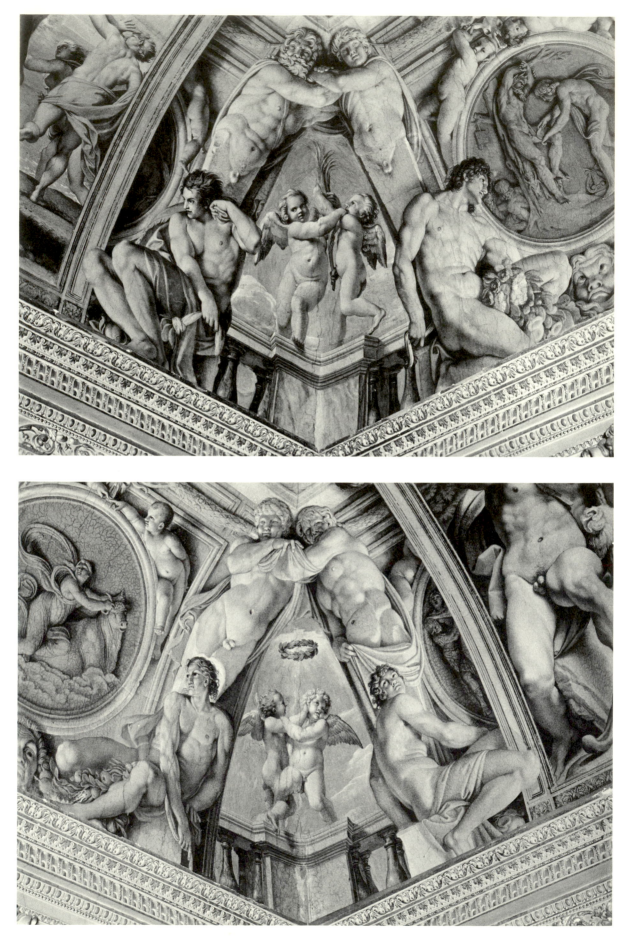

39-40. *Contest of Heavenly and Earthly Love*

41-42. *Contest of Heavenly and Earthly Love*

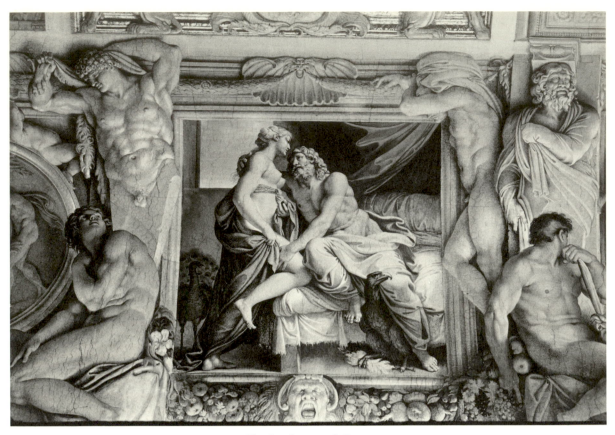

43. *Jupiter and Juno*

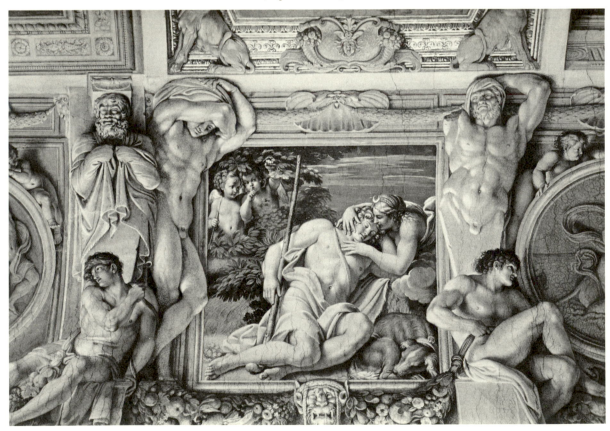

44. *Diana and Endymion*

45. *Hercules and Iole*

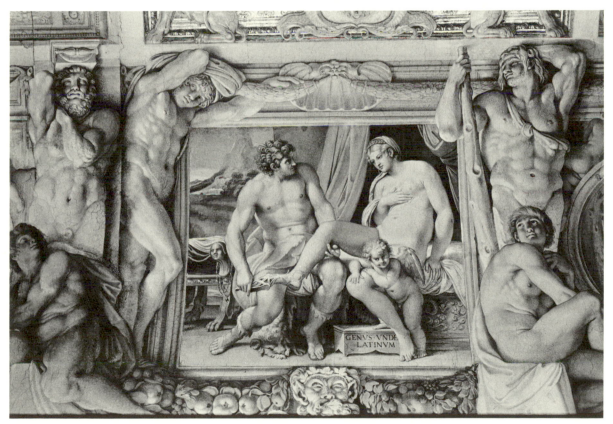

46. *Venus and Anchises*

47. Medallion with *Apollo and Marsyas*

48. Medallion with *Cupid and Pan*

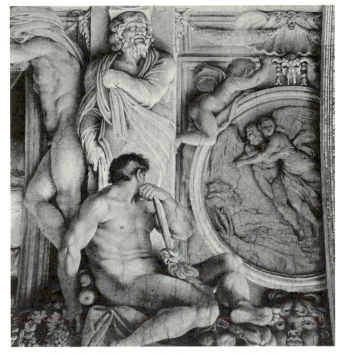

49. Medallion with *Boreas and Orithyia*

50. Medallion with *Orpheus and Eurydice*

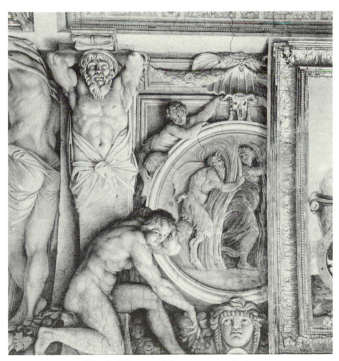

51. Medallion with *Pan and Syrinx*

52. Medallion with *Salmacis and Hermaphroditus*

53. Medallion with *Europa and the Bull*

54. Medallion with *Hero and Leander*

55. Medallion with a scene
of abduction

56. Medallion with *Jason and
the Golden Fleece*

57. Medallion with *Paris*

58. Medallion with *Pan*

59. *Aurora and Cephalus*

60. *Glaucus and Scylla*

61. End of vault, showing *Polyphemus and Galatea*

62. End of vault, showing *Polyphemus and Acis*

63. *Polyphemus and Galatea*

64. *Polyphemus and Acis*

65. *Pan and Diana*

66. *Mercury and Paris*

67. *Apollo and Hyacinthus*

68. *Ganymede and the Eagle*

69. *Triumph of Bacchus and Ariadne*

71. *Triumph of Bacchus and Ariadne* (detail)

70. *Triumph of Bacchus and Ariadne* (detail)

72. *Triumph of Bacchus and Ariadne* (detail)

74. *Temperance*

73. *Fortitude*

76. *Charity*

75. *Justice*

77. *Perseus and Andromeda*

78. *Combat of Perseus and Phineus*

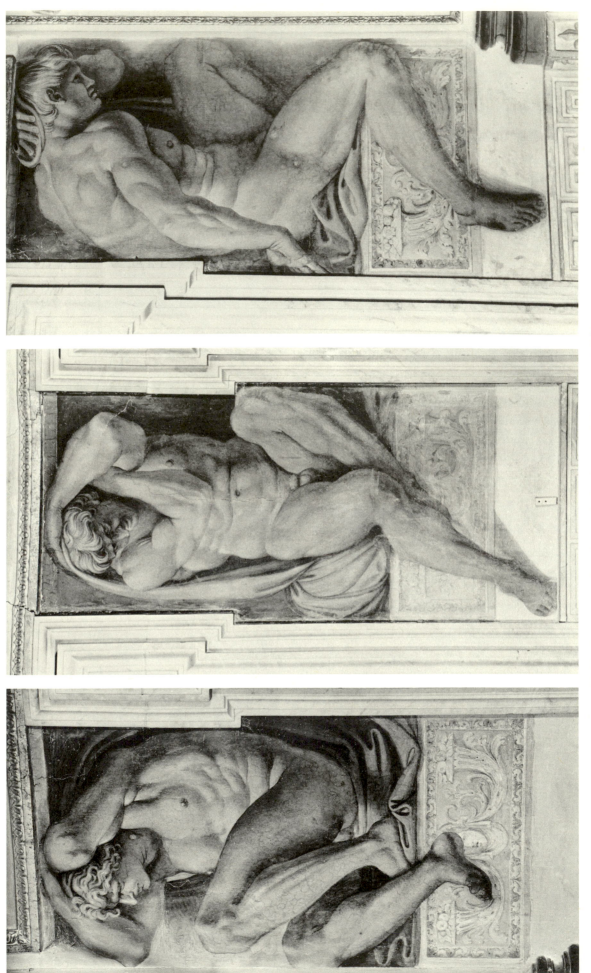

79-81. Bronze captives beneath the fresco of *Perseus and Phineus*

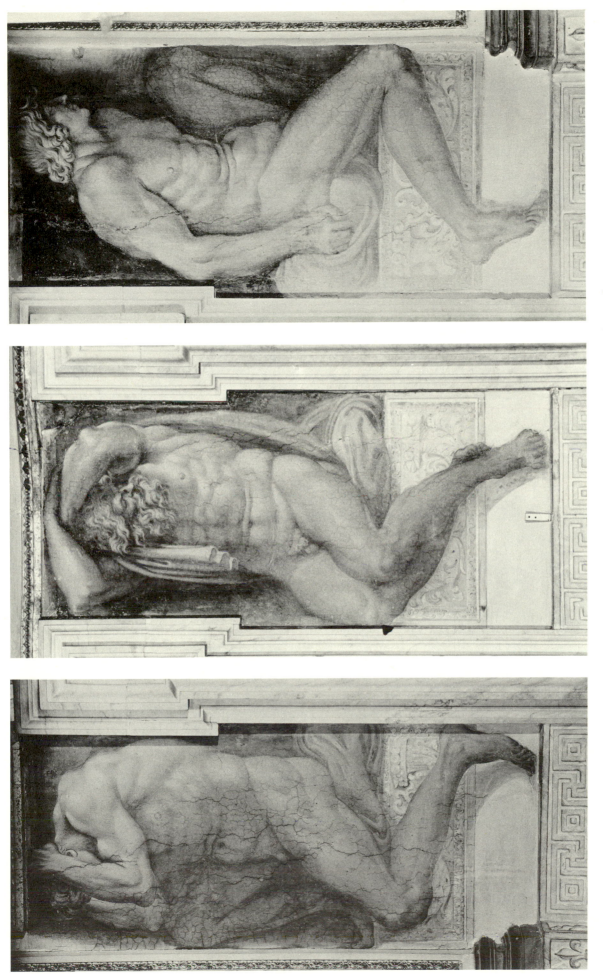

82-84. Bronze captives beneath the fresco of *Perseus and Andromeda*

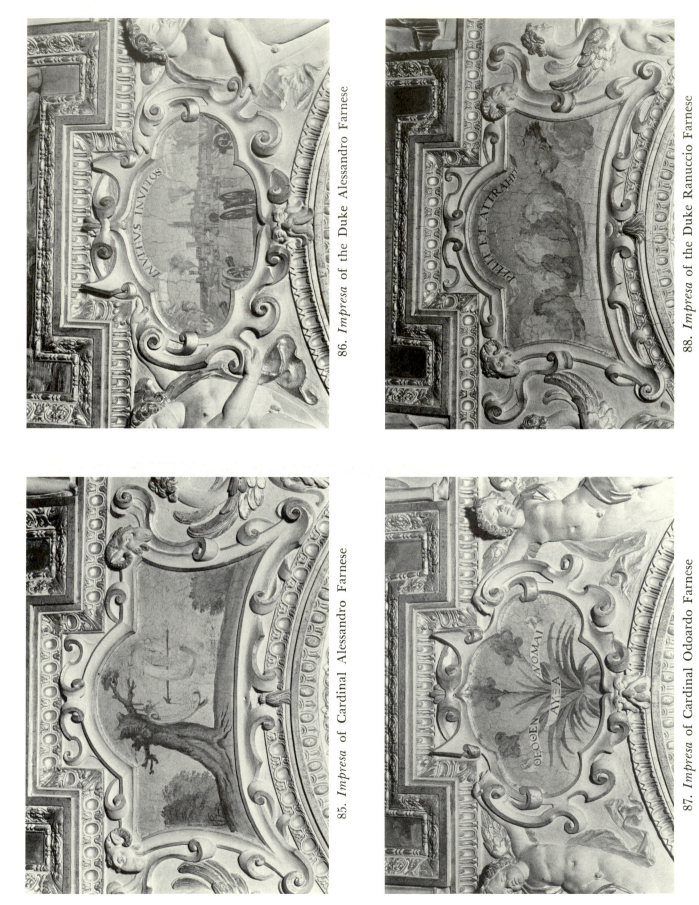

86. *Impresa* of the Duke Alessandro Farnese

88. *Impresa* of the Duke Ranuccio Farnese

85. *Impresa* of Cardinal Alessandro Farnese

87. *Impresa* of Cardinal Odoardo Farnese

89. *The Virgin with the Unicorn*

90-91. Decorative panels of window soffits

92. *Daedalus and Icarus*

93. *Diana and Callisto*

94. *Transformation of Callisto*

95. *Mercury and Apollo*

96. *Arion and the Dolphin*

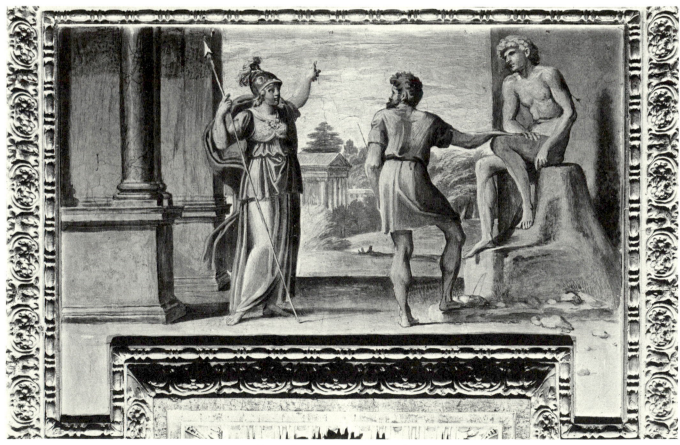

97. *Minerva and Prometheus*

98. *Hercules and the Dragon*

99. *Hercules freeing Prometheus*

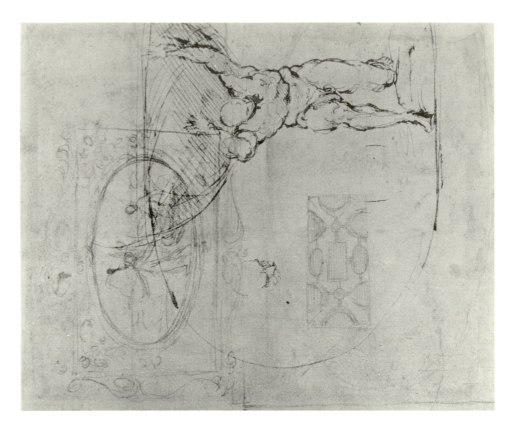

100-101. *Studies for the Camerino* (No. 1 recto and verso). Oxford, Ashmolean Museum

103. *Studies for the grisaille ornament of the ceiling*
(No. 30 verso). New York, Metropolitan Museum

102. *Design for the decorative framework of the ceiling (No. 2).*
Windsor, Royal Library

105. *Faun* (No. 3). Paris, Louvre

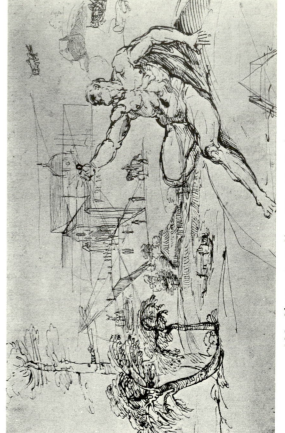

106. *Sheet of studies* (No. 7). Paris, Louvre

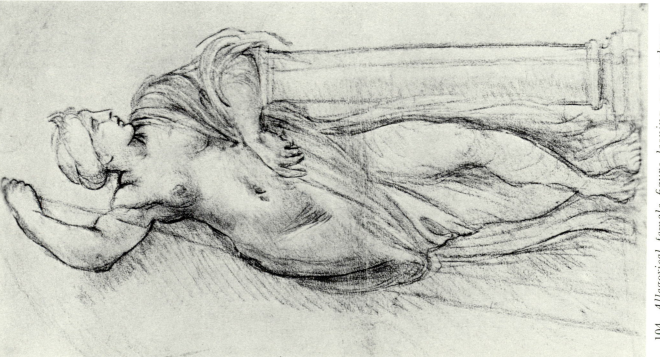

104. *Allegorical female figure leaning on a column*
(No. 6). Paris, Louvre

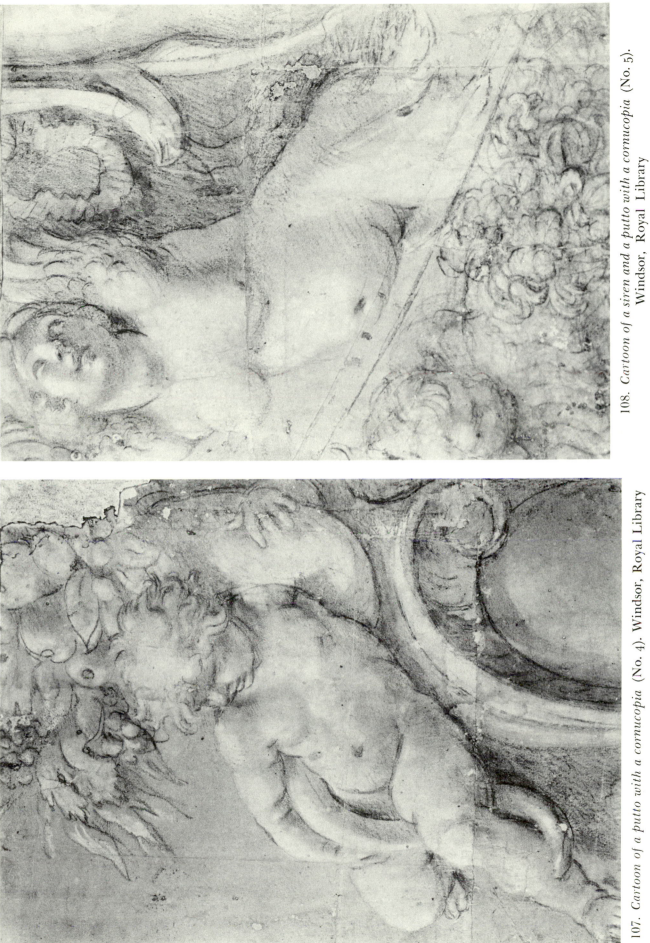

108. *Cartoon of a siren and a putto with a cornucopia* (No. 5). Windsor, Royal Library

107. *Cartoon of a putto with a cornucopia* (No. 4). Windsor, Royal Library

110. *Woman standing and pointing upward* (No. 8).
Besançon, Musée des Beaux-Arts

109. *Poet* (No. 11). Paris, Louvre

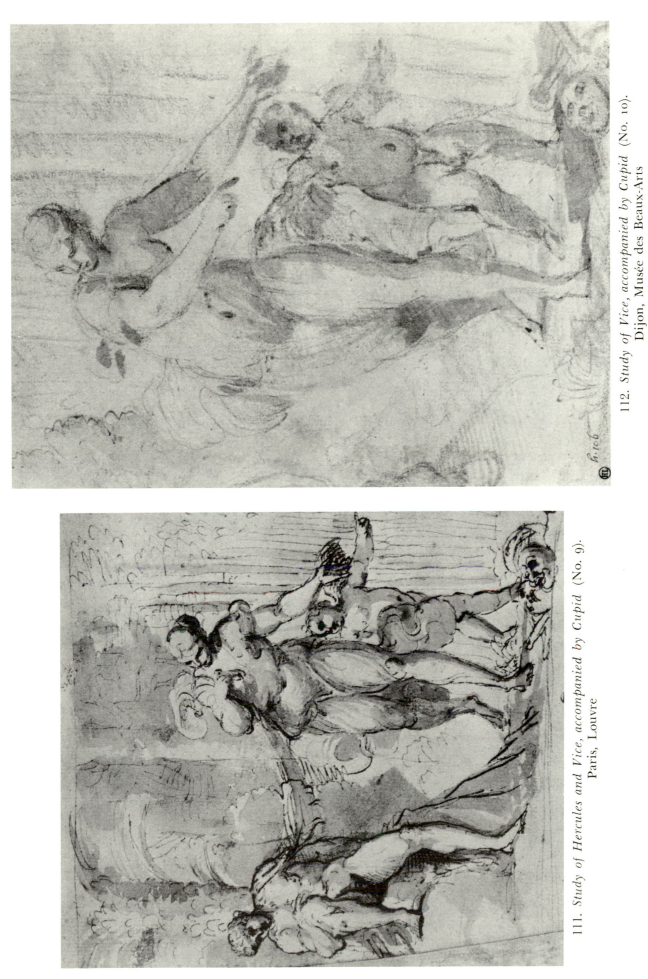

112. *Study of Vice, accompanied by Cupid* (No. 10).
Dijon, Musée des Beaux-Arts

111. *Study of Hercules and Vice, accompanied by Cupid* (No. 9).
Paris, Louvre

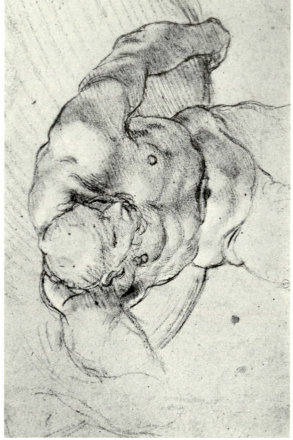

113. *Study for Hercules bearing the globe* (No. 36 verso).
     Turin, Biblioteca Reale
114. *Hercules with the globe* (No. 13). Turin,
     Biblioteca Reale
115. *Study for Hercules bearing the globe* (No. 12).
     Paris, Louvre

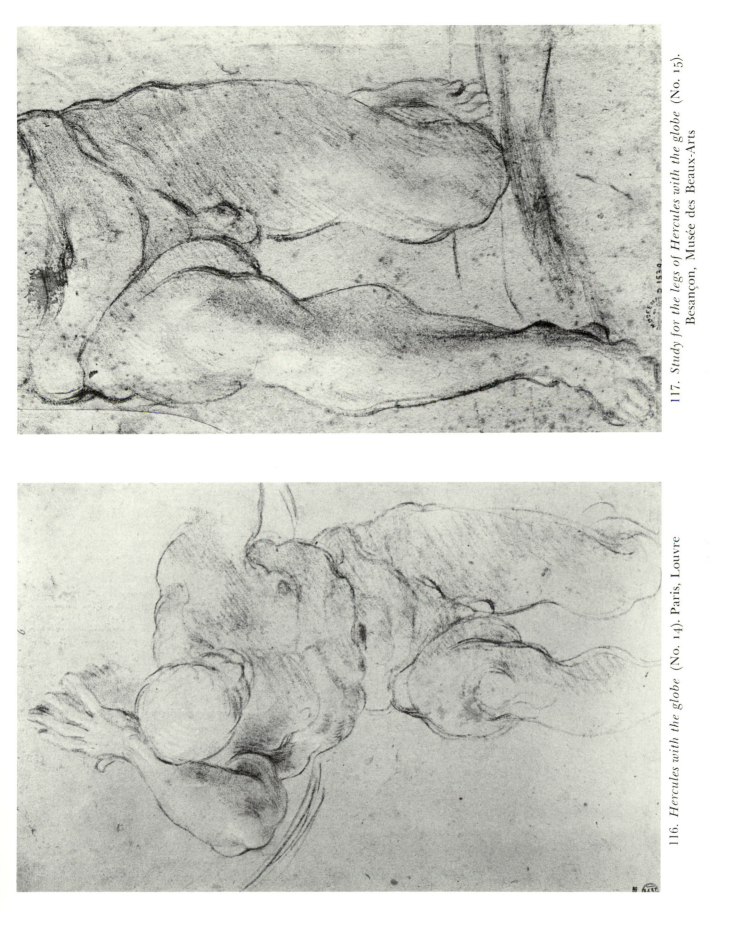

117. *Study for the legs of Hercules with the globe* (No. 15). Besançon, Musée des Beaux-Arts

116. *Hercules with the globe* (No. 14). Paris, Louvre

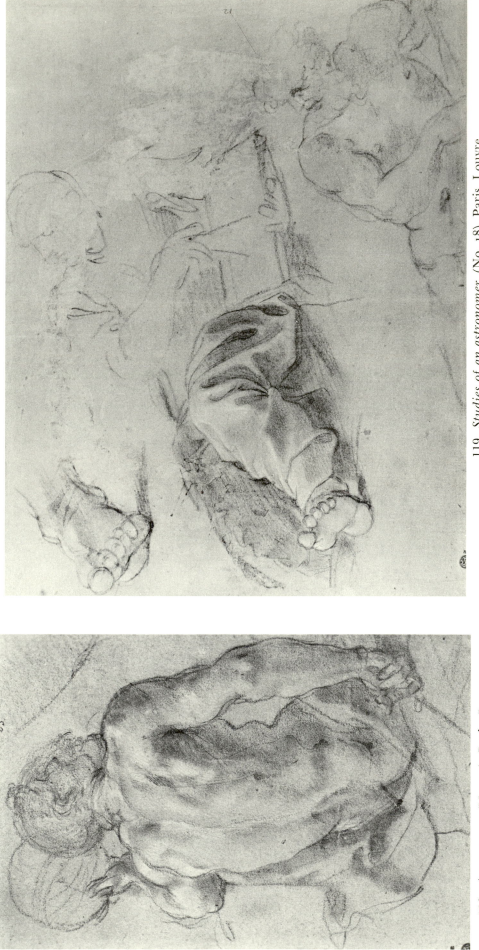

119. *Studies of an astronomer* (No. 18). Paris, Louvre

118. *Astronomer* (No. 17). Paris, Louvre

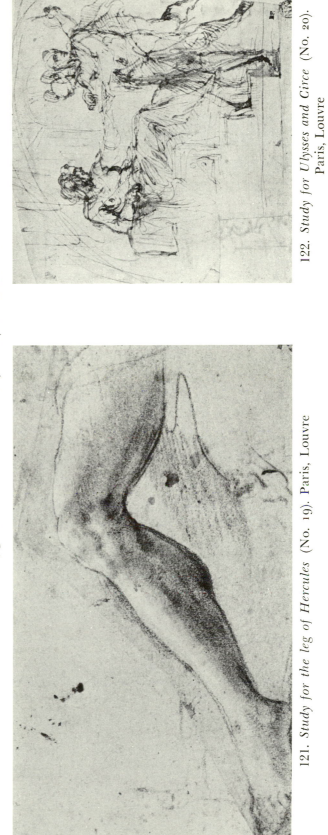

122. *Study for Ulysses and Circe* (No. 20).
Paris, Louvre

120. *Seated male figure with outstretched arm* (No. 16). Paris, Louvre

121. *Study for the leg of Hercules* (No. 19). Paris, Louvre

123. *Study for Ulysses and Circe* (No. 21 recto). Paris, Louvre

124. *Study for Ulysses and Circe* (No. 22). Paris, Louvre

125. *Circe* (No. 23). Windsor, Royal Library

126. *Mercury* (No. 24). Besançon,
Musée des Beaux-Arts

127. *One of Ulysses' companions* (No. 25). Paris, Louvre

128. *Studies for the Camerino* (No. 21 verso). Paris, Louvre

129. *Two oarsmen* (No. 26). Paris, Louvre

130. *Helmsman* (No. 27). Paris, Louvre

131. *Cartoon of a helmsman* (No. 28). London, British Museum

132. *Three Sirens* (No. 29). Windsor, Royal Library

133. *Study for Perseus and Medusa* (No. 30 recto). New York, Metropolitan Museum

134. *Medusa* (No. 31). Paris, Louvre

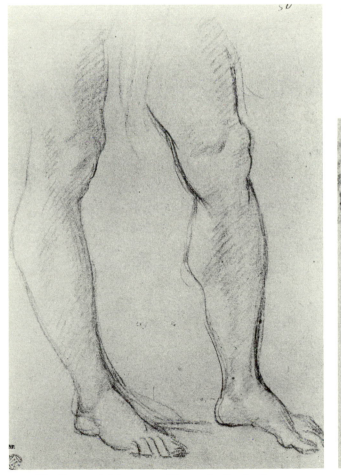

135. *Legs of Mercury* (No. 33). Paris, Louvre 136. *Head of Mercury* (No. 32). Paris, Louvre

138. *Bellerophon and the Chimera* (No. 40). Paris, Louvre

137. *Amphinomus carrying his father* (No. 34). Windsor, Royal Library

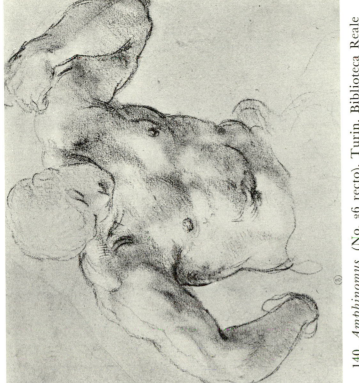

140. *Amphinomus* (No. 36 recto). Turin, Biblioteca Reale

141. *Study for the legs of Amphinomus'
father* (No. 37). Paris, Louvre

139. *Amphinomus carrying his father* (No. 35).
Montpellier, Musée Atger

142. *Study for the mother carried by Anapius*
(No. 39). Paris, Louvre

143. *Anapius* (No. 38). Paris, Louvre

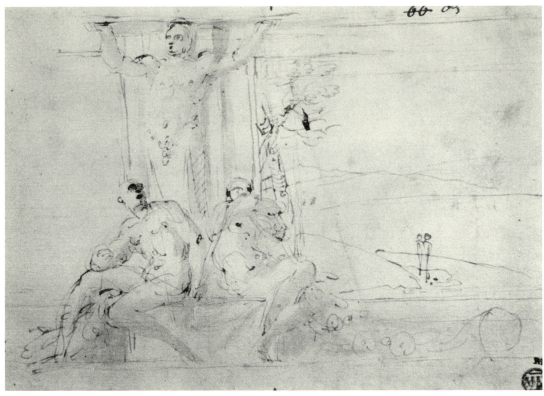

144. *Sketch for a decorative frieze* (No. 41). Paris, Louvre

145. *Study for the decoration of a ceiling* (No. 43). Paris, Louvre

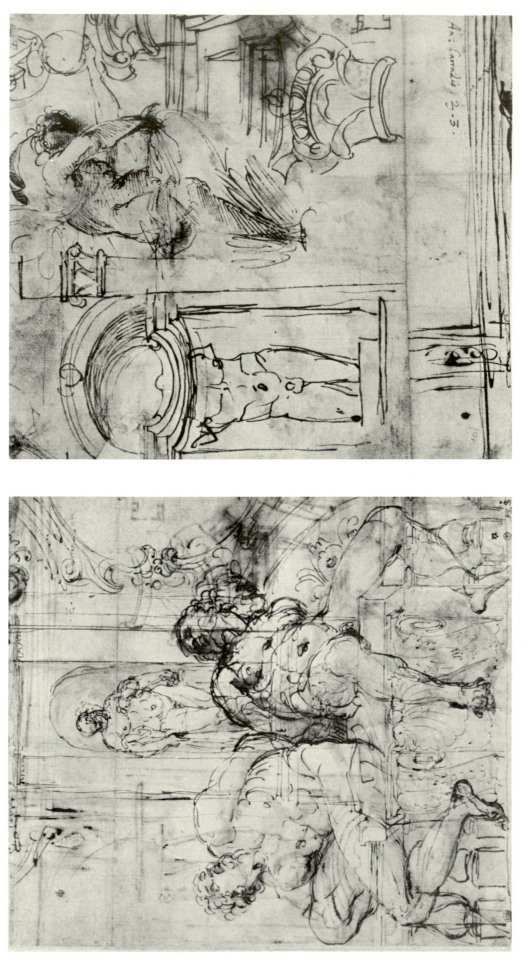

146-147. *Studies for a decorative frieze* (No. 42 recto and verso).
Paris, Ecole des Beaux-Arts

148. *Studies for the Farnese ceiling* (No. 44 recto). Paris, Louvre

149. *Studies for the Farnese ceiling* (No. 44 verso). Paris, Louvre

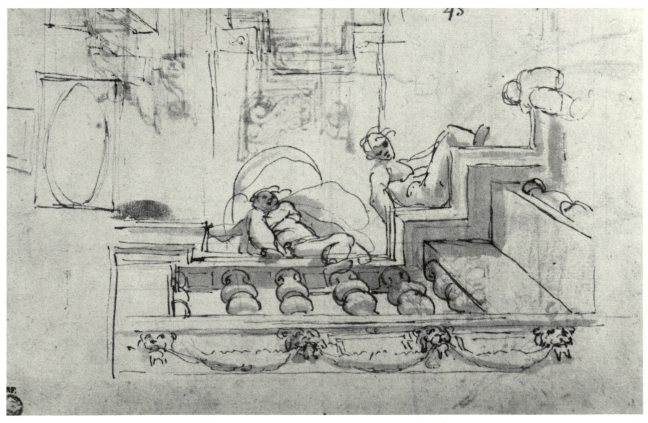

150. *Studies for the Farnese ceiling* (No. 45). Paris, Louvre

151. *Design for the Farnese ceiling* (No. 46). Paris, Louvre

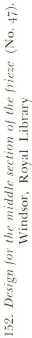

153. *Study for a decorative frame* (No. 49).
Paris, Louvre

152. *Design for the middle section of the frieze* (No. 47).
Windsor, Royal Library

154. *Studies for the frieze* (No. 48). Windsor, Royal Library

155. *Studies for the Farnese ceiling* (No. 50). Paris, Louvre

156. *Woman seated in a richly ornamented room* (No. 51).
Chatsworth, Devonshire Coll.

157. *Sheet of studies* (No. 52 verso).
Paris, Louvre

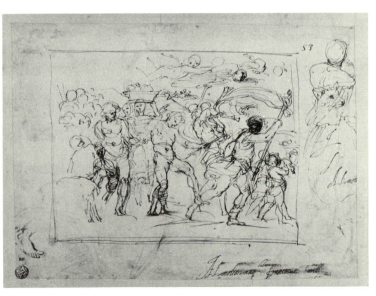

158. *Bacchic procession* (No. 53 recto).
Paris, Louvre

159. *Bacchic procession* (No. 54). Vienna, Albertina

161. *Triumph of Bacchus and Ariadne* (No. 56). Vienna, Albertina

160. *Bacchus in his chariot* (No. 55). Paris, Louvre

163. *Ariadne in her chariot* (No. 58). Vienna, Albertina

162. *Studies for the Triumph of Bacchus and Ariadne* (No. 57). Vienna, Albertina

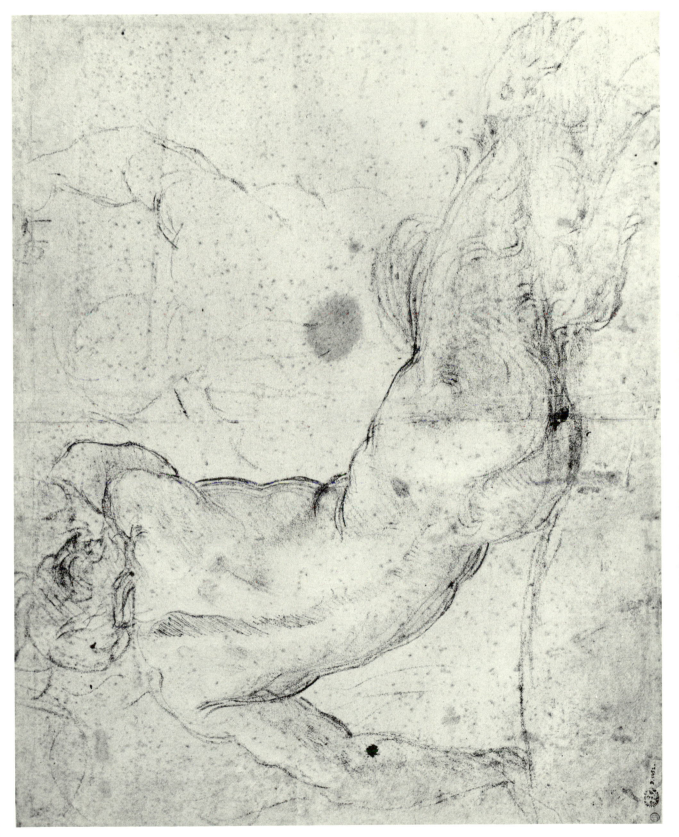

164. *Satyr* (No. 59). Besançon, Musée des Beaux-Arts

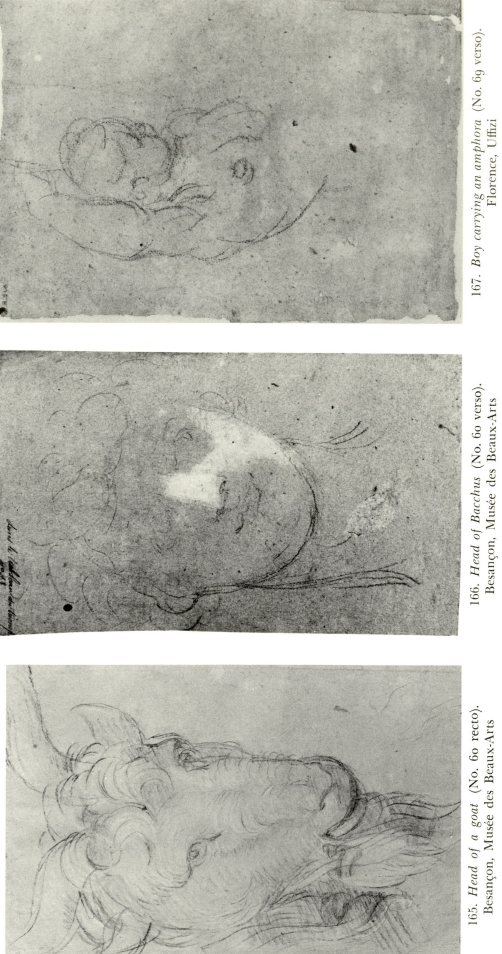

167. *Boy carrying an amphora* (No. 69 verso).
Florence, Uffizi

166. *Head of Bacchus* (No. 60 verso).
Besançon, Musée des Beaux-Arts

165. *Head of a goat* (No. 60 recto).
Besançon, Musée des Beaux-Arts

169. *Studies of goats* (No. 63). Windsor, Royal Library

168. *Ariadne* (No. 61). Florence, Gernsheim Coll.

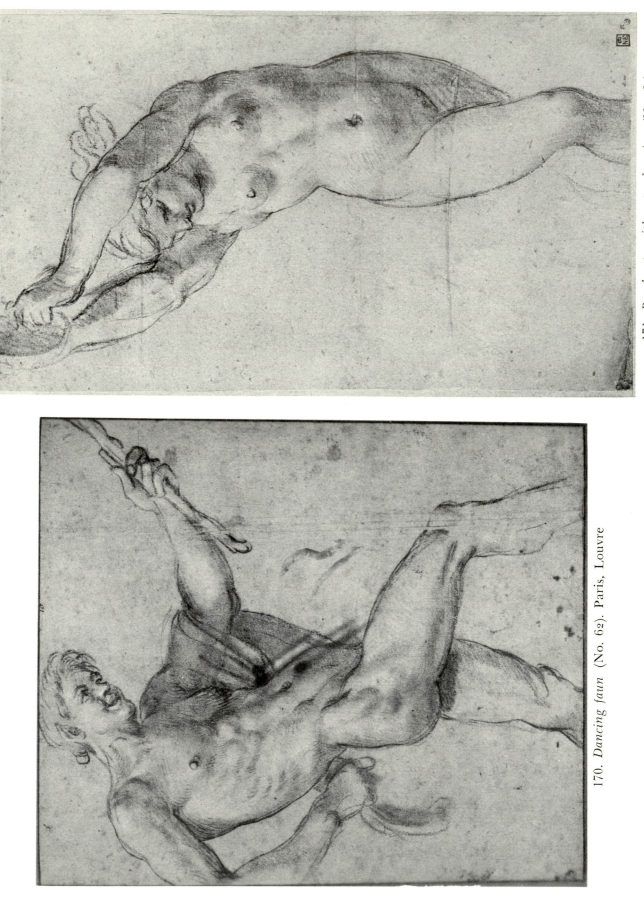

171. *Bacchante with a tambourine* (No. 64).
Budapest, Museum of Fine Arts

170. *Dancing faun* (No. 62). Paris, Louvre

173. *Silenus supported by a faun* (No. 66).
Turin, Biblioteca Reale

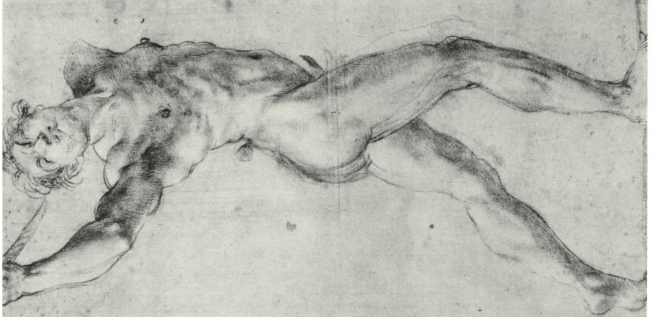

172. *Faun blowing a trumpet* (No. 65). Paris, Louvre

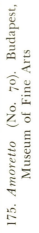

175. *Amoretto* (No. 70). Budapest,
Museum of Fine Arts

176. *Reclining male figure* (No. 68). Paris, Louvre

174. *Girl carrying a basket on her head* (No 67). Paris, Louvre

177. *Earthly Venus* (No. 69 recto). Florence, Uffizi

178. *Part of the cartoon of the Triumph of Bacchus and Ariadne* (No. 71).
Urbino, Galleria Nazionale delle Marche

179. *Pan and Diana* (No. 72). Chatsworth, Devonshire Coll.

180. *Pan and Diana* (No. 73).
Windsor, Royal Library

181. *Studies of Pan and an eagle* (No. 74 verso). Paris, Louvre

183. *Diana* (No. 74 recto). Paris, Louvre

182. *Pan* (No. 75). Paris, Louvre

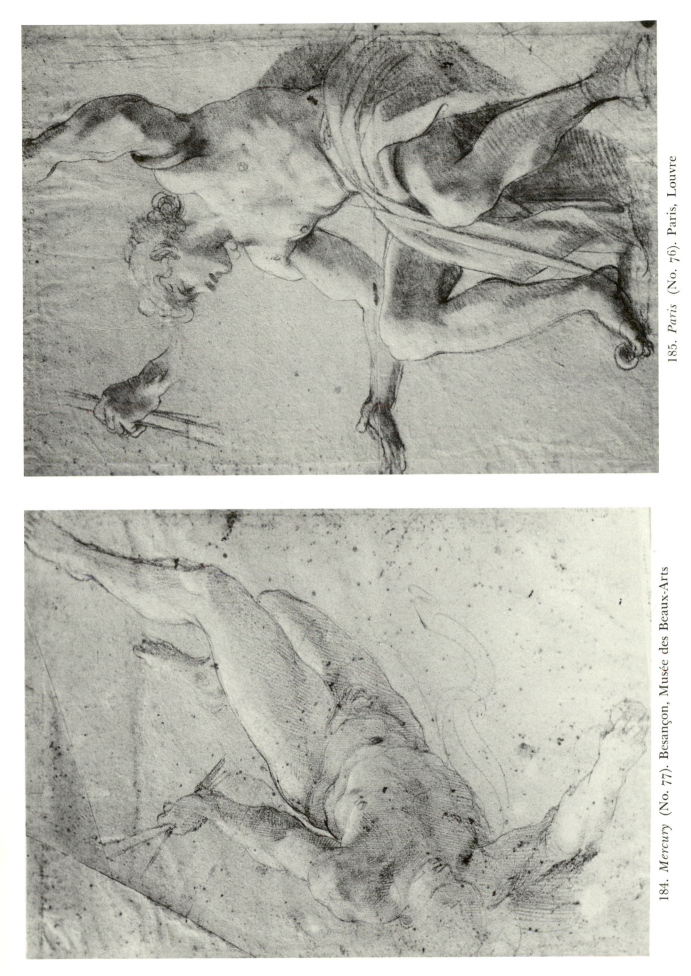

185. *Paris* (No. 76). Paris, Louvre

184. *Mercury* (No. 77). Besançon, Musée des Beaux-Arts

186. *Sphinx* (No. 78). Paris, Louvre

187. *Dog* (No. 101 verso). Besançon, Musée des Beaux-Arts

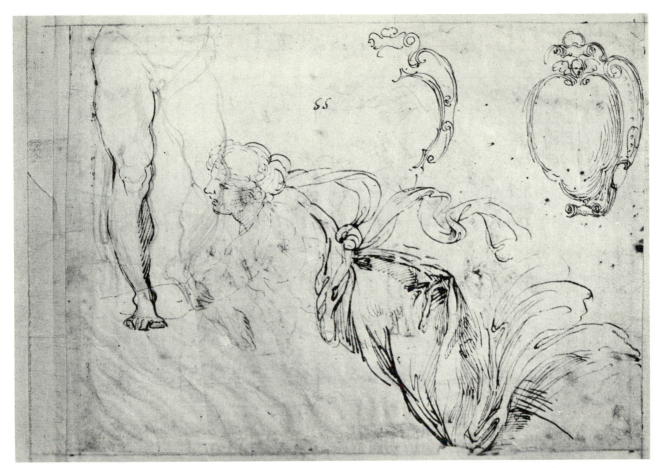

188. Agostino Carracci, *Studies of Aurora, a man's legs, and two cartouches*
(No. 53 verso). Paris, Louvre

189. Agostino Carracci, *Tithonus* (No. 79). Paris, Louvre

190. Agostino Carracci, *Cartoon of Aurora and Cephalus* (No. 80). London, National Gallery

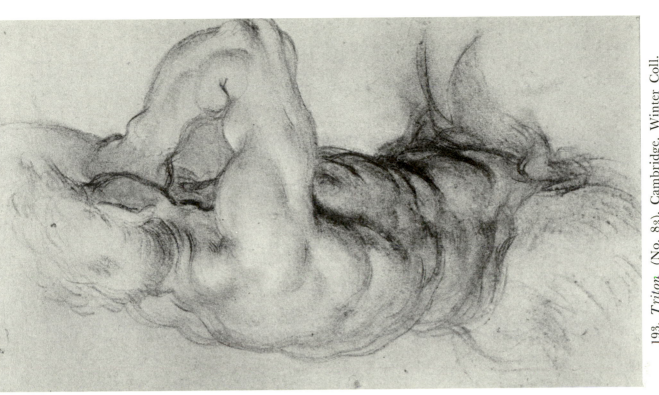

193. *Triton* (No. 83). Cambridge, Winter Coll.

191. Agostino Carracci, *Cupid* (No. 81 recto). Besançon, Musée des Beaux-Arts

192. Agostino Carracci, *Glaucus and Scylla* (No. 81 verso). Besançon, Musée des Beaux-Arts

194. Agostino Carracci, *Cartoon of Glaucus and Scylla* (No. 82). London, National Gallery

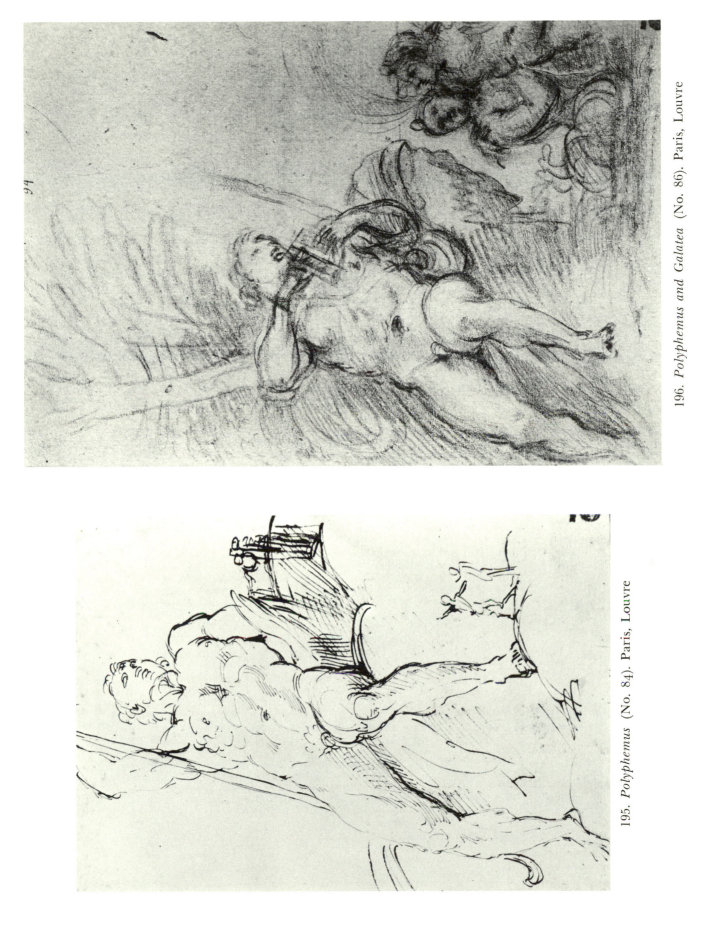

196. *Polyphemus and Galatea* (No. 86). Paris, Louvre

195. *Polyphemus* (No. 84). Paris, Louvre

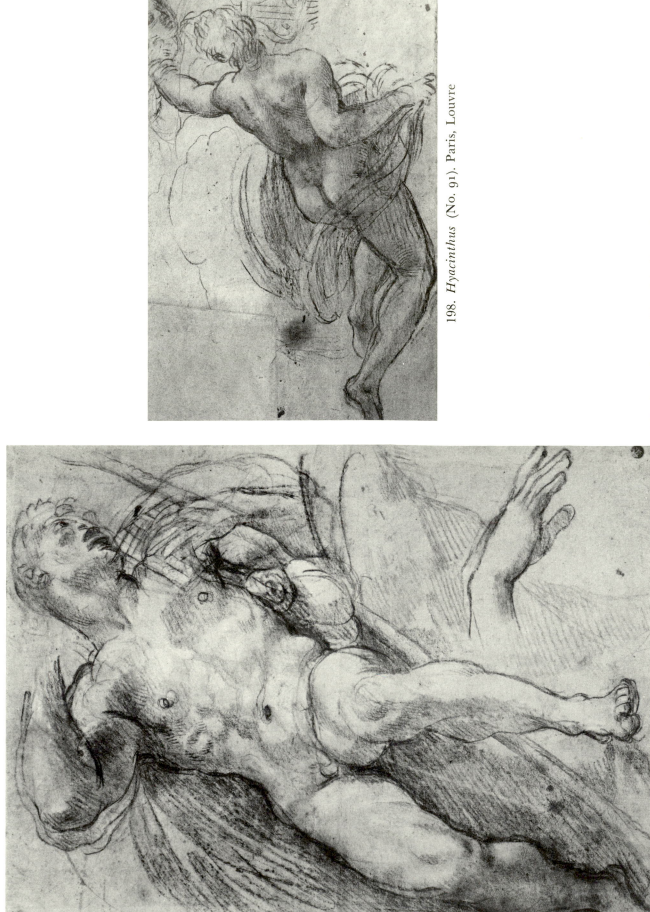

198. *Hyacinthus* (No. 91). Paris, Louvre

197. *Polyphemus* (No. 85). Paris, Louvre

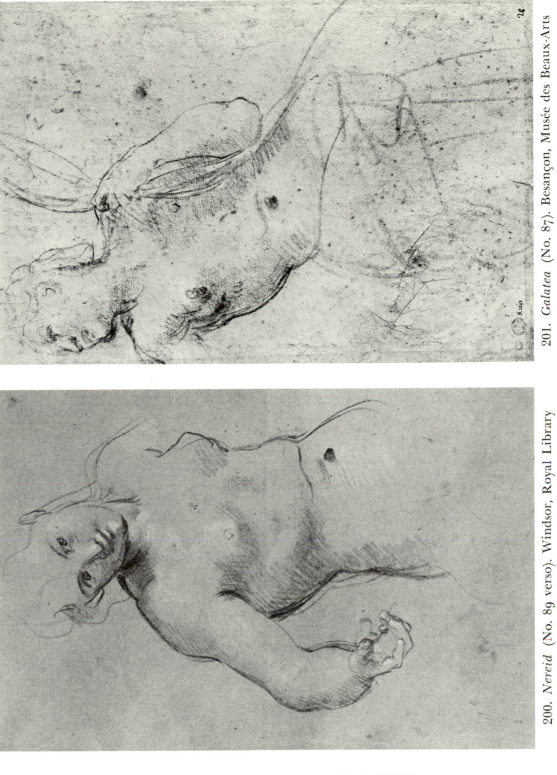

201. *Galatea* (No. 87). Besançon, Musée des Beaux-Arts

200. *Nereid* (No. 89 verso). Windsor, Royal Library

199. *Study of an arm* (No. 88). Paris, Louvre

203. *Juno* (No. 92). London, Courtauld Institute of Art

202. *Polyphemus* (No. 90). Windsor, Royal Library

205. *Juno* (No. 94 recto). Besançon, Musée des Beaux-Arts

204. *Jupiter and Juno* (No. 93). Ellesmere Coll.

206. *Studies of Jupiter* (No. 94 verso). Besançon, Musée des Beaux-Arts

207. *Study for the legs of Jupiter*
(No. 95). Paris, Louvre

208. *Iole* (No. 96). Besançon,
Musée des Beaux-Arts

209. *Dog* (No. 97). Paris, Louvre

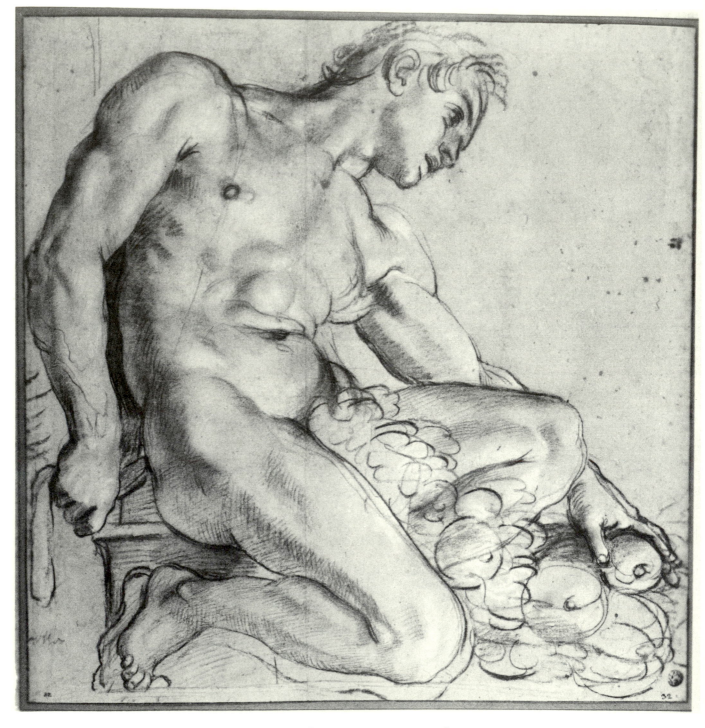

210. *Seated ignudo* (No. 98 recto). Paris, Louvre

211. *Seated ignudo* (No. 99). Paris, Louvre

212. *Seated ignudo* (No. 98 verso). Paris, Louvre

213. *Seated ignudo* (No. 100). Paris, Louvre

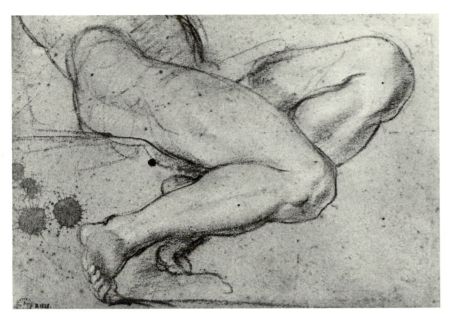

214. *Study for the lower part of a seated ignudo* (No. 101 recto).
Besançon, Musée des Beaux-Arts

215. *Seated ignudo* (No. 103).
Bremen, Kunsthalle

216. *Seated ignudo* (No. 102). Besançon, Musée des Beaux-Arts

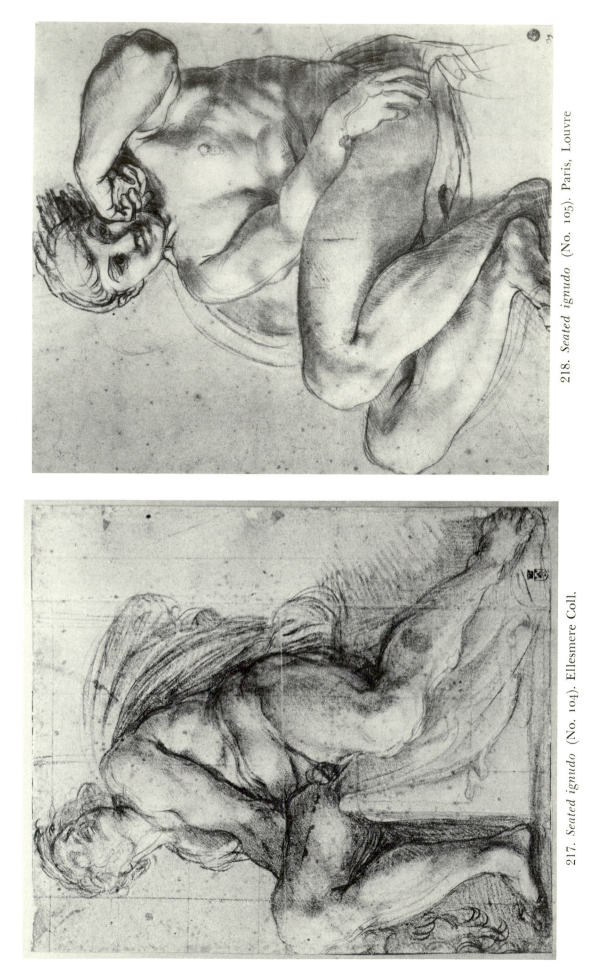

218. *Seated ignudo* (No. 105). Paris, Louvre

217. *Seated ignudo* (No. 104). Ellesmere Coll.

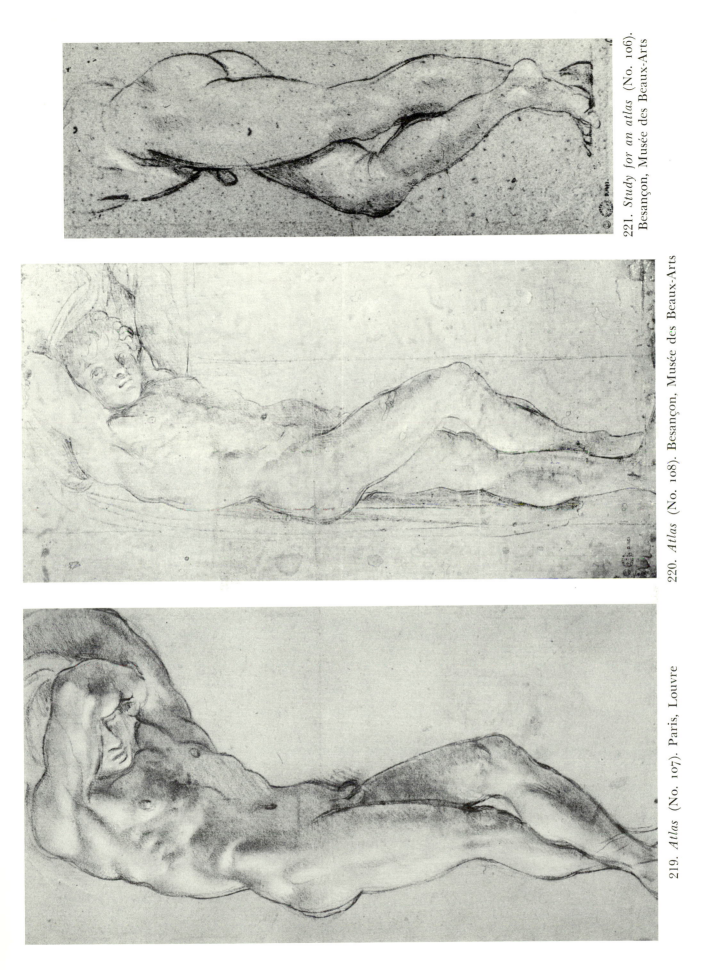

221. *Study for an atlas* (No. 106). Besançon, Musée des Beaux-Arts

220. *Atlas* (No. 108). Besançon, Musée des Beaux-Arts

219. *Atlas* (No. 107). Paris, Louvre

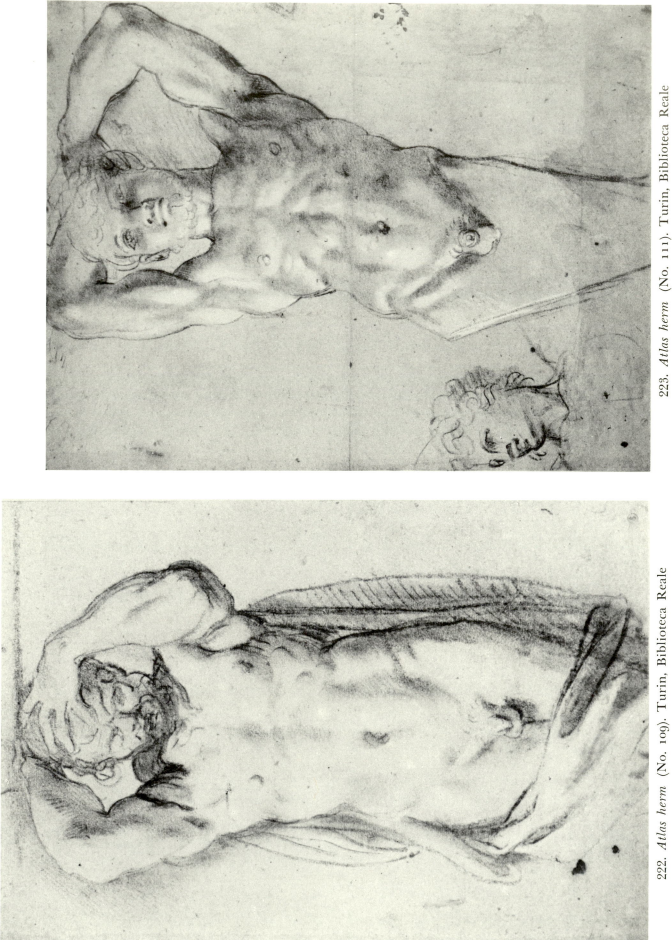

223. *Atlas herm* (No. 111). Turin, Biblioteca Reale

222. *Atlas herm* (No. 109). Turin, Biblioteca Reale

224. *Studies for an atlas herm and St. John the Baptist* (No. 110 verso). Windsor, Royal Library

225. *Atlas herm with a club* (No. 114). Florence, Uffizi

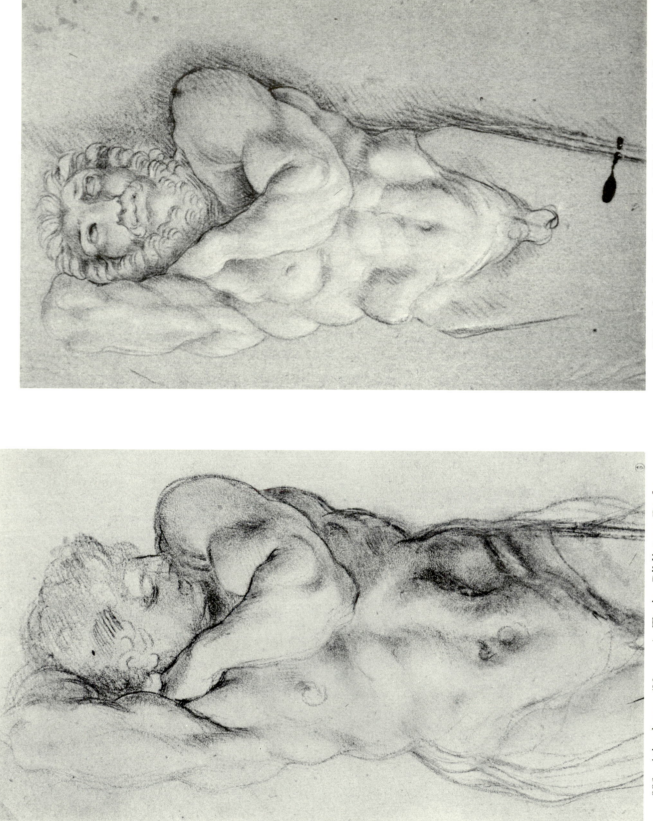

227. *Atlas herm* (No. 113). Windsor, Royal Library

226. *Atlas herm* (No. 112). Turin, Biblioteca Reale

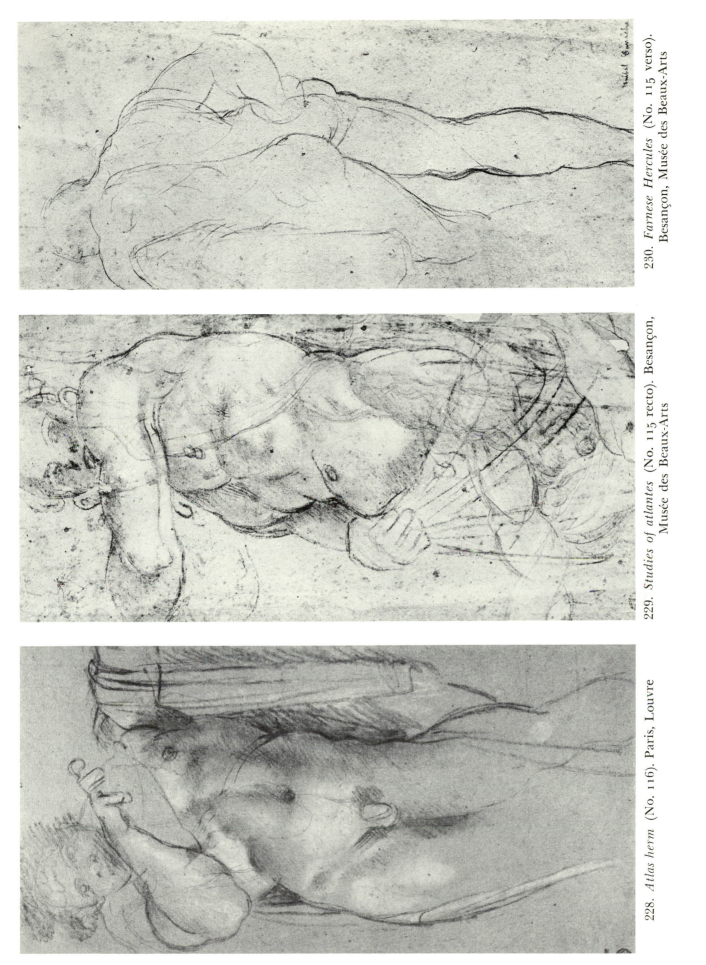

230. *Farnese Hercules* (No. 115 verso). Besançon, Musée des Beaux-Arts

229. *Studies of atlantes* (No. 115 recto). Besançon, Musée des Beaux-Arts

228. *Atlas herm* (No. 116). Paris, Louvre

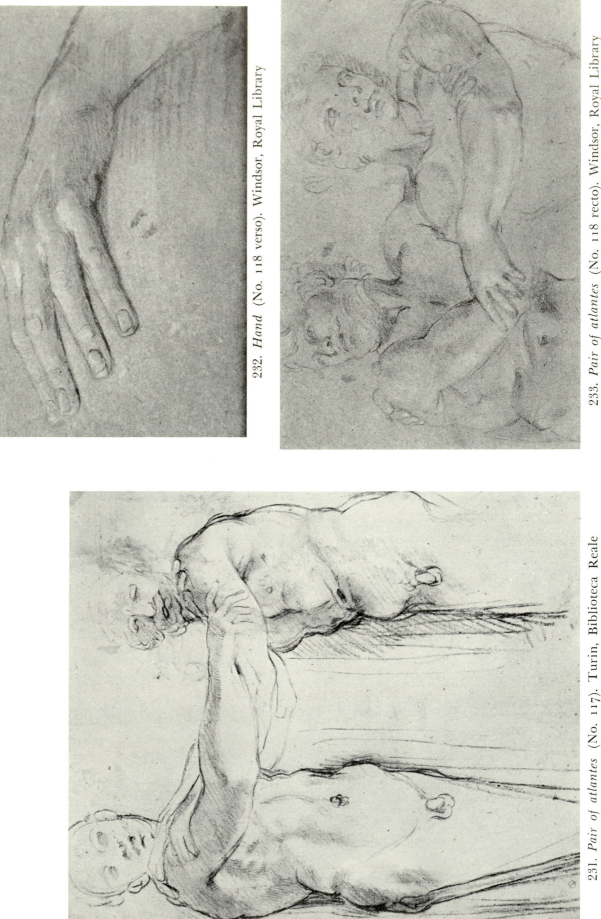

232. *Hand* (No. 118 verso). Windsor, Royal Library

233. *Pair of atlantes* (No. 118 recto). Windsor, Royal Library

231. *Pair of atlantes* (No. 117). Turin, Biblioteca Reale

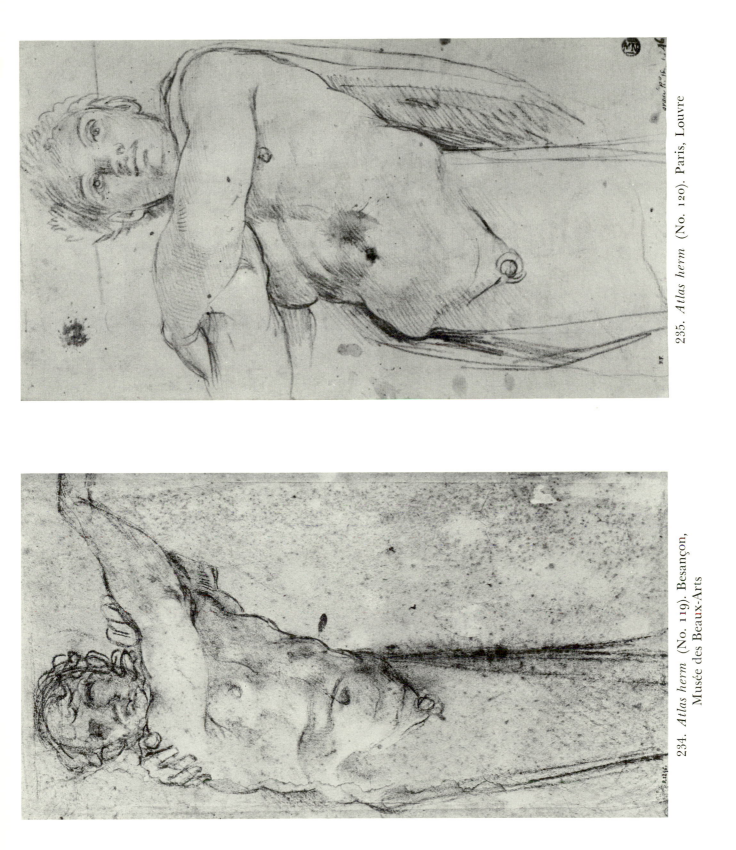

235. *Atlas herm* (No. 120). Paris, Louvre

234. *Atlas herm* (No. 119). Besançon,
Musée des Beaux-Arts

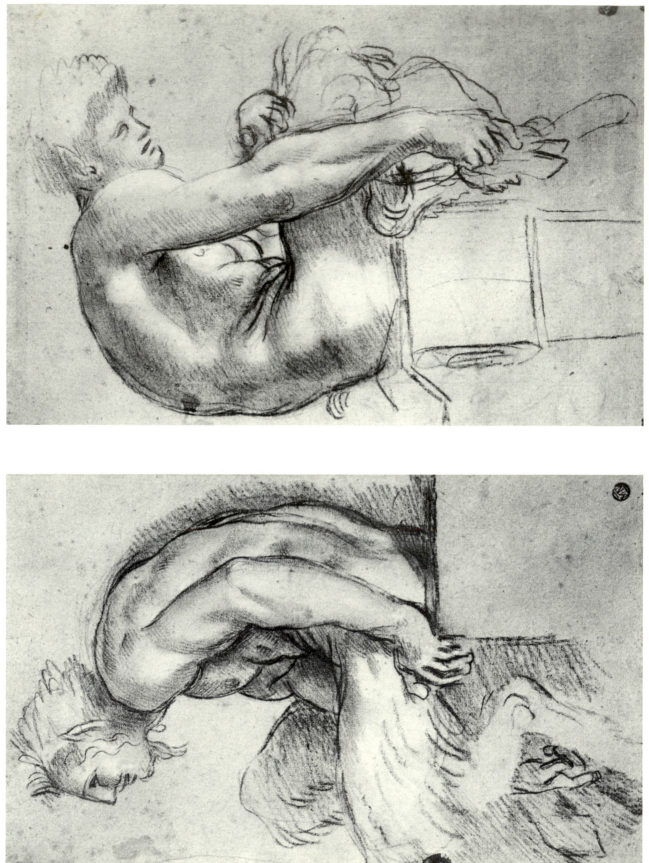

237. *Satyr* (No. 121). Paris, Louvre

236. *Satyr* (No. 122). Paris, Louvre

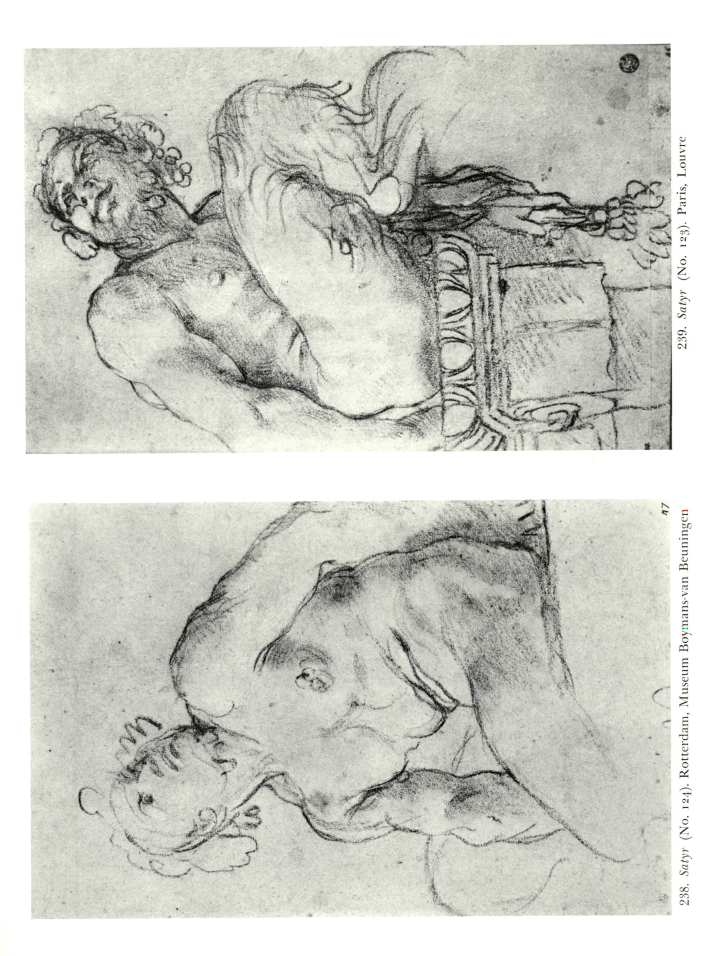

239. *Satyr* (No. 123). Paris, Louvre

238. *Satyr* (No. 124). Rotterdam, Museum Boymans-van Beuningen

240. *Two cupids carrying a third* (No. 125). New York,
Metropolitan Museum of Art

241. *Cupids fighting* (No. 127 verso).
Ellesmere Coll.

242. *Cupids fighting for a palm branch* (No. 126).
Paris, Louvre

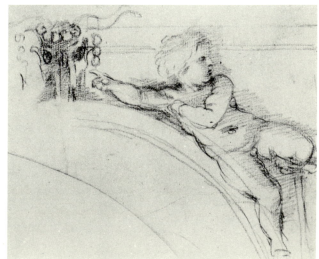

243. *Putto* (No. 132). Windsor,
Royal Library

244. *Cupids fighting for a torch* (No. 128). Besançon,
Musée des Beaux-Arts

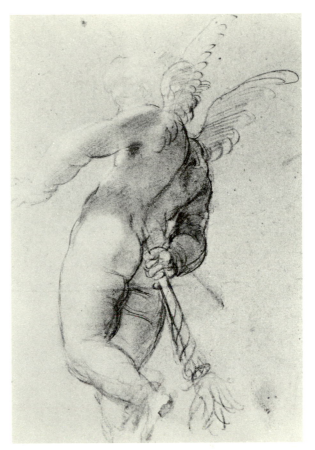

245. *Cupid with a torch* (No. 129).
Windsor, Royal Library

246. *Cupid* (No. 130). Windsor, Royal Library

247. *Cupids embracing* (No. 131 verso). Paris, Louvre

248. *Combat of Perseus and Phineus* (No. 133). Windsor, Royal Library

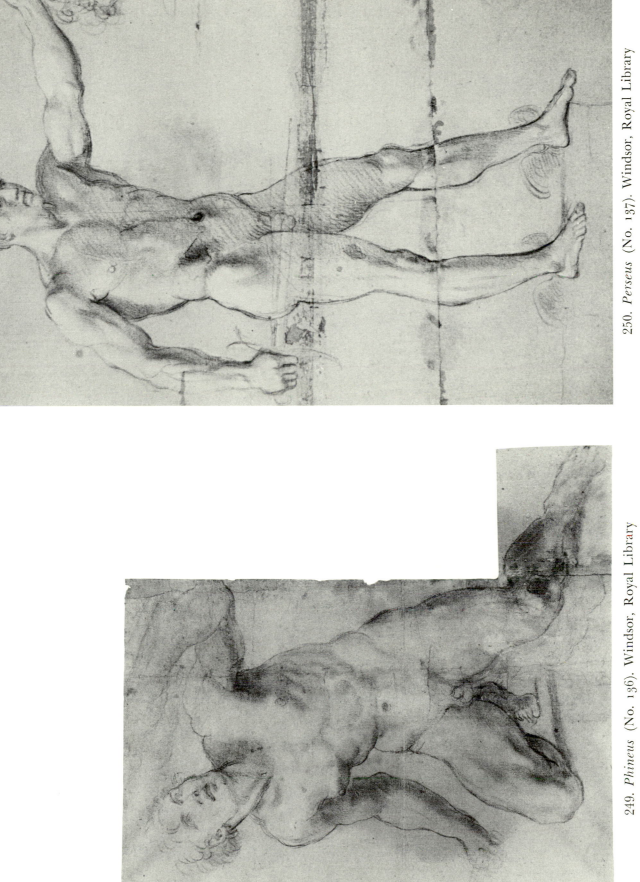

250. *Perseus* (No. 137). Windsor, Royal Library

249. *Phineus* (No. 136). Windsor, Royal Library

252. *Thescelus* (No. 135). Besançon, Musée des Beaux-Arts

251. *Thescelus* (No. 134). Windsor, Royal Library

254-255. *Studies for Perseus' warriors* (Nos. 138, 139). Windsor, Royal Library

253. *Man with arm raised* (No. 89 recto). Windsor, Royal Library

256. *Andromeda* (No. 140). Windsor, Royal Library

257. *Andromeda* (No. 141). Paris, Louvre

258. *Study for one of the Virtues* (No. 149).
Windsor, Royal Library

259. *Justice* (No. 150). Windsor, Royal Library

260. Domenichino (?), *Justice* (No. 151).
Windsor, Royal Library

261. *Mercury and Apollo* (No. 142). Paris, Louvre

262. *Mercury and Apollo* (No. 143). Windsor, Royal Library

263. *Arion and the Dolphin* (No. 144). Paris, Louvre

267. *Jupiter pursuing a nymph* (No. 148). Paris, Louvre

265. *Hercules and the Dragon of the Hesperides* (No. 146). Paris, Louvre

264. *Minerva and Prometheus* (No. 145). Paris, Louvre

266. *Prometheus freed by Hercules* (No. 147). Paris, Louvre

268. Carlo Maratti (?), copy after Annibale's cartoon
for *Hercules resting*. Whereabouts unknown

269. *Polyphemus and Galatea*. Paris,
Louvre, Inv. 7198

270. *Triumph of Bacchus and Ariadne*. Windsor, Royal Library, Cat. 305A

271. *Mercury and Apollo*. Paris,
Louvre, Inv. 8005

272. *Triumph of Bacchus and Ariadne*. Paris, Louvre, Inv. 7184

273. Simone Moschino, *Alessandro Farnese crowned by Victory*. Caserta, Palazzo Reale

274. Annibale Carracci, Detail from the frescoes of the Palazzo Magnani, Bologna

275. Pellegrino Tibaldi, Frescoes of the Sala d'Ulisse. Bologna, Palazzo Poggi

276. Agostino Carracci, *Omnia vincit Amor*. Engraving B. 116, dated 1599. New York, Metropolitan Museum. Gift of Miss Georgianna W. Sargent, 1924

278. *Repose of Hercules*, gem owned by Fulvio Orsini. From La Chau and Le Blond, *Description des principales pierres gravées . . .*, 1780

279. *Eros and Anteros*. Woodcut from V. Cartari, *Imagini dei Dei degli antichi*, 1581

277. Carlo Cesio after Annibale Carracci, *Salmacis and Hermaphroditus*. Engraving from *Argomento della Galeria Farnese . . . .*, 1657

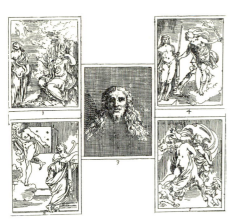

280. Emblematic pictures commemorating Agostino Carracci. Engraving by Guido Reni from *Il funerale d'Agostin Carraccio*, 1603. Collection of Mr. and Mrs. Philip Hofer

281. Perino del Vaga, *Triumph of Bacchus*, Paris, Louvre, Inv. 593

282. *Alessandro Farnese and the Siege of Antwerp*, medal. From Litta, *Famiglie celebri italiane*

283. *Alessandro Farnese and the Siege of Maastricht*, medal. From Litta, *Famiglie celebri italiane*

284. Bernard Salomon, *Perseus liberating Andromeda*. Woodcut from G. Simeoni, *Vita et Metamorfoseo d'Ovidio*, 1559

285. *Impresa* of Cardinal Alessandro Farnese. Engraving from G. Ruscelli, *Le imprese illustri*, 1572

286. Agostino Carracci, Drawing. Windsor,
Royal Library, Cat. 158

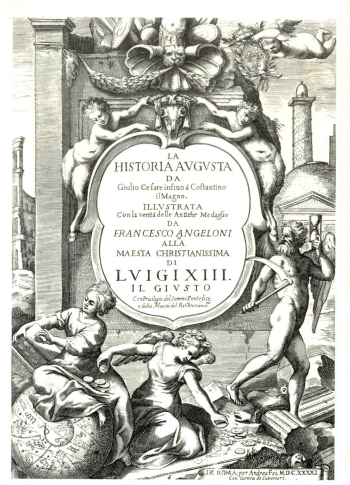

287. Title-page after Giovanni Lanfranco from
F. Angeloni, *La Historia Augusta*, 1641

289. Nicolas Poussin (studio of), *Hercules and the
Erymanthian Boar*. Windsor, Royal Library, Cat. 255

288. Peter Paul Rubens, Drawing. London, Victoria
and Albert Museum. Crown Copyright